In memory of our parents
Leonard Emmett Drewry and Bessie Boyd Drewry
and
Henry John Doermann and Alice Robbins Humphrey Doermann

STAND AND PROSPER

STAND AND PROSPER

PRIVATE BLACK COLLEGES AND
THEIR STUDENTS

Henry N. Drewry and Humphrey Doermann

IN COLLABORATION WITH

Susan H. Anderson

PRINCETON UNIVERSITY PRESS   PRINCETON AND OXFORD

Copyright © 2001 by Princeton University Press
Published by Princeton University Press, 41 William Street,
Princeton, New Jersey 08540
In the United Kingdom: Princeton University Press, 3 Market Place,
Woodstock, Oxfordshire OX20 1SY

Second printing, and first paperback printing, 2003
Paperback ISBN 0-691-11632-6

*The Library of Congress has cataloged the cloth edition
of this book as follows*

Drewry, Henry N., 1924–
Stand and prosper : private Black colleges and their students /
Henry N. Drewry and Humphrey Doermann in collaboration with
Susan H. Anderson.
p. cm.
Includes bibliographical references and index.
ISBN 0-691-04900-9 (alk. paper)
1. African American universities and colleges—History.   2. Private
universities and colleges—United States—History.   I. Doermann,
Humphrey.   II. Anderson, Susan H., 1947–   III. Title.
LC2781 .D74 2001
378.73'089'96073—dc21   2001019851

British Library Cataloging-in-Publication Data is available

Publication of this book has been aided by a
grant from the Andrew W. Mellon Foundation.

This book has been composed in Adobe New Baskerville by
Princeton Editorial Associates, Inc., Scottsdale, Arizona

Printed on acid-free paper. ∞

www.pupress.princeton.edu

Printed in the United States of America

3   5   7   9   10   8   6   4   2

Contents

List of Figures		ix
List of Tables		xi
Foreword		xv
Preface		xix
Acknowledgments		xxvii
Chapter 1.	Panorama	1
Chapter 2.	Major Historical Factors Influencing Black Higher Education	13
Chapter 3.	The Beginnings of Black Higher Education	32
Chapter 4.	Public Schools, High Schools, Normal Schools, and Colleges	41
Chapter 5.	Curriculum	57
Chapter 6.	Higher Education in a New Century	70
Chapter 7.	Two Decades of Desegregation	99
Chapter 8.	Talladega College: A Case History (1867 to 1975)	127
Chapter 9.	Leadership and Luck	160
Chapter 10.	The Graduates	181
Chapter 11.	The Students	196
Chapter 12.	Faculty: Challenge and Response	218
Chapter 13.	The Small Colleges	233
Chapter 14.	Student Aid	244
Chapter 15.	External Sources of Support	254
Chapter 16.	Leadership and Financial Independence	268
Chapter 17.	Stand and Prosper	280
Notes		289
References		311
Index		319

Figures

Chapter 7
Figure 7.1. Private Black Four-Year College Enrollment at
Five-Year Intervals from 1955 to 1975   106

Chapter 8
Figure 8.1. Percentage of Students Enrolled by Residence   142

Tables

Chapter 1
Table 1.1. Private Institutions Ranked by Endowment Assets
   per Full Time Equivalent (FTE) Student in FY 1999
   (Selected Colleges)   11

Chapter 2
Table 2.1. Ratio between Per Capita Expenditures for
   Teachers' Salaries by Race (in Dollars)   22
Table 2.2. Southeast Region Teachers' Salaries, 1916
   (in Dollars)   23
Table 2.3. Blacks in U.S. Population, 1800–1950   25

Chapter 3
Table 3.1. Number of Black Educational Institutions in the
   United States, 1866–1870   40

Chapter 4
Table 4.1. Advanced Schools and Colleges for Black Students,
   1870   47
Table 4.2. Black Schools Offering Secondary and College-
   Level Courses, 1915   52

Chapter 5
Table 5.1. Sources and Amounts of Income for Freedmen's
   Schools for Period July 1, 1869–December 31, 1869   67

Chapter 6
Table 6.1. "Higher Schools" for Black Americans at End of
   Each Decade, 1860–1950, and in 1915 and 1954   71
Table 6.2. Data on Black Colleges for Selected Years   73
Table 6.3. Percentage Increase/Decrease in Black Private
   Colleges and Enrollments for Selected Years   75
Table 6.4. Veterans Enrolled in Black Colleges (Private and
   Public) in Southern States, 1946–52   79
Table 6.5. Percentage of Colleges Ranked in the Top Fifteen
   for the Years and Categories Listed and Also Ranked
   among the Top Fifteen Colleges in 2000   80

Chapter 7
Table 7.1. Degrees Granted by Private Black Colleges, 1955,
        1966, 1970, and 1975   117
Table 7.2. Doctorates Awarded to Recipients of B.A. Degrees
        from Forty-Four Private Black Colleges   118
Table 7.3. Private Four-Year Black College Endowments, 1955,
        1967, and 1975   122
Table 7.4. Minimum, Median, and Maximum Salaries for
        Teachers at Private Black Colleges, 1971 and 1975   123
Table 7.5. Comparison of a Group of Private Black Colleges
        and Private White Colleges, 1970 and 1975   124

Chapter 8
Table 8.1. Talladega College Enrollment   141
Table 8.2. Presidents of Talladega College, 1867–1999   145
Table 8.3. Graduates Who Earned B.A.s in Each Decade from
        1889–98 to 1979–88   156
Table 8.4. Institutions from Which Advanced Degrees
        Received by Talladega Graduates   157

Chapter 9
Table 9.1. Selected Characteristics of Three Colleges, 1997   161
Table 9.2. Enrollment, Mean Verbal Aptitude Scores, and
        Class Rank in Three Colleges, 1966–95 (Selected Years) 163
Table 9.3. Risk Tolerance at Spelman, Xavier, and Stillman,
        1995   179
Table 9.4. Xavier University Enrollment, Classified by Racial
        and Ethnic Status, Fall 1996   180

Chapter 10
Table 10.1. Black American Leadership in Ten Selected Cities
        (1998), Classified by Type of Undergraduate College
        Attended   183
Table 10.2. Distinguished Black American Lawyers and U.S.
        Military Leaders Who Graduated from Historically Black
        Colleges   185
Table 10.3. Collegiate Origins of Forty-Nine Senior Black
        American Officials in the U.S. Federal Executive Branch,
        1998   186
Table 10.4. Sixty MacArthur Foundation "Genius Grant"
        Awards to Black Americans, 1981–98   189
Table 10.5. Summary of Collegiate Origins for Selected
        Careers of Distinguished Black Americans   190

Table 10.6. Collegiate Origins of Black Entering Students in
    U.S. Medical Schools, 1997 versus 1978   191
Table 10.7. Collegiate Productivity Index for Medical Students   192
Table 10.8. Collegiate Origins of Black American Recipients
    of Research Doctorates, 1977–96, Selected Years   193
Table 10.9. Collegiate Productivity Index for Research
    Doctorates   194

Chapter 11
Table 11.1. Annual Freshman Surveys, 1975 versus 1995:
    Percentage of Students Who Received Average Grades of
    B+ or Higher in High School   198
Table 11.2. Freshmen Who Estimate They Need Remedial
    College Work in Particular Subjects   199
Table 11.3. Mother's Education and Occupation   200
Table 11.4. Father's Education and Occupation   201
Table 11.5. Miles from Home to College   202
Table 11.6. Percentage of Black Families with Incomes below
    the U.S. National Median versus Percentage of Families of
    Black Freshmen with Incomes below the National
    Median, 1971–95   202
Table 11.7. Percentage of Black Families with Incomes above
    the U.S. National Seventy-Fifth Percentile versus
    Percentage of Black Freshmen with Incomes above the
    National Seventy-Fifth Percentile   203
Table 11.8. Percentage of Black Families with Incomes below
    the National Thirty-Third Percentile versus Percentage of
    Families of Black Freshmen with Incomes below the
    National Thirty-Third Percentile   204
Table 11.9. Freshman Degree Plans and Life Goals   205
Table 11.10. Self-Confidence   207
Table 11.11. Percentage of Bachelors Degrees Awarded
    Classified by Major Subject Areas   209
Table 11.12. Percentage of Liberal Arts Bachelors Degrees
    Awarded to Students Majoring in the Natural Sciences,
    1966–96   210
Table 11.13. Percentage of All Bachelors Degrees Awarded to
    Students Majoring in Education and in Business and
    Management   210
Table 11.14. Satisfaction with Academic Experience   211
Table 11.15. College Choice: 1993 Black Freshmen in Four-
    Year Colleges Followed up in 1997, Compared with 1993
    Freshmen of All Races in All Four-Year Private Colleges   212

Table 11.16. Satisfaction with Facilities, Housing, and Support
Services 213
Table 11.17. Community and Diversity 214
Table 11.18. Percentage of 1991–92 Freshmen Who
Graduated Six Years Later 216

Chapter 12
Table 12.1. Opening Fall Enrollment, Private and Public Black
Colleges versus All Postsecondary Institutions, 1970–95
(in Thousands) 219
Table 12.2. National Private Foundation Grant Authorizations
for Faculty Development in Historically Black Private
Colleges, 1970–99 (in Thousands) 230

Chapter 13
Table 13.1. Ten Lowest-Enrollment UNCF Colleges, 1976 and
1997 235

Chapter 14
Table 14.1. Percentage of Freshmen Reporting "Major
Concern" about Ability to Finance Their Educations,
1985 and 1995 249
Table 14.2. Selected Federal Money Flows to Colleges as a
Percentage of Total Current Fund Revenues, 1984 and
1996 252

Chapter 15
Table 15.1. Percentage Distribution of Revenue Sources in
UNCF Member Colleges and in U.S. Private Colleges and
Universities, 1995–96 255
Table 15.2. Percentage Distribution of Revenue Sources in
UNCF Colleges, 1985–86 and 1995–96 255
Table 15.3. Private Gifts to the United Negro College Fund,
1995 and 2000 262

Chapter 16
Table 16.1. Educational and General Expenditure per FTE
Student at U.S. Private Colleges and at Private Black
Colleges (in Constant 1992 Dollars), 1976, 1988, and 1996 271

Foreword

IT IS A pleasure and a personal privilege to contribute a brief Foreword to this splendid book by Henry Drewry and Humphrey Doermann on private black colleges and their students. There is, to the best of my knowledge, no other study that combines an insightful examination of the history of these institutions and an analysis of their recent circumstances and prospects. This is, then, a study of the past and present of forty-five historically black four-year private colleges and universities that make up an important but poorly understood sector of American higher education.

From their founding in the immediate aftermath of the Civil War until *Brown v. Board of Education* in 1954, the historically black colleges and universities (public and private) were, with few exceptions, the only option for young black men and women who wanted to continue their formal education beyond the secondary level. This country's legacy of slavery and racism is stamped on these colleges as well as on their students—and, indirectly, on all of us. The special "space" that these colleges and universities occupy today can only be understood in the context of the recurring crises that they confronted during the decades when they were largely responsible for educating this country's aspiring black professionals and educators. The authors do not exaggerate when they write that "these institutions represent, in many ways, one of the most remarkable stories of education-against-the-odds of any set of schools in America." Their histories also speak to the adaptability of colleges and universities—and to the consequences of failing to adapt or of adapting too slowly to fast-moving changes in the society. The debates over curricular change that are described so vividly (industrial education, or "vocationalism" in modern parlance, versus emphasizing the liberal arts) have loud echoes today. As Chapter 9 explains, leadership and luck also played crucial roles in determining which of these colleges would evolve most successfully. The case studies presented in the book add depth and richness to the chronicle.

It would be unfortunate if this book were read only by those with direct knowledge of, and interest in, the historically black colleges and universities—fascinating as it will be to them. The reason is that it is impossible to understand the evolution and present circumstances of *any* part of America's variegated system of higher education without understanding the role that has been played by this neglected sector. To propose what I hope is not too far-reaching a comparison, my visit to China in 1974 opened my eyes to aspects of American society that I had never seen before in such sharp relief. Messrs. Drewry and Doermann have produced a book that should be essential reading for all students of American higher education and, for that matter, for those outside the United States who are interested in this country's continuing struggle to overcome its unlovely history of racial discrimination.

In more recent times, the sequence of events that began with *Brown* and that included the passage of the Civil Rights Act of 1964 and the Higher Education Act of 1965 altered fundamentally the structure of opportunities for black Americans and raised profound questions about the role of the historically black colleges. Prior to the *Brown* decision, about 90 percent of black students were enrolled in historically black colleges and universities; by 1970, slightly less than half of all black American undergraduates attended these institutions. Subsequently, the number of black Americans attending predominantly white colleges and universities grew markedly, and a number of people wondered if the historically black institutions would survive in the face of intensified competition for both students and staff.

The second half of this book demonstrates that, tough days notwithstanding, a number of these private four-year colleges have emerged stronger than before from this complicated period in the history of American higher education. They attract better prepared students, offer a wider range of curricular options, and are in stronger financial condition—which is certainly not to say that they are in any way affluent. Budgets are very tight, and to this observer, it is simply remarkable what is accomplished with such modest resources.

A recurring theme of the book is institutional diversity. As the authors explain eloquently, no one type of educational environment is right for everyone. Just as some women students prefer women's colleges to coeducational institutions, and some applicants prefer large urban institutions to smaller colleges in rural locations, some students prefer the distinctive character of the historically black college to living and learning in a predominantly white setting. In the authors' words: "Given relatively free choice, one should have a certain faith in the educational marketplace. In the end, most people will choose well enough in terms of their own needs."

The existence of a variety of institutional templates is no less evident within each of these broad groupings. The wide range of differences among the historically black private colleges and universities is striking. When these forty-five institutions are grouped by size, we find that the largest third enroll between 1,500 and 6,000 students and generally send a significant number of their undergraduates on to major graduate schools. The middle third enroll between 800 and 1,500 students and are likely to be found in middle-sized southern cities. The smallest colleges within this group frequently serve as important "second chance" opportunities for students who are less well prepared and lack the scores on standardized tests that would be expected at many other institutions. These are often first-generation college students who are likely to come from southern communities. An important finding is that the differences within the group of forty-five institutions studied here appear to be increasing, not diminishing. At the same time that the strongest institutions are doing very well by any standard, the smallest and most vulnerable of these colleges seem, if anything, more vulnerable today than they were three decades ago.

As we look ahead, in a new century, no one can be sure how all of these institutions will fare. It is easy to identify factors that pose serious challenges for them. A wave of retirements at predominantly white liberal arts colleges could make it more difficult for even the strongest black colleges and universities to retain and recruit faculty. The unprecedented growth in endowments at the wealthiest colleges and universities creates wider wealth disparities than we have seen in the past, and the uses to which these resources are put could add markedly to the competitive problems faced by both predominantly white institutions that are less well endowed and nearly all of the historically black colleges and universities. The impact of information technology on many aspects of life on and off campus could, if not well managed from a system-wide perspective, lead to new fears that at least some of the historically black colleges will be unable to keep up with developments at better-positioned peer institutions. Finally, it is ironic but true that attacks on affirmative action that are directed primarily at white institutions could have major adverse effects on leading black colleges and universities by reducing opportunities at the graduate level for their aspiring doctors, lawyers, and future academics.

However, in thinking about such questions, and many others that could be posed, it is helpful to refer again to the historical record presented so well in this book. These colleges and universities have proved to be remarkably resilient. The authors believe, and I agree, that with good leadership and a fair share of the luck on which all institutions have to depend, they will continue to "Stand and Prosper."

William G. Bowen

JASON COLEMAN spoke to *New York Times* reporter Tamar Lewin just after his freshman year at college. He offered her vivid memories of how, in his well-integrated New Jersey public school, he and his white friends pulled apart just as high school began. "We listened to different music, we played different sports, and we got interested in different girls," he said. "And we didn't have much to say to each other anymore." He soon found himself trapped between a black "hip-hop culture" and his honor studies classes, where the majority of students were white; between clashing ideas of black style and white style, black culture and white culture. As Lewin reported, "Although Blacks are now a slight majority in the school, he, like many of the black students, felt an underlying jostling about who really owns the school. And he felt dismissed, intellectually and socially, by some teachers and classmates."

When it came time for college, Jason made a choice that many good black students find themselves considering. He opted to go to Howard University, one of this country's forty-five historically black private four-year colleges, located in Washington, D.C. At Howard, that first year, he evidently found a space freer from the buffetings of racial currents that run through this society. He found he could relax and put his full energies into "studying hard to go to medical school, as his father and brother had." Although today most black American students go to predominantly white colleges and universities, a significant minority takes another route into higher education. Less than half a century ago, a school like Howard would probably have been Jason Coleman's only choice if he wanted a college education.[1]

America's private black colleges have undergone profound changes in their century-and-a-half-long history, as has the society in which they exist. Yet they continue to be, as they always have been, sanctuaries for young black Americans. From their beginnings, they were places of relative safety that allowed space for the discovery and strengthening of self, provided time and encouragement for intellectual journeys often discouraged elsewhere, and inculcated pride and interest in the preservation of the black experience. They provided support for and development of artists and scholars and they helped students prepare for and enter life as professionals. Underfunded, often ignored by the larger society, private black colleges have nonetheless never been far from the juncture points of conflict and change in America.

These schools emerged after the outbreak of the Civil War from the activities of abolitionists and especially from the overpowering urge of impoverished freed slaves, previously denied the simplest rudiments of learning. The urge was not just for an education but for access to every level of educational experience. The founding of black schools and colleges by antislavery white Americans and ex-slaves in the first chaotic years after the Civil War was part of the formidable task of converting the constitutional abolition of slavery into the reality of personal freedom and equality, a task—in very different form—still under way today.

For black Americans, this journey into higher education includes in more recent times heartening milestones as well as serious setbacks, moments of optimism and times of worry. In May 1954, the Supreme Court ruled unanimously in *Brown v. Board of Education* that public elementary and secondary education could not be segregated based on race, striking down the "separate but equal" doctrine that had ruled since the 1890s. That doctrine had long validated the tracking of black and white Americans into schools and colleges that were indeed separate but also distinctly unequal. Historic civil rights legislation followed the *Brown* decision in the mid-1960s, signaling the opening of previously off-limits careers to black Americans and so changing the nature of what professions college-bound black students might hope to be educated for. In the 1970s, black high school graduates for the first time began enrolling in large numbers in traditionally white colleges and universities nationwide—and the nature, the value, the very existence of black educational institutions was thrown into question.

It was hardly the first crisis black higher education had experienced. Black colleges are often enveloped in crisis; they are always at the edge. Their existence was dramatically in doubt from the moment that the first college program was offered early in the Civil War. In this book, we trace the development of private black colleges—four-year, baccalaureate-level schools, most founded to educate newly freed slaves in the South following the Civil War—from their enthusiastic but meager beginnings to the present. Private black colleges are a subset of the more than one hundred historically black colleges and universities (HBCUs)— public and private; four-year and two-year; undergraduate, graduate, and professional—all of which were founded prior to passage of the Civil Rights Act in 1964. We emphasize the history (without which black education loses much of its meaning), assess the changes that have occurred since the *Brown* decision, consider the complex racial environment of more recent years, and try to imagine what the future may hold for these institutions.

Most Americans know little about black colleges. There is much to suggest that, before the *Brown* decision, many Americans might have considered "black higher education" an oxymoron—if they had thought about it at all. Not surprisingly then, relatively little has been published on the subject—next to nothing before 1954.[2]

Even some of the changes that have taken place in black colleges over the past few decades hardly appear to have been noticed, unlike corresponding changes in traditionally white institutions. To take but one example, few know that majorities of white students are currently to be found at several public historically black colleges, but most Americans are aware that traditionally white colleges have significant numbers of black students.

After the *Brown* decision, some observers, including prominent black educators, wondered whether desegregation might render these colleges obsolete. But the colleges have more than persisted: they have developed in interesting and often expansive ways, in many cases growing stronger in the ensuing decades. They continue to serve as incubators for black business, government, and professional leaders. But no less importantly, they serve as places where black high school students with weak elementary and secondary school preparation can still find an opening, an opportunity for a college experience, and so establish a successful path into the larger society.

PATHWAYS TO OPPORTUNITY

One hears few doubts today about whether these colleges will survive or whether they are useful. Their record of accomplishment is so well established that voices expressing doubts about the continued need for them are rare indeed. Yet black higher education calls out for further attention—from educators, funders, and scholars. These institutions represent, in many ways, one of the most remarkable stories of education-against-the-odds of any set of schools in America.

Nowhere in our history has the paradox of American democracy and its subsystems of slavery and racial caste played out more clearly than in the area of black higher education. Consider the following widely accepted suppositions: the point of democracy is to provide genuine equality of opportunity; equality of opportunity in the nineteenth and twentieth centuries became increasingly dependent on access to education; slavery, racial segregation, and discrimination, by definition, sought to deny such access. From these suppositions it should follow, as philosopher John Rawls has suggested in his book, *A Theory of Justice,* that to help reduce the bias of contingencies in the direction of inequality of opportunity, greater resources should be devoted to the education of those previously denied equal opportunity.[3] Instead, until at least the 1960s (and much later in many cases), governments in the states where most black Americans lived chose to devote proportionally far greater resources to the education of whites than to black Americans. Indeed, state support for black higher education, practically nonexistent for half a century after the end of slavery, was still grossly inadequate well after the *Brown* decision.

The history of private black higher education is little known, and yet it is important for an understanding of how these schools developed and an assessment of what they are today. The first part of this book explores the black experience in higher education from the pre–Civil-War years—when it was illegal in many states to teach slaves to read and write—through the period of the Jim Crow laws in the South—when, on average, one black American was lynched every four days. It continues the story into the 1970s, when educators began to cope with the impact of desegregation on black colleges. Through these many dismal years, the faith of black Americans in education as the road to opportunity seems nothing short of extraordinary. So does the survival and continual adaptation of private black colleges to the needs of their students and to the highest standards possible under the most difficult conditions imaginable. Although the two authors consulted closely when writing this book, Henry Drewry is primarily responsible for the historical narrative recounted here.

Humphrey Doermann is primarily responsible for the chapters that make up the second part of the book, focusing on the state of the private black college in recent decades. In assessing the nature and future of modern private black colleges, we pay particular attention to the changing social and educational context within which the colleges exist, the growth and significance of government funding, their leadership patterns, and the changing origins and attitudes of their students. We also emphasize the accomplishments of their graduates, the ability of the smaller colleges among them—in a landscape of ever larger institutions—to provide real value to their students, and their "mission" or missions in the twenty-first century.

Viewed individually, some of these colleges have prospered and grown stronger in the past three decades, others are struggling (as so many of them have for the past century and a half), and a few have not fared well and have been forced to close. The authors believe, however, that in the aggregate, the record of the private black college, although it charts a precarious course, reflects a significant success story.

Compared with their status three decades ago, a number of these colleges draw more and better-prepared students, offer more choice in fields of study, and are in better financial condition. They are now more capable than they were two decades ago of competing directly with the stronger, predominantly white colleges and universities. That success does not appear to be in danger of vanishing any time soon. The smallest and most vulnerable of these colleges, however, seem, if anything, more vulnerable today. Their endowments are weak, their enrollments may not generate the levels of funding needed from tuition, faculty salaries remain unattractive, and plant and equipment are often in need of refurbishment. Yet by objective then-and-now measures, only a few of the most vulnerable of these schools appear to have lost ground. But the traditional measures applied to these schools in the past do not adequately reflect either the escalating costs of basic instructional technology or the costs of competition throughout higher education to hire new black faculty members.

What is important about this overall record of accomplishment? To begin with, over the years these colleges have made a great contribution to the formation of a significant black middle class—and continue to do so, even though black students now more often attend traditionally white colleges than black colleges. To an important degree, black colleges still provide a significant opportunity for the less well-prepared students, whose standardized test scores might have kept them out of many other four-year colleges, to progress and earn bachelors degrees. Black colleges have been and remain treasured keepers of black cultural history and of many of its documents, artifacts, and art works. They are a source of black pride and still offer a significantly different choice for many students who would prefer not to spend their undergraduate years in a majority white college. All of this has been and continues to be achieved on extremely lean budgets.

Viewed in a larger context, black colleges, Indian colleges, and women's colleges together make up a crucial component of America's complex and unique system of higher education, which features an unusual diversity of institutions with special origins, purposes, sizes, and clienteles. Less regimented than most national educational systems, the American system allows students greater possibility of changing directions, of shifting from one college or college subsystem to another, or of gaining a second chance, for students with weaker preparation or those recovering from false starts. Finally, the United States provides postsecondary opportunity to a relatively large share of its population. Such a system has been criticized for being more costly than the systems of other countries, for duplication, and for inefficiency. But such educational choice and opportunity—for every level of ability and preparation— seems of particular use in an economy that so clearly requires increasing numbers of well-educated people. According to the best current demographic projections, within the next thirty years, the adult workforce will include a far larger proportion of people of color, and many will not have attended well-financed college-preparatory schools. The colleges with long, successful histories of serving students of this description appear then to have particular, practical value to the nation, even as they contribute to increasing its institutional, creative, and human diversity.

If one values institutional diversity, then it is perverse to search for a single template for providing the best four-year undergraduate education. By the same logic, it may be counterproductive to try to assess whether a "better" education will be offered by a private college or a public one; whether women will be more effectively educated at women's colleges or coeducational ones; whether black Americans will be better educated at historically black colleges or predominantly white ones. Given relatively free choice, one should have a certain faith in the educational marketplace. In the end, most people will choose well enough in terms of their own needs.

The more interesting questions may be: Does this sector serve its students well? Does it add to the productivity, creativity, and strength of the total system? Answers are usually not as easy to come by as questions are. But these are the sorts of questions we hope to illuminate in this book.

We believe that as a group, private black colleges merit further strengthening in the foreseeable future; and more generally, that the nation gains much by supporting and maintaining institutional diversity among colleges and universities. The schools we studied have long provided pathways in this society otherwise unavailable to untold numbers of young black Americans. They still do. That service cannot be too highly valued. We are convinced that it is no less important to maintain and strengthen the kinds of student aid programs—governmental and private—that have made it possible for students to enroll and graduate anywhere their talents and energy permit. We can only hope that Congress will not lessen its three-decade-old direct interest in minority-serving institutions and will continue to authorize targeted, multipurpose support to black colleges, tribally controlled Native American colleges, and colleges serving large numbers of hispanic students. We also consider ways in which strong leadership exhibited by trustees, faculty, administrators, and alumni/ae of private black colleges can continue to strengthen the value of the black college experience.

AUTHOR PERSPECTIVE

This book concentrates on forty-five historically black four-year private colleges. Largely outside its scope—but included in the federal definition of historically black colleges and universities—are forty public four-year colleges and universities, ten public two-year colleges, and several private two-year colleges and private professional schools. Although these schools are similar to the four-year private colleges in many of their accomplishments and are important subjects for further study, as a group, private black colleges differ from them in governance, financing, and other matters. And private black colleges are what—given our backgrounds, interests, and careers—we know best. We chose to focus our energies on our strengths, although certainly much that we say about the private colleges applies at least in part to the other institutions as well, and some of our tables compare the public and private black college experience.

In the preface to his work *A History of Negro Education in the South*, Henry Allen Bullock commented that "every book is somewhat autobiographical in nature." Certainly, we brought our backgrounds and work experience—our "autobiographies"—to this task, for both of us in one way or another have spent significant parts of our lives associated with private black colleges. Both of our fathers held faculty and administrative posts at such colleges. Leonard E. Drewry was professor of education and principal of the Practice High School at Talladega College; Henry John Doermann was director of the Normal School and Academy at Hampton Institute (now Hampton University). Henry Drewry, who is black, spent several years of his childhood on the Talladega campus. He is a graduate and also a former trustee of Talladega. Both of us have worked for foundations that have dedicated part of their resources to the support of black colleges. Humphrey Doermann, who is white, acted as foundation program officer in a series of grants, which, beginning in 1977, the Bush Foundation, in cooperation with the William and Flora Hewlett Foundation, awarded to private black colleges. Doermann was president of the foundation until 1997, and is assistant to the president and research associate at Macalester College. Henry Drewry, as program associate and later senior advisor for higher education at the Andrew W. Mellon Foundation, had responsibility for grantmaking involving private black colleges and for a program of undergraduate fellowships for minority students preparing for doctoral studies in the arts and sciences.

As a result of our careers, a great deal of the information-gathering for our book was actually done prior to the evolution of the idea of writing it. While working for our respective foundations, we met regularly with presidents, administrators, and faculty members from most of the private black colleges during our visits to their campuses, their visits to our offices, or joint meetings of one sort or another that we all attended.

Once we decided to write the book, we visited fourteen private black colleges together or individually over two years to interview administrators, faculty, students, alumni/ae, and trustees on a range of topics. We also met with such figures as William Gray, president and CEO of the

United Negro College Fund, the late Leon Higginbotham, former federal judge and Harvard Law School faculty member, and Sisters Monica and Mary David of the Order of the Blessed Sacrament, which founded Xavier University.

We explored college archives, considered major federal studies of higher education, delved into contemporary material on the early years of these colleges, and read as wide a variety of secondary works—books, articles, and studies—on the area as was available. In addition, two special analyses of existing databases were commissioned for the book, one based on data from *Who's Who Among Black Americans* (1998–99), the other on the annual freshman surveys of the Higher Education Research Institute (HERI). The analyses of these databases appear throughout the book.

Black higher education has long borne a similar relationship to its parent field, U.S. higher education, as black American history, women's history, and Native American history have sustained to their parent field of U.S. history. In recent years, each of them has come into its own, as scholars recognize the importance of these subfields to understanding their parent field. It is time that the same happen for the black colleges—that they be recognized as an important part of the universe of American institutions of higher education. This study, whatever its faults or deficits, is a labor of love growing out of concern for a group of colleges too important to be left so long in the shadows.

Acknowledgments

THE IDEAS AND experiences that made the writing of this book possible developed from our years of visiting private black colleges as representatives of either the Andrew W. Mellon Foundation or the Bush and William and Flora Hewlett Foundations and, for one of us, from four rewarding years as a student at one of these colleges. However, writing this book would have been inconceivable without the help of many other people, only a few of whom are mentioned here. We are in debt to all of them, mentioned and unmentioned, and hope our efforts as authors will justify theirs as advisors and informants. More than any other single individual, William G. Bowen, president of the Mellon Foundation, influenced the project outcome through his initial support of the idea, his first-draft manuscript review, and his wise but restrained counsel about how to pace research and writing in a book of this scope.

Because one author was based in Princeton, New Jersey, and the other in Saint Paul, Minnesota, two related but separate support networks helped maintain progress in the joint project. In the Mellon Foundation's Princeton office, our collaborator Susan Anderson provided invaluable research assistance in locating bibliographical and documentary material and in keeping abreast of reports in the media regarding institutions included in the study. In addition, she formatted and proofread the manuscript, prepared the list of references, and provided service to the project in dozens of other ways. Kamla Motihar and Mary M. Rivera, the Foundation's librarians, also provided research assistance, as did two other Mellon staff members, Joseph Meisel and Roger Schonfeld, who read and commented on the manuscript. Roger also helped prepare the list of references. Roland Chin's quickness in solving important computer problems made it possible for the project to progress, and Joyce Pierre helped move messages and material between Princeton and Saint Paul. Others in this network included Mark Hicks, a graduate student in the department of higher education at Columbia University Teachers College, who served as research assistant during the early days of information gathering, and Mark's advisor, Professor Dawn Person.

In Saint Paul, Michael S. McPherson arranged an office and sponsored an author's part-time appointment at Macalester College, which allowed time for work on this project. McPherson read and commented on the last nine chapters, and offered important perspectives on federal policy in financing U.S. higher education. Sue El-Eid performed many administrative tasks, expedited the work flow, and converted raw drafts into final manuscript. Tatsuhide Kanenari, a Macalester College student research assistant, tabulated the collegiate origins of distinguished black Americans, conducted a literature search, and compared trends in recent financing of private black colleges with those in other U.S. four-year private colleges. Grants from the Andrew W. Mellon Foundation supported the project expenses at Macalester from 1997 through 2000.

Tom Engelhardt, freelance editor, and Peter Dougherty, executive editor of the Princeton University Press, both made important editorial contributions. Readers who view our credit to both as merely part of the publishing protocol make a serious error in this case. Dougherty provided sage advice and chaperoned us in all our painless and pleasant contacts with the Press. Engelhardt pressed us to perform much better in framing, organizing, and presenting our ideas than we could have without him. His awareness and sensitivity regarding most aspects of our topic helped us find the all-important common ground in our ideas at several points where we differed as to significance and emphasis. To say that these things are reflected in the finished work does not begin to express the important part Dougherty and Engelhardt played.

As the project developed, we sought and received information, advice, and support from a very large "advisory committee," even though its members never received appointment papers or met as a group. The first part of this group offered ideas about general strategy, read and commented on outlines and chapter drafts, and located essential data and information sources for us. The second part of the group, usually connected directly with private black colleges, shared with us what they knew and thought, and arranged for us to meet colleagues who could tell us more. The first advising-and-editing group included John Archabal, Anita Pampusch, and Stanley Shepard at the Bush Foundation; Oliver E. Allen, editor and author; Richard Hope, of the Woodrow Wilson National Fellowship Foundation; Clarence J. Jupiter, former development vice president at Xavier University of Louisiana; Verlyn Klinkenborg of the *New York Times;* Michael T. Nettles, at the University of Michigan; Julius S. Scott, Jr., former president of Paine and Wiley Colleges and of Albany State University; and Charles Willie of Harvard University. In the second group of major informant-advisors, many private black college presidents took time from busy schedules to talk with us when we visited their institutions, and arranged for us to speak with faculty, administrators, trustees, and students. These included William Harvey at Hampton University, George Johnson at LeMoyne-Owen College, Joseph Johnson and Marguerite Archie-Hudson at Talladega College, Joe Lee at Tougaloo College, Audrey Manley at Spelman College, Walter Massey at Morehouse College, Ernest McNealey at Stillman College, Haywood Strickland at Texas College, H. Patrick Swygert at Howard University, and

Dorothy Cowser Yancy at Johnson C. Smith University. Three long-service faculty members contributed to Chapter 12 their observations of change during the past thirty years: Ben E. Bailey (Tougaloo), Carrell P. Horton (Fisk) and Ann D. Taylor (Bethune-Cookman). Linda J. Sax and her colleagues at the Higher Education Research Institute, University of California–Los Angeles, provided the survey-based comparisons in student attitudes and backgrounds that form the backbone of Chapter 11. Richard P. Dober, planning consultant, provided much of the analysis of physical plant in Chapters 1 and 16. Other major informants included Washington, D.C., attorney William A. (Bud) Blakey; Alice Green Burnette, counselor on fundraising; Wayne Camara and Frederick Dietrich at the College Board; Robert D. (Danny) Flanigan, treasurer at Spelman; Professor A. Leon Higginbotham of Harvard University; Sister Mary David and Sister Monica Loughlin, presidents of the Order of the Blessed Sacrament (Xavier University's founding order); Donald M. Stewart, former Spelman president, now president of the Chicago Community Trust; and Thomas Wolanin of George Washington University. Throughout our work the United Negro College Fund Archives proved to be a valuable source of material and information.

Five persons cannot be properly assigned to either the major-advisor or major-informant group above because they made many major contributions of both kinds. These are Johnnetta B. Cole, former Spelman president now at Emory University; Norman C. Francis, Xavier's president; William H. Gray III, CEO at The College Fund/UNCF; and Alan H. Kirschner, a College Fund consultant, and Dean K. Whitla of Harvard University. There are in addition a number of students and alumni/ae of black colleges who met with us or shared their thoughts in writing.

Finally we wish to thank Annette Liberson and Betsy Doermann for their many contributions that played a vital part in the development of the book, most important of which has been their generous and steady support and encouragement throughout this project.

Henry N. Drewry
Princeton, New Jersey

Humphrey Doermann
Saint Paul, Minnesota

STAND AND PROSPER

Panorama

MOST AMERICANS have little direct contact with private black colleges, have not visited one, and are not sure what they should expect if they did. This first chapter sketches for the newcomer how these colleges appear today and outlines key forces and trends that shaped them during the past thirty years. For these institutions, however, early history is as important as recent history. In some ways more so. Prior to the 1950s and 1960s, black Americans lived a very different history of civil rights and educational opportunity than did white Americans. The difference is far greater than that portrayed in most U.S. history survey courses that are taught in secondary schools and colleges. Without appreciation of that difference, one cannot understand what an accomplishment of determination and faith the success of many of these black colleges represents today, nor can one properly judge the potential of these colleges for further service to the nation. This chapter ends with an introduction to that separate history. During the 1950s and 1960s, three changes in law altered fundamentally the role of black Americans and of private black colleges in American society. The first, noted in the Preface, was the 1954 U.S. Supreme Court decision in *Brown v. Board of Education,* which directed that public elementary and secondary schools be racially integrated, and which laid the legal foundation for later court rulings directing integration of public colleges and universities in the South. The second major change was passage of the Civil Rights Act of 1964; the third was the Higher Education Act of 1965. Prior to the 1950s, black public and private colleges were, with rare exceptions, the only colleges accessible to black Americans. Black students prepared for a relatively narrow range of professional careers, principally teaching and the ministry. By the 1970s, however, black students were enrolling in historically black and also in predominantly white colleges, with a far wider range of careers open to them than before. Owing to the federal student aid and direct institutional subsidy under the Higher Education Act, private black colleges suddenly found themselves supported by significant government money, and, also for the first time, confronted with aggressive national competition for able students and faculty.

In 1950, prior to the *Brown* decision, about 90 percent of black American college and university enrollment was in historically black colleges, public and private. By 1970 there were approximately 357,000 black American undergraduates, the majority in institutions where few if any

Blacks had enrolled previously. One hundred seventy thousand or 48 percent were in historically black colleges. Fifty-six thousand of these undergraduates were enrolled in private black colleges. During the next thirty years, the number of African American students choosing predominantly white institutions grew rapidly. Meanwhile, the number attending historically black colleges leveled off until the 1980s and then, with a sharp increase in women's enrollment, rose again to record levels in the 1990s.[1]

In the late 1960s and early 1970s, several foundation-supported assessments of the status and prospects of historically black colleges ranged in tone from near funereal to cautiously optimistic. Daniel C. Thompson, professor of sociology at Dillard University, a private black institution, wrote in 1973 that "Private black colleges are challenged to institute revolutionary reorganization or face progressive disorganization. Most of these colleges, which have performed so nobly in the past, are now threatened by extinction (progressive disorganization) unless they seriously examine themselves, find the constant support needed, and bravely make the program and structural changes necessary in order to be truly relevant."[2]

Vivian W. Henderson, president of Clark College, another private black college in Atlanta, wrote that "The historic Negro college will have the responsibility for educating a diminishing but significant proportion of black youth enrolled in higher education. . . . Negro colleges will be slow in attracting white students not because of the policy or lack of quality but because institutionalized and entrenched racism is a barrier to the movement of white youth."[3]

William J. Trent, Jr., executive director of the United Negro College Fund from 1944 to 1964, cautioned against belief in any simple projection: "People generally discuss Negro colleges as if they were all alike, with a common fate. This is nonsense. Negro colleges are located along a spectrum of quality ranging from excellent to poor, just as are other institutions. Further, what will happen to these Negro colleges will cover a broad spectrum of possibilities."[4]

Although Trent was correct in warning about the dangers of easy generalization, a broad description of this collegiate landscape is possible. Today's forty-five four-year historically black private colleges can be divided into three groups according to enrollment size. Ranked in thirds, by size, the largest of the colleges enroll between approximately fifteen hundred and six thousand students. These colleges offer a strong variety of well-taught liberal arts and precareer subjects, generally pay higher faculty and staff salaries compared with the smaller black colleges, and often send a significant number of graduates on to major graduate schools. In many respects, they are competitive with white liberal arts colleges of similar size. About half of the largest-enrollment private black colleges are also in the largest Southern cities: Atlanta, New Orleans, Washington, D.C., and Miami.

The majority of these colleges and universities do not concentrate on graduate studies, although several offer a few post-baccalaureate specialties. For example, Clark Atlanta University has a long history of Ph.D. work. Howard University, Washington, D.C., is a research university with a full spectrum of professional programs. Xavier University of Louisiana provides the only graduate pharmacy program in New Orleans. Hampton University and Tuskegee University recently launched doctoral programs in science, Tuskegee University trains doctors of veterinary medicine, and Virginia Union University offers doctoral study in theology. Several universities and colleges offer master's-level studies.[5]

The middle third of these colleges enrolls between eight hundred and fifteen hundred students. These colleges are more likely to be found in middle-sized Southern cities such as Tuscaloosa, Orangeburg, Nashville, and Augusta. Although they have enjoyed some of the same successes as the larger colleges, they have sometimes had to struggle harder to maintain enrollment growth and quality.

The smallest colleges in the final group enroll two hundred to eight hundred students. They more frequently welcome students not well prepared for college by their prior schooling. These often are first-generation college students and students from rural Southern homes. During the past three decades, some of these very small colleges languished for years at a time under indifferent leadership and a few narrowly escaped closing down. However, some of the same colleges at different times have enjoyed excellent leadership and showed a remarkable capacity for rapid improvement.[6]

The four-year accredited private black colleges are listed here, in the three different enrollment groupings based on 1995 enrollment statistics. If their past is a guide, several colleges in each of these groups will grow or shrink significantly, and so move into a different category. Perhaps because many of these colleges are relatively small, with few financial reserves, the volatility within this group is greater than one might encounter, for example, among the Associated Colleges of the Midwest, or the Ivy League:

I. Largest fifteen historically black private colleges	*II. Fifteen next-largest colleges*
Benedict College, Columbia, South Carolina	Claflin College, Orangeburg, South Carolina
Bethune-Cookman College, Daytona Beach, Florida	Fisk University, Nashville, Tennessee
Clark Atlanta University, Atlanta, Georgia	Florida Memorial College, Miami, Florida

I. (*continued*)

Dillard University, New Orleans,
Louisiana

Hampton University, Hampton,
Virginia

Howard University, Washington,
District of Columbia

Morehouse College, Atlanta,
Georgia

Morris Brown College, Atlanta,
Georgia

Oakwood College, Huntsville,
Alabama

Saint Augustine's College,
Raleigh, North Carolina

Shaw University, Raleigh, North
Carolina

Spelman College, Atlanta,
Georgia

Tuskegee University, Tuskegee,
Alabama

Virginia Union University,
Richmond, Virginia

Xavier University of Louisiana,
New Orleans, Louisiana

II. (*continued*)

Johnson C. Smith University,
Charlotte, North Carolina

LeMoyne-Owen College,
Memphis, Tennessee

Miles College, Birmingham,
Alabama

Morris College, Sumter, South
Carolina

Paine College, Augusta, Georgia

Paul Quinn College, Dallas, Texas

Philander Smith College, Little
Rock, Arkansas

Rust College, Holly Springs,
Mississippi

Stillman College, Tuscaloosa,
Alabama

Tougaloo College, Tougaloo,
Mississippi

Voorhees College, Denmark,
South Carolina

Wilberforce University,
Wilberforce, Ohio

III. Fifteen smallest-enrollment colleges

Arkansas Baptist College, Little Rock, Arkansas
Allen University, Columbia, South Carolina
Bennett College, Greensboro, North Carolina
Barber-Scotia College, Concord, North Carolina
Edward Waters College, Jacksonville, Florida
Huston-Tillotson College, Austin, Texas
Jarvis Christian College, Hawkins, Texas
Knoxville College, Knoxville, Tennessee
Lane College, Jackson, Tennessee
Livingstone College, Salisbury, North Carolina
Saint Paul's College, Lawrenceville, Virginia
Southwestern Christian College, Terrell, Texas
Talladega College, Talladega, Alabama
Texas College, Tyler, Texas
Wiley College, Marshall, Texas

Close inspection of the list reveals that even within the three enrollment groups there is much variety of purpose and clientele. Tougaloo College and Talladega College, for example, are not high-enrollment institutions, but have produced a significant number of graduates who subsequently earned doctoral and professional degrees. Although a majority of the largest-enrollment colleges draw more than half their students from out of state, three of them—Bethune-Cookman, Dillard, and Shaw—enroll more than 60 percent of their students from in-state.

NURTURING ENVIRONMENTS

Except for the different racial mix, a first-time visitor to one of these colleges will find much that looks familiar. Approximately 95 percent of the students and more than half the faculty and staff are African American.[7] As with colleges throughout the nation, most black colleges began with two- or three-story brick buildings with white wooden trim, often reminiscent of early New England colleges. But all are not the same. Dillard University in New Orleans mixes colonial and plantation-style buildings in an orderly, spacious campus plan. Urban colleges such as Morehouse and Xavier include both the early low-rise buildings and later urban high-rise design, reflecting a need to accommodate on limited city sites a larger enrollment than the founders anticipated. Tougaloo College, built on a former slave plantation, samples the architecture of several periods: the president's office is in the original plantation owner's house, next door to a large 1960s rough-concrete library, and a block from a utilitarian 1990s humanities building.

Like American colleges generally, many historically black colleges expanded in the 1960s, aided by low-cost federal construction loans. Their campuses contain occasional familiar-looking glass-and-steel box buildings—dormitories and classrooms—which looked modern and functional when they were built, but have since developed maintenance problems and may no longer meet modern building codes. Finally, as with most colleges today, the major new buildings on historically black college campuses have been designed with more attention to attractiveness and comfort—as well as to utility—than generally was true twenty or thirty years ago.

Richard P. Dober is senior consultant for a planning group that advises trustees and architects about campus design and college building projects in the United States and abroad. Over the past forty years, he has visited private black colleges many times, assessing their physical plant for The Ford Foundation in the 1960s, and reviewing building and renovation proposals for the Bush and Hewlett Foundations in the 1980s and 1990s. He finds the quality of planning and construction in recent years at private black colleges comparable to that on college campuses else-where. The campus for Spelman College, an elite private black college for women, is not the same as the campus for Bryn Mawr College, an elite, predominantly white women's college. Spelman has not enjoyed signifi-cant outside financial support for as long as Bryn Mawr. But Dober thinks their planning standards are comparable today in ways that were not true in the 1960s and 1970s. Here are his impressions:

> These private black colleges, often located in small and middle sized com-munities, are visible cultural centers, sources of jobs, and symbols of pride. Often to get to them, you cross the tracks, pass through modest if not impoverished neighborhoods, and enter the campus, surprised and experi-encing a more pleasant place.
>
> At some institutions, the older edifices were splendid examples of enter-prise and skill. Designed by the locals, built with bricks manufactured on the site and with lumber planed there, crafted and erected by the faculty, staff and students—their scale, detailing and simplicity were architecturally at-tractive. How sad, then, to see nearby the government regulated and funded, minimal contemporary structures that seemingly ignored the aes-thetic lessons evident in the historic buildings.
>
> Equally evident were the contrasting landscapes; the newer areas bleak, the older parts of the campus visually comforting in their tree cover, lawns and shrubbery.
>
> Worst of all, in memory, now and then, here and there, was the physical decay in the older and better architecture; the neglect explained away by financial difficulties which forced the campus administrators to give higher priority to people and programs than to physical spaces.[8]

Unfortunately, the financial difficulties are not just administrative ex-cuses. Private black colleges live on lean budgets—some extremely lean. Average tuition received per student in these colleges in 1996 was $6,347, or 62 percent of the amount received per student by all four-year private colleges. Yet private black colleges maintain approximately the same ratio of students to faculty as do most U.S. four-year private colleges (15 to 1 versus 15.6 to 1). Not surprisingly, faculty are paid less.[9] Among United Negro College Fund (UNCF) colleges, the average salary of a full professor was $48,145 in 1996–97 or 28 percent less than the average for full professors at other comprehensive four-year private institutions. The gap for instructors was 14 percent.[10] In 1996, private black colleges spent about 7 percent less per student on educational and general expenses than did all four-year private colleges and universities. As with private colleges throughout the nation, the percentage of faculty at private black colleges with doctoral or professional degrees increased significantly in the past twenty years: from 41 percent of all faculty in 1977 to 62 percent in 1997.

Many black college graduates, particularly from residential colleges, have said that their undergraduate years provided an important transition from family dependence to adult self-direction, and that their personal development in college was as important to them as their academic experience. More often than one might ordinarily expect, the authors in their conversations with alumni and with faculty at private black colleges encountered the word "nurturing," or personal anecdotes amounting to the same thing. A published example is in the autobiography of Andrew Young, former mayor of Atlanta and U.S. ambassador to the United Nations:

> In retrospect I realize my years at Howard were important to my personal development. I was mature enough upon graduation to regret the lackadaisical attitude I had toward my studies when I started college, but it was college that helped me mature. By the time I graduated from Howard, I had learned to embrace the strengths of the black middle class. I learned to interact in formal social settings, refined my manners and conversation skills, and began to carry myself with self-assurance. Howard picked up where Mrs. Bowen and Gilbert Academy left off. It was the same philosophy—academic achievement and exemplary behavior. I had not fully mastered either concept, but I had grown to appreciate the wisdom of having those abilities in one's repertoire.
>
> Had I failed to come to terms with my identity as a middle-class black person, I would never have accomplished very much in the civil rights movement or won elective office.[11]

William H. Gray III, president and chief executive officer of the United Negro College Fund, made a similar observation:

> I don't know how we measure the contribution of truly dedicated hardworking teachers. But I do know that when we ask how the graduates of historically black colleges and universities are so often able to compete with the graduates of the most prestigious universities in the nation, it always seems to come back to the faculty role models. . . . It would be difficult to overestimate the importance of faculty in the success of these colleges and their graduates.[12]

What can we say about these colleges and the major challenges their leaders faced in recent years? Put too simply, the 1970s were a particularly tough time to lead a private black college. The decade included continued social unrest, many demands for administrative reform, sharply increased competition for excellent students, and increasingly strong pressure to change what was taught and how. For most colleges, the 1980s and 1990s were less difficult, although certainly not easy. In these years, an improved national economy gave virtually all private colleges a chance to demonstrate their resiliency. Many private black colleges, like colleges elsewhere, used this time to assess and change their educational strategies: giving increased attention to writing skills and computer literacy, reducing reliance on lecturing, and adjusting course content to accommodate increased student interest in international affairs and in new career opportunities.

THE PAST THIRTY YEARS

During the 1970s, most experienced college presidents reported that the authority of their office was constantly being challenged—by students, by faculty, and sometimes by alumni. One effect of the Vietnam War and the Watergate years was that strong individual authority acquired a tarnished name. The Spelman College board of trustees appointed its first faculty trustee in 1970.[13] A few other private black colleges adopted a similar change, as did many predominantly white colleges. Student demonstrators occupied administrative offices to protest official college positions on everything from rules of student conduct to U.S. foreign policy. Decisions such as choosing a new president—once solely the province of private trustee discussions—were now initiated by broadly based search committees.[14] There is no question that in most colleges, the 1970s produced a fundamental change in the limits of individual presidential authority.

At the same time, the oil shortage of the mid-1970s triggered double-digit cost inflation, the most rapid within memory. Operating budgets were tight. With the general enrollment of eighteen- to twenty-four-year-old black freshmen experiencing a moderate downward trend in the private black colleges, many of their presidents faced the uncomfortable choice of experimenting with tuition increases, stretching operating budgets even further, or spending from endowment principal (if there was an endowment).[15]

An important new source of revenue did emerge in these years, but it proved to be a mixed blessing. Under the Higher Education Act of 1965, the federal government provided grants to students to attend college anywhere in the United States if they demonstrated financial need, were admissible, and maintained satisfactory academic records. Title III of that act also provided direct institutional subsidy to historically black public and private colleges. During the 1990s, according to one estimate, those federal funds together amounted to almost half of an average private black college's annual budget, either through direct payments, or from student tuition and fees financed with federal and state aid.[16] The "mixed blessing" part was that this same availability of student aid money helped northern and western predominantly white colleges to seek greater variety among their students, and thus stimulated an unprecedented recruitment competition for the best-prepared black high school graduates. During the same period, the flagship white public universities in the South also opened their doors much wider to black students. Any black college president who took the long view was unlikely to complain, since the new competition meant that for the first time, able black high school graduates enjoyed something like the same national range of college choice that had been reserved for Whites only a few years earlier.

But the effects of the new competition on many black colleges were severe. This was particularly true for colleges with strong academic reputations—those which were attractive recruitment targets—but which lacked either extra scholarship money or the recruitment organization to meet quickly the new challenge. For example, at Fisk University, enrollment dropped from 1,610 in 1974 to 1,149 in 1978 and to 694 in 1983. The average freshman SAT verbal scholastic aptitude score decreased from V412 in 1968 to approximately V340 in 1976, a signal that reading comprehension and independent study skills among entering freshmen were weaker than they had been. Fisk achieved partial recovery in the 1980s, at least as measured by the percentage of entering freshmen that ranked in the top fifth of their high school graduating class. Twenty-seven percent of Fisk freshmen in 1976 had been in the top fifth of their high school graduating class; by 1982, the percentage had risen to 44 percent.[17] Carrell P. Horton, former professor of psychology and dean of academic affairs at Fisk describes her observations of those years in Chapter 12.

The new government funds permitted all colleges to enroll more of the poor and needy. But they also permitted predominantly white colleges and universities to recruit black students so aggressively that the scholastic leading edge of black public and private colleges was temporarily blunted. Of all the changes of the 1970s, this probably provided the greatest challenge to the leadership of private black colleges.

Leaders of private black colleges during the 1980s seemed generally to have more control of their fate than in the prior decade. There were fewer new external challenges. However, there was continuing need to respond to the challenges that had flooded in during the 1970s. As noted earlier, part of the leadership energy would go toward adapting and improving educational programs. Presidents also stepped up their search for operating and capital funds. Many colleges raised tuition more rapidly than they had previously done, and some launched larger and more comprehensive capital fund drives. In colleges such as Spelman,

Clark, and Xavier, where great change took place, fundraising consultants from well-known national firms were retained and became regular visitors at their trustee meetings. In these colleges, admission staffs grew; fundraising staffs were enlarged and reorganized both to seek private capital funds, and to learn to deal with the federal agencies responsible for student aid, building construction loans, and Title III institutional subsidy. Despite a great deal of work, however, the tangible gains—such as improved operating budgets, or larger enrollments—seemed only slightly to outnumber the losses. A clearer answer to the fundamental issues of the 1970s would not emerge for a few more years.

Perhaps it is too soon to say what the results are for the college presidents of the 1990s. Certainly colleges everywhere continued to benefit from a national economy that featured extremely low inflation, full employment, and, for colleges fortunate enough to have an endowment portfolio, a sharply rising stock market. During the decade, several historically black private and public colleges reported informally that they were once again beginning to attract the kinds of students who had been so successfully recruited by the most selective northern and western colleges in the previous two decades. Respected national magazines and newspapers, including *Newsweek,* the *New York Times,* the *Washington Post,* and the *Wall Street Journal,* for the first time published feature stories about individual students who, faced with excellent college choices of all kinds, chose to enroll at private black colleges.[18] But the struggle for survival is not over. Faculty salaries and student financial aid budgets still must rise significantly to be competitive with those of predominantly white colleges and universities. Teaching loads in most historically black private colleges remain heavy enough so that little time and energy remain for such things as reorganization of curriculum or large-scale implementation of new teaching techniques. These things could be said of most of the colleges in the nation, except perhaps the most prosperous ones. However, the private black colleges—even in the best of times—make up a collegiate network that is low on reserve assets. So much energy is required to meet the challenges of earlier years and to keep current programs respectable that, in most instances, the colleges' reserve strengths are limited.

Many long-term observers of these colleges say that the most noticeable occurrence of the past fifty years is that private black colleges are, among themselves, much less alike than they were in the 1950s.[19] Several colleges, favored by location, leadership, and good fortune, have grown in size, attractiveness, and financial strength. Others, with different locations and circumstances, and with less adaptability, by comparison still appear to be struggling. However, fifty years ago it would have been foolhardy to predict that even a few private black colleges would become sufficiently successful at attracting and managing endowment funds so that, on an endowment-dollars-per-student basis, they now are comparable to well known universities elsewhere. Table 1.1 shows that among 344 private institutions surveyed, three private black colleges made it to the middle of such a ranked list, and one appears near the end. These four are Spelman College, Hampton University, Howard University, and Bethune-Cookman College.

We think it is reasonable to expect that several other private black colleges within the next decade will, in such matters as endowment, faculty qualifications, and student career achievement, measure increasingly well compared with many other nationally respected colleges and universities. To do this, they will need to continue to define a clear vision of purpose. In different ways throughout the book, this emphasis of the authors is repeated and becomes almost a refrain: if their leaders can maintain vision and focus, the private black colleges will remain significant and also will carry forward a distinctive history that is important to the institutional diversity of American higher education and to the texture of American society.

The next seven chapters turn to history: the history of black higher education, and the unusual difficulties that were so important to its development. For some readers, this may be more history than seems necessary. For most, however, these chapters will add to a better understanding of both the present status of private black colleges and their role in all U.S. higher education. Richard Kluger, author of a history of the Supreme Court's decision in *Brown v. Board of Education*, explains at

TABLE 1.1

Private Institutions Ranked by Endowment Assets per Full Time Equivalent (FTE) Student in FY 1999 (Selected Colleges)

National Rank	Private Black Colleges and Universities	Other Private Colleges and Universities	Endowment Assets ($) per FTE Student
1		The Rockefeller University	7,197,143
2		Princeton University	1,007,978
111	Spelman College		96,648
113		Carnegie Mellon University	94,885
144		Barnard College	68,203
171		Tulane University	53,415
216		New York University	36,537
219	Hampton University		35,435
228	Howard University		31,206
324	Bethune-Cookman College		10,416

Source: Cambridge Associates, Inc., *1999 NACVBO Endowment Study* (Washington, D.C.: National Association of College and University Business Officers, 2000), Exhibit 5.

the beginning of his book why this close examination of background is important.

> From the start, the United States aspired to far more than its own survival. And from the start, its people have assigned to themselves a nobler destiny, justified by a higher moral standing, than impartial scrutiny might confirm . . . .
>
> Of the ideals that animated the American nation at its beginning, none was more radiant or honored than the inherent equality of mankind. There was dignity in all human flesh, Americans proclaimed, and all must have its chance to strive and to excel. All men were to be protected alike from the threat of rapacious neighbors and from the prying of coercive state. If it is a sin to aspire to conduct of a higher order than one may at the moment be capable of, then Americans surely sinned in professing that all men are created equal—and then acting otherwise.[20]

As an example, the Declaration of Independence in 1776 said clearly and simply: "We hold these truths to be self-evident, that all men are created equal, that they are endowed by their Creator with certain inalienable Rights, that among these are life, liberty, and the pursuit of Happiness." However, fifteen years later the U.S. Constitution and its Bill of Rights permitted continuance of the institution of slavery for almost a full century. Many states during that time passed laws making it illegal to teach Blacks to read and write. In 1857, the U.S. Supreme Court said that Dred Scott, a slave, was property, not a citizen, and without standing to sue in federal court.

Soon after the Civil War, three amendments to the Constitution promised equal rights to black Americans. The Thirteenth Amendment (1865) abolished slavery everywhere in the United States. The Fourteenth Amendment (1868) provided that "No state shall deprive any person of life, liberty or property without due process of law; nor deny to any person . . . the equal protection of the laws." The Fifteenth Amendment (1870) stated that the right of citizens to vote "shall not be denied or abridged . . . on account of race, color, or previous condition of servitude." But during the ensuing decades, Blacks who attempted fully to exercise these rights encountered denial, hostility, and little help from the courts.

The emergence of nationally competitive, distinctive black colleges seems impressive under any circumstances. It is doubly so when one observes the large discrepancy between promise and reality—in human rights and in educational opportunity—that existed for black Americans during most of the nation's history.

CHAPTER 2

Major Historical Factors Influencing Black Higher Education

SLAVERY AND RACISM

THE RELATIONSHIPS that evolved between black and white Americans over the two and a half centuries from 1619 to 1865 have influenced every aspect of the life of black Americans, education being no exception. The first Africans who arrived in the English colonies were sold as indentured servants in Jamestown, Virginia, in 1619. Many Europeans would arrive in the New World in much the same way, but what happened to them thereafter would prove quite different. Unlike those of their European counterparts, agreements with Africans for a period of service routinely became lifetime indentures and those obligations were then extended to their children. In 1671, there were approximately two thousand African servants in Virginia, all with indentures that covered their lifetimes and those of their offspring. They and their children were slaves. By the end of the seventeenth century, there were approximately twenty-eight thousand Africans in twelve of the thirteen colonies, all in the same condition of servitude. Each colony except Georgia—whose governor owned slaves in a neighboring colony—recognized slavery as legal. Georgia legalized slavery in 1749. This process of enslavement was reflected in various laws enacted in the British colonies. Virginia, for example, passed legislation in the 1660s requiring "that all children born in this country shall be held bond or free according to the condition of the mother" and that "baptism doth not alter the condition of the person as to his bondage or freedom . . . [so that owners] may more carefully endeavor the propagation of Christianity by permitting children, though slaves . . . to be admitted to that sacrament."[1] A Maryland law provided that the children of European women married to Africans would be slaves as their fathers were and that the women would also be slaves as long as their husbands remained alive.[2] By the beginning of the 1670s, a firm link between African background and slave status had been established in the minds of European colonists. In the next century, laws in southern states would classify slaves as chattel—personal property—and make it illegal to teach slaves to read or write.

At the start of the American Revolution, more than half a million African slaves resided in the colonies, concentrated mainly in large agricultural units in the coastal lowlands and piedmont of the area stretching from Virginia to Georgia. The concept of the "rights of man," heralded by the Revolution in the Declaration of Resolves of the First Continental Congress in 1765 and then in the Declaration of Independence, had little if any effect on these people held in bondage. Some northern states, where slaves were few, abolished the institution soon after the Revolution, but elsewhere the number of slaves only increased and the oppressive nature of the slave system continued to grow. Under pressure from southern states, the new nation in its Constitution recognized slavery as legal, failing to perceive that it would spawn a series of political crises that would end in a cataclysmic civil war. Along this troubled course, in 1820 and again in 1850, southerners and non-southerners negotiated compromises that sought to draw boundaries limiting new territories into which slavery could spread, and to establish a procedure that allowed white Americans living in a territory to decide whether slavery could exist there. The fragile nature of these compromises was reflected in the case of *Dred Scott v. Sanford*. Scott, a slave, claimed his freedom because his master took him from Missouri, a slave state, to the free state of Illinois and the free territory of Wisconsin, and back to Missouri. In 1857, the U.S. Supreme Court denied Scott's claim that he had become free when taken into free territory and had lived north of the boundary line for slavery established in 1820. But the Court went much further. It stated that as a Black, Scott was not even a citizen and so could not sue in federal court; that slaves were property, and could be taken into any territory by their owners. The effect was to heighten the developing bitterness between those who supported the expansion of slavery and abolitionists who opposed slavery on moral grounds or because of the threat it posed to free labor. Only three years later, a state of civil war existed between eleven secessionist southern states and the rest of the Union.

The development of a system of chattel slavery seems incongruous in a country whose government was based on the political ideals expressed in the Declaration of Independence and the Constitution. That many of the individuals who developed this political system were also slave owners created fundamental logical and moral conflicts that remain difficult to resolve. To reconcile the simultaneous acceptance of chattel slavery and a belief in "liberty, equality, and the pursuit of happiness"[3] required the founders to view the people retained in bondage as inferior to those who held them and therefore neither entitled to be judged by the same morality nor to enjoy the same societal benefits. The deep-seated nature of such a rationalization helps explain why some periods of American history that are praised for advancing the concept of democracy were also times when the oppressiveness of slavery and discrimination against

Blacks actually increased. Laws were passed in Alabama, Virginia, and other southern states during the period of Jacksonian democracy (1829– 41) that made it illegal to teach Blacks to read or write. Large numbers of black Americans were lynched during the Populist period (1892–96). Jim Crow reached its fullest development during the Progressive era (1890–1917). Each democratic upsurge in the country made it more difficult to justify the existence of slavery and so more important to establish the rationalization that black Americans were undeserving of the considerations to which other Americans were entitled.

Even in 1865 as the Civil War was drawing to its end, many white Americans of all classes, northern as well as southern, believed that the long enslavement of Blacks was evidence that they were intellectually inferior beings on whom any serious investment in education would be wasted. As that famed French visitor to the United States, Alexis de Tocqueville, observed in *Democracy in America*, "the prejudice of race appears to be stronger in states that have abolished slavery than in those where it still exists; and nowhere is it so intolerant as in the states where servitude has never been known."[4] Despite the existence of strong anti-slavery feelings in the northern states, racist attitudes continued to run deep in the region, as shown by the violent New York City Draft Riots of 1863, when opposition to the draft resulted in the death of about a dozen Blacks, and by the destruction of black-owned property and the restrictions placed on black voting rights in some Union states during the Civil War.

RACISM AFTER SLAVERY

The Thirteenth Amendment to the Constitution ending slavery, passed by Congress on January 31, 1865, in the wake of the Union victory in the Civil War, produced little or no immediate change in the attitudes of most white southerners. Embittered by defeat, they sought to restore as closely as possible in the South the political and social patterns that had existed before the war. In late 1865, "Black Codes"—laws quite similar to pre-war Slave Codes—were passed in each state of the former Confederacy. The next year, former Confederate Vice President Alexander Stephens, six former cabinet members, and four ex-generals of the Confederacy were elected to seats in Congress. Black Americans were barred from voting in the elections. Steps were taken in several states to establish public schools with provisions that excluded black Americans or minimized their access to education.

The reaction of the Republican majority in Congress to the appearance among them of former Confederate officials was immediate. They refused to seat the elected southerners and took control of the reconstruction of the occupied South out of the hands of Andrew Johnson, the former governor of Tennessee and states-rights Democrat, who had succeeded the assassinated Abraham Lincoln as president. The Fourteenth Amendment was then passed by Congress and ratification made a mandatory step for southern states seeking readmission to the Union. The amendment defined citizenship, extended it to black Americans, prohibited states from denying the privileges and immunities of citizenship to any citizen, and guaranteed due process to all citizens. It also provided for the reduction of state representation in the U.S. House of Representatives in proportion to any limitations placed on the rights of black Americans to vote in that state.

Both Republicans and Democrats recognized that for the first time in the existence of the United States, the number of members of the House of Representatives allocated to each southern state would be based in part on the total number of black Americans counted in the upcoming 1870 census rather than on the three-fifths-of-all-slaves rule, as previously mandated by the Constitution.[5] As a result, southern members of the House of Representatives would increase in number and northern Republicans feared they might lose control of the federal government. If black Americans were prohibited from voting, Republicans would certainly lose their majorities in southern state legislatures and would see fewer members of their party elected to both houses of Congress. This specter of a southern-based Democratic Party stronger in Congress in 1872 than it had been in 1860 led to the adoption of the Fifteenth Amendment in 1870. It provided that "the right of citizens of the United States to vote shall not to be denied or abridged by the United States or by any State on account of race, color, or previous condition of servitude." That it would take almost another century before the federal government was willing to act on this amendment indicates how limited the national commitment actually was for these equal rights for black Americans.

Black Americans were politically active in the South during Congressional Reconstruction. There were 241 black Americans among the 976 delegates who took part in ten conventions held in 1867 to draw up new state constitutions prior to rejoining the Union.[6] In South Carolina, black Americans were a majority of the convention members. Overall they constituted 25 percent of all representatives. They were also a significant presence in state legislatures. Two were elected to the U.S. Senate and fourteen served nineteen terms in the House of Representatives between 1870 and 1877. Southern Whites generally expressed their opposition to these changed relations in a variety of ways.

Over several decades, violence or the threat of violence intermingled with political maneuvering as white Americans labored to reassert their pre-war dominance over black Americans and the political dominance of the Democratic Party in the South. Acts of violence by the Ku Klux Klan,

Regulators, Jayhawkers, Rifle Clubs of South Carolina, and other organized groups were directed against freedmen, white Republicans, or anyone viewed as supportive of Blacks. A report of a Congressional Investigating Committee found the Ku Klux Klan, the most active of these white supremacy groups, involved in violence that resulted in the deaths of 373 freedmen between 1866 and 1868. The report also provided detailed information on nine counties in South Carolina where over a six-month period in 1871, the Klan murdered thirty-five, beat up 262, and destroyed the property of 101 Blacks. Testimony before the committee indicated that extortion, intimidation, and terror were common throughout the southern states in those years.

Passage of the Amnesty Act of 1872 further strengthened the South in its opposition to civil rights for black Americans and to the influence of the Republican Party. The ban on former Confederate officials being involved in politics was ended and their return to the voting rolls gave a boost to the Democratic Party. At the same time, the demise of the Freedmen's Bureau—a federal agency created to assist black Americans in their transition from slavery to freedom—left the masses of impoverished former slaves without the advocacy or crucial services the bureau had provided. In its absence, freedmen, who often worked as tenant farmers on land owned by white Americans, were more easily intimidated into a withdrawal from politics by the threat of losing their homes, livelihood, and lives. Recognizing that the political situation was favorable to their interests, white Americans sought successfully to oust Republicans from state legislatures and to secure the removal of the remaining federal troops in southern states.

The presidential election of 1876 provided exactly the opportunity southerners sought. All but three southern states had already returned to Democratic Party ranks: Republican majorities remaining only in Florida, Louisiana, and South Carolina. In the election, neither Republican candidate Rutherford B. Hayes of Ohio, nor the Democratic candidate Samuel Tilden secured a majority of the electoral votes. In the three Republican-controlled southern states, both parties claimed victory. A federal commission with a Republican majority was set up by Congress to determine the winning party. In 1877, it awarded all twenty disputed votes to Hayes. The Democrats accepted the commission's decision in return for Republican agreement to remove all federal troops from the South. This Compromise of 1877 brought the twelve years of Reconstruction to an end. A generation of white southerners, the losers in a war, had successfully restored the status quo ante through political action and private terror.

Not surprisingly, the success of the Democratic Party increased the terror and intimidation. Between 1886 and 1916, 2,605 Blacks were lynched in the southern states—an average of one person every four days over a period of three decades.[7] Systematic disenfranchisement resulted in a precipitous decline in black elected officials in Congress—from sixteen in the seven-year period ending in 1877 to seven in the thirty-three-year period between 1877 and 1910. After 1877, southern states and municipalities accelerated enactment of legislation to separate all aspects of civic life by race. Historian C. Vann Woodward provides an excellent sense of the spirit of the times in *The Strange Career of Jim Crow.* "Up to the year 1898," he wrote,

> South Carolina had resisted the Jim Crow car movement which had rapidly swept the western states of the South completely by this time. In that year . . . the Charleston News and Courier, the oldest newspaper in the South and a consistent spokesman for conservatism, fired a final broadside against extremists on behalf of the conservative creed of race policy. "As we have got on fairly well for a third of a century . . . without such a policy," wrote the editor, "we can probably get on as well hereafter without it. . . . If we must have Jim Crow cars on the railroads, there should be Jim Crow cars on the street railways. Also on all passenger boats. . . . If there are to be Jim Crow cars, moreover, there should be Jim Crow waiting saloons at all stations, and Jim Crow eating houses. . . . There should be Jim Crow sections of the jury box, and a separate Jim Crow dock and witness stand in every court—and a Jim Crow Bible for colored witnesses to kiss. It would be advisable also to have a Jim Crow section in county auditors' and treasurers' offices for the accommodation of colored tax payers. . . . There should be a Jim Crow department for making returns and paying for the privileges and blessings of citizenship. . . ." In resorting to the tactics of reductio ad absurdum the editor doubtless believed that he had dealt the Jim Crow principle a telling blow with his heavy irony. . . . But . . . apart from . . . the Jim Crow witness stand, all the improbable applications of the principle suggested by the editor in derision had been put into practice—down to and including the Jim Crow Bible.[8]

Emboldened by the unwillingness of the federal government to support the freedmen and by the absence of large-scale objections from northerners, southern lawmakers took other major steps toward their goal. They began to put in place the legal underpinnings for "white supremacy," relying on ostensibly nonracial categories, from which they nonetheless managed to exempt white Americans from legislation that might negatively affect them. A classic example was legislation regarding suffrage that passed in a number of southern states beginning in the late 1890s. These laws established poll taxes, property requirements, or literacy tests as the basis for the right to vote, which might have prevented the poor and illiterate—black and white—from voting. However, "grand-father clauses" exempted those whose fathers or grandfathers had been eligible to vote before January 1, 1867. Naturally no black Americans in any southern state was able to meet that requirement. States then held that poor, illiterate, propertyless white Americans were not being exempted due to race but to a historical tradition of voting eligibility. Once the disenfranchisement of black Americans had been achieved, nothing but action by the U.S. Congress or the federal courts could have prevented the passage of any laws thought necessary to maintain racial segregation.

But northern interest in the plight of the freedmen waned at the very time that such steps to maintain segregation were being taken. For some Americans, the new survival-of-the-fittest theories of Social Darwinists served as justification enough for the developing racial caste system and for the growth of monopolistic business practices at home and policies of imperialist expansion in Latin America and Asia. By the end of the nineteenth century, few white voices rose in opposition to violations of the civil rights of black Americans. Tradition, local ordinances, and state laws had undone the political and social advances of the Reconstruction era.

Appeals to the courts brought no relief. In fact, a series of Supreme Court decisions between 1873 and 1896 undermined the actions taken by Congress between 1865 and 1875 to protect the rights of black citizens. Provisions of the Civil Rights Enforcement Act of 1870 were declared unconstitutional; state governments were generally supported when in conflict with the federal government over equal-protection-of-the-law issues; and discrimination against individuals in public places was sanctioned, even when committed by businesses that served the public at large. In two 1880 decisions, the Supreme Court provided what amounted to a "how-to-do-it" course in discriminating against black Americans without running afoul of the federal judiciary. In a West Virginia case, the Court declared that a state law excluding black Americans from serving on juries was a violation of the Fourteenth Amendment. However in a Virginia case, heard in the same session, it held that systematic exclusion of black Americans from service on juries was not a violation, as long as it was not actually embedded in law.[9] In such cases, proof would then be required that black Americans had been excluded solely because of race and relief would have to be sought in those very same state courts that practiced the exclusion.

In 1890, Louisiana passed legislation requiring that railroads provide separate cars for Blacks and Whites and that passengers be required to use the coaches provided for their racial group. Black Americans, feeling that there was a chance to overturn the new law, made plans to test it. On June 7, 1892, Homer Plessy boarded an East Louisiana Railway train and took a seat in a car designated for Whites. Asked to move, he refused to do so.[10] The conductor sought police assistance. Plessy was arrested and charges were brought against him in a local New Orleans court presided over by Judge John H. Ferguson. Plessy promptly challenged the 1890 law in federal court, charging that it violated his Thirteenth Amendment rights and the Fourteenth Amendment's equal protection guarantee. R. L. Desdunes, the publisher of the *Daily Crusader,* a black-owned New Orleans newspaper, expressed support for Plessy, reflecting the sense of optimism many Louisiana Blacks felt about the outcome of the case:

> We venture nothing by saying that there are signs which indicate that the country is growing weary and disgusted over this race legislation, and our legislators would do well to place themselves in harmony with the new dispensation which means to establish in America National citizenship and a "peace of the United States."
>
> We think it can be logically shown that common carriers are compelled to accommodate travelers whatever may be their color, and that a law which is intended to deny travel under any circumstances is clearly unconstitutional and intolerable.[11]

It was not until 1896 that the Supreme Court heard the case of *Plessy v. Ferguson.* The decision, written by Justice Henry Billings Brown, made it obvious how misplaced the *Daily Crusader's* optimism regarding the readiness of the federal government to protect the rights of black citizens had been. It upheld the state law requiring separation by race on railroads operating in Louisiana, provided equal facilities were offered for each racial group. Regarding the Fourteenth Amendment, Brown wrote:

> We cannot say that a law which authorizes or even requires the separation of the two races in public conveyances is unreasonable, or more obnoxious to the Fourteenth Amendment than the acts of Congress requiring separate schools for colored children in the District of Columbia, the constitutionality of which does not seem to have been questioned, or the corresponding acts of state legislatures.
>
> We consider the underlying fallacy of the plaintiff's argument to consist in the assumption that the enforced separation of the two races stamps the colored race with a badge of inferiority. If this be so, it is not by reason of anything found in the act, but solely because the colored race chooses to put that construction upon it.[12]

A single dissenting (and prophetic) opinion in *Plessy v. Ferguson* came from Justice John Marshall Harlan, who had owned slaves in his native Kentucky but firmly supported the Union. He believed that the intent of the framers of the Constitution and common sense should be the basis of all legislation:

> Everyone knows that the statute in question had its origin in the purpose, not so much to exclude white persons from railroad cars occupied by Blacks, as to exclude colored people from coaches occupied by or assigned to white

persons. . . . The thing to accomplish was, under the guise of giving equal accommodation for Whites and Blacks, to compel the latter to keep to themselves while traveling in railroad passenger coaches. No one would be so wanting in candor as to assert the contrary. . . .

In my opinion, the judgment this day rendered will, in time, prove to be quite as pernicious as the decision made by this tribunal in the Dred Scott case. . . . It seems that we have yet, in some of the States, a dominant race— a superior class of citizens, which assumes to regulate the enjoyment of civil rights, common to all citizens, upon the basis of race.[13]

Although *Plessy v. Ferguson* dealt with public transportation, both proponents and opponents recognized its implications for education. So bleak did the post-decision climate seem that some black Americans saw in the "separate but equal" clause a dim ray of hope. *Plessy*, they believed, might at least put an end to efforts in several state legislatures to end all state appropriations for black education. Black public schools would then have the funds needed for their continued existence. But even this prospect—that some bit of moral good might flow from an immoral ruling—was not to materialize.

Plessy's implications for private higher education became clear as a result of a ruling in the 1908 case of *Berea College v. Commonwealth of Kentucky*. In 1904, the state of Kentucky had passed a law requiring segregation in all state schools, both public and private. Berea, a small private institution in eastern Kentucky that had admitted both Blacks and Whites since its founding in 1859, challenged the constitutionality of a law (obviously aimed solely at the school, as there were no other unsegregated educational institutions in the state). For the hearing before the state Supreme Court, Kentucky provided an openly racist brief, suggesting that "if the progress, advancement and civilization of the twentieth century is to go forward, then it must be left not only to the unadulterated blood of the Anglo-Saxon-Caucasian race, but to the highest types and geniuses of that race." Seven of the sitting Justices in the *Berea* case had participated in *Plessy*, six of them concurring with Justice Brown's decision.[14] Thus the decision not to overturn the Kentucky Supreme Court's ruling was not surprising; nevertheless, it broke new ground by permitting states to outlaw voluntary as well as obligatory contact between the races. Yet another step was taken in the creation of a full-fledged racial caste system.

Such Court decisions as *Berea v. Kentucky* provided the go-ahead for state and municipal lawmakers to separate the races without considering *Plessy*'s call for equal facilities. In the private sector, businesses discriminated against black Americans in employment, charged higher premiums for insurance, and often refused to provide mortgages on black-owned property. Most unions refused to admit black American members.

During President Woodrow Wilson's administration, segregation in the
federal workplace became the rule in Washington. The president even
turned down a modest proposal by northern liberals to establish a federal
commission to study the race problem, apparently assuming that the
matter did not warrant study.

In the early years of the twentieth century, "separate" had increasingly
come to mean "unequal," especially in the realm of public education.
Few would deny that the allocation of educational resources is a sensitive
measure of the priorities of those in control of the purse strings. The
distribution of financial resources under the dual system of schools required in all the southern states provides insight into the relative value
state governments and the educational bureaucracy placed on educating
black and white Americans.

As a region, the South spent less on public education than did other
areas of the country. State funds were distributed to counties based on
the total number of students they were educating. But the counties were
then free to distribute those funds to schools or school districts as they
saw fit. Table 2.1 shows the growing inequality in per-student expenditures for black and white teachers' salaries (the major annual expense for

TABLE 2.1

Ratio between Per Capita Expenditures for Teachers' Salaries by Race
(in Dollars)

Year	Black Student	North Carolina White Student	Alabama White Student	Lowndes County, Alabama White Student
1875–76	1.00	1.03	0.89	na
1880–81	1.00	0.94	1.04	na
1885–86	1.00	1.08	1.17	na
1890–91	1.00	1.14	1.23	na
1895–96	1.00	1.05	na	na
1900–01	1.00	1.38	na	na
1905–06	1.00	1.91	na	na
1910–11	1.00	2.44	5.83	29.39
1915–16	1.00	2.89	5.69	30.08
1920–21	1.00	2.70	5.35	33.22
1925–26	1.00	2.67	4.85	29.50
1930–31	1.00	2.30	4.09	25.26

Source: Horace Mann Bond, *The Education of the Negro in the American Social Order* (New
York: Prentice-Hall, 1934), pp. 153–59.

Notes: na indicates that data are not available.

TABLE 2.2
Southeast Region Teachers' Salaries, 1916 (in Dollars)

County Group: Percentage of Blacks in Population	Aggregate White Teachers' Salaries	Aggregate Black Teachers' Salaries	Per Capita White	Per Capita Black
< 10	7,755,817	315,579	7.96	7.23
10–25	9,633,674	1,196,788	9.55	5.55
25–50	12,573,666	2,265,945	11.11	3.19
50–75	4,574,366	1,167,796	12.53	1.77
75	888,749	359,800	22.22	1.78

Source: Thomas Jesse Jones, *Negro Education: A Study of the Private and Higher Schools for Colored People in the United States* (Washington, D.C.: U.S. Bureau of Education, 1917).

schools) in selected years from 1875 to 1930. It tallies the amounts spent on white students for every dollar spent on black students in North Carolina, Alabama, and Lowndes County, Alabama. Table 2.2 provides data on the aggregate salaries of white and black teachers based on the percentage of Blacks in the population of the county.

Three trends are clearly reflected in the tables. First, salaries for teachers of white students rose precipitously compared with those for teachers of black students. Second, the higher the percentage of black Americans in a county, the greater the difference in per capita spending. And third, per capita spending for teachers' salaries directly reflects patterns of increasing disenfranchisement, segregation, and discrimination in political and social life between the end of Reconstruction and World War I.

CONDITION OF THE FREEDMEN

In 1790, when the first national census was taken, there were more than 758,000 Americans of African descent in the United States, many of them foreign born. In the 1860 census, the black population was found to have increased by a factor of 5.9 to 4,442,000—few of them foreign born—while the white population had increased by a factor of 8.4. The number of black Americans who became citizens as a result of the Fourteenth and Fifteenth Amendments—92 percent of whom had spent their entire lives as slaves—had declined as a percentage of the total population by 5 percent.

The South would remain the home of over 90 percent of the black population until the 1880s and over 50 percent would still be living in that region midway through the twentieth century. One-third of the population of the South would be black American throughout the nineteenth century. Census data show that more than three-quarters of black Americans—currently the country's most urban ethnic group—lived in rural areas in 1900, already a decline from Reconstruction (see Table 2.3). Literacy—estimated at 5 percent—existed almost solely among free Blacks in the northern states, and occasional individuals who either were taught by Whites or attended a rare pre-war clandestine school operated in the South by a black teacher. By the late 1860s, large numbers of Blacks were economically destitute and often worse off physically than before the war. The vast majority had worked on white-owned plantations that produced staple agricultural crops of cotton, tobacco, or rice. As slaves, they had not profited from their labor. They were unable to accumulate private property or to benefit from the wealth they had helped produce.

Freed in 1865, they were without resources to purchase land on which to use their agricultural skills for their own benefit. There was much talk about grants to freedmen of "forty acres and a mule" with which they could establish economic self-sufficiency. The more militant abolitionists and supporters of civil rights backed the idea of the federal government distributing among former slaves land that had been abandoned by or confiscated from the military and civilian leaders of the Confederacy. But no such general policy was ever put into effect, even though the federal government owned considerable land in the South. In the few instances where the confiscated lands of Confederate military or political officials had been distributed to black Americans, the lands were eventually returned to their pre-1865 owners.

The overwhelming majority of nineteenth-century black Americans had neither personal experience living as free persons nor living relatives who had such experience. They had been taught "on the job" to perform the limited tasks assigned them by those who held them in bondage. Lack of experience in managing their own affairs left them vulnerable when dealing with aggressive or unscrupulous Whites, large numbers of whom were hostile toward any organized activity on the part of Blacks, including school attendance. This hostility extended to any missionaries or teachers who worked with Blacks. Those Blacks who endured the condescension of well-meaning Whites were hardly better off than those who faced outright hostility.

The limited demographic information available about freedmen after the Civil War provides crucial insight into the effects of slavery on the personalities and attitudes of those held in bondage, but it cannot fully explain the overwhelming interest shown in education among large numbers of black people of all ages. Contemporary sources often cannot help explain this interest because those in closest contact with Blacks—other

TABLE 2.3

Blacks in U.S. Population 1800–1950

Census Year	Number of Blacks (000)	Percentage of Total U.S. Population	Percentage of Blacks Living in South	Percentage of School-Age Blacks Enrolled	Percentage of Black Rural Population	Percentage of U.S. Rural Population	Percentage of Blacks in Southern Population
1800	1,002	19	91.6	na	na	na	35.0
1820	1,772	18	92.7	na	na	na	37.2
1840	2,874	17	91.9	na	na	na	38.0
1860	4,442	14	92.2	1.9	na	na	36.8
1880	6,581	13	90.4	33.8	na	na	36.0
1900	8,834	12	89.6	31.1	77.4	60.3	32.3
1920	10,438	11	85.3	53.5	66.1	48.7	27.1
1940	12,866	10	76.9	68.4	52.1	43.3	23.8
1950	15,042	10	67.9	74.8	38.3	na	21.8

Sources: U.S. Bureau of the Census, *Historical Statistics of the United States: Colonial Times to 1957* (Washington, D.C.: Government Printing Office, 1960), pp. 9–11; U.S. Bureau of the Census, *Negro Population in the United States 1790–1915* (Washington, D.C.: Government Printing Office, 1968), pp. 44–47; Thomas Snyder, *120 Years of American Education: A Statistical Portrait* (Washington, D.C.: Government Printing Office, 1993), pp. 11–12.

Note: na indicates that data are not available.

Blacks, former slave owners, and their agents—either had limited skills in maintaining records or had strong cultural biases about Blacks that hardly made for accurate reportage. Those who opposed education for Blacks—with its promise of freedom and equality—reflected with astonishing unanimity the view that freedmen were dangerous to society unless controlled as free citizens in much the same fashion as when they had been slaves. The general view dominating the southern press was that Blacks not only should remain in a slave-like state but were congenitally incapable of handling a better status. George Fitzhugh, a Virginia lawyer who regularly wrote articles for the *De Bow's Review,* proved quite typical when in 1866 he assured his readers that "immemorial usage, law, custom and divine injunction, nay human nature itself, have subordinated inferior races to superior races. Never did the black man come in contact with the white man, that he did not become his subordinate, if not his slave."[15] This unflattering view would be widely echoed over the following century in the press and reflected in state and federal policies nationwide. The scholarly community, North as well as South, proved no exception. Typical among pre–World War II American historians was the following passage on black Americans in the widely used 1937 to 1950 editions of Samuel Eliot Morison's and Henry Steele Commager's text, *The Growth of the American Republic.* Discussing the period from 1820 to 1850 they wrote:

> As for Sambo, whose wrongs moved the abolitionists to wrath and tears, there is some reason to believe that he suffered less than any other class in the South from its "peculiar institution." The majority of slaves were adequately fed, well cared for, and apparently happy. . . . Although brought to America by force, the incurably optimistic negro soon became attached to the country, and devoted to his "white folks."[16]

There was less unanimity among those who supported serious efforts to provide educational opportunities for black Americans. Some supporters viewed education as inextricably connected to freedom and were simply committed to the application of the principles of the Declaration of Independence to all U.S. citizens. Others pushed education and rights for black Americans as a useful strategy to help maintain political control in the South. Still others believed that freed black Americans should be educated, but only in limited ways, to prepare them for the kind of menial jobs they were believed capable of performing and for an acceptance of their subordinate place in society.

Recognizing the cultural biases in contemporary reports on freedmen in the post war years improves our ability to make use of them, but a great deal more remains to be done. Important assistance in understanding the states of mind of those just released from the slave system has come from sophisticated sociological and psychological probes by social scientists into how the populations of total institutions behave, feel about themselves, and respond to the expectations those in control have of them.[17] In *Total Institutions,* Samuel E. Wallace provides a reasonable definition of such a place:

> All institutions in society—the church, family, courts of law or care-giving centers—have some power over the individual. . . . When any type of social institution—religious, educational, legal or medical—begins to exercise total control over its population, that institution begins to display certain characteristics: communication between insiders and outsiders is rigidly controlled or prohibited altogether; those inside the institution are frequently referred to as inmates—subjects whose every movement is controlled by the institution's staff; an entirely separate social world comes into existence within the institution, which defines the inmate's social status, his relationship to all others, his very identity as a person.
>
> In part total institutions are created because we feel some individuals in our society need to be given, forcibly if necessary, a new identity.[18]

American slavery was obviously such an institution. Information gained from studies of twentieth-century total institutions provides a background for probing the actions of slaves in the previous century. A review of descriptions of slave behavior, examined with the insights provided by studies of inmates in twentieth-century prisons, concentration camps, asylums, and military organizations, supports some assumptions about the feelings and attitudes of slaves that were not part of the thinking of either a Fitzhugh or such historians as Morison and Commager.

For a host of reasons the slave system, like other total institutions, was never fully successful in molding the personalities of its "inmates" to the degree desired by those in authority. This could have been due to the inefficiencies found in all human organizations or to the tendency of those having absolute authority to believe that the doctrines they formulate (in this case, of white supremacy) actually do define reality. Deferential behavior is often mistaken for an internalization of assigned institutional roles. The existence of subversive subculture structures within total institutions that support values and expectations different from those of the authorities, although feared, are often not recognized. Rather than one personality type of stereotypical, submissive "Sambo," slavery unsurprisingly produced a rich variety of personality types. Only with this in mind can the remarkably enterprising spirit of many freedmen be explained. In truth the range of attitudes of the freedmen ran the gamut from the view that the end of slavery was a license to avoid work to that of parents who surprised contemporary white observers by establishing schools at almost untold sacrifices to themselves so that their children might attend. And thousands of all ages, as soon as they were free, sought education with considerable passion.

POLITICAL AND ECONOMIC INSTABILITY IN THE SOUTH

Many historians, from John Elliott Cairnes writing in 1862 to Allan Nevins in 1947 and James McPherson in 1988 consider slavery to be the underlying cause of the Civil War.[19] The war's immediate cause was the success of the Republicans—the party opposed to the expansion of slavery into new territories—in the presidential election of 1860. Slavery had dominated southern life for decades, formed much of the wealth of its ruling class, and provided the labor for cotton, one of the country's major exports. The institution tended to corrupt both slaves and slave owners. It threatened the economic position of poor Whites in the South and the possibility of its spread threatened the economic position of poor Whites in the North. Only at the radical fringe—among relatively small numbers of Abolitionists—was there serious concern for the rights of those held as slaves.[20] Even President Abraham Lincoln was initially willing to support a constitutional amendment permitting the continuation of slavery in the states where it already existed. It is probable that southerners understood better than northerners that the emancipation of slaves was primarily an action taken for military reasons and that the Union lacked the resolve to enforce the provisions of the constitutional amendments conferring citizenship on former slaves and guaranteeing equal protection under the law.

In 1865, the South's economy was as unstable as its politics. More than 358,000 southerners (2 percent of the population and 32 percent of the armed forces) had been killed or wounded during the Civil War.[21] The region's overall financial loss from the war years has been estimated at more than two billion dollars.[22] In addition, the Fourteenth Amendment invalidated the Confederate debt so that individuals could not be paid for services rendered or loans made to them. In any case, Confederate money was worthless. Many homes and other structures were destroyed. The railroads were in ruins. Almost the entire black population was poverty stricken. Prior to 1865, much of the region's wealth had been in land and slaves. The Emancipation Proclamation and the Thirteenth Amendment freed the slaves without compensation to their owners.

In 1861, over five million bales of cotton—the South's major crop—was produced and sold at thirteen cents a pound. In 1866, the production of fewer than two million bales had briefly pushed the price up to forty-three cents, but as production increased the price steadily declined, reaching thirteen cents again in 1876. But the situation of a large landowner planting cotton was not the same in 1876 as fifteen years earlier. Labor was now provided by sharecroppers or farm laborers who either received a share of the cotton or an agreed-upon amount for their labor. Even given the minimal sums paid out, the cost of producing cotton had risen without the use of slave labor, and cotton prices would only continue to decline, reaching under nine cents per pound in 1901.[23]

The appearence of political stability in the South by the end of the nineteenth century was achieved at great cost to the region as a whole and particularly to black Americans. In denying them their new constitutional rights, the country engaged in a profound waste of human talent and created a host of problems that sapped the strength of the southern region for decades and laid the foundation for further destabilization. Disenfranchisement decreased the percentage of black Americans registered to vote from 66.9 percent of those of voting age in 1867 to 5.7 percent in 1892. The conformity that came to be required on all matters related to race placed severe restrictions on the free expression of opinion in politics, education, and any other areas of life that affected both Blacks and Whites. For all practical purposes, there was no two-party system in the "solid [Democratic] South."

As historians have noted then and since, Whites in their organized and systematic oppression of Blacks brought out the worst in themselves. The appearance of stability was not the same as racial peace. There were, for instance, a staggering 491 lynchings of southern Blacks between 1896 and 1900 alone. The South (and other regions of the country) experienced major race riots: Statesboro, Georgia, and Springfield, Ohio, in 1904; Atlanta, Georgia, and Brownsville, Texas, in 1906. Each riot followed a similar pattern. Whites, angered by reports or rumors of criminal activity by Blacks, lynched the real or alleged perpetrators, also beat and killed other Blacks in the area and destroyed property owned by Blacks. This pattern repeated itself in another upsurge of anti-black violence following World War I apparently intended to make clear that the Allied victory in the war "to make the world safe for democracy" did not include the world in which they lived in the United States. Race riots in Longview, Texas; Chicago; Knoxville, Tennessee; Omaha, Nebraska; and Elaine, Arkansas, in 1919; in Tulsa, Oklahoma, in 1921; and in Detroit, Michigan, in 1925 rocked the country. Lynchings, although not as numerous as in the late 1890s, increased in number in the 1910s and Congress failed on several occasions to pass legislation making lynching a federal crime.

Several new organizations opposed to racial segregation and discrimination were established. The Niagara Movement, predecessor to the National Association for the Advancement of Colored People (NAACP), was organized in 1905. At its first annual meeting, it adopted a resolution demanding full citizenship rights for black Americans. The introduction to the resolution, written by W.E.B. Du Bois, reflected a new aggressiveness that would only build over the next several decades:

> In the past year the work of the Negro hater has flourished in the land. Step by step the defenders of rights of American citizens have retreated. The work of stealing the black man's ballot has progressed and the fifty and more representatives of stolen votes still sit in the nation's capital. . . . Never before in the modern age has a great and civilized folk threatened to adopt so cowardly a creed in treatment of its fellow-citizens, born and bred on its soil. Stripped of verbose subterfuge and in its naked nastiness, the new American creed says: fear to let black men even try to rise lest they become the equals of Whites. . . . The blasphemy of such a course is only matched by its cowardice.

The NAACP's initial program included a crusade against lynching, as well as efforts to secure greater police protection for southern Blacks and to gain improved educational and job opportunities for Blacks nationwide. In establishing branches in northern and southern cities and in directly challenging segregationists, it would be recognized as the leading civil rights organization. It would also experience far greater opposition than did the National Urban League, established in 1911, whose activities in large cities focused mainly on improving job opportunities for Blacks. Urban League organizers, like those of the NAACP, included both Blacks and Whites.

In 1911, Marcus Garvey also founded the Universal Negro Improvement Association (UNIA) in Jamaica. In 1917, he moved it to New York City, to which numbers of southern Blacks had been drawn by job opportunities during World War I. The UNIA, drawing its following mainly from southern and Caribbean migrants to urban areas, developed into the first black mass movement in the United States. Like the leadership of the NAACP and the National Urban League, Garvey urged Blacks to organize their own businesses but also to unite as a "nation," and to consider establishing independent states in Africa.

Although the effectiveness of the UNIA declined in the mid-1920s after Garvey was charged with using the mail to defraud and sentenced to five years in prison, the NAACP and the National Urban League increased their activities in this period. Unsurprisingly, both organizations struggled to keep afloat through the years of the Great Depression. Confronted by a 1913 "cotton depression" and a 1915 cotton crop devastated by boll weevils, the South, which did not benefit from the boom years of the 1920s, was already depressed when the Great Crash occurred in 1929.

The political and financial situation in the southern states and the poverty and deep-seated discrimination that were an ongoing part of life for most black southerners hardly seemed propitious conditions in which to establish—much less nurture—a new system of education. From this perspective, a decline from a 79 percent illiteracy rate among Blacks in 1870 to 11 percent in 1940 is striking in itself, but the development of approximately one hundred black institutions concerned with higher education, many of them in the private sector, is astonishing.[24]

CHAPTER 3

The Beginnings of Black Higher Education

FOR ALL PRACTICAL purposes, black higher education began in institutions established in the South just after the Civil War. Prior to that, however, a few Blacks had attended traditionally white colleges and a small number of institutions had been established before the war to provide higher education for Blacks.

Higher education in British North America had itself begun in 1636, when the Massachusetts General Court appropriated the monies for the establishment of Harvard College, whose aim it was "to advance learning, and perpetuate it to posterity."[1] Other institutions of higher learning—Yale, William and Mary, Brown, Dartmouth, Columbia, Princeton, Rutgers, and the University of Pennsylvania, each affiliated with one of the several Protestant denominations in the New World—were established before the American Revolution. Several state institutions were founded soon after the Revolution but only one, the University of North Carolina, awarded baccalaureate degrees in the eighteenth century.

The first black students entered American colleges and universities almost two centuries after the founding of Harvard. Although records tell us that a few black Americans like Francis Cardoza (who served as South Carolina's secretary of state and Mississippi's state superintendent of education during the Reconstruction era) attended university in Europe, John Chavis was the first to be involved in American higher education. He studied privately under President John Witherspoon of the College of New Jersey (later Princeton University) in the late eighteenth century. Although never formally enrolled, Chavis was apparently successful in his academic work, for he later operated a school in Virginia that prepared students for college.

The first degrees earned by black Americans were awarded to Edward A. Jones and John Russworm in 1826. Jones, who graduated from Amherst College in Massachusetts, became an Episcopal priest in Sierra Leone, where he helped to found the first college in the region. Russworm graduated from Bowdoin College in Maine, went to Liberia—a settlement established by former American slaves—to be Superintendent of Education and where he served as the governor from 1836 to 1851.

From the graduation of Jones and Russworm to the end of the Civil War—by which time the black American population of the United States had reached 4.4 million—twenty-eight Blacks (including Jones and Russworm) received baccalaureate degrees. Oberlin College in Ohio, founded in 1833, enrolled women and Blacks in the late 1830s and became outspoken in its admissions policies. Among its distinguished alumni was U.S. Senator Blanche K. Bruce (1875–81), one of a small number of black Americans elected to that body. It is reasonable to assume that other northern Blacks who sought admission to various northern colleges were unsuccessful. In any case, the twenty-eight graduates are all we can account for before 1865.

The first of the small number of pre-war institutions established for the purpose of providing higher education for black Americans was founded around the same time and for the same reason as colleges for white women: both groups were excluded from or had limited access to existing institutions of higher education.[2] The first of the schools established for Blacks was the Institute for Colored Youth in Philadelphia, founded in 1837, the same year as the Mount Holyoke Female Seminary was founded in Massachusetts for white women. Four other institutions for Blacks were established before the Civil War: Avery College in Allegheny, Pennsylvania (founded in 1849); the Ashmun Institute in Chester County, Pennsylvania (1854); Wilberforce University in Ohio (1855); and an academy for black girls in Washington, D.C. (1851), which became Miner Teacher's College in 1860. Following a pattern common to many other institutions of higher learning at the time, these schools offered preparatory programs, and sometimes primary-school work, for students aspiring to attend college. With the exception of Miner Teacher's College, these institutions were located in areas where considerable anti-slavery feeling existed. Quakers, generally opposed to slavery, were a strong influence in Pennsylvania; northern Ohio also showed strong abolitionist sentiments.

There is no record of any of the black institutions awarding baccalaureate degrees before the end of the Civil War. Ashmun Institute awarded its first bachelors degree in 1865 (and renamed itself Lincoln University the following year); as evidently did Wilberforce University. The absence of information on degrees granted by Avery College and an 1870 description of Avery in a Freedmen's Bureau Report as "excelled by no high school in the country" makes it reasonable to assume that it too awarded no degrees before 1865. The Institute for Colored Youth granted its first degree in 1932, nineteen years after moving to Cheyney, Pennsylvania, and changing its name to Cheyney Training School for Teachers. The first degree from Miner Teacher's College was not issued until 1933.[3]

Although the first colleges for women and for Blacks were established in the same period, there were great differences in the educational backgrounds of the two groups that affected the nature of the institutions created to serve them. According to the 1860 census, for each one hundred of their group between ages five and nineteen, there were fifty-seven white females and fewer than two Blacks (male and female) enrolled in school.[4] According to the 1890 census, for each one hundred of their group, fifty-seven black males and sixty-five black females over thirteen years old were illiterate. For white females, the comparable number was nine.[5] The absence of statewide systems of public elementary and secondary education in the South and the high level of hostility toward higher education of any sort for black Americans only exacerbated the situation. Thus many white women were far ahead of all but a few Blacks in their level of education before institutions of higher learning were in place for them, and hostility to educating them was far lower. At a time when southern Blacks constituted 94 percent of the black American population, and when 90 percent of them could not read or write, the effort to establish simultaneously elementary schools, secondary schools, and colleges where none had previously existed created a unique situation with a unique set of problems.

FREEDMEN'S SCHOOLS

Progress in elementary and secondary education, without which development of higher education was difficult, proved painfully slow in the South during the post–Civil-War years. The very idea of free public schools for any racial group was opposed by most large landowners in the region. Although white businessmen and white small farmers, as well as the vast majority of Blacks, all supported their establishment, the majority of white southerners of all classes proved unsympathetic or hostile to education of any sort for the former slaves. This opposition expressed itself in ways ranging from legislative inaction on matters involving schools for Blacks to violent attacks on white teachers of black students, the destruction of school buildings, and the harassment of parents whose children attended school. The widespread opposition suggests why the private and not the public sector took the lead in providing black education.

Northern efforts to provide such education in the slave states began as Union forces took control of various parts of the Confederacy. The American Missionary Association and regional and state Freedmen's Aid societies undertook work of this nature in parts of the South occupied by Union troops as early as 1861. General William Tecumseh Sherman is often credited (and perhaps given more credit than he deserves) with planting the idea that set in motion an organized effort to establish schools for Blacks in the South. He publicly called on philanthropic people to assist in addressing the needs of the masses of black Americans flocking to the Union army as it moved from place to place. The numbers of these refugees—as the freedmen who followed the Union troops were appropriately called—increased to such a degree that they began to interfere with the conduct of the war. "To relieve the government of the burden that may hereafter become insupportable," wrote Sherman, "and to enable the Blacks to support and govern themselves in the abandonment of their disloyal guardians, a suitable system of cultivation and instruction must be combined with one providing for physical wants."[6] The idea of establishing schools had also received a boost from a June 1863 report by the Freedmen Bureau's Inquiry Commission to the Secretary of War that described the difficult conditions under which freedmen lived and the corruption of southern civil officials in their dealings with them. Thanks in part to the report, volunteers in northern cities began providing food and clothing for the refugees in the South, and in 1865, Congress, after two years of heated debate, established the Bureau of Refugees, Freedmen, and Abandoned Land, commonly referred to as the Freedmen's Bureau.

The legislation that created the Freedmen's Bureau as a branch of the War Department made no specific mention of education. The terms of the legislation gave the Secretary of War the power to "direct such issues of provisions, clothing, and fuel as he may deem needful for the immediate and temporary shelter and supply of destitute and suffering refugees and their wives and children, under such rules and regulations as he may direct."[7] It also gave the Bureau responsibility for managing southern land that had been abandoned or confiscated as a result of the war.

In March 1865, President Andrew Johnson appointed General Oliver Otis Howard as the Bureau's first commissioner. His annual salary was set at $3,000 and those of assistant commissioners at $2,500, but no appropriation was made for the operation of the Bureau. As a result, all positions except those of the assistant commissioners were filled by personnel borrowed from the army. Provisions for destitute freedmen often came from military supplies. Hampered from the beginning by these financial arrangements, the Bureau suffered a major setback when President Johnson returned all confiscated lands to their pre–Civil-War owners. Some of these properties had been sold or rented to freedmen and the funds generated used to operate the Bureau. This loss of financing essentially destroyed the Bureau's efforts to assist freedmen in establishing a self-sufficient economic base in agriculture, which served to exacerbate the difficulties to follow.

For the next six years, until it ceased to exist in 1872, the Bureau was the sole federal agency to embrace the cause of freedmen's rights. Some twentieth-century historians have viewed the Freedmen's Bureau as having had little impact because of the weakness of its organizational structure, its lack of funds, and white southern opposition. In the economic and political spheres, there is much to support this view. The same cannot be said about its influence on education. It was here that the Bureau made its most significant contribution. The January 1970 reports of John W. Alvord, superintendent of schools for the Bureau, provide ample evidence of the Bureau's involvement with volunteer groups to set up or assist in the establishment of 4,207 schools, employing 8,967 teachers, and serving 210,618 pupils "of all kinds [graded schools, high and normal schools, night schools, and Sabbath schools]."[8] As he wrote at the time:

> When our armies entered the South and the facts there were brought to light, two important things appeared: first, a surprising thirst for knowledge among the negroes; second, teachers in large numbers volunteering to instruct them. Hence, as soon as access could be obtained, schools among the colored people were successfully established. Many, indeed scoffed; more doubted; but it is a remarkable fact that the earliest efforts to impart knowledge to these darkened minds found them fully prepared for its reception. . . .
>
> The earliest school in the South for freedmen, or "contrabands," as they were then called, was commenced by the . . . [American Missionary Association] at Fortress Monroe September 17, 1861. During the day it was for children, and at night for adults. . . .
>
> The first determination of the Commission was not to take this great charity from the hands of its voluntary patrons. The people of the North had been pouring our supplies for suffering soldiers, and this general flow of philanthropy was not to subside. It turned naturally to the freedmen. To lift them up by education, was legitimately the work of the people. . . .
>
> The Commissioner, therefore said, . . . "The educational and moral condition of the people will not be forgotten. The utmost facility will be offered to benevolent and religious organizations and State authorities in this maintenance of good schools for refugees and freedmen until a system of free schools can be supported by the reorganized local governments."[9]

Had the Freedmen's Bureau not been established it is unlikely that any federal agency would have worked on behalf of the former slaves, and volunteer educational activity by religious and secular antislavery activists would not have been as effective. It is also highly unlikely that at any time soon after the war, state governments, controlled by white southerners, would have recognized the region's interest in black education and so appropriated sufficient tax funds to educate the former slaves.

DENOMINATIONAL GROUPS AND FREEDMEN'S AID SOCIETIES

Actively working with the Bureau in support of education were private northern freedmen's aid societies and religious missionary groups, including the American Baptist Home Mission Society, the American Missionary Association of the Congregational Church, the Freedmen's Aid

Society of the Methodist Episcopal Church, the Board of Missions for Freedmen of the Presbyterian Church, the African Methodist Episcopal Church, and various groups of Quakers and Lutherans, as well as the American Church Institute and Episcopal Board. The African Methodist Episcopal Church Zion, the Colored Methodist Episcopal Church, and several black Baptist groups also cooperated with the Bureau. Although these groups worked closely with the Freedmen's Bureau, they only occasionally collaborated with each other. As a result, some cities or towns had several Protestant-supported schools of different denominations while hundreds of other towns and rural areas had none. The joint support of three Freedmen's schools in Kentucky by the American Missionary Association and the Western Freedmen's Union Commission proved a rare exception.

The American Missionary Association in particular brought impressive credentials to its efforts to provide education for freedmen. Its existence was due in part to an 1839 incident involving the Spanish ship *Amistad,* which sailed for North America with a cargo of African slaves in violation of an international agreement regarding foreign slave trading, of which both the United States and Spain were signatories. Near Cuba the Africans mutinied, killed the captain and most of the crew, and attempted to force one of the crewmembers to steer the ship back to Africa. Due to his trickery, the ship eventually made landfall in the area of Montauk, Long Island, in New York State, and the mutineers were captured in Long Island Sound and incarcerated in New Haven, Connecticut. Antislavery advocates organized a legal defense for the captives. In 1841, the case reached the U.S. Supreme Court, where former President John Quincy Adams argued on behalf of the Africans. In an opinion written by Justice Joseph Story, with only one justice dissenting, the Court held that the Africans were not slaves but persons kidnapped in violation of international law and so were free to return to Africa. The Africans' supporters, including many Congregationalists who wanted their denomination to take a stronger anti-slavery position, maintained the organization that had been developed to defend the mutineers and, in 1849, incorporated it as the American Missionary Association. This organization became one of the most productive religious groups working to establish black schools and colleges. As late as 1915, it supported thirty institutions serving seven thousand students in eleven southern states.

Historians of the late nineteenth and early twentieth centuries devoted considerable attention to the motives and actions of northern Whites who took part in the Reconstruction process in the South, tending to lump together northern missionaries, teachers, merchants, and politicians as "carpetbaggers." Among many other criticisms, these historians accused the so-called carpetbaggers of pressing Blacks to engage in educational activities beyond their abilities and so worsening relations be-

tween the races.[10] More recently, historians take a very different view of
the long-term consequences of such educational activity among freedmen. Despite woefully inadequate facilities, these efforts to provide education had clearly positive results for individual students, their descendants, freedmen as a group, the South, and the country as a whole.

There is no reason to doubt that southern Whites felt oppressed or
that some of the so-called carpetbaggers were motivated by greed, political ambition, and anti-southern sentiments. It would be surprising if
victors did not sometimes belittle the vanquished. But it is difficult to
identify another civil war in which the defeated side suffered less in the
aftermath of defeat. Tennessee was readmitted to the Union one year
after the war ended; six other states followed two years later. By 1870, all
the former Confederate states were back in the Union. No fines, long
prison terms, or death sentences were imposed on the Confederacy's
political and military leaders and by 1872, amnesty had been granted to
all former Confederates. No indemnities were levied on the states that
had seceded. Most of the violence that occurred during the postwar
period was initiated by the Ku Klux Klan and similar anti-black organizations. Land that had been confiscated and distributed to former slaves
during and immediately after the war was returned to its pre–Civil-War
owners.

The Union's approach to Reconstruction of clemency and respect for
the inalienable rights of peoples in the defeated area may be the policy of
preference in any war, especially a civil war in a democracy. The Union
was restored and steps were taken toward the reconciliation of North and
South, but this progress was carried out at the expense of the constitu-
tionally guaranteed rights of black Americans who, through no fault of
their own, had been unable to secure an education or accumulate the
material resources vital to their success as citizens.

In this context, it is amazing how consistently contemporary reports
reflected a high interest in education among former slaves. A Union
officer reported, "The most hopeful sign in the Negro was his anxiety to
have his children educated. The two or three hundred boys and girls I
used to see around the Bureau schoolhouse—attired with a decency
which had strained to the utmost the slender parental purse, ill spared
from hard labor necessary to support their families, gleeful and noisy
over their luncheons of cold roasted sweet potato—were proofs that the
race has a chance in the future. Many a sorely pinched woman, a widow
or deserted by her husband, would not let her boy go out to service,
'because,' they said, 'I wanted him to have some schooling'."[11]

School Superintendent Alvord of the Freedmen's Bureau described a
conversation overheard in a railroad car in 1865: "One man [most probably white] asked another how things were working in his neighborhood.

'Everything is wrong,' said the second; 'everything is going crazy. The negroes, old and young, little and big, have all gone mad about schools. That fool T. (the county superintendent [of education]) has ruined everything'."[12] Hortense Powdermaker, an anthropologist interested in issues of race, makes the same point when she describes the trust Blacks placed in education as "much like the faith of those Americans who set up the public school system. They looked to education as the great indispensable foundation of democracy."[13]

A few southern Blacks, putting themselves at considerable risk in a hostile society, had even operated illegal schools in Georgia, Louisiana, Tennessee, Virginia, and other states before and during the war. In areas where Union troops gained control, freedmen's education societies sprang up immediately and groups of freedmen petitioned state and local governments to establish schools for their children. Black Americans elected to conventions to write new state constitutions and black members of state legislatures gave high priority to initiating and supporting legislation to establish statewide public school systems.

Education was hardly imposed upon freed black Americans by northern "do-gooders." The evidence suggests rather that freedmen generally viewed education as crucial to their freedom and progress, and vital to their sense of who they were. In making it illegal to teach slaves to read and write, southerners communicated a powerful sense of the value of both and so inadvertently fostered a deep-seated belief that education was related to freedom, higher social status, wealth, and power. This message was certain to stir interest among ambitious freedmen (and poor white Americans) seeking to share in those things society prized. Longtime citizens who could make use of previously developed specialized intellectual and technical skills, important familial connections and friendships, or accumulated wealth passed down from ancestors, were obviously at a clear advantage. To the four million slaves who acquired citizenship as a result of the Civil War, to whom none of these advantages were readily available, education appeared to be the most promising avenue to advancement.

The Freedmen's Bureau invested five million dollars of government funds in freedmen's education. It was a paltry sum given the scale of the need, but was nonetheless a valuable investment. To the Bureau funds were added the contributions of church groups, secular freedmen's associations, and individual donations that established many of the private schools and colleges for Blacks, including a number that exist today. Table 3.1 shows the growing number of black educational institutions established between 1866 and 1870.

Census data on black youth aged five to nineteen show an increase in school enrollment from 1.9 per 100 persons in 1860 to 9.6 in 1870.

TABLE 3.1

Number of Black Educational Institutions in the United States, 1866–1870

Year	Number of Schools	Number of Teachers	Number of Students
1866	740	1,314	90,589
1867	1,839	1,087	111,442
1888	1,831	2,295	104,327
1869	2,118	2,455	114,522
1870	2,677	3,300	149,581

Source: Thomas Jesse Jones, *Negro Education,* p. 289.
Note: Comparable data for the years 1861–1865 are not available.

Equivalent data for all white youths show a decline from 50.6 youths per 100 persons in 1860 to 48.4 in 1870.[14]

Valuable as the efforts of northern teachers and the contributions of the Freedmen's Bureau were, they had a temporary, emergency quality to them and could not be long sustained. By the end of the war, thoughtful observers recognized that neither the federal government nor northern church groups were likely to maintain the level of financial support needed for the long haul. If particularly higher education was to be available to black Americans on a permanent basis, observers assumed that pre-college preparation would have to be supported by public funds from state governments, a point made in the final report of the Freed-man's Bureau superintendent of schools:

> This Bureau has only inaugurated a system of instruction, helping its first stages, and which should be continued and perfected. . . . It should not be arrested in mid career; should rather be aided from some source to make its final showing. . . . Nearly a million and a half of [freedmen's] children have never as yet been under any instruction. Educational associations, unaided by Government, will of necessity largely fall off. The states south, as a whole, awake but slowly to the elevation of their lower classes. No one of them is fully prepared with funds, buildings, teachers, and actual organizations to sustain these schools. . . . With sorrow we anticipate, if the reports of super-intendents can be relied on, the closing of hundreds of our school build-ings, sending thousands of children, who beg for continued instruction, to the streets, or what is far worse, to squalid, degraded homes. . . . The several States will ere long, we hope, come nobly forward in duty to their children.[15]

Private financial support for all black higher education was also viewed as unsustainable. State-supported colleges would also be needed.

CHAPTER 4

Public Schools, High Schools, Normal Schools, and Colleges

PUBLIC SCHOOLS

PUBLIC SCHOOLS of the type first established in New England in the seventeenth century were slow indeed to develop in the South. None of the constitutions of the states that formed the Confederacy contained any provision for supporting public education, and before 1860, measures to establish statewide systems of public schools for white students failed to secure the necessary votes in the legislatures controlled mainly by large landowners. Typically, southern state constitutions merely included a "pauper-school" clause, under which funds were provided to pay tuition for children to attend private schools if their parents declared themselves unable to pay. Only North Carolina maintained tax-supported public schools of the sort that existed in all northern states by 1850.

When the political influence of large landowners weakened in the aftermath of the Civil War, businessmen, small farmers, and other white supporters of public schools were finally able to press an education agenda. Legislation establishing public schools was passed in several states, beginning with Florida. Some of this legislation included prohibitions against the use of public school funds to support the education of Blacks. The rationale for these discriminatory arrangements was that public-school funds came from taxes on property. Because black Americans owned little or no property, it was reasoned that their schools should not be allowed to draw support from such funds. That only months earlier Blacks had been slaves and could not own personal property was not taken into account. Black schools were to be supported entirely by special taxes paid by black Americans and by tuition paid by parents. Whites who did not own property were usually allowed to send their children to the new public schools without paying a special tax, whereas property-owning black Americans were not exempt from paying taxes into the fund for schools that their children were barred from attending.

Congressional Reconstruction changed the political landscape in which decisions about public education were made. An article providing for public education was included in each new state constitution. There were now sufficient numbers of black and white supporters of public education in the reconstituted legislatures to turn the school issue from whether to how statewide systems would be organized.

In the constitutional conventions and state legislatures, the fiercest debates on education were over issues of compulsory school attendance and racially mixed versus racially separate schools. Opposition to compulsory attendance revolved around the untraditional nature of the idea in the South, the needs of families for the labor of school-age children, and the folly of such a requirement when existing facilities and the teacher supply could not accommodate the school-age population. On these matters, convention delegates did not divide strictly on racial lines. As a result, some states did include compulsory attendance in their constitutions.

Debates over the racial composition of schools were far more heated. The vast majority of white Americans categorically opposed integrated schools under any circumstances. Most black Americans, however, opposed constitutional provisions requiring racially separate schools, but often disagreed over whether to include articles making it illegal to exclude students from any school because of race. They argued over whether this was the only way to ensure equality of educational opportunity. Black members of the South Carolina convention pressed the issue and managed to include an article providing for the establishment of racially mixed schools. In other states, black Americans simply sought to prevent any mention of the racial makeup of schools. Proponents of this position indicated that they did not necessarily wish their children to attend racially mixed schools but objected strongly to any constitutional prohibition. They reasoned that constitutional silence on the issue would put pressure on public school officials to provide Blacks with facilities not inferior to those provided for Whites.

Most of the constitutions ultimately took no position on the subject and as schools were established, they were simply informally identified as serving one racial group or the other. This was no less true in South Carolina despite the mixed-race provision in its constitution. In one instance, white students withdrew from an Orangeburg, South Carolina, school when black students insisted on entering. Even today that school has an almost entirely black enrollment.

The desire of white businessmen and small farmers to secure passage of public school legislation placed them in a peculiar situation. Although in general as opposed as large landowners were to the use of tax revenues to support schools for Blacks, they knew they would be unable to get the legislature to appropriate funds if opposed by a *de facto* alliance of Blacks and large landowners. As a result, they often found themselves making common cause with Blacks and so supporting black schools established and maintained with public funds. The creation of statewide systems of schools was an accomplishment of Reconstruction, but the South continued to lag behind other regions on most indicators of school effectiveness: per capita spending for education, percentage of school-age students enrolled in school, teachers' salaries, length of school year, and the percentage of students completing high school.

Widespread unease among Whites over changing racial relations produced frequent upsurges of education-related violence. Black schools were burned; teachers and students harassed or attacked; and black parents fired from jobs if their children were known to be attending school. At no other time in American history has there been so much anti-school violence or such widespread and sustained expression of hostility to education. Numerous examples are documented in the records of congressional hearings, the National Archives, and the War Record Office. Typical are two incidents that occurred in 1870:

> On the fourth of October the [school] house was completely destroyed by fire, nothing being saved but a few benches, and the Sunday School library. . . . The fire was undoubtedly the work of an incendiary as it occurred at midnight and no fire had been kindled within the building. . . . It would be difficult for anyone who does not know the poverty of the freedman and his intense zeal for education to conceive the disheartening effect of such a calamity upon the poor people who had denied themselves every luxury, and with unprecedented liberality had given one half their wages, week after week, for the construction of this house for themselves and their children.[1]
>
> In many counties . . . there is still great bitterness of feeling against the schools and all those engaged in the work and bands of K.K.K. [Ku Klux Klan] armed and disguised men, have committed most atrocious outrages. About the last of November Mr. R. H. Gladdings who has been teaching . . . at Greensboro, Green Co. was driven away. The man with whom he boarded (a white man) was taken out of his house in the night and unmercifully whipped and Mr. Abram Colby (colored) a member-elect of the legislature and one of Mr. Gladdings strong supporters in the school work, was taken out of his house and beaten nearly to death. Mr. Gladdings was warned to leave and appealed to the Mayor for protection to prevent any outrage upon him, he was therefore obliged to leave. . . . Notwithstanding the difficulties the school work goes on with increased efficiency. The freedmen pay more liberally than ever toward the support of their schools.[2]

The view of education as a pernicious influence on Blacks leading them to see themselves as the equals of Whites was widely held even by Whites of relatively more moderate views. The following is an example from an 1867 exchange of letters between Anna Gardner, a northern teacher in a black school in Virginia, and James C. Southall, editor of the *Chronicle,* a Charlottesville, Virginia, newspaper.

> Mr. J. C. Southall.
> Having heard colored people speaking of you as a true friend to the cause of education among them, I take the liberty, on their behalf, of requesting you to make a donation to the Jefferson School, in the form of printed diplomas, stating that the graduate is qualified to commence teaching the rudiments of an English education, &c.
> Yours Respectfully
> Anna Gardner

> Miss Gardner,
> I take as deep an interest in the welfare of the Negro race as anyone. I am anxious to see them educated, and am prepared to give any aid to further these objectives. The impression among white residents of Charlottesville is that your instruction of the colored people who attend your school contemplates something more than the communication of ordinary knowledge implied in teaching them to read, write, cipher, etc. The idea prevails . . . that you come among us . . . as a political missionary; that you communicate to the colored people ideas of social equality with Whites. . . . [This] we regard as mischievous, and only tending to disturb the good feeling between the races.
> Respectfully
> James C. Southall

> Mr. J. C. Southall, I teach *in school and out* . . . . "Whatsoever ye would that men should do to you, do ye even so unto them."
> Yours Respectfully
> Anna Gardner[3]

The widespread hostility toward the nineteenth-century beginnings of higher education for Blacks was quite different from the respectful acceptance of the seventeenth- and eighteenth-century beginnings of higher education in British North America. Nevertheless, there were notable similarities in the early histories of these educational institutions. In both cases, early institutions were privately controlled and usually church-related, with curricula modeled on what their founders had studied. Such private colleges developed not only before public colleges but also in advance of systems of public elementary and secondary schools. Here the similarities end. Most historically black colleges were located in the South, but only one of the colonial colleges was southern. Colonial colleges enrolled only males, whereas in early black colleges, coeducation was common. And, of course, the political and social environment in which the students at colonial colleges and black colleges spent their pre-college and college years differed radically. Furthermore, a relatively high degree of literacy existed among European-Americans in New England and the mid-Atlantic region in the seventeenth and eighteenth centuries, whereas not more than five out of one hundred black Americans could read or write in 1865 and only seventeen out of one hundred could do so five years after the end of slavery.[4]

The delineation between different educational levels was not as clear in the nineteenth century as it is today. It was not unusual for students at the secondary and college levels to attend the same institutions and be taught by the same teachers. Thus, according to a Bureau of Education survey, 33 percent of all students enrolled in U.S. colleges in 1890 were actually doing secondary school work.[5] All early black colleges initially provided secondary and occasionally even elementary schooling, because of the nearly simultaneous founding of all levels of school for black students. The more advanced schools offered students the only opportunity available to take the basic preparatory courses needed to begin college-level work.

NORMAL SCHOOLS, HIGH SCHOOLS, AND COLLEGES

John Alvord's semi-annual Freedmen's Bureau reports contain most of what information we have on how many of these early "advanced institutions" there were, how many students and, in some cases, teachers they had, and what sort of coursework they offered. In his 1870 reports, for example, seventy-nine normal schools, high schools, and colleges are listed and brief descriptions are provided about some of them.[6] The description of Howard University contains the following:

> This institution is rapidly assuming the character which its name indicates. It now has nearly four hundred students pursuing academic and professional branches, besides about four hundred residents of the city who four evenings every week are instructed in common branches by advanced pupils from the normal department. . . .
>
> The following departments are now either fully or in part organized, viz: Normal, preparatory, (under one organization), collegiate, law, medical, theological, agricultural, military, commercial, and musical, besides the Lincoln night school. . . .
>
> In the college department the sophomores and freshman classes are fully organized. The course of study is similar to that of first-class institutions in the country.
>
> The law department has constantly increased in numbers and importance since opening. About fifty students, representing fourteen different States,

besides the District of Columbia, are enrolled. . . . The course pursued here is thorough.

The medical department now comprises a full faculty of seven physicians and surgeons, with 28 regular students.

The remaining departments above named are all in a more or less advanced state of organization, and work accomplished by them is most satisfactory. . . .

Taken altogether these institutions are now the most interesting feature of the freedmen's education, and give assurance of its continuance. Many hundreds of teachers and leading minds have already been sent forth from them to commence a life work, and make their mark upon the coming generation. These hundreds will be followed by thousands.[7]

But how appropriate was it to devote scarce human and financial resources to the establishment of "colleges" when the population for which these were intended was for the most part desperately poor and without formal education of any sort? The designation of "college" or "university" exaggerated the status of most of these early institutions; however, then as now the colleges and secondary and primary schools were mutually dependent. To postpone the establishment of institutions of higher learning until well-organized systems of pre-college education were firmly in place would have retarded the development and progress of the group the educational institutions were meant to serve. W.E.B. Du Bois, a graduate of Fisk University (one of these early institutions of higher education) and the first black American to receive a Ph.D. from Harvard University, spoke to this point. In his book *The Souls of Black Folks,* Du Bois wrote, "The culture of the university has been the broad foundation stone on which is built the kindergarten's A B C. . . . The function of the university is not simply to teach bread-winning, or to furnish teachers for public schools, or to be a centre of polite society; it is, above all, to be the organ of that fine adjustment between real life and the growing knowledge of life, an adjustment which forms the secret of civilization."[8] Charles Eliot, then President of Harvard, agreed. "The only way to have good primary schools and grammar schools in Massachusetts is to have high and normal schools and colleges, in which the higher teachers are trained. It must be so throughout the South; the Negro race needs absolutely these higher facilities of education."[9] Little in the pre–Civil-War life experience of black Americans had furnished the "fine adjustment" to which Du Bois refers and which early colleges sought to provide.

Teacher education programs were a critical part of the curriculum of most early freedmen's colleges. Many elementary and secondary schools included normal school programs in recognition that simple replacement of northern teachers (whose numbers were in any case beginning to wane by the early 1870s) was not sufficient to meet the needs of the increased number of students seeking an education. The work of expanding the pool of available teachers was reflected in the programs of a majority of the "advanced institutions" in existence in 1870. The July 1, 1869, semi-annual report of the Freedmen's Bureau superintendent of schools comments on Howard University that "This institution . . . closed its first school year with 172 students. Of this enrollment 139 were in the normal and preparatory department."[10]

The data on students and teachers in normal and high schools and colleges from a July 1, 1870, report to the Freedmen's Bureau reflect the limited ability of northern volunteers to meet the educational needs of freedmen, in spite of the diligent work of those associated with the Bureau (see Table 4.1). Five years after the end of the war, the Bureau identified only one state in which more than ten normal and high schools and colleges had been established. No post-elementary institu-

TABLE 4.1
Advanced Schools and Colleges for Black Students, 1870

State	Number of Institutions	Number of Students	Number of Students per School	Number of Teachers	Number of Teachers Per School
Alabama*	6	314	62.8	13	2.3
Arkansas	2	249	124.0	4	2.0
Delaware	1	41	41.0	1	1.0
District of Columbia*	4	545	181.7	35	14.3
Florida	2	598	299.0	11	5.5
Georgia*	7	134	26.8	9	1.8
Kansas*	2	150	150.0	2	2.0
Kentucky	6	785	130.8	22	3.6
Louisiana*	5	447	149.0	9	3.0
Maryland*	2	78	78.0	2	2.0
Mississippi*	4	293	293.0	7	7.0
Missouri	2	164	82.0	4	2.0
North Carolina*	20	846	47.0	44	3.0
Ohio*	1				
Pennsylvania*	4	332	166.0		
South Carolina*	9	1,477	295.4	39	7.8
Tennessee*	9	977	139.6	23	4.8
Virginia*	8	452	64.6	10	2.7
West Virginia	1	161	161.0	6	6.0
Total*	**95**	**8,043**	**101.9**	**231**	**3.3**

Source: Alvord, *Freedmen's Schools*, pp. 64, 52–54.

Note: *Indicates one or more schools for which information is unavailable. These schools were not used when determining the number of students or teachers per school.

tions are identified in Texas, a state with 6 percent of the South's black population. With 522 students, the Howard School, a high school in Columbia, South Carolina, had the largest enrollment. Howard University's 400 students and thirty-five teachers was the largest post-secondary enrollment, and the only institution having more than ten teachers, as well as the only one established soon after the Civil War that had a four-year college program with a significant number of students enrolled in it.[11] Twelve of the seventy-one schools in the Freedmen's Bureau report employed a single teacher and had enrollments which ranged from twelve to sixty-six students.

A systematic study of black education was undertaken in 1915 by the U.S. Bureau of Education in cooperation with the Phelps-Stokes Fund, a philanthropic organization founded by Miss Caroline Phelps-Stokes. Its purpose was "to supply through an impartial investigation, a body of facts which would be available to all interested, showing the status of Negro education by an examination of all private and higher schools for colored people in the United States." The study, reporting on 653 existing institutions, included all private schools and colleges and all public secondary schools and colleges. Of this number, 294 were rated as "large or important." Names and locations were given for each of these, as well as information on enrollment, staff, value of property, income, and expenses.[12] The report calls attention to the limited number of public and private facilities for school-age youth, the inadequacy of their equipment and level of support, and the overall weakness of many of the institutions identifying themselves as colleges or universities.

The 1915 study made an important contribution by providing reliable statistical data on facilities and resources for black Americans developed over half a century. Many of the report's assessments were sound. The rapid expansion in the number of "colleges" and "universities" far outpaced the human and financial resources needed to ensure their success.[13] These significant shortfalls in resources forced some institutions to compromise their curriculum focus in order to attract donations.

The report, however, suffers from a number of serious deficiencies. In spite of the observation that "the sound development of 10,000 [black] people requires every type of education," it reflected the contemporary southern preference for "industrial education"—schooling limited to training black Americans to do the kinds of work they had done as slaves in agriculture, mechanics, commerce, and domestic service—over academic curricula in private secondary schools and colleges. Its tone was frequently condescending and its criticisms of private academically oriented institutions excessive, given their difficult circumstances. The opening paragraphs identified the North, the South, and the Negro as "three elements in race adjustment": "Negroes" were presented as "the primary element that give rise to the problem"; white southerners as "large and powerful in number, wealth, education, and experience . . . part of the group most concerned in this problem"; and northern states as "not so immediately concerned in the education of the Negro race as the South or the Negroes themselves . . . [but] as essential to the proper solution of the vexed problem." The future of the South, it suggested, depended on the training of black and white workmen "however serious may be the problems of sanitation and education developed by the Negroes."[14]

This document was as positive and sympathetic a report as supporters of black education could have expected in 1915 and yet its impact provided another obstacle for the struggling normal schools and colleges to overcome. Its fallacious indictment of Blacks as the "primary element giving rise to the [race] problem" negatively influenced black education. Its preference for industrial education retarded attempts to improve the quality of black higher education and impeded the development of social and political equality of the races. "Though the facilities for all types and grades of education are strikingly inadequate, a large number of the colored leaders have been much more eager for the literary and collegiate type of schooling than for the teacher-training, agricultural, or industrial institutions," the author of the report remarks, in effect demanding that black schools lower their sights and accept educational inferiority:

> While the failure to understand the purposes of industrial and agricultural education is thus easily explained, it is none the less unfortunate. The real purpose of industrial education, as conceived by Gen. [Samuel C.] Armstrong and advanced by his pupil, Booker T. Washington, was the adaptation of education, whether literary or industrial, to the needs of pupils in the community.
>
> The extravagant and high-sounding names of a large number of colored schools have led to a misconception of the grade and type of work done by them. Frequently they represent only the hopes of the founders. In other cases the names have been selected to satisfy the ambitions of the colored people or to attract the support of the white people. In these instances, the terms "university," "college," and "literary" usually indicate that the financial support is partly from Negroes; the titles "industrial," "agricultural," and "rural" constitute a bid for sympathy and contributions from white people. Some schools in their eagerness to offer college courses not only hamper their general work but also bring ridicule on efforts to maintain college classes.[15]

Although the report is correct that "college" or "university" in the titles of early black institutions did reflect aspirations rather than reality, in many cases those aspirations were subsequently fulfilled. Forty-five of eighty-eight private institutions identifying themselves as colleges or universities in 1915 are still in existence. Seven institutions identifying themselves in 1915 as schools, institutes, or seminaries currently appear on the list of historically black colleges. All fifty-two are now certified by their regional accrediting associations. State governments or the District of Columbia now operate five of them. Three are junior colleges.

Among important developments reported in the 1915 study is a greater rate of increase in the number of public institutions established between 1870 and 1915, even though in absolute numbers, more private sector "advanced" institutions were founded in this period. Although private schools continued to outnumber public institutions by a large margin, the number of state-sponsored schools rose from two in 1870 (Bowie State College in Maryland and Fayetteville Normal School in North Carolina) to twenty-seven by 1915. In those same years the number of private institutions had increased from fifty to about 235. Public institutions existed in all states of the former Confederacy, as well as in Delaware, Kansas, Maryland, New Jersey, Ohio, and Oklahoma, an increase due in large part to the federal Land Grant Act of 1890. In the initial Land Grant Act of 1862, Congress appropriated funds to support one college per state that stressed the importance of agriculture and the "mechanical arts." In states with dual systems of education, the colleges established under the 1862 legislation were for white students. The 1890 Act called for the distribution of land-grant funds on an equitable basis. As a result, Alcorn College, which had been established in Mississippi in 1871, became the first of sixteen black land-grant institutions. In some cases, new racially segregated institutions were established in such states as Kentucky, Missouri, and West Virginia, which had remained in the Union during the Civil War. This reflected the increased separation of black and white Americans taking place everywhere in the country.

Curriculum in the new state-supported institutions focused mainly on teacher training and industrial education, as reflected in the appearance of "normal" and "mechanical and agricultural" in the names of twenty-one of the twenty-seven institutions. In 1915, there was a total of fifty-two students doing college-level work, all located at two of the twenty-seven public institutions, whereas 2,595 students were engaged in such study at thirty-one private colleges. The focus on industrial education and the smaller number of college-level students in state-supported schools reflect an important difference between public and private institutions at the time. Private black colleges became in essence the sole providers for black Americans of higher education as we think of it today.

STUDENTS

For most Americans, college attendance was the exception rather than the rule before the mid-twentieth century. Those who attended were mainly the children of "well established," financially secure families. In the South, the close connection between college attendance and class status and the limited availability of public secondary education meant that white students who pursued higher education were generally the children of families who could afford tutors or private elementary and secondary schools. Going to college was nearly impossible for black Americans in the years following emancipation. The secondary schools they could afford were few. Rarely was there a family member or friend who had attended college and even the modest cost of tuition was beyond the means of most black families. Nevertheless, the numbers of black Americans attending secondary school, a prerequisite for entering college, increased significantly between 1870 and 1915. Census data show that for every one hundred young people of school age, the number enrolled in all levels of school rose from ten in 1870 to thirty-four in 1880; after dropping slightly over the next two decades, the number rose to forty-five in 1910 and fifty-three in 1920.[16] The information for 1870 shows enrollment of 8,043 students in seventy-four of the ninety-five institutions identified as high schools, normal schools, or colleges. The number of students taking courses at the elementary school level is unknown, but such students may have been in the majority. No enrollment data are available for twenty-one of the ninety-five institutions included in Table 4.1. By 1915, secondary school enrollment had increased by approximately a factor of 9.5 and many more of these students were doing genuine secondary school work.

Table 4.2 provides some detail on enrollments in the 747 private and public institutions for Blacks existing in 1915.[17] Private institutions accounted for 83 percent of this total and enrolled 87 percent of elementary and secondary school students. The 2,585 students enrolled in thirty-one of these private institutions accounted for 98 percent of the total black college enrollment, although they represented only 22 percent of the students enrolled in all private institutions. Only at Howard University and Lincoln University were a majority of the enrolled students engaged in college-level work.

The fifty-two college-level students attending the public institutions represented 0.7 percent of their total enrollment. Forty of these students attended the state of Ohio's Combined Normal and Industrial Department, which was administered by Wilberforce University, a private institution. The other twelve students attended Florida Agricultural and Mechanical College, the only public institution in the South enrolling black

TABLE 4.2

Black Schools Offering Secondary and College-Level Courses, 1915

	Number of Schools	Number of Elementary Students	Number of Secondary Students	Number of College Students
Private	626	70,564	11,927	2,585
Independent	119	12,273	2,241	1,738
Northern denominational	354	43,605	7,188	719
Black denominational	153	14,686	2,498	128
Public	121	9,812	12,262	52
Land Grant	16	2,595	2,268	12
State	11	1,466	1,132	40
City	67	0	8,707	0
County training	27	5,751	155	0
Total	747	80,376	24,198	2,637

Source: Hill, *Traditionally Black Institutions*, p. 4.

college students a decade and a half into the twentieth century. Most of the other students enrolled in the public institutions were engaged in industrial education at a pre-college level.

Some private black colleges in the South, including Howard University and Talladega College, made a point of accepting students without regard to race and enrolled small numbers of non-black Americans in the nineteenth and early twentieth centuries. Native Americans attended Hampton Institute, their education being part of the stated mission of that institution. Children of white American faculty sometimes enrolled in elementary schools, secondary schools, and (more rarely) colleges where their parents taught. Observing such a situation during an inspection of Atlanta University in 1887, the State of Georgia University Board of Visitors reported "in attendance . . . a number of white students of various ages and sexes. . . . [And] that it is the avowed intention [of members of the faculty] to receive all white children who apply for admission." When Atlanta refused to put an end to the attendance of white students, it lost an annual eight-thousand-dollar appropriation. Although prohibited by state laws from doing so, white nuns from the Sisters of the Blessed Sacrament, the order that founded Xavier University, took courses toward their baccalaureate degrees at Xavier. It was not until after 1954, however, that non-Blacks appeared at any one institution in significant numbers. Approximately two hundred are now enrolled at Xavier University, and Whites compose a majority at several historically black public colleges, including West Virginia State College and Bluefield State College in West Virginia.

FACULTY AND ADMINISTRATORS

A typical teacher in a freedmen school during the decade following the Civil War was a well-educated, white, middle-class, Protestant woman from New England. The presidents of the early colleges fit the same profile except that all were men (as were the majority of teachers at the preparatory and college levels) and almost all were clergymen. Some northern black Americans were among the teachers but, for obvious reasons, their numbers were few. Charlotte Forten (1837–1914) was one of this small number of black Americans. She was born in Philadelphia and studied and taught school in Massachusetts before joining the movement to work in the South from September 1862 to May 1864. The diary of her years in Port Royal, South Carolina, provides a picture of the life of a "schoolmarm" in a freedmen's school:

Wednesday, November 5 [1862]. Had my first regular teaching experience, and you and you only friend beloved, will acknowledge that it was *not* a very pleasant one. Part of my scholars are very tiny,—babies, I call them—and it is hard to keep them quiet and interested while I am hearing the larger ones. They are too young even for the alphabet, it seems to me. I think I must write home and ask somebody to send me picture-books and toys to amuse them. . . .

Sunday, November 30 [1862] I am in a writing mood to-night and think I will give to you . . . a more minute description of the people around [me]. . . . First there is old Harriet. . . . Her parents were Africans. She speaks a very foreign tongue. Three of her children have been sold from her. Then there is her daughter Tillah. Poor creature, she has a dear little baby, Annie, who for weeks has been dangerously ill with whooping cough and fever. . . . Harry is another of her sons. I have told you dear A., how bright, how eager to learn, he is. . . .

The Oaks. Monday morn. April 13 [1863]. Came hither last eve., and spent the night. In the night was sure I heard some one try my door. Asked "Who's there?" No answer. The noise was repeated—the question asked again. Still no answer. Woke Miss W[are] who had the adjoining room. She lit the candle and took out our revolvers,—all ready for rebels. Waited awhile. Then as all continued quiet, put our pistols under our heads and composed ourselves to sleep.[18]

Forten returned to South Carolina in 1871–72 to teach at the Shaw Memorial School in Charleston, after which she taught at Dunbar High School in Washington, D.C.

Historian James McPherson reports that of 1,013 early teachers and the seventy-six presidents whose homes have been identified, approximately half were born in New England, an area that in 1870 constituted only 15 percent of the northern population.[19] The region's impact was even greater if those who studied in New England or went to college in areas settled by New Englanders are included.

The recruitment, placement, and support of northern teachers in the South constituted one of the first social-action movements of its kind in U.S. history, not unlike the Civil Rights Movement and the Peace Corps a century later. Work in freedmen's schools was far from easy and was sometimes dangerous. In spite of the organizational networks that church mission societies and freedmen's aid societies provided, these groups paid small salaries and individual teachers had to be self-reliant and deeply committed. Local white Americans reacted with hostility to these teachers, some of whom arrived on the heels of the victorious Union army. Communication with colleagues in adjoining towns and counties required considerable time and effort. Most worked alone or in small groups. Freedmen's Bureau records for 1870 show 231 teachers staffing sixty-six "advanced schools and colleges," an average of 3.1

teachers per institution.[20] If the six institutions with more than eight teachers are excluded—Howard University had thirty-five; the others, nine or ten each—the average number of teachers per school falls to 2.4. Reporting on all black educational institutions (elementary, secondary, and college), the consolidated school report of the Bureau of Refugees, Freedmen, and Abandoned Lands cites a total of 3,300 teachers operating 2,677 schools, serving 149,581 students in 1870, which works out to an average of 1.2 teachers per school and 45 students per teacher.[21]

There were some benefits to the situation in which most teachers found themselves. Their social lives were confined almost entirely to the communities in which their students lived. This separation from a larger community at least partially broke down many barriers: northern and southern, black and white, educated and illiterate. There were frequent opportunities for contact with students and their parents outside the classroom, and so opportunities for informal instruction, which are rare today in any urban or large suburban school system. It may be one of the ironies of the period that in private schools and colleges established in the South after the Civil War, out-of-school contacts between predominantly black students and predominantly white teachers were more frequent and of better quality than at any other time in U.S. history.

As the number of teachers in black educational institutions and Blacks holding college degrees increased, so did tensions related to the racial makeup of school faculties. Believing that black colleges should educate students for professional and leadership positions, black Americans in the 1880s began to press for the appointment of Blacks to faculty and administrative posts. Northern teachers and administrators were sometimes condescending to their students, claiming that black Americans were not yet prepared for these professorial positions. These patronizing attitudes toward Blacks followed a familiar pattern in the history of missionary activity. Because most early black colleges were founded by missionary groups and staffed by white Americans motivated by religious commitment, it is not surprising that these groups sought to maintain control over and administration of "their" institutions and did so within the racial framework of the times. Nor is it surprising that black Americans sought change, although with only modest success. In some private schools, the number of black teachers did grow at a rate faster than that of the total teaching population. Increases in black staff members were slower at the secondary level, and slowest at the college level. By 1915, however, they constituted 71 percent of all teachers at private institutions.

The data for 1915 also show that school staffing patterns depended on the school's denominational affiliation. The percentage of black faculty was highest (91 percent) in institutions established by three black denominational groups, African Methodist Episcopal, African Methodist Episcopal Zion, and Colored Methodist. The next highest percentage (70 percent) was found in colleges controlled by northern Baptists and Methodists, denominations with large numbers of black members in the South. Colleges with independent boards of trustees affiliated with northern denominational groups with few black members ranked third. The American Missionary Association of the Congregational Church, the most active of the denominational groups, had the lowest percentage of black faculty (30 percent). The relative positions of these four groups remained the same between 1895 and 1915, although the total number of black faculty increased between 25 and 30 percent.[22]

Institutions supported by northern denominations were far slower to consider Blacks for administrative than for teaching posts. Only three of twenty-nine institutions affiliated with white denominational groups had black presidents in 1895, increasing to eight in 1915. The American Missionary Association, among the leaders in setting up schools and colleges in the South, had white presidents in both 1895 and 1915 in all five of its institutions that had college students enrolled in these years.[23]

There was no unanimity of opinion on the staffing issue among supporters of black higher education. Some supporters, even among black educators, insisted that more time was needed before Blacks would be ready to hold these positions; others viewed such appointments as a natural extension of the institutions' missions. In some black colleges, the views had hardly changed half a century later when in 1964—with the Civil Rights movement in full swing—President Adam Daniel Bittel at Tougaloo College retired, ending an unbroken ninety-five-year-long string of white presidents.

Faculty hiring and presidential appointment practices were criticized at one time or another in most of the colleges founded by northern denominational groups. Typical of the attitudes of graduates of these institutions are those expressed by W. E. B. Du Bois. In *Dusk of Dawn,* he described his fond memories of and appreciation for the efforts of his white college professors, even though some years earlier he had criticized Fisk for not hiring more black faculty and not appointing a black president.[24] For anyone who experienced life as a student at a black college, there was no inconsistency in believing that Whites were able teachers and administrators and simultaneously urging change in the racial composition of the staff.

CHAPTER 5

Curriculum

THE MAJORITY of white Americans attending college in the nineteenth century had the luxury of doing so without concern for immediate employment. This was not the case for freedmen, who had considerable skills and wisdom in the ways of surviving in a hostile environment, but had neither income nor wealth to sustain them. Moreover, the pervasive efforts to exclude them from intellectual development, their high rates of illiteracy, and their scant preparation for formal education placed the freedmen, through no fault of their own, at a serious disadvantage when competing for positions requiring literacy. It soon became clear, however, that such problems as illiteracy were more easily managed than the problems of crafting curricula that would promote a sense of self-worth and personal freedom, and of avoiding curricula intended to maintain the racial caste system that had been in existence during the two centuries of slavery.

The strong New England influence among the founders of and teachers at freedmen's schools shaped both the formal curriculum and the general character of early black schools and colleges. Northern teachers brought to these institutions not only a social consciousness reflecting a commitment to the abolition of slavery and the work ethic of evangelical Puritanism, but also a course of study encountered in their own student and teaching experiences. They assumed that this curriculum, which provided moral and intellectual preparation for civic life in New England, would be no less appropriate for achieving similar purposes among freedmen. Thomas J. Morgan, a Union officer and abolitionist who became secretary of the Baptist Home Mission Society, was typical when he wrote of the relative importance of knowledge, skills, and character as the goals of a curriculum and asserted that the latter of these was the most important:

> If a man goes out of school depraved in heart and deficient in will power, all his learning and skill and intellectual qualities may be a curse and not a blessing. Students must be trained to be honest, truthful and pure-minded . . . industrious, thrifty, faithful to the performance of duty, intelligent, moral, progressive, public spirited and self-respecting. . . . Ignorance fosters idleness, thriftlessness, wastefulness and vagabondage; education encourages industry, thrift, frugality and home keeping.[1]

With rare exceptions, the courses of study were carbon copies of those followed in New England academies and colleges. Latin and Greek held the place of honor, with serious attention also given to mathematics and grammar. Dean of the Howard University Graduate School Dwight Oliver Wendell Holmes's description of the requirements for admission to the freshman class at his institution in 1868–69 included "two books of *Caesar,* six orations of *Cicero,* the *Bucolics,* the *Georgics,* six books of Virgil's *Aeneid,* Sallust's *Cataline,* two books of Xenophon's *Anabasis,* and the first two books of Homer's *Iliad.* In addition . . . the student was required to pass examinations in higher arithmetic, algebra to quadratics, the history of Greece and Rome, ancient and modern geography, and English grammar."[2] Critics of classical education for black Americans—such as Samuel Chapman Armstrong—argued that this curriculum did not prepare early graduates well for the practical necessities of southern life. On the same topic, Horace Mann Bond, professor of education at Fisk University and dean at Dillard University, wrote that "No provision was made in the curriculum for electives. . . . Cicero, Livy, Horace, Quintilian, Tacitus, and Prose Composition afforded a rather full fare in Latin, while Greek could hardly be said to suffer neglect when every student was expected to read Xenophon's *Memorabilia,* Homer's *Iliad,* Sophocles' *Antigone* and other Greek tragedies, the New Testament in Greek, Thucydides, Plato's *Apology* and the *Crito,* and Demosthenes' *On the Crown.* Mathematics courses were as extensive as those in the classical languages, and the few classes in history, natural science, and moral philosophy were organized and taught in the approved fashion of the time."[3] His description was equally true of black and white students seeking the baccalaureate degree in the late nineteenth and early twentieth centuries.

Although the academic curriculum resembled that followed in northern institutions, huge differences existed in the social setting within which that curriculum was implemented. Missing was the sense of belonging to a cohesive community that was typical of the northern student's experiences. Far more common was an oppressive feeling that those in the neighborhood with power and influence were opposed to the very existence of the school—an opposition that served to hinder the progress of some students and drove others to strive harder. The support that came from northern individuals and groups, although considered a valued necessity, produced an uncomfortable sense of dependency in those who felt regret or shame over their inability to support their children's education, and a pernicious sense of entitlement in others. White teachers in early "advanced schools" dealt with students from a racial group with which they had had little if any previous contact. Teachers and students were often painfully isolated from the white majority in the locality.

But the curriculum itself, rooted in the Western classical tradition, also presented problems. When copying this curriculum for use with their black American students, white teachers could not duplicate the objective that had determined the choice of content for white students in northern classrooms—to promote an understanding of the history, cultures, and geographic origins of the people from whom the students were biologically and culturally descended. In freedmen's schools, no serious effort was made to temper the European-based content of humanities and social science courses with an infusion of information about the history, cultures, and geographic origins of the freedmen's ancestors. Although recognizing the problems with this choice, black Americans nonetheless generally accepted the necessity for and the values of a European-based curriculum.

In the 1930s, historian Horace Mann Bond spoke to its positive aspects for freedmen's academies and colleges:

> Boys and girls came from the environment of slavery and were transported to a place where the students of Mark Hopkins, Theodore Woolseley, Charles Finney, and Henry Fairchild sought to do with Negro students what these men had done with them. They succeeded in an uncommon way. If the colleges took students from "life," it was from a life in which there was no idealism and very little intelligence. The teachers insisted that the institutions they managed should have both.[4]

W. E. B. Du Bois offered a sensitive and eloquent reflection on the complexity of this issue in an *Atlantic Monthly* article in 1897:

> One ever feels his two-ness,—an American, and a Negro; two souls, two thoughts, two un-reconciled strivings; two warring ideals in one dark body, whose dogged strength alone keeps it from being torn asunder. The history of the American Negro is the history of this strife—this longing to attain self-conscious manhood, to merge his double self into a better and truer self. In this merger he wishes neither of the older selves to be lost. He would not Africanize America, for America has too much to teach the world and Africa; he does not wish to bleach his Negro blood in a flood of white Americanism, for he believes—foolishly, perhaps, but fervently—that Negro blood has yet a message for the world. He simply wishes to make it possible for a man to be both a Negro and an American without being cursed and spit upon by his fellows, without losing the opportunity of self-development.[5]

In varying degrees black institutions took steps to include information on the history and culture of black Americans but only occasionally— mainly in history and sociology—did they offer specific courses focused on the black experience. Howard University, for instance, introduced two such electives in 1918–19. One was *Race Problems,* a sociology course open to underclassmen, that dealt with "Growth, distribution and tendency of the Negro population. Segregation, occupation, crime, vital statistics, marriage, divorce . . . [and] the progress of the Negro in home ownership, education, religion, and business." The other, *The Negro in American History,* an elective for seniors and graduate students (who had had the two English history courses required of history majors), dealt with slavery, the Civil War, Reconstruction, and "efforts at racial adjustment and the struggle of the Negro for social justice."[6]

The black experience also became part of the academic life of the colleges through organized activities that brought students from other black colleges, outside artists, public figures, and scholars to campuses for debates, lectures, and recitals. Knoxville, Morehouse, and Talladega Colleges, for instance, formed a Debating Triangle in 1911 that included among the topics it debated public issues related to race in the United States. In another example, Talladega established a lecture recital program in 1922 that brought black and white artists, poets, scholars, and writers to its campus. Included among them were such well-known black Americans as Horace Mann Bond, William Stanley Braithwaite, Langston Hughes, and Hale Woodruff. But the major infusion of the experiences and concerns of black Americans into the academic life of the colleges would have been difficult if not impossible to keep out: it took place in discussions both in and outside classes, in work done on research papers, and in conferences with professors in the sciences and humanities. Nevertheless, it would take more than half a century before faculty at black colleges and at other institutions of higher education would focus serious attention on addressing the black American experience in the curriculum.

In line with existing practices, black schools and colleges prepared mission statements that set forth the goals their institutions sought to reach through their curricula. Virtually all institutions highlighted the task of moral and intellectual development of students, as did northern schools. A unique feature of the institutional statements of late nineteenth- and early twentieth-century black colleges was the inclusion of "race progress" as a crucial part of their mission. The following excerpt from the 1904 Tougaloo College catalog is a typical:

> The Aims of the School.
> The ideal toward which the school is working may be expressed in these words from an address by the President, "If I might sketch a program for racial elevation it might be this: Manual Training in connection with the ordinary common and high school studies for all, with trade schools for those manifesting some degree of skill in handicraft, and technical schools for the more scientific, in order that a strong foundation for general intelli-

gence and material prosperity may be laid: Higher Education, collegiate and professional, for all who can attain it, that thus the best of the world's thought may be transmitted to the mass, and the individual come to the fullest intellectual life; the whole lit by morality and transfused with the religion of the Christ, to the end that it may attain the highest of goals.[7]

It was on the matter of how best to promote "race progress" that a major conflict developed in the early twentieth century over whether black schools and colleges should emphasize academic education or industrial education. The approach of most black colleges prior to 1900 had been that of a "generalized emporium of learning" that provided elementary, secondary, normal, college, industrial, and professional studies. Speaking in May 1950, an alumnus of Talladega gave his view of one of these early multipurpose college programs, as it existed in the four years before his graduation in 1900:

Observing deficiencies in every department of the life of . . . [its] new charges . . . [the faculty] set up within the limitation of meager resources a sort of educational department store over the entrance to which he might well have put the legend, "Merchandise to fit every social and economic need." In marketing his wares, moreover, he refused to be defeated by the tragic poverty of his constituency.

In spite of this all-things-to-all-needs philosophy, however, it was still a college he envisioned even though its academic reach far exceeded its temporary grasp. An inventory of the items composing its study program appeared to present a picture wholly unrelated to any rational design. But a closer view would disclose that a distinctive thread of purpose ran through the all, and while this seemingly planless plan was difficult to reduce to a blueprint, it was equal to the demands of the necessary spade work for social efficiency. And, withal, the ultimate objectives were never obscured by the imperatives of the immediate situation.[8]

Academic and industrial education had in fact, coexisted in black institutions since the 1860s. Most early institutions had little practical choice but to include some elements of vocational training in a situation where students sometimes had to build part of their own campuses or work on the college farm to pay their tuition and fees. In some cases, as at Hampton Institute, vocational training was the central element in the curriculum. In others it provided a way for students to gain practical experience and possible trades that offered hope of a post-academic living in an economically constricted world. For impoverished institutions, it held out the possibility of reducing critical costs of maintaining their campuses.

Three events help to explain how and why the peaceful coexistence of academic and industrial education was transformed into a serious clash of concepts, approaches, and educational philosophies. The first was a speech by Booker T. Washington in September 1895 at the Cotton States Exposition in Atlanta, Georgia. The second was a series of conferences held by educators at Capon Springs, West Virginia, between 1898 and 1903. The third was the publication in 1903 of W.E.B. Du Bois' groundbreaking book *The Souls of Black Folk*.

In its primary focus on industrial education, Hampton Institute in Hampton, Virginia had long differed significantly from most other early black colleges. Its white founder, General Samuel Chapman Armstrong, had been sent to Hampton by the Freedmen's Bureau during the Civil War to ease difficulties that had developed between black and white residents in an area that had come under control of the Union army. Envisaging freedmen in the role of industrial workers of a future South, Armstrong decided that a suitable model for their education would be a manual training school he had run in the Hawaiian Islands. He opened Hampton Institute in 1868 with a curriculum built around the concept of industrial training. The three-year course of study that followed elementary school included in the first year, "Geography, vocal music, rhetoric, gymnastics"; in the second, "elementary business, agriculture, chemistry, soil analysis, and exercises in teaching"; and in the third, "English, reading and composition, oration, and book-keeping and practice teaching."[9] The aims and methods of Hampton are reflected in this description of course work in home economics and agriculture:

> In the farm work, under the constant direction of an educated practical farmer, the graduates of this institution will have learned both the theory and practices of the most profitable methods of agriculture.
> The female students do all the home-work of the boarding department. Thus, in the home, on the farm, and in the schoolroom the students have their opportunity to learn the three greatest lessons of life—how to live, how to labor, and how to teach others.[10]

Armstrong presented his views to a national audience in an 1872 speech to the National Education Association, describing the major goal of black education as offering "uplift through labor." Teachers would train students for work in agriculture, mechanics, and household services and for teaching positions in schools that offered such instruction. His speech attracted white northerners and southerners who supported "appropriate" education for black Americans that would indeed improve their skills in labor and service without altering their social and economic subordination in the newly developing "white rule" southern state governments. Some of these backers would provide significant financial assistance to Hampton in the years to come.

Booker T. Washington enrolled as a student in Hampton Institute in the year that Armstrong gave his speech. He completed his studies in 1875 and after a brief teaching stint in West Virginia, returned to Hampton as head of its night school. In 1881, with Armstrong's recommendation, he was appointed principal of the Tuskegee Institute, a normal school being established in Tuskegee, Alabama. Modeled after Hampton, it opened its doors the following year. Washington's administrative abilities and his accommodating views on segregation attracted notice within the region and drew financial support to the Institute. As a result, he was invited to speak at the 1895 Cotton States Exposition—a trade fair of states producing large quantities of cotton—in Atlanta. His views on race relations and education favorably impressed southern white Americans, brought wider attention to Tuskegee, and national prominence to its founder. The essence of the speech is reflected in the following excerpt:

> To those of my race who underestimate the importance of cultivating friendly relations with the Southern white man who is his next door neighbor, I would say, cast down your bucket where you are, cast it down in making friends, in every manly way, of the people of all races by whom you are surrounded. Cast it down in agriculture, in mechanics, in commerce, in domestic service, and in the professions. . . . The wisest among my race understand that the agitation of questions of social equality is the extremist folly, and that progress in the enjoyment of all privileges that will come to us must be the result of severe and constant struggle, rather than of artificial forcing.[11]

In the minds of many white Americans, such a compromise in which black Americans would accept social and political segregation in return for an education that would equip them to hold menial jobs made Washington the leading spokesman on black education. Both black and white Americans perceived the alternative as no provision of public education for the descendents of freedmen. For black Americans, this created a new and serious problem. Education, initially established to aid in assimilating black Americans into the national mainstream, would now be structured to prevent that assimilation from taking place, and it was the black principal of a well-known educational establishment who was mapping out the way to accomplish this goal. Washington had charted the path onto what Henry Bullock, in *A History of Negro Education in the South*, has termed "the Great Detour" in black education.[12]

The spread of the idea of industrial education was helped along by a series of factors. In 1896, the U.S. Supreme Court rendered the "separate but equal" decision in the case of *Plessy v. Ferguson*. Laws requiring racial segregation in public and private life were subsequently enacted in southern states and efforts were renewed to end public support for the education of black Americans. Industrialization, the "manifest destiny" of the United States on a global stage, and the new doctrine of Social Darwinism increasingly attracted the attention of Americans. Active white support for civil rights and education for black Americans declined markedly. Opposition to prevailing southern views on race and education all but disappeared. Beginning in 1898, northern and southern educators, among whom were several white presidents of black schools and colleges, came together to work out the future of black education in a series of annual meetings at Capon Springs, West Virginia. In 1903, the group arrived at a consensus: the educational philosophy of Samuel Chapman Armstrong and Booker T. Washington would be the basis for a special kind of schooling deemed particularly appropriate for Blacks. This would be presented to the southern white Americans in terms of the benefits of teaching black Americans to perform more efficiently urgently needed agricultural and mechanical labor. As a result of the Capon Springs conferences, industrial education increasingly replaced the classical academic curriculum in black public precollege and college education. Public elementary and secondary institutions became training schools and southern institutions of higher education would now commonly be identified as "agricultural," "mechanical," or "normal" schools.

The majority of the better-established private institutions nonetheless continued to focus on the value of an academic education as the core of a secondary school and college experience. Its spokesmen held that "race progress" required the development of an able community leadership. For this, it was essential that schools and colleges not limit students' outlook to the opportunities available in a segregated system. This group looked for its educational models to the most respected academies and liberal arts colleges in the country.

Differences on this issue were reflected in the thirty-seven schools and colleges established between 1900 and 1915. Nineteen of these—just over half—identified themselves as "agricultural and mechanical" schools. The available information is not sufficient to determine the degree to which these institutional names represented actual agreement with the principles of Armstrong and Washington or, as stated in the Bureau of Education's 1915 report, a perception that such designations increased the chances of securing white financial support. For educators at the time, the financial significance of a school's designation would certainly have seemed self-evident. Records for 1915 show $7,726,338 as the total value of the endowments of 121 black high schools, normal schools, and colleges. The combined value of the Hampton and

Tuskegee endowments—$4,651,457—accounts for 60 percent of this total, more than double the $2,312,553 value of the combined endowments of the thirty-two private institutions that had students taking college level courses in 1915. The remaining eighty-five schools and colleges had endowments of $762,328, a rough average of $9,000 each.

W. E. B. Du Bois was the leading proponent of traditional liberal arts curricula in preparatory and college education. He expounded his views as editor of the *Crisis,* the official journal of the NAACP, from 1910 to 1934, as a member of the faculty at Atlanta University from 1934 to 1944, and with great clarity in *The Souls of Black Folk*. In a chapter entitled "Of Mr. Booker T. Washington and Others," he vigorously opposed the idea of establishing industrial schools as the only postsecondary educational option available to black Americans. A classical liberal arts higher education, he insisted, was essential to the development of black leadership without which he saw little chance for race progress. Objecting to the notion of any assumed inferiority or moral inadequacy in Blacks as a race, he rejected Washington's economically focused and socially accommodating position. He believed that without education and political rights, black Americans would never gain political and social equality, or be able to take advantage of opportunities to establish economic security. At the same time, he was less optimistic than Frederick Douglass—the former escaped slave and foremost voice of the abolitionist movement in the nineteenth century—that an integrated society would follow in a reasonable period of time after emancipation. Instead, Du Bois argued that the role of black schools should be to educate a "talented tenth"—the most able and forward looking students—for leadership positions. Du Bois was not opposed to vocational education as an option for students desiring it or unable or unwilling to pursue a rigorous academic program.

The Washington camp showed no comparable acceptance of or tolerance for traditional liberal arts education. In "What Is the Matter With the Atlanta Schools," an article that appeared in the November 1907 issue of *Colored American Magazine* (which Washington controlled), the writer attacked the classical curriculum generally, and the private black colleges in Atlanta specifically, describing them as possibly harmful to black Americans. "As we understand, in our system of education, the college or university is of no more service in educating people than it makes itself helpful in the education and uplift of the masses. The college that shuts itself off from the masses, and fails to be felt in the community life where it is located, falls far short of the purpose of higher education, and its influence contributes more to the destructive than to the creative."[13]

Despite these clashing views on curriculum, most black colleges offered a blend of liberal arts and industrial education courses. The curriculum at institutions devoted to the liberal arts typically offered much that was professional or vocational as well as some courses that would qualify as industrial education. Fisk University, ranked among the foremost adherents to an academic curriculum, accepted financial support from the Slater Fund in the 1880s to instruct girls in household duties and to teach printing, and Howard University offered courses in Foods and Cookery, Plain Sewing, and Printing in 1917–18. Likewise, public and private institutions committed to industrial education required some academic courses. Even during the most intense period of the industrial/academic debate, Hampton and Tuskegee, as well as some black state-supported institutions, moved slowly but steadily to increase their academic offerings. Nevertheless, the differences in philosophy were important. It was the liberal arts rather than the industrial arts that did most to promote concepts important for a more humane society. It was the colleges committed to the liberal arts that challenged the concept of training black students for careers that reinforced social separation, economic dependency, and political impotence.

PHILANTHROPY

Under the best of conditions it would have been difficult to establish schools and colleges to accommodate the more than one million southern black Americans of school age for whom no schooling had been provided before 1865. In spite of this situation, however, the percentage of five- to nineteen-year-olds enrolled in school increased by more than 35 percent between 1865 and 1915, while enrollment for all five- to nineteen-year-olds increased by about 16 percent. What financial resources there were for black education came from the Freedmen's Bureau, tuition, the religious organizations that played a major role in establishing schools and colleges, and a few secular philanthropic foundations devoted to black education. Freedmen's schools took in an average of $1.8 million a year from 1867 to 1870, almost half from the Freedmen's Bureau (Table 5.1).

From 1870 into the twentieth century, however, denominational groups were the major sources of financial support. As the 1915 Bureau of Education report made clear, tuition provided less than half the total income for 96 percent of the high schools, normal schools, and colleges. More than half of these institutions depended on their affiliated denominational boards for 50 percent or more of their income.[14]

In the late nineteenth and early twentieth centuries, three philanthropic foundations unrelated to specific Protestant religious groups also demonstrated a special interest in black education: the John F. Slater Fund, the General Education Board, and the Phelps-Stokes Fund. In

TABLE 5.1

Sources and Amounts of Income for Freedmen's Schools for Period July 1, 1869–December 31, 1869

Source	Amount ($)
From school fund	4,887.50
From refugee and freedmen's fund	4,500.00
From appropriations fund	520,121.83
For transportation of superintendents and school books (estimated), charged to "transportation account" on books of distributing officers	2,500.00
Total from Bureau	532,009.33
From benevolent societies, churches, individuals, and foreign countries (estimated)	350,000.00
From freedmen (estimated)	180,000.00
	530,000.00
Total income from all parties	1,062,009.33

Source: Alvord, *Freedmen's Schools,* p. 10.

addition, a significant contribution was indirectly provided by the Peabody Education Fund. Established in 1867, the Peabody Fund focused on the development of public schools in the South and made no direct contribution to black higher education. It was, however, dissolved in 1914, at which time it donated a lump sum of $350,000 to the John F. Slater Fund, whose primary focus was black elementary, secondary, and college level education.

In 1882, John F. Slater—a Connecticut cotton and woolen manufacturer—set aside a sum of one million dollars, the income from which was to be used for the education of Blacks in the Southern states. Recently retired President Rutherford B. Hayes served as first president of the Fund's board of trustees. Over the next decade, the Fund made grants only to institutions that offered industrial training, which profoundly affected the nature of black education. Because of financial constraints, many black colleges seeking support adjusted their curricula to meet the Fund's requirements. From 1894 to 1914, the Fund donated more than $956,000 to black colleges, 35 percent of which was given to Hampton and Tuskegee. The funds going to these two institutions declined after James H. Dillard became general agent and president of the Fund in 1910 and were discontinued in 1928. In 1931, the last year of Dillard's tenure, grants to colleges and universities reached their highest level ($52,000 for the year). Between 1882 and 1932, the Fund made grants totaling $3.8 million, of which $1.2 million went to colleges and universities.[15]

John D. Rockefeller established the Southern Education Board in 1903 to promote "education within the United States of America, without distinction of race, sex, or creed." The grant-making function of this organization was delegated to its trustees and became known as the General Education Board. From its founding to 1914, it gave black institutions approximately $700,000 out of a total of $15.8 million issued in grants. In contrast, black education was the primary if not the exclusive interest of the Phelps-Stokes Fund, established in 1911. Its primary impact on higher education in the early twentieth century was not due to its grant activity but to its cooperation with the Bureau of Education in conducting the Bureau's 1915 study on "Negro Education." The nature of the cooperation between the Fund and the Bureau is described in the introduction to the study:

> The trustees [of the Phelps-Stokes Fund], believing that . . . a report of existing conditions would prove invaluable to southern educators and legislators, to philanthropists interested in Negro education, to the principals and trustees of schools for colored youth, and to various education boards . . . asked the Commissioner of Education if he would accept the cooperation of the Phelps-Stokes Fund in making such a study on condition that the expenses of the agents should be paid by the fund.[16]

The result of that cooperation was a body of useful data but also a set of recommendations suggesting that industrial education should be the primary recipient of funding. Foremost among these recommendations intended to "indicate the changes that are possible and most immediately necessary rather than to summarize all the improvements that ideal conditions require" is the following:

> The most vital test of educational effort is in the extent to which it provides for the economic, intellectual, and spiritual needs of the individual and community. The principle of adaptation to pupil and community needs requires decreasing emphasis on educational courses whose chief claim to recognition is founded on custom and tradition. The recommendations herewith made are based on such community necessities as health, home comforts, civic responsibilities and rights, and teachers with knowledge and vision.[17]

The actions of the various denominational groups and of these secular philanthropic organizations are an outstanding example of domestic benevolence. Without them, there would have been fewer black schools and colleges, they would have been less well equipped and staffed, and their student bodies even worse off. Meaningful black higher education might well have been delayed another half century or more. That being said, the directed nature of the funding provides a cautionary notice to modern funding institutions of the power of modest sums (relative to the educational funds needed) in a money-starved environment. Such sums can decisively shape the paths that institutions can afford to take, whatever their educational goals may be. The funding institutions of this era did very little to directly influence the number of black Americans in positions of administrative and instructional leadership in colleges affiliated with northern denominations. Moreover, they did even less to improve the quality of administration in colleges affiliated with black denominations, in which the sometimes ineffective clergy was heavily involved.

Far more significantly, placing what money there was largely into industrial training programs warped and narrowed the development of black educational institutions for years to come. It helped to formalize the half-spoken doctrine of separate but unequal status in the very structure of the new black education system just as this doctrine was being formalized in the larger society. Black Americans were to be educated, but largely subordinately in a system whose very curricula would be "practical" for the "Negro race" and so conceptually inferior to those of white schools and colleges. It would take black and white educators of a more humanistic bent—who were more sensitive to and supportive of intellectual development, social justice, and racial equality—years to dig out from under the "industrial" label. And yet given the nature of American society at that time, given white attitudes and sensibilities, it would be unrealistic to assume that other paths were open to the funders. The choice was most often between funding for industrial education and no funding at all and in that context, the philanthropists of the period played an important role in the progress of black higher education.

However much funding set an agenda, lack of funding set its own agenda as well. The very existence of black schools and colleges was often dependent on the religious interests and sectarian rivalries of various Protestant denominational groups. Despite the enormous region-wide need for schools, several denominations established what amounted to rival schools and colleges in the same towns and cities. By 1915, six institutions existed in Nashville, and two to five in thirty-three other cities. Education for the freedmen and their descendants might have been improved by more thoughtful planning and by joint financing of single institutions, as occasionally happened. The location of the 626 private institutions existing in 1915, mostly small and inadequately funded, represented overexpansion in some areas and an absence of schools in many others. It is from the colleges and stronger high schools and normal schools that made up a third of this group that the current private four-year black colleges emerged.

CHAPTER 6

Higher Education in a New Century

GROWTH

To UNDERSTAND the growth of black higher education in its second century of existence, one must turn once again to the 1915 Bureau of Education study, *Negro Education*. It provides a baseline of information on black schools at the edge of the modern era. Little other information is available because the nature and health of black schools of any sort were of remarkably little interest to the majority of the population. The Southern Association of Colleges and Secondary Schools, for instance, refused even to evaluate black institutions until 1931, when some schools were finally placed on its "approved list."

The 1915 report provides, as a letter transmitting it to the secretary of the interior put the matter, "a detailed statement, on the basis of a geographical arrangement, of the facts pertaining to . . . all schools for Negroes of secondary or higher grade, and of all schools, of whatever grade, which receive appreciable support from private individuals, church organizations, boards of education, and other organized societies.[1]

Site visits had been made and descriptions provided of all of the "large and important" schools. The fullest descriptions and most favorable assessments were, unsurprisingly, given to two secondary-level industrial arts schools. The report placed no special emphasis on postsecondary education. Colleges were treated almost as an aside both in terms of their numbers—4.2 percent of the total—and in the importance assigned to them. They are lumped under the term "higher schools," which was used to refer to all institutions offering postelementary education. The term is sometimes used interchangeably with "higher education," which, in its current usage, refers only to postsecondary education. Although little concerned with higher education, the 1915 report provides previously unavailable information on the small number of institutions that had college-level programs.

Of 653 black "private and higher schools," only twenty-seven were publicly supported.[2] Five hundred ninety-five of these schools were located in the states of the former Confederacy; the remaining fifty-eight were in the Border States, Ohio, Pennsylvania, and the District of Columbia. Two hundred fifteen are identified by name as normal schools, high schools, or colleges, although some schools that had "college" in their name never offered postsecondary courses. Table 6.1 takes the numbers of "higher schools" for Blacks forward to 1954, the year of *Brown v. Board of Education* (the Supreme Court desegregation decision). There is a significant rise in the number of these schools before 1915 and a decline after 1915, largely due to the growth of segregated public high school systems throughout the South.

It would be a mistake to apply this pattern, however, to black colleges. The study identifies thirty-one private institutions that enrolled college students in 1915.[3] Although "private higher schools" reached their peak number in 1920, it was the pre-college institutions among them that declined drastically thereafter, whereas the number offering college courses tripled by the 1940s.[4] It should be noted, however, that some colleges continued to operate elementary and secondary schools into the 1950s. In many southern school districts, these were the only institutions that offered college preparatory work to black students.

Table 6.2 provides information on the growth of colleges between 1915 and 1954, as well as the number of students enrolled and degrees granted (where the information is available).

Several factors contributed to both the decline in pre-college "higher schools" and the growth in the number of institutions of "higher education." Most important was the increase in the number of public second-

TABLE 6.1

"Higher Schools" for Black Americans at End of Each Decade, 1860–1950, and in 1915 and 1954

Year	Number of Institutions	Percent Increase/Decrease
1860	5	
1870	100	1900
1880	118	18
1890	155	31
1900	172	11
1910	192	12
1915	215	12
1920	217	1
1930	130	−40
1940	93	−28
1950	92	−1
1954	92	0

Sources: T. J. Jones, *Negro Education;* U.S. Office of Education, *Survey of Negro Colleges and Universities* (New York: Negro Universities Press, 1928), No. 7; U.S. Office of Education, *National Survey of the Higher Education of Negroes* (Washington, D.C.: Government Printing Office, 1942), pp. 40, 41.

ary schools in the South. This led to a significant increase in the number
of black high school graduates, even though most of these public schools
were of poor-to-average quality, lagged badly behind the better private
black schools, and received far less financial support than white public
schools. Many of them emphasized industrial arts training and often did
not go beyond grade ten. Even with the proliferation of public high
schools in the 1920s, there were still only fifty-nine accredited high
schools for black Americans in the South in 1934. Twenty of these were
private. Of the remaining thirty-nine, ten were in North Carolina. Alabama and Florida had two each. South Carolina, the state with the second largest percentage of black Americans in its population had only one
accredited high school, and Mississippi, with the largest percentage of
black Americans, had none. That this situation represented an improvement is an indication of how bad the situation had previously been.

The establishment of public secondary schools gave an option to black
parents who had previously been forced to accept that their children's
formal education would end short of high school graduation. It also
offered the possibility of financial relief to parents of children who would
have attended private schools. Now, those in straitened circumstances
could choose a free, if unimpressive high school education for their
children and had the option of saving their meager funds for college.
Thus public high schools provided an alternative that increased the feasi-
bility of attending college. The number of black students enrolled in
high school shot up more than six-fold between 1917 and 1932—from
19,242 to 135,981—significantly enlarging the potential pool of college
applicants. However, this striking increase in high school enrollment
seems less impressive if overall access to secondary school is taken into
account. In 1932, black high school students made up only 5.8 percent of
their age group. The comparable number for white Americans was 17.7
percent.

But the growing number of black secondary schools and consequently
of high school graduates became in itself a major factor in the growth of
colleges. Earlier in the century, when preparation for pre-college teaching could be completed within a normal school program that was the
equivalent of secondary school, such an increase might have had less
effect on black college enrollment. In the 1910s and 1920s, however,
some southern states raised the requirements for certification as a
teacher to two years of college and, in the second quarter of the century,
to a college degree. As one of the few professional jobs open to black
Americans, teaching had been, before 1900, the career path chosen by
one-third of the almost 2,000 black college graduates. Thus, the expanding number of teaching positions available and the higher state requirements for certification both contributed to growing college enrollments.

TABLE 6.2

Data on Black Colleges for Selected Years

	1914–15	1926–27	1935–36	1942–43	1953–54
Private Institutions					
Number of four-year institutions	31	56	58	58	54
Number of two-year institutions	0	0	28	33	11
Total private institutions	31	56	86	91	65
Enrollment in private institutions					
Male	na	na	na	na	13,662
Female	na	na	na	na	17,110
Total	1,643	10,396	20,138	na	30,772
B.A. degrees granted	na	818	1,970	na	4,935
Faculty*	4,640	na	na	na	3,278
Public Institutions					
Number of four-year institutions	2	21	28	29	36
Number of two-year institutions			7	4	5
Enrollment in public institutions					
Male	na	na	na	na	17,597
Female	na	na	na	na	25,522
Total	52	3,464	13,605	na	43,119
B.A. degrees granted	na	165	1,490	na	6,968
Faculty*	na	na	na	na	4,024

Sources: Data for 1915, 1927, 1936, and 1954 are from Hill, *Traditionally Black Institutions.* Data for 1943 are from U.S. Office of Education, *National Survey of the Higher Education of Negroes.*

Note: na indicates that data are not available.

*Includes 1914–15 faculty teaching at all levels and 1953–54 faculty teaching at college level.

The opening of public secondary schools for black Americans in the South also gave an unexpected financial boost to private institutions for which higher education had always been the primary objective. To provide pre-college courses had always been no more than a necessary step toward the accomplishment of their mission, not the mission itself. Publicly supported secondary schools raised the possibility of refocusing their resources on support for college-level work. Although the poor quality of most public secondary schools made this a difficult decision, economic problems resulting from a decline in denominational support and later from the impact of the Great Depression (which hit the South earlier than the rest of the country) most often decided the matter. Nevertheless, not until after mid-century had all of these colleges closed their secondary schools.

For private black high schools and normal schools, as well as the financially weaker colleges, the new competition with the free public schools for students often proved devastating during the Depression. As Table 6.1 reflects, their mortality rate was high. Of the 217 in operation in 1920, more than 124 had closed their doors by 1940. However, some that had served only pre-college students in 1915 successfully made the transition to college status, completing the difficult job of securing faculty, developing curricula, and establishing reputations as college-level institutions. Among them were Tuskegee Institute, Oakwood Manual Training School, and Stillman Institute in Alabama; Saint Augustine School and Scotia Seminary in North Carolina; Voorhees Industrial School in South Carolina; and Hampton Institute and St. Paul Normal and Industrial School in Virginia. All were part of the growth of degree-granting institutions from thirty-one in 1915 to fifty-four in 1954, and are today four-year colleges.

Hampton Institute and Tuskegee Institute were the two best known of these elementary/secondary schools. Together they had enrolled 1,762 elementary and 900 secondary students in 1915, ranked second and third in enrollment behind Howard University and first and second in endowment. By the mid-1920s, however, in response to public high schools with curricula modeled on Tuskegee's and Hampton's and the rise in certification requirements for teaching careers, each began its college level program. The following passage in Tuskegee's 1927–28 catalog announced its decision to move in this direction:

> Under the modified social and economic conditions following the close of the World War, it has become necessary that Tuskegee Institute should simply intensify the instructional processes, to make more thorough the methods of educational procedure and raise the degree of academic and technical attainment required in a more exacting economic environment.

Therefore, in addition to those courses of secondary grade, in the specialized vocational schools, leading to special diplomas, there have been added . . . new courses on the college level.[5]

Eventually both schools closed their elementary and secondary programs.

For the stronger of the private colleges, the situation was also problematic because the growing pool of applicants from public institutions had frequently completed less rigorous courses of study than had graduates of private high schools. To address this difficulty, private colleges built on their traditional strengths: the ability to identify talent and commitment in students, and the motivational and pedagogical skills needed to work successfully with students whose pre-college schooling was below average. These strengths of the black colleges would allow a dozen or more of the private institutions to post impressive records in both academic standards and number of students during the 1930s, 1940s, and 1950s.

During slightly more than a decade from 1914 to 1925, the number of colleges increased 81 percent and their student populations increased an astonishing 533 percent. Enrollment increased more than 50 percent even during the period from 1936 to 1954, when the number of colleges decreased 7 percent. Table 6.3 shows these changes in selected time periods from 1914 to 1953.

Public colleges were not a significant factor in black higher education before the 1920s. Although it is not our purpose here to trace their development, their rapid growth and the importance of their role beginning in the 1920s requires some mention. By 1926, enrollment had dramatically increased sixty-five-fold to 3,464 college students. The growing significance of public colleges was reflected in the changing student ratios. In 1914, there had been forty students in private college for every one in a public college; by 1926, the ratio had dropped to three to one; and by 1935, 1.5 to one. By 1953, thirty-six public institutions constituted 40 percent of all black four-year colleges and enrolled 57 percent of all black college students. The private colleges maintained a reputation for more demanding academic programs, but by mid-century they had lost their dominance in enrollment.

TABLE 6.3
Percentage Increase/Decrease in Black Private Colleges and Enrollments for
Selected Years

	1914–1925	1926–1935	1936–1953
Colleges	78	4	−7
Students	533	94	53

Between 1910 and 1950, both private and public college enrollments grew faster than the 18 percent increase in the black population.[6] But the numbers for Blacks still lagged behind those for college attendance for all Americans in the eighteen- to twenty-four-year-old age group at the time: only 5 percent of men and 4 percent of women were enrolled; the comparable figures for Whites were 15 percent and 8 percent of young men and women, respectively.

The effects of two world wars and the Great Depression on the transformation of black Americans from the most rural to the most urban of the country's ethnic groups had a key, albeit indirect, influence on black education. The large-scale migration of southern black Americans to industrial cities outside the South began during the First World War. What had been a trickle of former slaves moving northward in the late nineteenth and early twentieth centuries increased exponentially as wartime needs for urban labor grew and European immigration practically came to a halt. For black Americans, however, the magnet was more than jobs and pay. Segregation, which prevailed in every aspect of southern life, was less intrusive in northern cities; discrimination was less overt; and northerners appeared less prone to violence than southern Whites. Just as important to migrants with children—for some a major factor in the decision to move to the North—was the availability of better public schools. In turn, their improved economic situation, thanks to better paying jobs, made it possible for some black families to pay for a college education for their children. By the late 1920s, student rosters at several private black colleges in the South showed increased numbers of students from Buffalo, Chicago, Cleveland, Detroit, New York, and other urban centers. A small but growing number of children of black college graduates now began appearing at their parents' alma maters or at other black institutions—a new and momentous development in black education. College attendance was increasingly viewed by students and their families as an important step toward equality of opportunity and by many as an obligation to the "progress of the race."

In 1927, the Federal Bureau of Education undertook a second study on black education, published as the *Survey of Negro Colleges and Universities*.[7] The document speaks of both "a heartening presentation of the facts" and "a gloomy side of the picture." Among the "heartening facts" were an 81 percent increase in the number of colleges since 1915 and a five-fold increase in the number of college students enrolled. On the "gloomy side," it stressed the immediate need for "more education, better education, and higher education." This is a remarkable change in attitude since the 1915 report, reflecting the degree to which, in little more than a decade, the black college had managed to put itself on the map of white educational consciousness. In 1929, the year the study was published, the stock market crashed, worsening the conditions that had depressed southern agriculture for almost a decade. The wholesale price of cotton—the region's main crop—dropped from 33 cents per pound in 1920 to 6.4 cents in 1932. These developments had an immediate effect on the large percentage of black families still working in agriculture, and specifically in cotton production. The average annual income of families of students in black colleges in 1927 was an exceedingly low $199, but this was more than 2.5 times the average student tuition at the twenty-one black state-supported colleges then in existence.

When the Depression hit full force, these figures changed. Private colleges were forced to cut faculty salaries, financial aid, and other operating expenses. Elementary and secondary departments were closed down, reducing students enrolled in pre-college programs from 24 percent to 17 percent of all students at black colleges.[8] To increase income, colleges were forced to raise tuition and fees, increases that some students could not afford. Among the perverse outcomes of the Depression years was that more black students completed secondary school because of job shortages for teenagers but, for a time, the increased graduation rate was not reflected in college enrollment because of severe financial difficulties.

Concerned about the development of their member institutions, the Association of Colleges and Secondary Schools for Negroes (established in 1913) requested that the federal government authorize another study of black higher education. In response, Congress in 1939 charged the Office of Education (then a division of the Federal Security Agency) with conducting a study published as the *National Survey of the Higher Education of Negroes*.[9] The findings were published in 1942, by which time the United States was engaged in World War II. To a stark description of the precarious situation of black schools and colleges as the Depression years ended, the report added a dismal view of the preparation for college that public schools provided for black Americans.

According to the study, of the twelve million black Americans in the United States, three-quarters still lived in the South, where the per-pupil funds allocated for the education of a black student averaged little more than one-third that allocated for a white student. The school year for black students was one to three months shorter, and black teachers with comparable education and experience received lower salaries. For colleges facing these conditions, mere survival was a formidable challenge. Segregated public high schools and normal schools left much to be desired in their physical facilities and the academic quality of their course work. As a result, black college teachers continued to face intellectually able but poorly prepared students and they had severely limited opportunities to upgrade their professional skills through further formal study. At only three private institutions in the South—Atlanta University, Fisk University, and Howard University—could Blacks, whether already faculty members or not, enroll in graduate school before the 1950s. Several southern states eventually established programs of financial assistance for black Americans attending graduate schools outside the region, but these were insufficient to offset the financial hardship of being unable to attend the public graduate schools that their state taxes helped to support. War-related expenditures coupled with discriminatory policies ensured that increased public funding would not be made available for black education.

Matters leading up to World War II commanded the attention of faculty and students at black colleges, who were much concerned about fascism in Europe. Although it is doubtful that Hitler's *Mein Kampf* was widely read by black or white students, black experiences, especially in the South, formed the basis for a special sensitivity to reports of Italian attacks on Ethiopia in the early 1930s and later of German mistreatment of Jews.

When the United States entered World War II, black college students strongly supported the war effort and criticized the government's hesitancy to admit black Americans into combat units. They hoped that in the end these positions would build support toward the "double V"— victory over racism not only abroad but also at home. Black Americans registered for the military and volunteered for service, as did other Americans. Between 750,000 and one million black Americans served in the military during the war. About half were stationed abroad in all the theaters of operation and found themselves, however unintentionally, engaged in the often eye-opening experience of contact with people in foreign countries and cultures without histories of institutional racism directed against Blacks.

During the war years, the involvement of students and faculty in the military reduced by almost half the male presence on black campuses. A 1945 survey of black enlisted men indicated that 40 percent of those with one to three years of college and 24 percent of those who had completed four years of high school planned to continue with their education at the conclusion of the war. Five percent of those who had completed four years of college planned to do the same.[10] There does not appear to have been a follow-up study to determine the degree to which they followed through on their plans, but as shown in Table 6.4, veterans did indeed enter or re-enter college in large numbers beginning in 1946.

The four decades after 1915 were hardly years for which an observer would have confidently predicted the growth that took place in private black colleges or the levels of academic quality that some of them at-

TABLE 6.4

Veterans Enrolled in Black Colleges (Private and Public) in Southern States, 1946–52

Fall of Year	Number of Veterans	Total Students	Percent of All Students
1946	18,216	58,842	31
1947	26,306	74,173	35
1948	22,526	70,644	32
1949	19,320	70,431	27
1950	13,562	69,651	19
1951	7,985	66,290	12
1952	4,222	68,375	6

Source: Hill, *Traditionally Black Institutions,* p. 13.

tained. Yet most were sounder institutions in 1954 than they had been in 1915, and some had established enviable records under the most grueling conditions.

With the exception of Howard, Hampton, and Tuskegee, the relative status of individual private black colleges showed considerably more variability and their development was much more difficult to predict in the first half of the twentieth century than in the second half. The data in Table 6.5 help to make this clear. Identifying the top fifteen colleges in the areas of enrollment, market value of endowment, per-student value of endowment, and degrees awarded in the years 1915, 1955, 1967, and 1975, Table 6.5 shows the percentage of those colleges in each year and category that also appear among the top fifteen colleges in 2000. A total of forty institutions appear in one or more categories and years in this table.

Of the fifteen largest colleges in 2000, thirteen appear fairly consistently in the rankings for the latter half of the twentieth century.[11] Although only seven appear in the rankings for 1915, the number grows to eleven in 1955. In 1955, 1967, and 1975, ranked colleges listed among the top fifteen constituted less than 50 percent in only one category in one year. That not one of the sixteen different institutions that appear in one or more of the 1915 rankings is among the fifteen largest in 2000— whereas from the mid-1950s on, we see a consistent presence in the rankings of a sizeable majority of the fifteen largest—underscores the point that rankings prior to 1955 were less good predictors of an institution's future than rankings in 1955 and later.

To call attention to a relationship between rankings and the operational success of these institutions is not to overlook the relative vulnerability of all private black colleges. Bishop College, which ranked

TABLE 6.5

Percentage of Colleges Ranked in the Top Fifteen for the Years and Categories
Listed and Also Ranked among the Top Fifteen Colleges in 2000

	Year				
Category	1915	1955	1967	1975	1955, 1967, and 1975
Enrollment	27	47	60	73	47
Endowment	33	67	60	60	60
Per-student endowment	na	53	67	67	40
Degrees granted	na	67	53	73	27

Source: National Science Foundation WebCASPAR database system.
Note: na indicates that data are not available.

among the top ten in enrollment in 1955, 1967, and 1975, closed its
doors in the 1980s. Fisk University, one of the leaders in degrees granted
in 1915 and in the top five in endowment in 1955 and 1967, dropped to
eighteenth in endowment in 1975. Howard, Hampton, and Tuskegee,
which placed no lower than fourth in any of the rankings for 1955, 1967,
and 1975 (except for Hampton's and Howard's per-student endowment
in 1955) maintained their position throughout the period. The same is
true for Benedict, Bethune-Cookman, Morehouse, and Spelman Colleges, and Dillard and Virginia Union Universities. But two decades after
the *Brown* decision, the overall picture was much the same as it had been
for more than a century. Some private black colleges teetered financially
on the edge of dangerous cliffs. Some developed relatively firm foundations on safe ground. And others stood hopefully, if a bit unsteadily,
somewhere in between.

CHANGE

Between 1915 and 1954, private black colleges experienced qualitative
changes in institutional character, in the interactions among various
campus constituencies, and in the relations among the institutions themselves. The thirty-one colleges existing at the time of the first Bureau of
Education study might be characterized as New-England-style schools
established by white Americans to provide higher education for black
Americans, even though black denominational groups established five of
them. The presidents and faculty members of those five colleges were
black, but their combined college-level enrollment in 1915 was only 115

students. The remaining 26 colleges, with college-level enrollments total-ing 2,522, were established by—and received a substantial part of their income from—northern denominational groups. Most of their presi-dents were White and white church groups determined college policy. Over the course of the next half-century, however, they became "black colleges" in a fuller sense. Not only were their students black but their policies and curricula came to be shaped and implemented largely by black administrators, faculty, and trustees. Their leadership shared with their students the experience of living as Blacks in the United States.

During this period of change, there were no organized efforts by black staff or students to reduce what might be called white cultural influences or to discard the existing college and curriculum models. At the same time, subtle but profound changes were taking place in the climate of these institutions. Blacks on campuses, as elsewhere, felt a growing con-sciousness of "otherness" imposed by American society, and of the need to involve more Blacks in setting policy and determining the direction of the few institutions that were meant to serve them. Greater efforts were made to relate what was happening in college to what was happening in the lives of black people elsewhere in the United States. Paradoxically, this recognition of "otherness" and "difference," as it became embedded in an institutional mission and life, generated a new sense of comfort among students on campus.

The experiences of those who served in the armed forces in World War I, both in the United States and abroad, helped form postwar attitudes and agendas that produced changes in the character of the colleges. Of the four hundred thousand black Americans who served in the military during the war, many had not previously been outside their states or their counties. For them, military service provided an introduction to a wider world that was unlike the rural South. The two hundred thousand who were part of the American Expeditionary Force in France, especially those who served in combat, experienced race relations that differed markedly from those shaped by American laws and customs. Contacts with French citizens did not carry the same assumptions of authority and racial superiority or inferiority that dominated almost all contacts be-tween black and white Americans in the United States. Nothing perhaps stamped the significance of foreign contacts on the psyche of black Americans more than white Americans' opposition to such contacts.

This was brought to public attention by the publication in the May 1919 issue of the NAACP's magazine *Crisis* of a 1918 document entitled "Secret Information Concerning Black American Troops." Issued by the French Military Mission stationed with the American Army in France and circulated among French officers, it advised:

It is important for French officers who have been called upon to exercise command over black American troops, or to live in close contact with them, to have an exact idea of the position occupied by Negroes in the United States.

The American attitude upon the Negro question may seem a matter for discussion to many French minds. But we French are not in our province if we undertake to discuss what some call "prejudice." American opinion is unanimous on the "color question" and does not admit of any discussion.

Although a citizen of the United States, the black man is regarded by the white American as an inferior being with whom relations of business or service only are possible.

We must prevent the rise of any personal degree of intimacy between French officers and black officers. We may be courteous and amiable with these last, but we cannot deal with them on the same plane as with the white American officers without deeply wounding the latter. We must not eat with them, must not shake hands or seek to talk or meet with them outside the requirements of military service.[12]

Almost all such contacts were between French officers and enlisted men of the American Expeditionary Force. (There were only 639 black officers in the U.S. armed forces and few of them were in Europe.) Because contacts between French officers and their own enlisted men did not proceed on a basis of equality, there was no reason to expect those with black American servicemen to do so. Nevertheless, compared with black-white relations in the American South, there was in these relations a previously unknown level of mutual respect. The black community was well aware that white Americans objected to such civility abroad and that the closest thing to such civilities in the South most often involved white staff in the world of private black education.

The experiences of those assigned to combat duty also influenced black thinking. As part of the American Expeditionary Force, black Americans were ordered into combat against white Europeans in a war whose purpose—from the American point of view—was to "make the world safe for democracy." Black Americans, familiar with the common practices of southern police and courts of treating all incidents involving black-white violence as black criminal activity, found themselves occasionally commended as individuals and units for their actions against enemy soldiers. When returning from the war, these veterans found only familiar patterns of prejudice and discrimination that, if anything, had intensified, as if to warn black Americans not to expect improvements in race relations at home just because they had fought the Germans in Europe. Several veterans in uniform were among the more than seventy Blacks lynched in 1919. That same year, race riots occurred in Elaine,

Arkansas; Washington, D.C.; Millen, Georgia; Chicago, Illinois; Omaha, Nebraska; Chester, Pennsylvania; Knoxville, Tennessee; and Longview, Texas. But the veterans were changed by their experiences in ways that made it increasingly difficult to adjust to the contradictions they faced. Their wartime experiences played a part in shaping attitudes among black Americans that were reflected in reactions to the race riots that took place in 1919. In these riots, black Americans fought back with a new audacity, and defended themselves with the result that in Chicago— the most serious of the conflicts—and in other towns and cities, there were significant casualties on both sides.

The force of such experiences abroad and back home spread throughout black communities, finding voice among the small but growing groups of black intellectuals connected with one or another of the colleges, as well as with the black writers and artists of New York City's Harlem Renaissance.

Perceptive observers predicted such developments. New Englander John Underwood, who wrote the column "From an Andover Window" for *The Andover Townsman* (a Massachusetts paper) made such an observation in 1907:

> I always keep my eye out for the coming of these colored quartets . . . and so of course I went to hear the quartet from Atlanta University. . . . Their voices had the soft, velvety quality which the Negro voice has by right. Yet something was lacking, which I think I remember in the jubilee singers whom I used to hear years ago. I decided that it was the note of infinite sadness,— the sadness of slavery, in which the plantation melodies were born and with which they were sung. That was gone, and with it something of the old, haunting charm and pathos was gone from the rendering of "Swing Low, sweet chariot," and others. The singers were college boys . . . and they sang with college boys' hopeful and happy voices. As a result, the modern "lullaby" with which they closed the concert was the best thing they gave. Was I sorry for the loss? Would I have had it otherwise? On the contrary, I would not have it otherwise if I could prefer the American collegian to the American slave; and I wish every man in this country could listen to such singers and could realize that the grandson of the slave has become a college boy.[13]

Opposition to pre-war patterns of authority and status developed among black students along with a new confidence and strength that comes with education and organization. There was, however, a measure of uncertainty in this college generation as to where to direct their energies, and who and what their proper targets should be. With little or no experience of organized opposition, they initially focused on life within the institutions they attended. One of the issues that attracted the attention of black faculty, as well as alumni/ae and students, was the need to appoint more black Americans to faculty and administrative positions, a stance that appeared especially compelling in light of the limited opportunities for black Americans in traditionally white institutions. In 1914–15, Whites still outnumbered Blacks on the faculty at sixteen of twenty-eight four-year colleges controlled by independent or northern denominational boards, and occupied the presidency at eighteen of them. It had been well understood that the near absence of black Americans holding graduate degrees necessitated the appointment of white faculty and administrators in the years after 1865. Half a century later, however, given the number of college graduates and graduate degree holders, the failure to consider black Americans for these positions was less defensible and distinctly out of line with the missions of these institutions.

The dates of the first appointments of black Americans as college presidents show how much more slowly the process moved than the availability and quality of candidates warranted. Mordecai Johnson, holder of B.A. degrees from Morehouse College and the University of Chicago, a bachelor of divinity from Rochester Theological Seminary, and a masters of sacred theology from Harvard became the first black president of Howard University in 1926. John Hope, who received B.A. and M.A. degrees from Brown University, became the first black president of Morehouse College in 1906 and of Atlanta University in 1929. Lincoln University in Pennsylvania selected Horace Mann Bond, holder of a Ph.D. from the University of Chicago, as its first black president only in 1945. Charles S. Johnson, a noted sociologist, took over as the first black president of Fisk University in October 1946, a month before he was scheduled to travel to Paris as a U.S. delegate to the new United Nations Educational, Scientific, and Cultural Organization. He had recently returned from Japan as a member of a group making recommendations for changes in Japanese education. Not until 1953 did Spelman College appoint a black, Albert Manley, North Carolina College's dean of arts and sciences, as its president. In 1960, Tougaloo was the last black college to appoint a white president.

The changed consciousness many black Americans experienced—the increased sense of empowerment and possibilities that wartime service and access to new jobs and educational opportunities in the North held out—subtly changed the atmosphere in which all decisions were made in black educational institutions. Although organized protests by faculty, alumni/ae, or students in support of black candidates for college presidencies were rare, and seldom were protests the primary reason for such appointments, it is difficult to find an instance in which the issue of race did not factor into the selection of a black to succeed a white president.

Even the least obvious example—John Hope's 1929 appointment to the presidency of prestigious Atlanta University—reminds us that the very openness of white funders and trustees to such a change reflected a new atmosphere on black campuses and so among their supporters. Hope's predecessor, Myron Winslow Adams, had served Atlanta University well from 1919 to 1929. There was no significant opposition to his administration and no organized movement in support of a black American as his successor. In a 1929 meeting between John Hope, then president of Morehouse College, Atlanta University trustee Will W. Alexander, Jackson Davis of the General Education Fund, and Beasley Ruml of the Laura Spelman Rockefeller Fund (the latter three White), there was a discussion of the value of greater cooperation between Atlanta's black colleges. Alexander later described the conversation to Clark Foreman, nephew of the editor of the *Atlanta Constitution,* who suggested, "Why don't you elect Dr. Hope president of Atlanta University, and he'd be president of Atlanta University and Morehouse College. The campuses join; with one president over the two of them, you might bring the others in." In his history of Atlanta University, Clarence Bacote adds, "This suggestion was so logical and so simple that it seems strange that it had not been made before."[14] But it was logic, involving as it did the idea of appointing a black to run a new joint institution (a merger that did not take place), that would have seemed far less compelling to white funders and backers only a decade before; and Hope's subsequent appointment would be accomplished with a matter-of-factness and smoothness that would have been inconceivable at the time of the 1915 Bureau of Education report. It also represented a significant early step in efforts to encourage collaboration among the black colleges of Atlanta.

The 1926 appointment of Howard University's first black president did follow a student strike the year before, but there is no real evidence that opposition to President J. Stanley Durkee had played a role in the strike or that it was specifically in support of a black appointee. The situation surrounding the appointment of Horace Mann Bond at Lincoln University was somewhat different. More than a decade of alumni-led protest against a white-only policy for faculty appointments and the refusal of the trustees to appoint a black member to its board of trustees preceded it. In early June 1926, the trustees offered the position of president of Lincoln to a Philadelphia minister Walter Greenway. On June 27, candidate Greenway delivered a sermon in which he criticized the mayor of Philadelphia for rejecting an application by the local Ku Klux Klan to march in the Philadelphia Sesquicentennial Celebration, a matter actively covered in the black press. The alumni organization then expressed such serious opposition to Greenway that the board withdrew the offer and in November 1926, William Hallock Johnson, a white graduate of Princeton University and Princeton Theological Seminary, was appointed instead. In an effort to improve relations with the alumni, Johnson supported the election of Eugene P. Roberts of New York City as the first black trustee in 1927. During the next school term, Langston Hughes, the future poet who was then a senior at Lincoln, conducted a survey of student opinion on the desirability of opening faculty positions to Blacks. He discovered that the new postwar consciousness had not fully penetrated the campus. Astonished that the survey results showed startling majorities opposed to the idea, he wrote, "The mental processes of the hat-in-the-hand, yes-boss, typical white worshipping Negro is, to my mind, very strongly shown in the attitude of some of the students here toward an all-white faculty. [That] sixty-three per cent of the members of the upper classes favor for their college, a faculty on which there are no Negro professors . . . indicates that the college itself has failed in instilling in these students the very quality of self-reliance and self-respect which any capable American leader should have, —and the purpose of this college, let us remember, is to educate 'leaders for the colored race.' "[15] Several years before he retired in 1936, Johnson supported a resolution establishing a new policy, according to which faculty members would be selected without regard to race. His successor, Walter Livingstone Wright, also white, had been the candidate supported by the alumni in 1926. He served as president for nineteen years, conscientiously managing Lincoln, although he was not considered an outstanding leader. He saw the school financially through the toughest days of the Depression and, after World War II, established it as one of the Pennsylvania institutions of higher education for which the state made annual appropriations. But strong feelings persisted among the alumni that the day for black leadership of Lincoln was long overdue. This undoubtedly was a factor in the appointment of Horace Mann Bond in 1945.

From the 1920s on, alumni took a growing interest in the governing boards of their institutions. The issue was not simply the presence on boards of trustees of those who were graduates, but also the appointment of persons selected by alumni/ae to officially represent them and their interests. Arrangements were made for such appointments at several colleges between 1915 and 1954, although these did not always produce the desired results. Alumni/ae trustees occasionally expressed views on key issues that were contrary to those held by alumni/ae organizations, and the trustees sometimes neglected to pursue any other means of assessing the views and attitudes of graduates.

Student dress, curriculum issues, and parietals, as well as decisions related to campus social life captured students' attention and sometimes resulted in strikes or organized protests. Typical were a 1925 strike protesting the fierce regulation of student life by Fisk University President Fayette McKenzie's strict rules and a strike against compulsory chapel at Howard University in the same year. Both were settled with "little effort but, especially at Fisk, with some ill feeling."[16]

Rules and regulations dealing with students' social life reflected the way administrators and faculty construed the religious and moral standards of the day or of the religious group with which the institution was affiliated. As an example, the statement on student social life in the 1919 Howard University catalog appeared under the heading "Religion and Morals," and is typical of the general approach taken at most black colleges:

> The charter [of the University] contains no religious test or limitation. The University, however, is distinctly Christian in its spirit and Work. . . . The Young Men's Christian Association is the organization within the University which aims at (1) the promotion of the religious life of the men students . . . (2) the securing of employment for students; (3) the providing of wholesome recreation and social life as a substitute for undesirable resorts in the city.
>
> The Young Women's Christian Association is an affiliated branch of the National Association, and aims to develop among young women of the University high standards of character and conduct.[17]

Howard and Fisk were among the few institutions not affiliated with a denominational board, but this made little or no difference in institutional standards for determining what was appropriate in contacts between male and female students, entertainment, church attendance, and other matters. At one time or another students at most black colleges found themselves at odds with the rules and regulations. Three examples of restrictions that students in this period found to be egregious and unwarranted intrusions are: women could not receive male callers at Tougaloo College; the matrons at Storer College maintained the right to inspect incoming mail; and rules at Lane College stipulated what students were to wear right down to their undergarments! Student governments existed in most of these colleges by the 1930s and often gained modest authority to set rules regulating some social activities—subject to approval by the administration. Social dancing was banned on a few campuses, especially those affiliated with the Baptist Church. By the late 1940s, the bans on smoking—but not on drinking—had been lifted. Even with some liberalization of campus rules, black college students visiting northern, traditionally white college campuses in the 1940s were surprised by how relatively few institutional regulations governed students' out-of-class activities.

In the 1920s, Greek letter sororities and fraternities began replacing the YMCAs and YWCAs as centers of campus social life. By 1954, they existed on the campuses of most four-year colleges. Although their guidelines for membership were criticized as elitist and their initiation procedures were sometimes rough and crude, they remained immensely popular. Such fraternal and sororal organizations partially satisfied the desire among students to have more control over their social lives. The fraternities and sororities were increasingly seen as places for making valuable social contacts for the future—with alumni/ae brothers and sisters. The fraternities had come to be considered as focal points for social mobility. "Race progress" had not disappeared as a collective goal for the private black college and its students, but it increasingly competed with hopes for individual advancement and upward mobility. However subtly, this too reflected a new postwar consciousness based in part on the hairline cracks in the system that was meant to keep Blacks subordinate in America.

A mood of cautious optimism prevailed among black college students throughout the period in spite of pervasive segregation in the South and the intensity of discrimination that existed throughout the country. It was expressed by intellectuals and artists—in novels like Jean Toomer's *Cane,* in Langston Hughes's poem "The Negro Speaks of Rivers," and in the sculpture of Sargent Johnson—supported by an expanding body of art and scholarship dedicated to recovering black American history and culture. Industrial education was in distinct decline in the 1930s. There was a growing pride and comfort in black racial identity, vividly expressed by many of the artists of the Harlem Renaissance. Black poets and writers were frequent visitors to black college campuses. It was all part of a process that Nathan Huggins refers to as the "birth or rebirth" of a people and historian Henry Bullock refers to as "burying Uncle Tom."[18]

Most black intellectuals and artists of the period held baccalaureate degrees from black colleges. For scholars holding graduate degrees, black higher education now provided opportunities to teach, do research, and write that were not yet available at many traditionally white colleges and universities. The presence of black scholars on campuses gave reality to student dreams of a more expansive future for themselves, just as works of writers and artists, sometimes studied in these colleges, gave shape and meaning to those dreams. The best known of these pioneering black scholars are listed below, with the institutions from which they received baccalaureate degrees and the institutions and fields in which they received their graduate degrees. It was largely through the models they provided that private black colleges came of intellectual and scholarly age:[19]

	B.A. Degree	*Advanced Degree*
W.E.B. Du Bois	Fisk University	Harvard University (1895, Sociology)
Lewis B. Moore	Fisk University	University of Chicago (1896, Greek and Latin)
Benjamin Brawley	Morehouse College	Harvard University (1908, English)
George E. Haynes	Fisk University	Columbia University (1912 Social Economy)
Carter G. Woodson	University of Chicago	Harvard University (1912, History and Government)
Ernest E. Just	Dartmouth College	University of Chicago (1916, Physiology)
Alain Locke	Harvard University	Harvard University (1918, Philosophy)
Thomas W. Turner	Howard University	Cornell University (1921, Biology)
Charles Houston	Amherst College	Harvard University (1923, Law)
William A. Daniel	Virginia Union	University of Chicago (1925, Sociology)
Charles H. Wesley	Fisk University	University of Chicago (1925, History)
Henderson H. Donald	Howard University	Yale University (1926, Economics)
Lorenzo Turner	Howard University	University of Chicago (1926, English)
Laurence Foster	Lincoln University	University of Pennsylvania (1931, Anthropology)
Edward Franklin Frazier	Howard University	University of Chicago (1931, Sociology)
Abram Lincoln Harris	Virginia Union	Columbia University (1931, Economics)
Dwight O. W. Holmes	Morehouse College	Columbia University (1934, Education)

W.E.B. Du Bois, scholar, author, and activist, was in many ways the singular precursor of both the intellectual and literary strands of the post–World War I consciousness. *The Souls of Black Folk,* which he published while he was a member of the faculty of Atlanta University, pursued a theme repeated by the writers and poets of the 1920s and 1930s. It was the painful anomaly of experiencing segregation and discrimination at the hands of those whose theories of a democratic society and much of whose culture one respected and admired. In *The New Negro,* published in

1925, Alain Locke, professor of English and philosophy at Howard University and the first black Rhodes Scholar revisited this theme: "The Negro mind reaches out as yet to nothing but American wants, American ideas. But this forced attempt to build his Americanism on race values is a unique social experiment, and its ultimate success is impossible except through the fullest sharing of American culture and institutions." Poet Claude McKay, who studied at Tuskegee Institute before transferring to Kansas State University, made much the same point in a poem that appeared in *Harlem Shadows,* the first collection of his poems published in the United States:

> Although she feeds me bread of bitterness,
> And sinks into my throat her tiger's tooth,
> Stealing my breath of life, I will confess
> I love this cultured hell that tests my youth.[20]

Although the prevailing view was that conditions would improve and that the private black college would have a crucial role to play in the improvement, some black Americans were not optimistic that the full rights of a citizen would ever be secured or that a traditional higher education was a path worth pursuing. The leading advocate of this position in the 1920s was Marcus Garvey, who made no effort to attract college-educated Blacks to his mass movement. Du Bois and Garvey openly disapproved of each other. Carter G. Woodson, who founded the Association for the Study of Negro Life and History in 1916 to collect, preserve, and promote black history, was also pessimistic about the sort of education provided for black Americans in America. In his 1933 book, The *Mis-Education of the Negro,* he criticized both liberal arts and industrial arts education, likening the experiences of black Americans to a man traveling in a strange country who at the fork of the road takes the wrong way. The longer he travels, the worse off he is.

One important change in the black college landscape involved the development of far closer relations between previously unrelated institutions, thanks in part to attempts to improve effectiveness and keep costs within bounds by consolidation. The period before 1915 could be characterized primarily as a time of independent operations and rivalries among institutions. But to think of the post-1915 consolidation that occurred as an organized movement of black colleges would be to assign it more structure and purpose than it possessed. In reality, the tendency to consolidate resulted from the reactions of individual institutions to the pressure of change combined with the desire to improve academic services and the need to stretch meager financial and human resources.

Often, however, consolidation—joining together for purposes of strengthening—followed or went hand in hand with experiments in collaboration. A significant part of the consolidation that took place in the universe of private black colleges simply involved the closing of institutions that were no longer viable. Table 6.1 shows the rapidity with which this took place after 1920. Many of those that closed were colleges in name only. Some, however, had operated successful college programs for years before being forced to close by various, mainly financial, problems. In this latter group were Lincoln Institute of Kentucky and Simmons University in Kentucky; Kittrel College in North Carolina; Walden College, Morristown Normal and Industrial College, and Roger Williams University in Tennessee; and Hartshorn Memorial College in Virginia. Unfortunately, decisions to close were rarely made in a way that allowed remaining assets to be passed on to other institutions. A few private colleges were taken over by the state and continued to operate as publicly supported institutions. The earliest of these was Lincoln University in Jefferson City, Missouri, in 1879. The most recent was Lincoln University in Lincoln University, Pennsylvania, in 1972.

The institutions that continued to operate as private colleges varied considerably in quality and resources, but in general were viewed as more effective and deserving of support than those forced to close their doors. Although the survival of some colleges was influenced by parental desires to send their offspring to institutions with a specific religious connection, this factor declined in importance as the century progressed. Overall, it seems reasonable to suggest that the more successful private colleges had clearer visions of their missions and more able leadership than the institutions that did not survive. In the difficult environment within which all black colleges existed, however, they also needed a considerable dose of good fortune.

The importance of institutional mission received the attention of Dwight Oliver Wendell Holmes, dean of the graduate school at Howard University, in his book *Evolution of the Negro College* and of the U.S. Department of Education in *The National Survey of the Higher Education of Negroes*. In 1934, Holmes wrote:

> Another serious defect is the lack of definite and clear-cut objectives on the part of the several colleges. There is a fairly unanimous agreement among these institutions that they must meet the requirements of some accrediting body. The answer to the question "To what end?" is not always so certain. It is impossible, of course, for all these schools to offer all desirable forms of educational opportunity. . . . A few may become university centers, but the majority must confine themselves for many years to limited and well-defined objectives.[21]

Speaking of both private and public institutions in 1942, the *National Survey of the Higher Education of Negroes* suggested that a black college had not only the responsibility of educating American youth but for educating youth who will be denied some of the goals and forbidden some of the values which the society itself have set up. It deals with a specific group of youth who have all the problems of white youth plus many more that are particularly their own.

One of the first problems any college faces is that of defining its function as a specific type of institution. It must have a conception of itself as a liberal arts . . . college, and must see its responsibility as . . . a 4-year college.

Furthermore, as an institution serving a minority group whose social and economic position is rapidly changing, the college must have a conception of desirable goals in terms of the ultimate position of Negroes in the American social order and some idea of the effective means, direct or indirect, toward the desired ends. If it has no clear conception of itself as an institution for training Negro youth, or if it fails to take account of the minority group status of its students its program will, to that extent, lack both reality and specific direction.[22]

The process of focusing mission and resources on college education was well under way by the 1920s. Seminaries at Clark, Morris Brown, Morehouse, Talladega, and other institutions were separated from those colleges or closed. Elementary and secondary schooling had begun to disappear from campus, as did most nursing schools. Shaw University even closed its medical school. Industrial education lost much of its attraction well before World War II. By 1954, these institutions had become exclusively schools of higher education.

Closer coordination among institutions, especially those located in the same cities or affiliated with the same denominational groups also led to consolidation. Collaborative activities began modestly, with such experiments as holding joint summer sessions, sharing staff and consultant services, and joint use of buildings and stadiums. In 1913, seven black colleges had organized the Association of Colleges for Negro Youth (ACNY), with three important purposes: first, to have their work approved by a recognized accrediting agency; second, to use the accreditation procedure as an aid in improving academic and administrative programs; and third, to exercise collective pressure on such organizations as the American Medical Association to abandon the practice of issuing lists of approved colleges on the basis of ratings given by regional accreditation agencies, from which black colleges in the South were excluded.

The target was the action of the Southern Association of Colleges and Schools (SACS), the accrediting agency for the region, that refused to admit black colleges to its membership or even to evaluate their academic programs. Black college graduates wishing to pursue graduate or professional study at traditionally white universities were placed at a distinct disadvantage by this refusal. Only continuous petitioning by ACNY members and other black colleges finally convinced SACS to agree, in 1931, to evaluate the colleges and issue a list of those who met its standards. As it continued to press for inclusion of black colleges in SACS, the ACNY dissolved and replaced itself with a new organization, the Association of Colleges and Secondary Schools. This group, similar in structure and purpose to SACS, extended membership only to colleges on approved lists developed by SACS or by other regional associations. But SACS continued to refuse membership to black colleges until 1957, three years after the Supreme Court declared racial segregation in schools unconstitutional.

The many smaller-scale, experimental, and sometimes fumbling attempts at collaboration and cooperation led in 1944 to the creation of what is arguably the most influential association in the history of private black colleges, the United Negro College Fund (UNCF).[23] It was the brainchild of Frederick D. Patterson, third president of Tuskegee Institute. The year before World War II ended, anxious about the financial viability of black colleges in the postwar world, Patterson introduced the idea of a membership association having as its primary purpose the raising of unrestricted annual operating funds—funds unencumbered by instructions for how they should be used—for its members. Patterson believed that a nationwide united appeal would raise more for the black colleges taking part than the total they might collect in individual campaigns. Twenty-six other presidents of private four-year colleges joined the effort. They understood from personal experience that large foundations were becoming increasingly unwilling to contribute unrestricted funds to their colleges and that the presidents were spending unacceptable amounts of time on fundraising. The twenty-seven member colleges, representing the academically and financially strongest of the fifty-eight four-year institutions, took part in the first collective drive in 1944. Despite the involvement of John D. Rockefeller, Jr., and a public endorsement from President Franklin D. Roosevelt, the UNCF raised only three-quarters of a million dollars, one-half of the announced goal. However, the amount contributed by corporate, nonprofit, and individual donors was several times the total raised by the institutions individually in previous years.[24] As a result, a permanent office and paid staff were in place by 1948 and the College Fund Drive became an annual activity and a crucial source of income for its members.

The first executive director of the UNCF was William J. Trent, Jr., a graduate of Livingstone College, where his father had been president since 1925. Trent Jr., who had taught at Livingstone and Bennett Colleges (both in North Carolina), served from 1938 to 1944 as an advisor on negro affairs and as race relations officer in the Washington office of

Secretary of the Interior Harold L. Ickes. He took up his post at UNCF in 1944 and in 1951, under his direction, the Fund began planning a four-phase capital campaign to begin in 1953 and to run concurrently with the annual campaigns. The capital campaign was to help colleges raise funds for needs other than annual operating expenses, such as new buildings, major renovations, and new heating systems. Phase one got off to a good start with a five-million dollar donation from John D. Rockefeller, Jr., and substantial gifts from other important past donors to black colleges. When the campaign ended in 1956, it had raised $14.6 million, a significant sum, but less than the $27 million the planners hoped to secure. In 1956, Paul Younger, a UNCF fundraising consultant, commented on the possible effect on the campaign of the Supreme Court's May 1954 desegregation decision in the case of *Brown v. the Board of Education:*

> The reaction to the Supreme Court decision . . . of many potential donors to the capital fund reflected doubt over the permanence of the member colleges. Many indicated a reluctance to make a capital investment in a group of institutions whose future, in their minds, was not clear. This attitude was particularly apparent to the Texas campaign where a number of potential donors had indicated major support but now adopted a policy of "wait and see."[25]

It is not clear just how much effect the decision had on the campaign, because the records show that by the end of 1953, it was behind its Phase-2 goal for contributions from large corporate donors, Phase 3 was called off after the decision was rendered, and Phase 4 raised one-third more than its goal, but mainly in contributions from individuals and small groups. In the 1960s, the UNCF conducted a second capital campaign and raised $33 million, impressive testimony that Supreme-Court–induced worries about the disappearance of the private black college had been allayed.

UNCF was the first educational organization to undertake cooperative fundraising in American education. Between 1944 and 1954, it raised $24 million for its member institutions, whose number had grown to thirty.[26] The pioneering model it forged has been widely copied by other groups of educational institutions including the Native American Indian Fund and cooperative fundraising programs for several state university systems. In recent years, the Fund has taken on a wide variety of fundraising challenges. Included among these are support for a program of administrative support for members and the operation of the Frederick Patterson Research Institute, formerly the Research Department of the UNCF, which has the responsibility for gathering and disseminating information on member institutions and black higher education generally.

Given the haphazard growth of black colleges from their beginnings and, until the arrival of the UNCF, their limited ability to find funding, it is hardly surprising that various types of adjustments occurred over time. The closing of some institutions was part of this adjustment process, and the merging and affiliating of others just another aspect of the same process. Examples of these are to be found throughout the history of black higher education but those occurring between 1915 and 1954 were of particular importance.

Atlanta was the location of five black colleges—Atlanta, Clark, Morehouse, Morris Brown, and Spelman—each affiliated with four different denominational groups. All of them still enrolled elementary, secondary, and college students in 1915. According to the report of the Bureau of Education, Morehouse and Spelman had by then already worked out collaborative arrangements "whereby [Spelman] pupils desiring college work attend Morehouse College. In return Spelman Seminary maintains a full-time instructor at Morehouse."[27] A more significant step toward collaboration grew out of the activities leading to the appointment of John Hope as president of Atlanta University. Twenty-five years earlier, he had put forth a concept of collaboration among Atlanta schools. In an article published in 1904, two years before he became president of Morehouse College, Hope wrote, "When the time comes, the Atlanta schools, so close together and aiming at the same thing—the education of the Colored people—will probably come to some agreement. Out of this community of interest will develop spheres of influence. In view of present tendencies in some, if not all, of these schools, is it Utopian to forecast the following division of labor?" He then described spheres of interest that would allow for building on existing strengths and reducing much of the existing duplication of courses and overlap of activities. Hope continued, "With such division of labor as this, each school . . . would have a better guarantee of progress and permanency."[28]

Soon after Hope's appointment to Atlanta University in 1929, a formal agreement was worked out between his institution, Morehouse, and Spelman, which included the following provisions: Atlanta University would limit its offerings to graduate-level work. Morehouse and Spelman would offer no graduate-level courses. Each institution would retain its president and board of trustees. Spelman and Morehouse would each appoint three members to the Board of Atlanta University, and additional board members would be elected at large. The result would be a graduate school, an undergraduate college for women, and an undergraduate college for men.

The constituencies of Morehouse, Spelman, and Atlanta University did not unanimously support this plan, and supporters of Clark and

Morris Brown were critical of the failure to include their institutions in the arrangement. Even Hope's popularity among Morehouse alumni did not leave him immune from criticism on this matter. As a result, the overall structure he envisioned was only partly realized. Almost half a century later, formal steps were taken toward closer working relations of the sort he had once imagined. In 1972, Atlanta University, Morehouse, Spelman, Clark, Morris Brown, and a sixth institution, the Interdenominational Theological Center (ITC) organized the Atlanta University Center (AUC), a new corporation with an executive director and its own board of trustees. The Center had responsibility for any activities that involved two or more of its member institutions. Its major programs consisted of operation of the Robert W. Woodruff Library, providing academic and administrative computing services, establishing a dual-degree program in engineering, operating the Dolphus E. Milligan Science Research Institute, and establishing a Career Planning and Placement Center.

Three noteworthy collaborative developments related to AUC deserve mention even though all occurred after 1954. The first was the creation of the Interdenominational Theological Center, which, before becoming a charter member of AUC, was itself an interesting example of the tendency toward institutional consolidation even when different denominations were involved. The ITC was formed in 1958 by the merger of four independent seminaries representing four separate denominations. Seminaries affiliated with Clark, Morehouse, and Morris Brown joined the freestanding Phillips School of Theology. Johnson C. Smith Seminary joined in the 1969–70 year and the Charles H. Moson Theological Seminary was added in 1970. Considering that denominational rivalry had been a longstanding impediment to consolidation and collaborative agreements, it may seem strange indeed that seminaries representing six Protestant groups—Baptist, United Methodist, African Methodist Episcopal, Christian Methodist Episcopal, Presbyterian, and Church of God in Christ—would have so aggressively sought convergence, but they were driven by the actions of a number of colleges in closing or cutting loose their seminaries, and the realization that as independent institutions, each had little chance of surviving. It was in this context that the seminaries took steps that few colleges had been willing to consider.

The establishment of Morehouse School of Medicine was the second major collaborative development connected to AUC, although one with which only Morehouse College was initially involved. Founded in 1975 as a medical program within Morehouse and admitted as an independent member of AUC, the medical school received full accreditation to award the M.D. degree in 1985, at which time women made up the majority of its students and it had the highest proportion of women at any medical school in the country.

The third collaborative development had the potential to cause discord within AUC. It involved the merger of Atlanta University and Clark College, two institutional members of AUC. As frequently happens when significant changes occur in the status of entities within a collaborative operation, the Clark Atlanta University merger was accompanied by some tension and a period of unease. Clark trustees appeared to dominate the board of the newly merged institution, and Morehouse and Spelman, with whom Atlanta University had a formal agreement dating from 1929, were not involved in the decision regarding the merger. That this bilateral arrangement appears not to have caused major disturbances in the functioning of AUC itself is both a testament to the stable structure of the umbrella organization and to the importance that the individual institutions attached to the collaboration.

Several other mergers involved institutions in different locations. Two Presbyterian women's schools—Scotia Seminary in North Carolina and Barber Memorial Seminary in Anniston, Alabama—joined together in 1930, when Barber Memorial moved to North Carolina. Neither had offered college courses in 1915 and both enrolled many more elementary than secondary students. In 1945, the new Barber-Scotia College awarded its first baccalaureate degree.

Another 1930 merger, an early example of denominational collaboration, involved two colleges in New Orleans. New Orleans College was established by the Freedmen's Aid Society of the Methodist Episcopal Church in 1869, the same year that the American Missionary Association established Straight College. Both had similar origins and histories; both had elementary, secondary, and college divisions; and in 1915, both had plans to expand their college activity. Philanthropic foundations from which both sought financial assistance encouraged negotiations toward a merger. The new institution was named Dillard University for James H. Dillard, who served with distinction as general agent and president of the Slater Fund from 1910 to 1931. During part of that time he also served as president of the Anna T. Jeanes Fund, which was established with $200,000 given in 1905 by Anna T. Jeanes to the General Education Board to help improve rural schools for black Americans in the South.

The creation of LeMoyne-Owen College resulted from yet another collaboration between different denominational groups. The American Missionary Association established LeMoyne Normal Institute in 1869 in Memphis, Tennessee, with a gift of $20,000. By 1915, it had an enrollment of 402 elementary and secondary students. Postsecondary courses were first offered in 1924 and the institution became a four-year college

in 1930, awarding its first baccalaureate degree two years later. Owen
College was founded as a junior college in 1954 by the Tennessee Baptist
Missionary and Educational Convention. The two institutions merged in
1968, and the resulting four-year liberal arts college was assisted jointly
by the United Church Board for Homeland Ministries of the United
Church of Christ (formerly the Congregational Church) and the Tennessee Baptist Missionary and Education Convention. Other mergers
produced Bethune-Cookman College in 1923, Florida Memorial College
in 1941, and Huston-Tillotson College in 1952.

This movement toward the union of colleges or institutions that
evolved into colleges was in part responsible for the severe reduction in
the number of single-sex institutions from twelve to three. Of seven
women's schools in 1915, only Bennett and Spelman remained after
1954, when Barber-Scotia College began to admit male students. Of the
other female-only schools, Miner Teacher's College and Daytona Normal
and Industrial Institute had become part of coeducational institutions,
and Hartshorn Memorial College and Mary Allen Seminary had closed.
Morehouse alone remains from among five male-only institutions. Cookman College merged with Daytona Institute; Johnson C. Smith University, Lincoln University (in Pennsylvania), and Morgan College became
coed institutions, the latter two moving from private to public control.

Although close to one-quarter of the four-year private colleges existing
in 1954 had merged with or were affiliated with another institution, this
number was smaller than might be expected, given the painfully limited
resources of most of the institutions. Too little information is available to
be definitive and it would be an oversimplification to speak of any one
process as the solution to the problems faced by those black colleges that
closed between 1915 and 1954. But the examples suggest that consolidation offered a reasonable and reasonably successful way for hard-pressed
schools to address problems caused by small size, limited financial resources, and low enrollment. One might wonder what would have happened to black higher education had such arrangements been more
widely experimented with as alternatives for institutions that otherwise
had to shut their doors. Although alumni/ae with strong school ties and/
or denominational loyalties appear to have built-in difficulties in considering consolidations and mergers, the history of private black colleges
in this century suggests that considerable benefit accrued from carefully
conceived moves of this kind.

CHAPTER 7

Two Decades of Desegregation

BROWN v. BOARD OF EDUCATION

ON MAY 17, 1954, fifty-eight years after *Plessy v. Ferguson,* Chief Justice Earl Warren delivered the decision by a unanimous Supreme Court on the merits of segregated public schools. He was almost two-thirds of the way through when he answered the question foremost in the minds of listeners:

> We come then to the question presented: Does segregation of children in public schools solely on the basis of race, even though the physical facilities and other "tangible" factors be equal, deprive the children of the minority group of equal educational opportunities? We believe that it does.
>
> We conclude that in the field of education the doctrine of "separate but equal" has no place. Therefore, we hold that the plaintiffs and others similarly situated for whom the action has been brought are, by reason of the segregation complained of, deprived of the equal protection of the law guaranteed by the Fourteenth Amendment.[1]

Finally, it seemed *Plessy* was to become history. The *Brown v. Board of Education* decision surprised most of those who applauded as well as those who bemoaned its conclusions. In the years between the *Plessy* and *Brown* cases, the Court had moved ever so slowly and hesitantly along a route that only became clear on that May day in 1954. Prior to the 1930s, it had, in fact, firmly upheld the "separate" provision of *Plessy,* even as it ignored the "equal" provision and downplayed any federal role in protecting a citizen's rights. Justice David Brewer put it succinctly in 1905, when he advised black Americans "to take their chances with other citizens in the states where they made their homes."[2] In the 1930s, however, the Court had begun to inch toward enforcement of the "equal" as well as the "separate" provisions of *Plessy* in cases involving professional education. In *Missouri ex rel. Gaines v. Canada* and *Sipuel v. Board of Regents* (both in 1938), the Court ruled that in the absence of equal educational facilities, the states of Missouri and Oklahoma were required to admit Blacks to previously all-white state law schools.[3] These cases raised a serious problem for segregationist states. Historian Loren Miller described their dilemma:

All of . . . [the Southern states] had undergraduate colleges for Negroes. . . .
They did not have similar graduate and professional schools, and it was
extremely difficult to provide them because of very limited demand for their
use. Under the Gaines case they could not escape their dilemma by out-of-
state scholarships; under the Sipuel case, they could not require Negroes
to wait until they could establish the requisite graduate or professional
schools.[4] Nevertheless, southern states continued to take action to avoid
admitting Blacks to graduate and professional schools.[5]

In early 1951, the NAACP adopted a strategy aimed at securing a Court
ruling on the legality of segregation itself. With the NAACP's advice and
guidance, black parents in several states brought legal cases against
boards of education for depriving their children of the equal protection
of the law guaranteed under the 14th Amendment. The case brought
against Topeka, Kansas, by Oliver Brown and eleven other parents was
later consolidated with cases in Delaware, the District of Columbia, South
Carolina, and Virginia. They would appear on the Supreme Court docket
as *Brown et al. v. Board of Education of Topeka et al.*

The NAACP strategy was wisely formulated. The five cases had been
chosen so that they would include states in the South, a Border State, a
state where slavery had never existed, and the District of Columbia. In
these jurisdictions, segregated education had been provided for in state
constitutions, by statute, or had been made an option (invariably taken)
for individual school districts. The lead lawyer for the plaintiffs was
Thurgood Marshall, the NAACP's chief counsel and a 1933 graduate of
Lincoln University in Pennsylvania. His counterpart for the defendants
was John W. Davis, a graduate of Washington and Lee University and a
well-known constitutional lawyer who had been the Democratic Party
candidate for the presidency in 1924. The black college community reacted to the news of the decision with a combination of exultation and
concern. Their exultation arose from their beliefs that the decision was
the right and moral thing to do; that it validated the constitutional rights
of black Americans to pursue opportunities outside racial caste lines; and
that integration, as most college communities saw it, was the most promising long-range solution to problems resulting from prejudice, discrimination, and bigotry. The concerns were embodied in a number of rarely
articulated but omnipresent questions about the world of black higher
education to which these communities were so deeply committed: In the
wake of *Brown,* might black colleges in an integrated society wither and
die? If not, what would be their role in a nation of otherwise integrated
public and private higher education? Whom would they serve? How
would they compete for students and faculty with institutions with
greater status and higher levels of public and private support? Such

questions had undoubtedly been on the mind of W.E.B. Du Bois some two decades earlier:

> Theoretically, the Negro needs neither segregated schools nor mixed schools. What he needs is Education. What we must remember is that there is no magic, either in mixed schools or in segregated schools. A mixed school with poor and unsympathetic teachers, with hostile public opinion, and no teaching of truth concerning black folk is bad. A segregated school with ignorant placeholders, inadequate equipment, poor salaries, and wretched housing, is equally bad. Other things being equal, the mixed school is the broader, more natural basis for the education of all youth. It gives wider contacts; it inspires greater self-confidence; and suppresses the inferiority complex. But other things seldom are equal, and in that case, Sympathy, Knowledge, and the Truth outweigh all that the mixed school can offer.[6]

As it turned out, he had seen the future—educationally speaking—that awaited the post-*Brown* black college.

The Supreme Court did not—perhaps could not—deal with many important issues of inequality that had developed in tandem with segregated public schools: poorly trained teachers, widespread public hostility to equal education for black Americans, inadequate equipment, low salaries, and substandard physical plants. The remedies for these matters were left to the very same states that had, for the better part of a century, consciously created this difference in quality. Would they have the will to merge racially separate and grotesquely unequal schools into integrated systems that served the needs of both black and white students?

That it might have "the full assistance of the parties in formulating decrees," the Supreme Court placed the *Brown* case on its next docket and requested that the parties involved present further argument on the way that the actions required by the decision should be implemented. In a May 31, 1955, enforcement decree ordering the defendant states to move with "good faith compliance at the earliest practical date," the Court broke new ground again, but in this instance by taking a step backward. Having previously held that constitutional rights were inherent to individuals, the Court's unequivocal decision in the *Brown* case should have entitled the plaintiffs to claim their rights immediately. However, the 1955 ruling allowed the constitutional right it declared inherent to all citizens to be doled out to black children in a time frame that lower courts—many of which had consistently found in favor of segregation—would determine. The 1954 decision had been a monumental step toward a more democratic society. The 1955 enforcement decree suggested that the rights of plaintiffs could be subject to the convenience of defendants.

In 1954, the patterns of racial separation at all levels of education were as firmly established in the South as they had been in 1896, and in the former Confederate states almost no action was taken toward desegregation for several years. Meanwhile, de facto segregation in education actually increased in areas outside the South and not until 1956 were the provisions of *Brown v. Board of Education* even applied to higher education. With rare exceptions, another decade passed before the *Brown* decision had much effect on the day-to-day life of private or public black colleges. Not until the late 1960s would the casual observer of life in private black colleges see evidence that significant changes were under way.

When it became clear that legally segregated educational institutions would not continue to exist, opposition to continued support for black colleges developed in the South as well as in other areas of the country. The expression of this opposition that received most national attention was provided not by southerners but by two university professors in New England—the region that had once figured so importantly in the establishment and development of private black colleges. In a 1967 article in the *Harvard Educational Review,* professors Christopher Jencks and David Riesman described most black colleges as inferior, unnecessary, and undeserving of continuing support. Intellectually, financially, and scholastically, they describe the better "Negro colleges [as] . . . comparable to those of small and not distinguished sectarian colleges or fairly typical state colleges." As for the other black colleges, "By almost any standard, these colleges are academic disaster areas. Underpaid as their faculty members usually are, many of them could not make as much elsewhere. Some indeed could not get any other academic job."[7]

Judged by the most frequently used indices of educational quality (endowment, physical plant, professional standing of faculty, standardized test scores of students, and professional success of graduates), the best of the historically black colleges were of poorer quality than the best traditionally white institutions and, more generally, black colleges were found to be of poorer quality than white colleges. But such an assessment failed to give sufficient attention to both the histories of these colleges and the complexity of race relations and their effect on education. What the two professors were saying, in effect, was that the longest established and the wealthiest colleges in the country were superior to those established to serve the poorest racial minority during the last century, a century when a racial caste system dominated all aspects of social life. Neither gave any consideration to what value these institutions added to the educational development of their students, most of whom might not have obtained a college education of any sort.

For a century black college presidents had called attention to the inequality under which they labored, to the need for greater financial support for their institutions, to the deleterious effect of low income on the ability of graduates to give financial support, and to the need for more graduate and professional opportunities for their graduates. They noted that many in the country's academic communities were unmoved by the plight of black colleges, that some steadfastly held that segregated public black colleges were not unequal to their white counterparts, and that thoughtful comparisons between private black and white colleges of similar size and with similar financial resources were rarely if ever made. Nevertheless, during the *Brown* era, they struggled against views widely held among white Americans that black colleges were ipso facto inferior and had been justified only because segregation was necessary (according to segregationists) or legally required (according to those less willing to state a personal view). In addition, many white Americans believed that the desire of black Americans to attend white colleges, as indicated by their fierce opposition to segregation in education, proved that there was no reason for maintaining existing black institutions. Those who held such views for the most part targeted support for public institutions, but they did not waste time distinguishing between public and private. As a result, black colleges increasingly felt the necessity to justify their existence to a degree that had not been the case for half a century.

Presidents and trustees of black colleges publicly presented reasons for continued support, relying on their historical influence and the current needs of young black Americans. They emphasized that these private institutions, operating with scant financial resources, had been the major force in reducing illiteracy from over 90 percent to less than 10 percent between 1865 and 1915. Throughout their existence, they argued, they had identified students of considerable ability but poor schooling and contributed to their social mobility by helping prepare them for successful careers. These developments occurred in regions where the political and economic leadership had historically sought to build academic and intellectual inequality into the system of black education and where there was still little commitment to quality education for black Americans. Advocates noted that because poor pre-college schooling was not limited to black students, non-Blacks often needed the kind of services that private black colleges had traditionally provided. The leadership role of students and graduates of private black colleges in the civil rights movement and the increasing number of advanced degrees earned by graduates were extolled as examples of the effectiveness of the private black college.

Desegregation in higher education opened up the possibility that both black and white colleges might now serve both black and white students. Except where prohibited by state laws, private black colleges had always been open to students of all races. The charters of some contained provisions that no student was to be denied admission because of race, with the result that white students were occasionally enrolled throughout the post-Reconstruction period and a few of these schools actively sought to enroll non-black students after 1954. In 1976, there were 2,852 Whites enrolled in forty-six black colleges: 42 percent of them at Howard University; 17 percent at Huston-Tillotson College, Tuskegee University, and Xavier University combined; and 41 percent in the remaining forty-two colleges.[8] Several public black colleges attracted larger numbers of white students, with the result that by 1999 at West Virginia State College and Bluefield State College, also in West Virginia, a majority of the students enrolled were white.

ACCREDITATION, CRISES, AND FEDERAL ASSISTANCE

One result of *Brown v. Board of Education* was that the Southern Association of Colleges and Schools (SACS) no longer had a basis for refusing membership to black colleges. In 1957, SACS finally agreed to accept applications for membership from black colleges. SACS nonetheless insisted that those on their approved list undergo evaluation again, even though it had consistently denied allegations that it used different criteria in assessing black colleges for its approved lists and white colleges for membership. Of the fifty-nine black colleges that SACS had approved, only eighteen were admitted to membership following the second assessment. Thirty-nine others, more than two-thirds of those previously on the approved list, were returned to their unaccredited and unapproved status of 1930. Two conclusions can be drawn from this, both of which are feasible given the history of SACS' dealings with black colleges. One is that SACS discriminated against black institutions in 1957 by having them undergo a second assessment not required of traditionally white colleges admitted to membership at the time the black colleges received approved status. The other is that SACS had previously acted in an unprofessional, irresponsible, and discriminatory manner in improperly approving institutions that did not meet its criteria and by failing to provide the sort of recommendations that could have helped to remove the problems whose alleged existence in 1957 prevented those colleges from receiving accreditation and membership status.

By the mid-1960s, *Brown* and its implementing provisions were increasingly affecting many aspects of life at private four-year black colleges. In some ways, this was beneficial; in others it intensified problems and challenges the colleges already faced. Among the benefits was a growing sense of hopefulness among black students for whom *Brown* proved a validation of opposition to segregation and discrimination. The possibility of a future less influenced by racial prejudice brought with it an increase in self-esteem and the prospect of expanded career opportunities that gave added value to the investment of time and effort in higher education. The resultant increase in the number of black Americans attending college and graduate school raised enrollments in private black colleges even as public black college enrollments rose and increasing numbers of black Americans entered traditionally white colleges for the first time. The hiring of black faculty at traditionally white colleges also expanded job opportunities for black Americans holding graduate degrees.[9]

Foremost among the problems facing black education was the increased hostility that some individuals and groups expressed as reflected in a nascent opposition to what later came to be referred to as affirmative action and in efforts in some southern states to close public black colleges. Additional problems for private colleges included the need to raise student-aid funds for an increasing number of students from low-income families, to pay salaries for additional faculty, to construct new buildings for growing student bodies, and to support the remedial programs needed by some students. And by the mid-1960s, when traditionally white colleges began enrolling increasing numbers of black students nationwide, there was a new problem: the loss to those schools of many of the ablest students and almost no chance of replacing them with a corresponding number of non-black students. This will be discussed in Chapter 12.

Enrollment in the forty-six private four-year colleges increased from roughly 30,000 in 1955 to 61,000 in 1975 (see Figure 7.1). There were five institutions with more than 1,000 students in 1955, and twenty-two such schools by 1975. During these years, issues of race and education continued to operate with considerable force at every level. The withdrawal of large numbers of white students from desegregated schools suggests a widely held feeling among white Americans that greater comfort would be found in a school setting where their racial, religious, or ethnic group formed the majority and had significant influence on the school's cultural norms. It is not unreasonable to suppose that many black Americans, even those who felt especially strongly about the desirability of desegregation as public policy, also desired that a similar option remain open for black high school graduates.

Since small endowments and a large percentage of students needing financial assistance were characteristic of all private black colleges, enrollment growth always necessitated finding additional sources of revenue. Although colleges increased tuition and fees, the rise in the median income of black families during this period (from $4,700 in 1955 to $8,000 in 1974) was of little assistance for two important reasons. First, the purchasing power of $4,700 in 1955 was approximately equivalent to

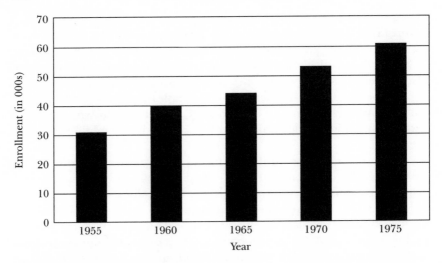

Figure 7.1. Private Black Four-Year College Enrollment at Five-Year Intervals from 1955 to 1975

Source: Hill, *Traditionally Black Institutions.*

$8,000 in 1974.[10] Second, children from families with incomes above the median were more likely than those below the median to attend selective traditionally white colleges (with sizable financial aid budgets) or strong public colleges.

A rising cost of living in the post-*Brown* era also contributed to the problems of private black colleges as they tried to raise tuition and fees in an effort—deeply circumscribed by the financial state of their student bodies—to increase revenues. In 1955, the average charge per student reported by black four-year private colleges was $695; the highest was $976 at Xavier University and the lowest $456 at Barber-Scotia. By 1975, that average had doubled to $1,385 with Rust College in Mississippi having the highest tuition and fees at $2,200.[11] For a median-income black family in 1974, paying tuition for two children attending Rust College would have required 54 percent of pretax family earnings. For such families (and for many non-black families as well) this was impossible without substantial scholarship support.

It is probable that some private colleges would not have survived to the end of the 1970s without the direct and indirect assistance provided by several new federal programs. In 1958, Congress passed the National Defense Education Act (NDEA) primarily in reaction to the Soviet Union's success in launching *Sputnik,* the first man-made satellite, into orbit. This event, which aroused fears that the United States was losing "the educational Cold War" to the Russians, led Congress to authorize the appropriation of federal money to support college science and foreign language studies. Subsequent federal programs provided funds for other areas determined to be important for national defense. The amounts received by black colleges were relatively small, but they still represented a welcome infusion of money at a time of great need in the history of black higher education. Although these funds were not specifically earmarked for black or financially needy institutions, black colleges were able to use the funds to strengthen their programs in designated areas of science, mathematics, and language training. Sometimes, however, financially desperate colleges were forced to give higher priority to improving cash flow by any means than to pursuing only those grants that fitted well with their institutional mission.

The Higher Education Act of 1965, in providing basic education opportunity grants (BEOGs) to disadvantaged students, was the first federal government program since the post–World-War II G.I. Bill of Rights to make grants directly to students who sought to continue their education. Along with subsequent federal grant and loan programs, it helped reduce the extent to which poverty limited the opportunity of students to pursue a college education. In 1959, the first year for which data are available on poverty in the population, almost 9.9 million black Americans were classified as poor. Had the rate of poverty among white Americans been equivalent to that of black Americans, there would have been approximately 88 million poor white Americans instead of the 28.3 million reported by the Census Bureau. By 1974, the number of black Americans living in poverty had declined by 2.2 million, largely because of the earnings of wives who had not previously worked, but poverty among white Americans had declined at a faster rate.[12] As a result, the percentage of black Americans classified as poor actually rose from 26 percent to 29 percent of the total population.[13] Not surprisingly, then, federal BEOGs became a critically important part of the financial package of many students at black colleges.

Title III of the Higher Education Act proved to be equally important. Under this legislation, government funds were allocated for use by "developing institutions" for faculty and curriculum development programs, exchanges of faculty and students between colleges, student services, and improvements in administrative structures. Because of their marginal financial status, most private black colleges qualified for assistance under Title III, about which more will be said in a later chapter. Federal funding, which had a major impact on higher education throughout the United States, was of special importance to private black colleges. Because of Title III and the large percentage of students qualifying for financial aid, federal grants during this period became the largest source of income for some college budgets.

The possibility of securing federal grants sometimes contributed to the creation of new problems. A typical example was the successful efforts of Talladega, a small, traditionally liberal arts college, to secure a grant to establish an academic program in criminal justice. The primary objective was less an interest in criminal justice than in securing income to ease cash-flow problems. Staff was hired and the program put into operation. Within a few years, before the modestly funded program was even securely established, federal support was discontinued and the institution, faced with the need to dip into its limited reserve, terminated the program.

To the fundraising efforts of individual colleges, the activities of the UNCF, federal appropriations to colleges, and grants and loan programs for students must be added grants from philanthropic foundations. Prior to 1954, the Julius Rosenwald Fund, the John F. Slater Fund, and the General Education Board made important grants to private black colleges. Between 1955 and 1960, the Ford Foundation, the Kresge Foundation, and the Pew Charitable Trust all recognized the continued importance of those colleges by giving them an average of about $1 million a year. The Kellogg and Mott Foundations joined these foundations in the 1960s. Foundation contributions averaged $2.3 million a year between 1961 and 1965, increasing to $2.9 million a year between 1966 and 1970, and to $5.8 million between 1971 and 1975, when the Andrew W. Mellon Foundation added its support to private black colleges. During the twenty-one years after the *Brown* decision, these six foundations made grants to private black colleges totaling $61.7 million. The Ford Foundation contributed 78 percent of this amount. Most of the grants were made to strengthen endowments (with grantees required to raise matching funds), to support faculty development, or to support the construction of new facilities.[14]

THE CIVIL RIGHTS REVOLUTION

The influences of the Civil Rights Act of 1964 and the Voting Rights Act of 1965 were less direct but no less important than judicial decisions. Both were passed, at least in part, as a result of protest activities in which black college students played an important role. In fact, the leading role students at black colleges would play in the civil rights movement of the 1960s, like the leading role that graduates of black colleges—lawyers, ministers, doctors, organizers—had played in civil rights events from the

1950s onward was an implicit confirmation of the importance of those colleges in American life.

The passage of the various civil rights acts in Congress and the impact of civil rights protests on the national consciousness in turn brought black colleges to the attention of a wider range of white Americans and had a powerful effect on the campuses themselves. Not only did these events stimulate a belief that racial justice might actually be attainable in the United States, but they infused a new sense of confidence and pride in students and faculty.

The 1964 Civil Rights Act contained separate sections, commonly referred to as "titles," dealing with voting, public accommodations, public facilities, public education, and fair employment practices. It authorized the attorney general to take legal action on behalf of plaintiffs whose civil rights were violated. Allocation of federal funds for education to segregated schools and colleges was now prohibited for the first time. Institutions were required to sign a statement of compliance with desegregation directives to qualify for such funds. In the summer of 1964, segregationists in the Senate mounted a filibuster to prevent a vote on the civil rights bill, but failed when the Republican Party shifted away from its traditional position of cooperation with southern Democrats on issues related to race. Minority Leader Everett Dirksen of Illinois explained the Republicans' actions: "This is an idea whose time has come. It will not be stayed. It will not be denied." Since Dirksen was hardly a traditional supporter of civil rights for black Americans, his statement confirmed the growing success of opponents of segregation in influencing public opinion on the issues considered in the legislation.

The sit-ins that began in 1960 are perhaps the most famous of the daring initiatives taken by black college students in cracking open the segregationist system and influencing public opinion. On February 1, four students from North Carolina Agricultural and Technical College, a public institution in Greensboro, took seats and asked for service at an all-white lunch counter of a Woolworth's store. When instructed to leave, they refused. The manager halted food service, but the students continued to sit at the counter until the store closed. Although their actions were modeled on the nonviolent, direct-action approach developed by Martin Luther King, Jr., during the Montgomery, Alabama, bus boycott, the students added what might be called an "in your face" element. They returned to the lunch counter the next day, were again refused service, again remained seated at the counter, and so on. News of the sit-in spread quickly from campus to campus. Within days, students from black colleges in Charlotte, Durham, High Point, and Elizabeth City, North Carolina, took similar action. Within months, the movement had spread to campuses in Atlanta, Nashville, Tampa, and other cities in the South.

The media carried pictures of students peacefully requesting service at lunch counters, being physically abused by segregationists, and carted off to jail by the police. Lunch-counter sit-ins expanded to include similar nonviolent protests at segregated libraries, parks, churches, and swimming pools. Ministers of black churches, free of the economic pressure applied to black Americans employed in white-dominated public and private institutions, publicly supported these actions. Although college presidents anxious about funding rarely supported the sit-ins openly, they seldom failed to make adjustments when scheduled campus activities conflicted with the protests. Black people of all ages in surrounding communities, and subsequently a small percentage of white students, joined black students in these demonstrations.

What had begun as a series of local protests and efforts to work within the judicial system became, within a decade after *Brown,* a nationwide movement (not inappropriately referred to as the "black revolution") in both the North and the South, which challenged de facto as well as de jure segregation. Looking back, it is difficult and unpleasant to imagine an America that had not experienced the civil rights movement and almost as difficult to imagine what a black revolution might have been like, had public and private black colleges not existed.

Challenges to discriminatory practices in political, economic, and social life multiplied, becoming the subject of daily news coverage in many parts of the country and a part of the education of college students. The riots in Harlem in 1964, in the Watts section of Los Angeles in 1965, and in Detroit in 1967 escalated national tensions, as did the June 1966 shooting of James Meredith, the first black American to be admitted to the University of Mississippi. Speaking at a protest rally in Greenville, Mississippi, days after the shooting of Meredith, Stokely Carmichael, chairman of the Student Non-Violence Coordinating Committee (SNCC), used the term "black power." It seemed to express a mood of frustration with the pace of change and with the perceived passivity of the religiously oriented nonviolent approach of Martin Luther King, Jr., and the Southern Christian Leadership Conference. "Black power" immediately caught the attention of the crowd in Greenville and of young black Americans throughout the country.

The initial responses of the three best-known civil rights groups— the National Association for the Advancement of Colored People, the National Urban League, and the Southern Christian Leadership Conference—were strongly critical of "black power." But the Congress of Racial Equality (CORE), another civil rights group, passed a resolution stating that "Black Power was not hatred but a means of bringing the

Black Americans into the covenant of Brotherhood and a reflection of racial pride in the tradition of a racially diverse nation." In Carmichael's words, "black people in this country are oppressed . . . and black power just means black people coming together and getting people to represent their needs and . . . stop that oppression."

Clearly the term meant different things to different people. To critics it was, at best, a poor choice of a term during a volatile period in race relations and, at worst, much the same as "white supremacy." To those who were attracted to the concept, the two words were invested with a range of meanings, including awareness by black Americans of the power of the ballot, of the necessity of registering to vote and take an active part in all aspects of the democratic process. To others, it meant black control over schools and other institutions in black communities or a revival of the Black Nationalism and separatism that had characterized Marcus Garvey's Universal Negro Improvement Association. Widely shared by proponents of the concept was the view that black power represented a collective frame of mind similar to that held by any group of people who have undergone a long period of oppression and are beginning to express a growing appreciation of their identity, history, and culture. The significance of this view—often called "black consciousness"—was in the emphasis it placed on black Americans' understanding of and respect for themselves, an emphasis largely absent during the two centuries of slavery and the century that followed emancipation.

The concept of black power served as a catalyst, highlighting the idea that how black Americans thought about themselves could be a determining factor in their ability to deal with the forces that had a powerful stake in preserving the country's racial caste system. In this phase of the civil rights movement, many black Americans felt certain that without this consciousness, without a sense of self-respect and togetherness, there would be no chance to attain racial equality. Black consciousness also exercised a significant influence on education at all levels and resulted in an increased body of scholarly works in the social sciences and humanities by and about Blacks. Thanks to the civil rights movement, the voices of a large minority of people with a long history in this country began to make themselves heard in the general intellectual discourse on political, social, and economic issues and in the arts.

BLACK STUDIES

What impact did the civil rights movement, black power, and black consciousness have on academic and intellectual life on black college campuses and on the preservation and stimulation of interest in black culture and history? Their influences are clearly visible in three major areas: expansion of the curriculum to include a wider range of professional studies; increased attention to black history and culture within the curriculum; and a declining black-college faculty role (compared, at least with their pre-1970s predecessors) in the production of scholarly works related to black culture and history.

Black scholars at private black colleges had carried on most of the scholarly research in black history and culture prior to World War II. Among the leading figures in this area were W.E.B. Du Bois, Carter G. Woodson, Benjamin Brawley, Charles Wesley, and Charles S. Johnson. Woodson was the first to champion what would come to be called "black studies" while, between 1896 and 1914, Du Bois directed a series of conferences at Atlanta University that produced reports on various aspects of black life, later published as a series of monographs by the Atlanta University Press.[15] Although some of the early impetus to study black life was lost during the disastrous Great Depression, studies in the social sciences and humanities continued, although at a reduced level, throughout the 1930s and 1940s. The Association for the Study of Negro Life and History urged black colleges to concentrate on black people in their research, curricular, and teaching efforts. In line with this view, President Joseph Rhoads of Bishop College in Texas called on black scholars to break with an academic tradition in which the culture and background of black people were ignored or treated as insignificant when dealing with American life. Scholars of black life clustered at Howard University, including Ralph Bunche, E. Franklin Frazier, Julius Lips, and Edwin E. Lewis, launched the Howard University Studies in the Social Sciences in 1938. During and immediately after World War II, Bunche, William Hastie, Robert Weaver, and other black scholars focused more of their efforts on influencing national and international policies than on research and publication focused on the black experience. Hastie served as civilian aide to the secretary of war and Weaver was director of the Federal Negro Manpower Commission during the war. Bunche's earlier research on colonial administrations provided the credentials for positions he held in the State Department and as director of the trusteeship division of the United Nations.

In the 1960s, black studies evolved as a major component of the black power/black consciousness movement, expressing opposition to the status quo in education just as various forms of nonviolent direct action had expressed opposition to discrimination in political and social life. Civil rights activists viewed many existing laws and customs as supporting the special privilege traditionally held by white Americans in the society and as being used to rationalize discrimination against non-Whites. In a similar fashion, proponents of black studies saw in existing concepts in American education support for ideas favorable to the educational status of some groups while disregarding the disadvantages encountered by others. The development of black studies, ironically often occurring at traditionally white colleges and universities, played a major part in spurring the new social history of the 1970s, with its realization that to understand American history and culture it was necessary to understand the history and culture of *all* its component parts.

The civil rights movement helped increase the attention black and white scholars and students gave to the black experience in America. The creation of the first official black studies departments at such traditionally white colleges as Cornell, Wesleyan, and Yale was generally a direct response to student pressure, sometimes in the form of sit-ins, occupations of university buildings. Most of these student leaders were part of the group of black American applicants first sought out by those colleges in the late 1960s and early 1970s. Unlike the vast majority of their siblings and friends, who had entered all-black college only a few years earlier, they were part of very small minorities of much larger student bodies. Feeling the discomfort of their relatively new and often isolated situations in these schools and imbued with the militancy of the moment, they sought the courses, majors, and departments of black studies (as well as increased recruitment of black students and faculty members) that would give them, their backgrounds, and their history a genuine place on campus.

Although logically, it might have seemed that private black colleges, so long in the forefront of the effort to study black life and preserve black history, would be the obvious places to lead the way to a black studies curriculum nationwide, such was not the case. On the subject of black studies, they would prove more conservative than their harder-pressed white counterparts—and, as ever, they would have more immediate issues of survival to consider. Although their administrators, faculty, and students shared a desire to learn more about their past and to challenge the political, social, and educational status quo, they often differed as to the approach that institutions should take. As with their counterparts throughout the country, black students wanted a greater role in decision-making about curriculum, grading, student life, and other campus matters that were part of the black college experience.

Administrators and established faculty, especially those at institutions where content related to black history and culture had for some time been incorporated into the social science and humanities curriculums, held that their existing approaches were satisfactory. Students and younger faculty argued that such an approach did not encourage a critical enough examination of the foundations of the humanities and social sciences in America—and left them trailing traditionally white colleges in areas where they should have been in the forefront. They proposed the establishment of black studies programs composed of specifically designated groups of courses and activities. Differences on this issue played a part in student protests at some private black colleges, but because of the traditions of these institutions, black studies programs were generally a secondary issue in student-faculty confrontations. Some institutions established such programs and, on all campuses, additional courses on the black experience were added and issues related to the topic became an increasingly important part of intellectual discourse.

Two other developments connected the civil rights movement, black studies, and the black college intellectual experience of the post-*Brown* era. First, a burst of scholarly material dealing with black history and culture provided students with ready access to far more valuable information on the general topic than had previously existed. Major new studies of slavery, African history, the black family, black education, and the Harlem Renaissance began to appear. Second, much of this new thought and research was taking place among scholars, white as well as black, located at traditionally white colleges. This proved to be yet another example of movement in the direction of equal opportunity that produced less than desirable results for the institutions that over the years had suffered most from discrimination.

THE PROCESS OF DESEGREGATION

Court actions were slow to take action to alter the racial makeup of the student bodies at colleges in the South. All the white public colleges had signed a statement of compliance with desegregation, but few of them had translated these pledges into action. Three years after the *Brown* decision, only 2,400 black students had enrolled as undergraduates in publicly supported, traditionally white southern colleges. This number grew to 17,000 in the next seven years, by which time an additional 4,000 black students were attending traditionally white private colleges in the region. In colleges outside the South, close to 95,000 black students (roughly the same number attending public black colleges in the South) had been enrolled in traditionally white colleges by 1967, an increase of approximately 45,000 since 1950. By 1967–68, there were 38,659 black Americans enrolled in white colleges in the South and the Border States, about 21,000 of them in 329 four-year colleges.[16]

Beginning in the mid-1960s, the impact of the *Brown* decision finally began to be felt in the world of black higher education. We do not have records of the number of students who transferred from private black colleges to traditionally white institutions, nor do we have a way of estimating the number of graduating high school seniors who, in the absence of the *Brown* decision, would have entered private black institutions. If we assume that without *Brown* most of the 21,000 black students enrolled in traditionally white institutions would have chosen black public or private institutions in roughly the same percentage (57 percent public, 43 percent private) as they attended those institutions in 1967–68, one can postulate that private black college enrollments would have been 20 percent larger. Given the lack of significant enrollment of non-black students in private black colleges, by the late 1960s, the rate of growth of the black colleges was falling behind that of all colleges, creating an immediate crisis for some of the smaller black colleges in particular.

Major differences show up in the course of desegregation when various areas of the South are compared. In Alabama, Florida, Georgia, Mississippi, and South Carolina, desegregation moved at a snail's pace, characterized by overt hostility, active opposition, and major eruptions of mob violence. The remaining southern states of Louisiana, North Carolina, Tennessee, and Texas moved hesitantly forward, taking action only when pressed to do so. Desegregation moved forward with less fanfare or overt hostility in the Border States.

Evidence of the slow movement of desegregation is provided by the Supreme Court ruling in a 1973 case in which the NAACP Legal Defense and Education Fund sued the Department of Health, Education, and Welfare (HEW) for failing to enforce provisions of the 1964 Civil Rights Act that prohibited the allocation of federal funds to states operating dual systems of higher education. The Supreme Court agreed to hear the case and in 1977 found in favor of the plaintiff. The decision indicated the degree to which states had delayed taking the actions required for compliance with *Brown* and the hesitancy of the Nixon administration in enforcing existing federal civil rights legislation in the South. The Court ordered HEW to develop guidelines that states would use in preparing desegregation plans.

For a time, some faculty and administration in private black education felt a guarded sense of well-being. Congress had passed legislation, the Supreme Court had found that the administrative branch was not enforcing that law, their enrollments were increasing, and the federal government was providing increasing amounts of federal assistance to them and their students. More thoughtful college leaders, however, were fully aware of the need for black colleges to develop financial bases that were less dependent on the federal government and to present clearer views of their missions. A generalized goal of race progress might have sufficed a century earlier, but it was hardly enough in the 1960s and 1970s. They saw clarification of their reason-for-being as crucial in attracting students, gaining alumni/ae support, and securing foundation and corporate grants in an increasingly competitive educational marketplace. The loss of many of the most talented students from their candidate pools—soon to be followed by the most talented faculty—was a growing cause for concern.

By the 1970s, most black colleges had been or were becoming active in state, regional, and national higher education organizations. Exchange programs with some northern colleges and joint degree programs with southern graduate and professional schools were being established. Nevertheless, new or improved relationships hardly signaled that racial prejudice had ended or that feelings of distrust and disaffection had disappeared.

One example of such persistence can be seen in an incident that occurred when Talladega College joined the Alabama Federation of German Clubs (composed of the University of Alabama, Auburn University, and other state institutions of higher education that offered German courses) in the late 1960s or early 1970s. This was part of an effort by Talladega to strengthen a German-language program introduced into the curriculum in the 1930s, for which the college had recently received grant support through NDEA. In the late 1970s, the Talladega College German Club began winning first place in annual language competitions at the Alabama Federation of German Clubs' convention. In 1980, it took three of four first places in undergraduate level competition and won in German folk dance as well—quite an accomplishment for a program with only one faculty member, Professor Leslie Dominits, and no students in whose homes German was spoken. At the 1980 convention's closing session, a majority of the Federation's member institutions voted to discontinue the competition. In a discussion of this incident, Professor Dominits expressed his view that the larger, traditionally white public and private institutions in the Federation, including the state's two flagship universities, deemed it unacceptable that a small black college should dominate the competition. As a longtime resident of Alabama, he believed he had some understanding of the nature of the race issue in education. He said, however, that never had he felt the invidious nature of prejudice and discrimination so intensely as in the decision to terminate a competition intended to stimulate oral proficiency in a foreign language, solely because of the repeated success of the German Language Club at a small black college.[17]

DEGREES EARNED

In spite of the continued existence of strong cultural biases, by the mid-1960s, the idea that the goal of education for black Americans was to prepare them for the menial jobs traditionally open to them had few outspoken advocates left. The interest of black students in careers from which they were largely excluded had been clear before the start of the civil rights movement. It was considerably stimulated by the legislation of the 1960s, and was also reflected in the courses that students at private colleges selected and in their chosen major fields. Expansions in black college curricula followed on the heels of the civil rights movement of the 1960s.

Baccalaureate degrees awarded by private black colleges before *Brown* were overwhelmingly in the liberal arts. In the two decades between 1955 and 1975, however, over 40 percent of all degrees were awarded in professional areas, with business becoming the largest single major by the end of the period (see Table 7.1). The social sciences and life sciences were now the most popular majors in the liberal arts. Education majors increased only 2 percent between 1955 and 1975, but degrees in education were never a good measure of the number of students in private black colleges who were preparing to teach. Historically, large numbers of history, English, biology, music, math, physics, and other liberal arts majors also entered the teaching profession.

Expanded career goals in the two decades after *Brown* resulted in a rise in graduate school attendance by graduates of private black colleges. Unfortunately, there is no good overall record of recipients of B.A.s who went on to earn M.A. degrees (see Table 7.2).

There is scant information on the number of B.A. recipients each year from private black colleges who went on to earn Ph.D. degrees but enough data exists to enable us to draw some conclusions:

- Over seven thousand holders of B.A. degrees from forty-five private black colleges received Ph.D. degrees by 1995.

TABLE 7.1
Degrees Granted by Private Black Colleges, 1955, 1966, 1970, and 1975

Area of Degree	1955	1966	1970	1975
Liberal arts	1,662	3,256	4,787	4,505
(percentage of total)	55	56	59	51
Professional	1,359	2,556	3,293	4,112
(percentage of total)	45	43	41	47
Major unknown	0	26	35	143
(percentage of total)	0	0.4	0.4	1.6
All Areas	3,021	5,838	8,115	8,760

Sources: United Negro College Fund, *Statistics of Member Colleges, 1955–56 School Year;* National Science Foundation, WebCASPAR database system.

Note: 1955 numbers of liberal arts and professional degrees is an estimate based on 11 UNCF colleges for which this information is available.

TABLE 7.2

Doctorates Awarded to Recipients of B.A. Degrees from Forty-Four Private
Black Colleges

	1906–85		1986–95	
	Science	*Nonscience*	*Science*	*Nonscience*
Average per college	43	75	16	29
Average per year	24	44	79	142
Total number of students	1,875	3,313	709	1,275

Sources: Franklin & Marshall College, *Baccalaureate Origins of Doctoral Recipients;* Harry W.
Green, *Holders of Doctorates Among American Negroes* (Boston: Meador Publishing, 1946).
  Note: A total of 7,164 degree recipients are reported in the first source; eight degree
recipients are reported in the second source between 1906 and 1920.

- The yearly average numbers of Ph.D. degrees received were
  higher for thirty-two of the colleges in the 1986–95 period than in
  the 1906–85 period.
- Twenty-four colleges averaged more than one graduate per year
  who earned a doctorate during the sixty-five years from 1920 to
  1985, whereas thirty-three averaged more than one per year during the ten years from 1986 to 1995.
- The total number of doctorates earned by B.A. recipients from the
  leading black colleges during the 1920–1985 and 1986–1995 periods, respectively, are: Howard 1014 and 376; Tuskegee 380 and
  170; Spelman 171 and 157; Hampton 369 and 156; Fisk 351 and
  93; and Xavier 156 and 58.
- If adjustments are made for size of enrollment, the performance
  of some small institutions—notably Talladega with 136 and 39
  and Tougaloo with 132 and 58—is noteworthy.[18]

We can assume that all or most graduates of private black colleges who
received doctorates between 1986 and 1995 received B.A. degrees after
1954. This suggests that preparation for graduate study became a more
significant objective of these institutions in the post-*Brown* era and played
a greater part in the academic experience and campus lives of these
students. However, information is incomplete on the years in which Ph.D.
recipients obtained bachelors' degrees, their fields of concentration, and
the institutions from which the degrees were received. More detailed
information is needed before definitive conclusions can be drawn about
the effect of desegregation on the attainment of doctoral degrees by
graduates of private black colleges in these years. But it should be borne in
mind that the number of graduates earning advanced degrees is not the
primary measure of the value of a college or group of colleges.

Private black colleges found themselves in a peculiar position, in the context of what took place between 1954 and the mid-1970s. On the one hand, the reduction of racial barriers to college attendance and to teaching and administrative positions in traditionally white institutions was greatly prized within the private black college community. On the other hand, their faculties wished to think of themselves as continuing in the role of preparing Du Bois's "talented tenth," but found fewer easily identifiable members of this group among those who accepted admission to their institutions. Although the colleges reluctantly accepted that they would attract fewer of the most able black faculty and students and fewer white faculty for whom opposition to racism was a primary concern, they were also troubled that there would be less daily interaction with outstanding students and faculty than had previously been the case. In the kind of paradox not at all rare in matters involving race in America, private black colleges saw the goals they set for themselves constrained by developments they found to be not only acceptable but eminently desirable.

Institutional mission emerged as one of several major dividing lines between the more and less successful private black colleges of the 1970s. Some showed evidence of having allowed the segregationist ethos of the South to dictate much of their sense of who they were and where they were going. These institutions appeared to see their mission as nothing more than to provide higher education for those who, because of law and custom, were unable to attend other institutions. Such a view, even in the worst of times, had not proved adequate for black colleges. It was grossly inappropriate for the post-*Brown* era. Certainly, however, many black educators felt a pressing need to rethink the role of the private black college in this new era. For they feared that the private black college might be left not with an expanded mission in a changing world but with at best only half (and for many, what might be viewed as the lesser half) of its old mission. With traditionally white schools beginning to skim off many of the best black students, no longer would the private black college be training the talented tenth and at the same time offering opportunities to many of those from poor quality schools. Its role might only be remedial, as a lowly way-station for those students otherwise ill prepared to compete with students whose preparation was more rigorous and more in line with college requirements. Once again presidential leadership proved to be a crucial factor at those black colleges where such fears and changing circumstances were being faced more forthrightly and the historically unique mission of the private black college was being reconsidered in light of the civil rights movement, desegregation, the new competitiveness of previously white colleges, and the emergence of black consciousness and black power movements on campuses.

Commenting in 1990 on the future of black colleges in the post-*Brown* era, Robert Goodwin, former executive director of the White House Initiative on Historically Black Colleges and Universities wrote, "These are cataclysmic times. Having walked through the doorway of a new decade and standing now on the very threshold of a new millennium, we are faced with some remarkable challenges: to try to make sense of our frenzied, fitful, and in another sense, remarkable past—and then to have some influence on our onrushing future."[19] Such creative thinking was most likely to be found on campuses with strong presidents backed by reasonably united faculties and board of trustees. This is hardly surprising. After all, a college president is in the best position to articulate an institution's distinguishing characteristics and guiding principles for faculty, students, and alumni/ae, to instill these principles in new arrivals, and to convey the ethos of the college to the outside community. As A. Bartlett Giamatti, the former president of Yale, put the matter:

> Management is the capacity to handle multiple problems, neutralize various constituencies, and motivate personnel. . . . Leadership, on the other hand, is essentially a moral act, not—as in most management—an essentially protective act. It is the assertion of a vision not simply the exercise of a style: the moral courage to assert a vision of the institution in the future and the intellectual energy to persuade the community or the culture of the wisdom and validity of the vision. It is to make the vision practicable, and compelling.[20]

For the private black college with its often-weak financial underpinnings, modest plant, and—during those years—shifting faculty and student bodies, the leadership role of the president cannot be overemphasized. By the mid-1970s, the caliber of leadership and management was a crucial if not the deciding factor in enabling some private black colleges to move out in front, defining new institutional roles in a changing world.

The Warren Court made a contribution to the responsibilities of institutional leadership that is rarely applauded. Its *Brown* decision provided a wake-up call to even the most moribund leadership that traditional views on race and education would not suffice for a country undergoing intense social and economic change that was unmatched, in the area of race relations, since the abolition of slavery.

It is improbable that at the time of their founding, many of the private black colleges considered their raison d'être simply to be the provision of an education—any kind of education—to those to whom it had previously been forbidden. But it is easy to see that much in American life might have contributed to the development of such a limited mission. Most influential was the support for industrial education among white funders and the frequent hesitancy of denominational boards to appoint black presidents and trustees and hire black faculty.

The most effective presidents we encountered in our research were those who successfully engaged others in support of a well-conceived institutional mission, worked closely with administrators and faculty in developing and implementing a successful plan for moving toward desired ends, passionately believed in their institutions, and enjoyed a fair share of good luck. Problem administrations appear to have had difficulty conceptualizing and articulating what they wished their institutions to accomplish and how they intended to proceed once they found themselves in a more open and competitive educational environment. Chapters 8 and 9 provide four case examples from different institutions in different periods.

A final word about leadership. Presidents of black colleges have traditionally been characterized as authoritarian in style, although those holding the posts have in fact demonstrated a wide range of leadership and management styles. Nevertheless, there is some truth in such a characterization and it reflects the difficult conditions under which many presidents of black schools were forced to serve. Presidents of black public colleges operated under government agencies whose officials, until recent decades, showed little of the respect typically accorded to college presidents. The denominational boards that controlled many private black colleges often acted with less sensitivity and decorum than was desirable. Regrettably, some black leaders used as models white authority figures who made at most token efforts to show respect for those they supervised.

In addition, in colleges always strapped for funds, leadership often meant devoting staggering amounts of time to raising money, the success of which was frequently judged as the most important measure of a president. This, unfortunately, did not change with the post-*Brown* era. Black colleges continued to be seriously underfunded, even though the overall value of their endowments grew dramatically. For the more successful colleges such an increase in endowments could be significant both in market value and in constant dollars, with the result that assets for the first time came close to producing a reasonably stable level of annual income. For schools at the other end of the scale, however, endowment value actually declined between 1954 and the mid-1970s as reflected in Table 7.3, which shows the total, average, maximum, and minimum market value of private black college endowments and the value in constant (1975–76) dollars for the years 1955, 1967 and 1975.

Maintaining a stable quality faculty has been a challenge for black colleges throughout most of their history, although this was easier at some institutions than others. The academic strengths and attractive

TABLE 7.3

Private Four-Year Black College Endowments, 1955, 1967, and 1975

	1955	1967	1975
Total market value	6,215,000	137,683,000	142,614,000
Total value in 1975–76 dollars	3,185,000	86,944,000	142,614,000
Average market value	345,000	3,530,000	3,657,000
Average value in 1975–76 dollars	176,800	2,229,000	3,657,000
Individual institution			
Maximum market value	2,709,000	29,884,000	25,724,000
Maximum in 1975–76 dollars	1,388,000	18,871,000	25,724,000
Minimum market value	5,000	25,000	31,000
Minimum value in 1975–76 dollars	2,500	15,787	31,000

Sources: United Negro College Fund, *Statistics of Member Colleges 1955–56 School Year;* National Science Foundation WebCASPAR database.

settings of Howard, Fisk, and Atlanta Universities, the leadership at some of the small colleges, and the financial base of Tuskegee and Hampton made it easier for these institutions to attract candidates of their choice in the pre-1954 years. The growth of black public colleges after World War II increased the demand for teachers, but in this competition private colleges initially fared well. Where salary differences existed between private and public institutions, they were small and the amenities at private institutions regularly tipped the balance in their favor. This changed markedly in the 1960s. Salaries at state institutions rose faster than those at small private colleges. Although the number of black Americans holding doctorate degrees increased, the pace was much too slow to meet a demand driven by several factors, including attempts by black colleges to increase the number of faculty members holding doctorates, the hiring of black scholars by traditionally white colleges, and a new competitive environment in which traditionally white businesses for the first time competed in a significant way for black talent.

In its annual statistical reports, the UNCF has included data on the number of faculty at its member institutions and, from time to time, information on faculty degrees and salaries. These data show a 69 percent increase in faculty members at forty-one UNCF member institutions between 1958 and 1975. Faculty size at Claflin, Barber-Scotia, St. Paul, Talladega, Wiley, and other such small institutions ranged from twenty to forty. Larger institutions with more than one hundred faculty members included Clark, Morehouse, Morris Brown, Xavier, Hampton, and Tuskegee. The 350 faculty members at Howard constituted the largest instructional staff at any private black institution. Forty-one percent of 1974 faculty members held doctorate degrees. Blacks constituted 65 percent of faculty members at UNCF institutions and non-Blacks 35 percent.[21]

Table 7.4 provides information on minimum, median, and maximum average faculty salaries at private black colleges in 1971 and 1975. From the figures, it is evident that although these colleges attempted to be competitive in attracting the necessary entry-level candidates, they had to rely on factors other than salaries—such as commitment to the mission of the institution—to encourage faculty to stay. The level of financial remuneration was simply not a major attraction in drawing faculty to private black colleges in the 1970s.

In spite of overall low levels of faculty remuneration and other problems, a number of black colleges continued to be successful during the 1960s and early 1970s, judged by several indices. Spelman College's applicant pool, for instance, continued to draw from various regions of the country and scored well on national standardized tests. Dillard University maintained its physical facilities at an enviable level of appearance. Xavier University became increasingly adept at preparing students to gain entrance into top medical schools and graduate schools in the sciences. Fisk University and Stillman College survived periods of serious financial difficulty and, by decade's end, showed signs of rebounding. Hampton University's efforts to strengthen its financial resources placed its endowment first among black colleges. Several two-year institutions attained the status of four-year colleges and were accredited by SACS.[22] Twelve black colleges had over one hundred graduates who had earned Ph.D. degrees by 1986.[23]

But some black colleges did not fare well. Bishop College in Texas, Simmons University in Kentucky, Mississippi Industrial College, and Virginia Seminary and College closed during these two decades. As a group, however, private black colleges awarded a disproportionately high per-

TABLE 7.4

Minimum, Median, and Maximum Salaries for Teachers of Private Black Colleges, 1971 and 1975

	Teacher Salary		
Year	Minimum	Median	Maximum
1971 dollars	5,785	9,363	13,611
In 1999 dollars	24,496	40,165	57,636
1975 dollars	8,846	10,841	18,078
In 1999 dollars	27,953	34,187	57,009
Increase in 1999 dollars	14%	−15%	−1%

Source: National Science Foundation WebCASPAR database.

centage of all baccalaureate degrees granted to black students and a surprisingly large number of baccalaureate degrees received by holders of advanced degrees in these years. If the formula for determining success included adjustments for the available human and financial resources, the effectiveness of this universe of institutions in this era should be viewed with far greater respect than has been the case.

For a comparative view of small private black and white colleges in these years we identified nineteen institutions with 1995 enrollments of under 2,500 students and endowments of under $25.5 million. Included were eleven black colleges (Group A) and eight white colleges (Group B).[24] Data, which appear in Table 7.5, compares minimum, maximum, and average enrollment and endowment for the years 1970 and 1975.

The average 1995 enrollment and endowment of the colleges was 1,165 students and $13 million for group A and 1,497 students and $20 million for group B. These represent average endowments per student of $11,159 for group A and $13,360 for group B in 1995, a difference of just over $2,000. Per-student endowment for Group A was $360 less than for Group B in 1970 and $100 more in 1975. The differences between institutions in the two groups in 1970 and 1975 were significantly smaller than in 1995. In the black-college group, the average enrollment increased 16 percent between 1970 and 1975 and 18 percent between 1975 and 1995. Average endowment increased 115 percent between 1970 and 1975 and rose 495 percent in the twenty years that followed. In the white-college group, enrollment declined 4 percent between 1970 and 1975, followed by a 12 percent rise by 1995. The average endowment rose 30 percent from 1970 to 1975 and an additional 629 percent by 1995. The data show that these colleges, falling within relatively narrow enrollment and

TABLE 7.5

Comparison of a Group of Private Black Colleges and Private White Colleges, 1970 and 1975

Enrollment characteristics	1970		1975	
	Group A	Group B	Group A	Group B
Minimum enrollment	572	1,054	1,054	1,636
Maximum enrollment	1,402	1,654	1,062	1,547
Average enrollment	850	1,211	989	1,169
Minimum endowment	$ 113,000	$ 306,000	$ 199,000	$ 762,000
Maximum endowment	$2,200,000	$3,087,000	$11,457,000	$3,493,000
Average endowment	$ 938,000	$1,793,000	$ 2,198,000	$2,299,000

Source: National Science Foundation, WebCASPAR database.
Note: See text for makeup of Group A and Group B.

endowment ranges in 1995, already showed important differences in 1970s, differences that increased by 1975 and over the next two decades. Two black colleges appeared among the top ten of the group in both enrollment and endowment in 1970. In both 1975 and 1995, the top ten included three black colleges in endowment and five in enrollment. Over the two decades from 1975 to 1995, growth in enrollment in the black-college group exceeded that of the white-college group by 6 percent, but growth in endowment of the white college group exceeded that of the black college group by 611 percent. In addition, it is important to note that the data for Group A bear a greater resemblance to the low level of financial resources typical of the majority of private black colleges than the data for Group B bear to those of all other private traditionally white colleges.

It is a challenge to understand the combination of factors that explains the different degrees of success experienced by colleges whose histories have much in common. It is easy enough to produce a list of the obvious factors that characterize successful college communities. Those with adequate financial resources, well-kept physical plants, strong sports programs, rich histories, famous alumni/ae, and locations in towns or cities that enjoy an active and vital cultural life are clearly more likely than others to be attractive to students and faculty. Changing views of what is attractive may also play a role in the ultimate success of a college. Colleges located in rural areas and small-town communities and colleges offering little opportunity for electives appear far less attractive than they did in the early 1950s—the very isolation that once promised a kind of psychic safety zone and the sense of order experienced in a prearranged curriculum are now often viewed as boring or stifling.

Several trends of the last quarter of the twentieth century were already obvious by the mid-1970s. Viewed as a group, the student population served by private black colleges represented a much smaller portion of middle-class black Americans and a much smaller fraction of the academically strong black students graduating from secondary schools. The career paths of those choosing black colleges were more challenging than their 1950s counterparts, but for the most part, these schools would not be the chief sources of black students who went on to doctorate programs, medical schools, and law schools. Although before World War II, liberal arts outdistanced industrial education to dominate curricula, by the 1970s, the liberal arts were increasingly giving way to more professionally oriented majors. Students showed a rising interest in institutions located in or near cities and declining interest in those in small towns.

Relationships with the cities and towns in which colleges were located changed drastically. Local businessmen and elected officials now served more regularly as trustees of the private colleges. Fundraising among local black and white businesses reached a scale that rarely existed in the 1950s. Elected officials more often supported the interest of black colleges in their districts. As a result of improved opportunities to purchase and rent, faculty and staff housing was no longer restricted to campuses or to enclaves surrounding them. Undoubtedly this made for more comfortable accommodations for many, but something was lost from the sense of community that the earlier proximity of faculty homes to student dormitories had provided. Local officials more commonly appointed black college faculty to positions on boards and councils in the area and white Americans began to appear among the local people attending cultural affairs at black colleges.

One change that began during these years and continued in the decades to come was that the stronger private black colleges came to more closely resemble one another and to separate themselves from the more slowly developing private black colleges. They were, by and large, urban schools at a moment when the city was becoming a powerful draw for prospective students. Their growth generally outpaced that of other schools. Their endowments tended to be healthier and their facilities remained more intact. Naturally, then, they were best able to give serious consideration to and plan coherently for a future unlike any that private black colleges had faced in their previous hundred years. Thus they were in a position to strengthen their situation in the years to come.

CHAPTER 8

Talladega College: A Case History
(1867 to 1975)

AMONG THE approximately one hundred private black colleges that have existed since Cheyney School was founded in 1837, it would be hard to claim that any one was typical or could stand in for the rest. But whether they were in Mississippi or Tennessee, whether they were large or small, religious or secular, coed or single sex, with or without graduate programs, they all existed in a similar atmosphere. From 1837 to 1954 and beyond, every one of them to some degree faced a segregated, generally hostile society; lack of encouragement from the world around them; neglect and lack of funds; and an all-pervasive racism that had to be experienced to be believed. White American society imposed on them a uniformity of experience that could not be found in a group of traditionally white schools of similar range. You did not attend a private black college without being aware of the unwelcoming larger world that surrounded you. Often the difference between carrying on and shutting the college's doors forever was a donation that an Amherst, a Duke, or an Oberlin would scarcely have noticed. Often the difference between relative success and absolute failure was the leadership of a single figure, a president who stood between existence and collapse in the way few presidents of traditionally white colleges ever did. Black colleges were forced to look both inward and outward to a degree that their white counterparts had never contemplated. They scrapped and scrabbled to get by in ways few other colleges did. And they were aware of their own embattled history and came to take pride in it in a fashion that would have been less familiar at Beloit or Hobart, at Middlebury or Swarthmore. Although no single black college may be called representative of the whole, the experience of any of them offers a striking sense of what it was like to attend or work at a private black college anywhere.

As it happens, one of the authors of this book attended Talledega College from 1940 to 1948, with several years off for military service during World War II. And from 1926 to 1928, his father, Leonard E. Drewry, was a professor of education and the principal of the Practice High School that the college ran, which fed the best of its graduates into the college itself. He also directed the college theater and was responsible for writing and producing a pageant celebrating the sixtieth anniversary of the college's founding.[1] On Monday, November 14, 1927, The Talladega College Little Theatre Players, assisted by the teachers and other students presented the pageant, *Sixty Yesteryears,* to the college community. It was meant to remind those assembled of Talladega's history and its connection to a particular physical and social environment, and to encourage thoughtful consideration of the college's nature and role in the years to come.

The narrator's preface to major episodes depicted in *Sixty Yesteryears* conveys both the spirit and perspective that animated Talladega College and others like it in 1927, as the school considered its past, the society of which it was a part, and the future it faced. Those words of the time serve to introduce the college's history from its post–Civil-War beginnings. The excerpts from *Sixty Yesteryears* provide us with an opportunity to compare our views on the college's history up to 1927 with the views of those for whom that November fourteenth was the present.

Talladega was one of the early colleges established by the American Missionary Association of the Congregational Church, one of the most active northern denominational groups working in the South. Its history includes periods of remarkable progress as well as periods of difficulty in attracting students, faculty, and donations. Some of its leaders were impressive; others left much to be desired. Its unsophisticated, bucolic setting in east central Alabama was in turn a danger to those who lived at the college in its early years, an attraction, and a disappointment. Various aspects of its history have made it a pioneer among private black colleges at some times, and a laggard at others.

In 1927, Talladega had only recently become a college in our present sense of the term. Twenty years earlier, its ratio of elementary and secondary students to college students was 180 to one. By the year of the pageant however, it was already three to one and, five years later, one to one. In his foreword for the day's program, President of the College Frederick A. Sumner, a white Congregationalist from Massachusetts whose family had been famed for its abolitionism, reminded the community of its successes over sixty years and shared his vision of more successful years to come in the soaring language of race progress that was so typical of that era in black college history:[2]

> Stated in terms of the life of the great seats of learning, Talladega College is sixty years young. However, three score years have been sufficient time for this Institution to have become a potent factor in the remarkable development of a Race.
>
> Beginning as an elementary school with one building, four teachers, and one hundred and forty pupils, the progress of the College on its sixtieth birthday can be reckoned by its thirty-five goodly buildings, its sixty-one

teachers and officers, its six hundred students, and its plant worth more than one million dollars. Nor is this all. Mere externals such as plant and equipment and numbers are vain things in a College unless they visualize a corresponding achievement in real educational values.

Founded and fostered by The Great American Missionary Association whose first slogan was "Education without caste," Talladega through the years has set as its goal the development of a College—one which will require no apologies in the face of the strictest appraisal of its worth and work. In measurably achieving this ideal it has had the good fortune of an active and farseeing Board of Trustees, the deep interest of the American Missionary Association, the constant support of Alumni and friends, the co-operation of a consecrated and efficient body of teachers, and always the love and loyalty of an earnest body of students.

May the sixty yesterdays we celebrate prophesy even more glorious years to come.

Sixty Yesteryears then opened with two musical selections presented by a twenty-two-piece college orchestra, choir, and male chorus: first an overture, "For a Negro Pageant," composed for the occasion by the college's professor of music, Tourgee De Bose, a graduate of Fisk University and the Oberlin Conservatory, and then "Fair Talladega," the college anthem, composed by Harry T. Burleigh (described by Alain Locke as a pathbreaking ambassador of black music to the "musical elect"). Other music performed throughout the celebration reflected a variety of traditions: "Rain Dance," "Deer Dance," and "War Dance," acknowledged the Native American traditions of the area and the affinity of black and Native Americans as oppressed peoples; "Let Us Cheer the Weary Traveler," and "Nobody Knows the Trouble I See," the inheritance from the painful era of slavery; Rachmaninoff's "Prelude in C-Sharp Minor" and Mendelssohn's "Andante Maestoso," the European cultural traditions that were the basis for the school's curriculum; and the "Star Spangled Banner," black patriotism toward a country that had largely rejected black Americans.

In the prologue to the pageant, the narrator then spoke of the central elements of the college's mission—race progress, self-improvement, and efforts to offset the results of unhappy and unjust race relations:

I am Progress.
I am that urge that makes men yearn to be like God.
A foe to sloth I am,
A spur to ambition and ceaseless striving after perfection,
A stinging gadfly,
Purposing that the race shall not stand still.
I beget that spiritual uneasiness which makes men despise a mean estate,

And aspire to the utmost fulfillment of all their capabilities. . . .
And now I come,
And without guile, to tell a simple tale of mine:
Here on this spot, unheralded and unknown to fame,
Once a pious son of God began an humble school,
Not as the plaything of some bored and moneyed patron,
Not yet the whim of some social demi-god
Irked by a round of dull inconsequentialities;
But rather an offering upon the altar of consecration—
A penance for his race's sin to its darker brother man,
Earnest of the debt owed to a wronged humanity.

As in most other private black colleges, life at Talladega reflected much of the New England religious tradition's emphasis on good and evil, guilt and conscience, the Protestant work ethic, and a willingness to postpone gratification. These precepts were so much a part of those who founded and staffed the early institution—and of the Congregational clergymen who occupied its leadership positions for over a century—that they were passed on both consciously and in deeper, less conscious ways to its students. The task was dear to the minds of these men. As historian James McPherson has commented, "An AMA teacher who played a prominent role in the early history of Talladega College conceived of his mission as the founding in Alabama of 'a real New England civilization.' "[3]

The Narrator next introduced the pageant's first episode, "Talladega, Border Town of the Cherokees," calling attention to the history of the region before the arrival of both European Americans and African Americans:

First you must know in days long past
That Talladega was the red-man's Border-town
The out-post of his virgin realm
Wherein he kept the even tenor of his primitive ways,
Unblessed by the gifts of his pale-faced fellow-man,
And uncursed by his vices.

Talladega, the seat of government for a county bearing the same name, is still a small town located in north central Alabama, sixty miles east of Birmingham. Before 1819, when Alabama became a state, Talladega was part of the Mississippi Territory, a region that at the end of the Revolutionary War was populated largely by Cherokee, Chickasaw, Choctaw, and Creek tribes. After the war, white land-seekers began moving into Big Spring, the village that occupied Talladega's current site. To contend with the growing number of migrants into the area, the government's agent to the Native American tribes introduced a program of "civilization." Some Creeks and Cherokees accepted this "civilization" or Americanization, adopting European-American patterns of land ownership and use, and, in some cases, even purchasing slaves. Others sought to maintain their traditional culture and fought the encroachment of white farmers.

In the Creek War of 1813–14, the village of Big Spring gained national attention as the site of a victory by soldiers under the command of General Andrew Jackson (aided by some Creeks and Cherokees) against Creeks opposed to Americanization. When those Creeks were finally defeated, the survivors fled to join the Seminoles in Florida. Ironically, westward-moving settlers who were pressing to gain control of Indian lands made no distinction between Native American allies and enemies. All Creeks and Cherokees who remained were forced to sign a treaty giving up twenty million acres of land and in 1838 were forced out of the area.

The narrator continued his historical tale from a perspective that would undoubtedly have been expressed in few places but a black environment in 1920s America:

> Ere long the hapless red man yielded all
> To the white aggressor.
> Then, in the name of Civilization and a Christian's God,
> Came Human Slavery to this home of the Cherokees.
> For many, many years this thing lay
> A withering blight upon the fair land.
> At length Truth spoke, and it was gone,
> And they whose debt it was, had paid in full.
> All through the dark night the dauntless slave-man stood,
> Awaiting the dawn;
> Dreaming the dreams of a better day;
> Singing his sorrow-songs;
> And possessing his unconquerable soul.

The white farmers and planters from Georgia and the Carolinas who moved into the Talladega area realized that the rich soil, warm climate, and plentiful rainfall made the land especially suited for growing cotton and corn. They were almost uniformly pro-slavery. Even though few initially owned slaves, the economic, political, and social life of the region came to center around slavery and plantation life. Jeffersonian Democrats dominated in politics and Talladega would remain part of the "solid [Democratic] South" for more than a century.

> Man, the yearning son of God,
> Wills to be unfettered both in body and in soul.
> A bondsman he may be,

But with his scandent spirit unshackled still.
So to Mobile came the new freedmen to counsel
And to devise what ways they could attain a more abundant freedom,
And withal, a more abundant life.

The origin of Talladega College, like that of several schools in the area, can be traced to a meeting in Mobile, Alabama, where former slaves gathered to discuss their future in late 1865. Talladega and its five surrounding counties had no school for black Americans. Agreeing on the importance of establishing schools, those attending the meeting signed a document stating that "We regard the education of our children and youths as vital to the preservation of our liberties, and true religion as the foundation of all real virtue, and shall use our utmost endeavors to promote these blessings in our common country."[4] Acting on their commitment, two former slaves from Talladega County, Thomas Tarrant and William Savery joined with others to secure the use of a room in a residential building and to engage one Leonard Johnson, who had in some way acquired the rudiments of learning, to start a school. In the meantime, lumber obtained by dismantling a carpenter's shop was used to construct the first school building for black Americans in Talladega County. The group then turned to the Freedmen's Bureau for help in finding a better teacher and the Bureau did indeed help them secure the services of Mrs. C. M. Hopson, a northerner. Shortly thereafter, when the group learned that an abandoned brick structure was up for sale, members approached the American Missionary Association as well as the Freedmen's Bureau, and with their joint support, purchased the three-story brick building and thirty-four acres of land in the town of Talladega for the sum of $8,000. It was fitting that Thomas Tarrant, who as a slave had been part of the crew that constructed the building—which was to have been a "Baptist Academy for white gentlemen"—was instrumental in arranging its purchase as a school for black children.

Narrator: Now comes the Yankee Schoolmaster,
And, too, the staid New England ma'am,
To implant and foster here the love of liberty
And the stern virtues of the Pilgrims. . . .
Firm for Justice and uncompromising for the right, were they. . . .
From humble beginnings builded they with the years,
And lo! An unfolding plan—
A dream coming true—
A growing Talladega.

The school, with its newly acquired building, classrooms, and office space, opened its doors in 1867. According to the records, it was one of twelve institutions for black Americans established that year. With the help of the American Missionary Association, Henry E. Brown, a white minister from Oberlin, Ohio, was appointed principal. The school building was renamed Swayne Hall in honor of General Wager Swayne, assistant commissioner of the Freedmen's Bureau for Alabama. The charter, secured on February 17, 1869, states that "none would be refused admission because of race or creed."[5]

Because the establishment of the "college" resulted from the action of local people, it immediately became a center of community activity. It would, in fact, quickly transform itself into a regional school. The initial 140 students of various ages came from the town and county of Talladega and the surrounding counties where no schools existed. The entire teaching staff consisted of Principal Brown, Mrs. Hopson and one other teacher from the North. The curriculum began with the three Rs and extended through the *Third Reader,* which focused attention on articulation and punctuation in the development of language skills. Such a course of study was so typical of schools developing in the state that it rated no more than a passing comment in the semi-annual report of the superintendent of schools for the Freedmen's Bureau: "Our educational board has provided for four normal schools in the State, at the following points: Huntsville, Talladega, Marion, and Mobile."[6] College records confirm plans to organize a normal department to train teachers in 1869. Years later, a field agent for the AMA described the earliest selection process for normal school students:

Nine counties adjacent, thickly populated, had no school of any sort. The principal was importuned for teachers. He met some of the colored people in their log churches and told them there was but one way in which they could secure a teacher. "Pick out the best specimen of a young man you have for a teacher, and bring to church with you next Sunday all the corn and bacon you can spare for his living. I will take him into my school and make a teacher of him."

Following his advice some brought their corn, from a handful to four quarts . . . and laid it on the altar in front of the pulpit, singing as they marched around the aisle. Eight or nine young men were selected from the different localities and furnished with rations. These came to Talladega ten, twenty, and thirty miles on foot with sacks of corn and bacon on their backs. There were positively no accommodations in Talladega for them, and they were obliged to sleep on the floors of such cabins as could receive them and give them a chance to bake their corn bread by the fire. This they did. For their studies, they began with the alphabet, and after six months, by giving their whole time to one thing, were able to read in the Second and Third Readers, and had been taught "by practice upon other pupils in the school 'how to teach reading.'" In the summer these pupils went home to teach "bush" schools until the fall term opened, when they were back on time at Talladega and in force. The principal had applications from fifty more young men and women who wished to come.[7]

Within three years, it became obvious that the "college" aspired to do more than support the existence of a normal school serving day students. Foster Hall, a large brick dormitory for girls and teachers, was completed in 1870. During the next two years, a theological department was established and the college acquired another building named Graves Hall. In 1873, the normal school was officially launched and graduated its first students in 1876.

Augustus Beard in his history of the American Missionary Association, offered this description of Talladega, one of those mixed emporiums of learning, in 1879:

> [T]he institution, with a look forward to the beginning of a four years' college course, elected [as President] the Rev. Henry Swift DeForest, a graduate of Yale in the class of 1857, subsequently an instructor at that university, and who had been drafted into the army in the war between the North and the South. In his service as chaplain he made his first acquaintance with the South. His entrance upon his work at Talladega sixteen years later was his second visit. During his administration the regular college course was entered upon, though previous to this time certain college studies had been blended with the theological course. . . . Instruction was given in agriculture, gardening, woodworking (such as cabinet-making and carpentry with architectural drawing), ironworking, bricklaying, brickmaking, printing, and cobbling. The girls have been taught nursing, domestic science, such as housekeeping, millinery, and making of garments and laundering. These studies . . . [were] obligatory.[8]

Other sources of the time confirmed the existence of industrial training courses at Talladega, although they tended to downplay their importance.

Attorney and alumnus George W. Crawford (1903) eloquently described Talladega's educational situation in the context of the pressures of its era:

> From slavery to even an approximation of first class citizenship has represented a long and painful transition for the Negro which is still in progress. This transition has been marked by certain developments that fall into distinctive periods. The first of these was the period of groping. . . . Observing deficiencies in every department of the life of his new charges he [the missionary teacher] set up within the limitations of meager resources a sort of educational department store over the entrance to which he might well

have put up this legend: "Merchandise to fit every social and economic need."

In spite of this all-things-to-all-needs philosophy, however, it was still a College he envisioned even though its academic reach far exceeded its temporary grasp. . . .

The second period in the transition . . . was the period of emergence. In it there was no abrupt or precipitous change of pace. The evidence of progress lay rather in a more adequate self-containment by the group and in the development of certain fundamental social attitudes. Principally among the latter was an appreciation of the dignity of labor. . . . The free and genteel were not expected to work with their hands. And so the newly freed Negro having been habituated to compelled labor as a slave, might well have yielded to the easy assumption that its continuation after emancipation, even though voluntary, was a compromise of his new status. But he was spared that delusion. Both his friends and dire necessity took care of that. Therefore instead of viewing toil as a badge of degradation he saw it as his opportunity, and indeed it was. As frequently happens in such circumstances, the effort to assure that the subject unlearn the old lessons and reconstruct his thinking went to great extremes in over-emphasis. The result was that in a very short time the demand for vocational training for Negroes—"industrial education" in the language of the day—became insistent to the point of practically destroying interest in every other sort of education for him. Friend and foe alike, although for differing motives, embraced the idea as a panacea. . . . While the pendulum was thus swinging to the opposite end of the arc, what of Talladega? You know the answer. With characteristic Yankee genius for accommodation to any point short of the betrayal of fundamental principles, the managers of this enterprise set down in the least conspicuous corner of this campus a Slater Shop wherein to teach manual training . . . at the secondary school level . . . . For all of the flexibility and power of accommodation, the College catalogue even in those controversial days still declared: The aim "of the College is to secure for its students the highest possible development in body, and mind and spirit.". . . [No] amount of pressure [could] dislodge it from the basic thesis that making a living is subordinate to making a life.[9]

The crucial financial support that Talladega received during the 1880s and 1890s from the Slater Fund—whose general agent strongly favored institutions with curricula centered on industrial training—helps explain "the flexibility and power of accommodation" Crawford cites as required at the time.

Relations between the college and the local white community, although hardly cordial, only occasionally reached the level of overt hostility that characterized day-to-day relations in the "black-belt" counties of the state.[10] One reason for this was that students and faculty members had little direct contact with the white citizens of Talladega. The students rarely if ever moved about in the residential areas of the town in which white Americans lived and, except for the purchase of personal supplies, spent very little time in its small business district. In addition, the county was poor (72 percent of its agricultural workers were tenant farmers as late as 1940) and the college's purchases of goods and services were undoubtedly important to local merchants. No white students from the area attended the college, its charter provision notwithstanding, although the school-age children of a white faculty member were enrolled in the elementary and secondary school. In 1885, the State of Alabama assessed the college's property for back taxes. In a discussion with the state auditor, school treasurer Edwin Silsby made a convincing argument that such an assessment would lay open the state's white colleges, none of which were taxed, to similar assessments. Soon after a state law exempting college property from taxation was passed by the legislature.

The college had its own internal problems. Before 1908, principals, presidents, and faculty seemed unable to agree on a common goal or a stable set of principles for the institution, although several early principals saw theological and normal training—neither of which were college-level programs at the time—as the primary mission of the college. In addition, even though the AMA required that it be involved in almost all decisions, large or small, the college consistently had difficulty securing operational funds—including salaries—from the AMA. At the same time, the college community was not exempt from various kinds of unpleasantness and even violence directed against black Americans, black institutions, and those white Americans connected with them. In an angry letter written to the corresponding secretary of the AMA, James F. Childs, a well-known black citizen of Marion, Alabama, described how then principal Edward Lord set aside separate seats for white Americans at a concert, publicly embarrassing Childs and his guest by firmly asking that they leave the building if unwilling to vacate those seats. Childs expressed his view that "Our leaders must not respect us because others do or do not but because we are worthy of respect."[11]

There are records of several shootings into the homes of faculty and administrators. In the late 1890s, Professor of Theology John M. P. Metcalf suffered a serious eye injury from a firecracker thrown by a local White into a group of bike-riding faculty. But without doubt the most unsettling incident was the 1870 lynching of a Canadian, William Luke, who had been only marginally connected to Talladega. Luke had gone South to do missionary work and was recruited by Principal Henry Brown to supervise the construction crew working on the girls' dormitory. Later he took a job teaching in a black school in a small Alabama town. A shooting incident between local black and white Americans became the excuse for the Ku Klux Klan to seize five men, four black Americans and Luke, who were given makeshift trials, turned over to the sheriff, and placed in jail for the night. The next day they were taken out by the Klan and lynched.

In 1890, the first college course of study was announced and, five years later, the first baccalaureate degrees were awarded to two Alabama residents, Zachariah Jones of Mobile and John R. Savage of Snow Hill. Several new buildings were also added to the campus: in 1881, Stone Hall, a dormitory for boys and male teachers, a house for the president, and two faculty homes; in 1883, the Cassedy building, which became the primary and intermediate grades school; and in 1884, the Slater Shop, built to house the woodworking program.

From the start, the college's academic and physical development was matched by its involvement in the community beyond the campus. The year after the school opened, members of the college played an important part in establishing a Congregational Church in town. Two years later, the first Sunday school association was organized in the area. In the early 1870s, students from the theological department helped in the construction of twenty-five churches in Talladega and surrounding areas. Some students returned to their hometowns in the summers to teach local children. Talladega teachers organized the first county teachers' institute in Alabama in the 1880s and, in 1893, the college hosted the first countywide meeting of black farmers held in the state. In 1915, the college offered to give the town of Talladega property on which to build a public school for black students. These actions, together with the grassroots origins of the institution, produced a sense of community that encompassed black and white Americans at the college, as well as black Americans in the town and, to some extent, in the county. As far as these groups were concerned, town-gown conflict was practically nonexistent.

What was life like for turn-of-the-century students? The 1896–97 catalog provides some insight.[12] For example, it estimated monthly expenses for a student as follows:

Rent of furnished room	$1.00	to	$1.00
Board	$4.75	to	$5.00
Tuition	$ .50	to	$1.00
Fuel	$ .20	to	$ .50
Lights	$ .10	to	$ .25
College laundry	$ .75	to	$ .75
TOTAL	$7.30	to	$8.50

It also listed a set of "regulations" that offer a sense of how black colleges involved themselves in the lives and habits of their students:

Students, as far as possible, are taught self-control, appeal being made to their own sense of justice, propriety and honor, and they are understood, on entering, to pledge themselves to obey all regulations of the Institution.

It is the aim of the Institution to promote good scholarship and Christian character, and the following regulations have been adopted:

- Students are not allowed to use intoxicating liquors or tobacco in any form.
- All profanity, playing cards or billiards, and everything of an immoral tendency are strictly forbidden.
- Keeping or using firearms on the premises is forbidden.
- Cleanliness of rooms and person, good order and fidelity to duty is required.
- Students will not throw articles from the windows of any College building, and will deposit ashes, slop, papers, etc. in the appointed places.
- Students will be held responsible for damage done by them to College property.
- Only plain and simple clothing is to be worn. Tight lacing is forbidden. Expensive dress will not be allowed at Commencement, and parents are requested not to furnish it.
- A long experience proves that much evil comes from students receiving food from home. Friends will please not send it.
- Regular and punctual attendance upon all hours of study and recitation are required.

Students are required to attend punctually the following religious exercises: Church service and Sabbath school on the Sabbath, daily prayers at their boarding places, and in the morning at the chapel or school-room. There are other services at which attendance is optional, although it is earnestly desired, and is very general. These are the services of the Missionary Societies, Mission Sabbath Schools, and Class and General Prayer Meetings.

The college continued to move forward on several fronts in the early twentieth century. Carnegie Library was built in 1904 with a $15,000 gift from Andrew Carnegie; the Office of the Dean of the College was created the next year; and electrical service was installed in 1906. The first intercollegiate debate involving Talladega was organized in 1906 and in 1911 a "debating triangle" was formed with Knoxville College and Morehouse College. Two years later, Talladega joined with Atlanta, Fisk, Howard, Knoxville, Morehouse, Virginia Union, and Wilberforce to form the Association of Colleges for Negro Youth.

Comments on Talladega's developing academic program appeared in the Bureau of Education's 1915 study:

The college subjects and attendance on the day of visit were: English, 42 pupils; biology, 32; history, 26; mathematics, 20; German, 22; Latin, 6;

Greek, 3; chemistry, 6; economics and sociology, 8; religion, 9; psychology, 12; education, 15; logic, 12; and art, 8. There were also a few students in physiology. The course outlined in the catalogue for 1915–16 is intended to prepare pupils for active service in teaching or for further study in progressive professional schools. The entrance requirements are noteworthy in the amount of credit allowed in manual arts and in the freedom from overemphasis on foreign languages.[13]

The Bureau of Education had very different ideas than Talladega College leadership about the future role of the college (and black colleges generally). The frustration of the Bureau can be seen in its evaluators' description of Talladega's minimalist version of industrial education and in their general recommendations for private schools:

> While the [college's] large, well-cultivated farm serves as an example of good farming in the county, its cultivation forms only a small part of the educational program for students. Only the students who work on the farm to earn school expenses have an opportunity to gain farm experience.[14]
>
> *Theory and practice of gardening.* For a people 73 percent rural, the theory and practice of gardening are of first importance. Only recently have the schools of the country begun to recognize the educational and economic value of gardening. In too many schools the garden has been merely a weak adjunct of the boarding department, with practically no place assigned to it in the school curriculum. . . .
>
> According to this study the use of the farm as an educational factor has failed in the large majority of instances. . . . In view of this failure, it is important to consider the possibility of gardening not only for its educational value and economic returns to the kitchen, but also as a working laboratory for the agricultural course.[15]

The Bureau of Education report described the physical plant as "over 20 buildings on the grounds, including several large brick structures, a number of neat cottages, and a large model barn. A good sewage system is provided. Most of the buildings are in good repair. The school buildings and dormitories are clean."[16]

Between the years of the federal study in 1915 and of the pageant in 1927, yearly income from tuition and student fees increased from $5,965 to $47,957 and total income rose from $39,822 to $174,955. In 1919, a system of scholastic honors was established. The next year a department of biology was created and courses in business administration and journalism were offered for the first time. The curriculum was reorganized and eight academic departments were established. In 1922, a free lecture-recital program was initiated to bring outside scholars and artists to the campus. The dormitory Seymour Hall, Callanan Gymnasium which housed the first swimming pool on the campus of a black college,

Silsby Science Hall, and Sessions Practice School (which in 1926, completed the separation of instructional facilities for elementary, secondary, and college levels) were all built in these years

The narrator of *Sixty Yesteryears* ended by invoking the Talladega of his day:

> From humblest beginnings now quite grown
> To usefulness and place and power,
> Envisioned by its prophetic founders!
> The shoot at length becomes a tree.
> Then looks the husbandman with just pride upon the fruits of his labors
> Well remembering how through toilsome years he carefully tended the
>   growing twig,
> Dreaming the day when a hardy trunk and sturdy arms
> Would defy the storms and stress,
> And underneath their leafy boughs
> Give shelter to youthful adventurers
> Along the high-roads of life.

The college could take pride in its academic standing. At a time when the Southern Association of Colleges and Secondary Schools refused to evaluate black colleges, graduate and professional schools in many northern states fully recognized the Talladega baccalaureate degree. The federal Bureau of Education's 1928 *Survey of Negro Colleges and Universities* reported that the state departments of education of North Carolina, Texas, Louisiana, Georgia, and Tennessee also recognized Talladega as a four-year college, meaning that its graduates received full credit for four years of college work. With regard to graduate study, the report added the following:

> The Universities of Michigan, Iowa and Chicago are listed as graduate schools that have recognized the college since 1923. In 1924 the University of Chicago accredited Talladega College to the extent of accepting its honor graduates without examination. Two graduates have recently entered Howard University. Another graduate spent one summer at the University of Michigan and a year at Cornell University, where he received his master's degree with distinction. Still another graduate, required to take an entrance examination in chemistry at the University of Chicago, made an A grade, and continued with a high record in the Chicago University Medical School.[17]

All of this was extraordinary for a small private black college in the Deep South in the 1920s. In 1927, the buildings and the athletic fields occupied about fifty acres of choice property on both sides of Battle Street, the town's main east-west thoroughfare at a point where the land begins to rise into the foothills of the Appalachian Mountains. An additional 765 acres acquired by the school was farmed or used for pasture and woodland. By the time the pageant was staged, Swayne Hall, the school's original structure, was surrounded by three other buildings that contained classrooms, laboratories, and administrative offices; three student dormitories and one for single faculty; a library, dining room, chapel, gymnasium, hospital, primary school, practice high school, a central heating plant, and a dozen houses for faculty and administrators' families. One of the buildings, DeForest Chapel, housed a pipe organ given to the college by Andrew Carnegie.[18] The barn, referred to in the 1915 report, had been converted into the Talladega College Little Theatre. As shown in Table 8.1 the college enrollment of 187 was 52 percent higher

TABLE 8.1
Talladega College Enrollment

Year	Total Enrollment	College Enrollment	Percentage Increase	Percentage of Total	Number of College Graduates	Number of Faculty
1867	140	0	0.0	0	0	3
1869	231	0	0.0	0	0	6
1892	510	2	0.4	0	na	
1897	693	10	400.0	1.5	2	na
1902	534	23	130.0	4	0	na
1907	613	32	39.0	5	7	na
1912	722	30	−6.0	4	6	na
1917	711	73	143.0	10	11	43
1922	511	123	68.0	24	26	27
1927	563	187	52.0	33	32	25
1932	443	221	18.0	50	41	34
1937	535	261	18.0	49	45	46
1942	628	394	51.0	63	52	39
1947	670	426	8.0	64	45	46
1952	297	297	30.0	100	43	34
1957	272	272	−8.4	100	120	na
1962	450	450	65.4	100	68	na
1967	498	498	10.7	100	52	na
1972	476	476	−4.4	100	110	49
1977	575	575	20.8	100	104	45

Sources: Hill, *Traditionally Black Institutions;* Holmes, *Evolution of the Negro College,* p. 99; Talladega College Office of the Registar, September 24, 1999; Talladega College Office of Institutional Research; 1970 report of Talledega College President Herman H. Long; and United Negro College Fund, *General Statistics of UNCF Member Institutions, 1977–78* (New York: United Negro College Fund, 1979).

than it had been five years earlier and was continuing to grow. The total
number of graduates of Talladega between 1895—its first graduating
class—and 1975 was 2,991, an average of thirty-seven per year.[19]

The typical 1927 freshman was a nineteen-year-old resident of Alabama who had attended public state school. As shown in Figure 8.1, over
95 percent of the students were from nine southern states, the majority
from Alabama and the three states that surrounded it. Only small numbers came from the Northeast and mid-West.

The typical Talladega student's high school teachers and fellow students had been black.[20] His or her mother was a housewife; his or her
father's earnings were minimal. Family income was at a level that made
college tuition difficult to afford. Both the size and the culture of such
black colleges as Talladega made it easy to develop friendships with
schoolmates and often, with faculty. Eighty-nine freshmen enrolled the
year the pageant was presented. Fifty-eight were graduated four years
later. Enrollment patterns changed as the college enrollment grew. In
1916, except for one foreign national, all students came from nine southern states, but by 1930, enrollment from outside the South had increased
to 11 percent of the student body, and was 30 percent by 1940, before
dropping back to 12 percent in 1950. Twenty to thirty states were represented in the 1940s.

Despite the—to a modern viewer, at least—onerous and intrusive regulation of a student's private life, the Talladega campus had the distinctly

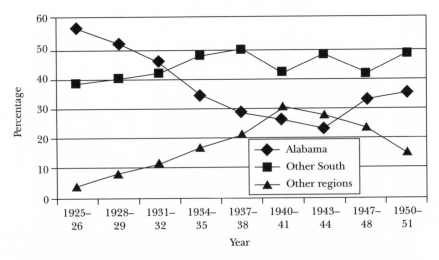

Figure 8.1. Percentage of Students Enrolled by Residence
Source: Talladega College Office of Institutional Research (September 24, 1999).

close-knit feeling of familial life, no small benefit for students living in an otherwise often hostile environment. The sense of pleasure and confidence that such an atmosphere engendered can be felt in the memories of its alumni/ae expressed many decades later. A member of the class of 1929 wrote characteristically:

All freshman girls lived in Foster Hall. At the start of junior year, our class moved to Foy Cottage that had been used as a Domestic Science building. The first floor had had two large rooms that were made into 4 to accommodate 3 or 4 girls each. I had two roommates. The blackboards had not been removed and we used them to study our math and chemistry problems. We wrote the chemistry problems on the board and studied while in bed. It was crowded but we enjoyed the togetherness!

Most of the cultural programs were in the Chapel. We could be escorted (with written OK'd permission) by our gentleman friend. This was known as "walking." The "Walk" was from Foy Cottage to the sidewalk, to the chapel and after the program back the same way to Foy where the matron was waiting to "Greet" the couples. Great Fun!

Teachers took a personal interest in students' education and work. My major was chemistry and Miss Standish was my professor. I recall an incident when she talked to me at length about her worry about my boy friend. She had heard that he "drank" so she thought he was not a proper "boy friend" for me. You can believe I stopped seeing him. It was as though my mother had spoken to me.

The dining room was another place where we got "training." Each table had a host and hostess (older students) who taught us "table manners" and general conversation. Many of us had come from homes where we learned these things but it did not hurt to have them repeated and practiced. . . . There was also the "Ys" where we learned to hold office and manage meetings, travel to conferences and meet other students and teachers.

The college provided national entertainers, vocalist[s], piano performers, movies, etc. These were required attendance and in many instances, a report was requested. Friends made at Talladega were lifetime—most of mine are now dead but I remember them with great favor.[21]

An alumna who entered the college in 1944 recalled her years as "important in building self-esteem. The elementary and high schools I attended in Chicago were integrated but prejudiced. Teachers equated intelligence with color of skin—the darker you were, the dumber you were. Being in Talladega helped to erase that concept. The small college environment encouraged one to be a 'doer' as well as an observer. The atmosphere promoted the 'take what you have and make what you want' approach to life. I found this to be very good for the development of creative thinking."[22]

Talladega's impressive development continued for an additional half century, largely because of the exceptional leadership provided from 1908 to 1976 by six successful presidents, all of whom had backgrounds as ministers. In addition, the institution demonstrated an ability to maintain over a period of several decades a core of outstanding faculty who set a tone and high standards of excellence for their younger colleagues and students. As with black colleges in general, the importance of quality leadership to Talladega's continued existence cannot be overemphasized. Table 8.2 lists all of the college's presidents.

The first in the remarkable string of presidents who saw Talladega through much of the twentieth century was John M. P. Metcalf, who took up his post in 1908. He had attended Oberlin College, as had a disproportionately high percentage of the school's early administrators and faculty. Metcalf came to Talladega as both its dean and professor of theology, for in the understaffed private black colleges of those years there was never a lack of jobs to be done. As president, he was instrumental in separating college from secondary school work. He replaced the college "department" with a college of arts and sciences, reduced the faculty's heavy teaching loads (previously as much as twenty-five to twenty-eight hours per week) and added a fourth year to the three-year college preparatory program. Greek, which with Latin had been compulsory, was dropped and students given modern language options instead.

Frederick A. Sumner, who took over from Metcalf in 1916, continued to strengthen the college program and finally placed the institution on a relatively sound financial footing. The endowment of $168,928 that he inherited reached $266,000 by 1927. The January 1931 issue of *The Talladegan* reported: "Through its President and Trustees, Talladega College is very glad to announce that the terms of the conditional gift of $500,000 from the General Education Board (organized in 1902 by John D. Rockefeller as a general holding board for his philanthropy in education) toward a permanent endowment of $1,000,000 have been met and that $500,000 has been pledged toward the conditional sum of $500,000 pledged by the General Education Board."[23] With the payment of these pledges and the receipt of the matching funds, by 1932 the endowment had risen to $650,000, which made Talladega the seventh ranked school among the private black colleges in the market value of its endowment. Only Hampton Institute and Tuskegee Institute, Spelman College, Howard University, Johnson C. Smith University, and Fisk University stood ahead of it. This was an impressive performance, given that Talladega was only fourteenth in total student enrollment and twentieth in number of college students attending.

TABLE 8.2

Presidents of Talladega College, 1867–1999

Name	Term	Undergraduate Degree	Graduate Degree
Henry E. Brown*	1867–69	Oberlin College	Oberlin College, University of Chicago
Albert A. Saffort*	1870–76	Oberlin College	na
Edward P. Lord*	1877–78	na	Yale Theological
Henry S. DeForest	1879–96	Yale College	Andover Seminary
George W. Andrews**	1896–04	Oberlin College	McCormick Seminary
Benjamin M. Nyce	1904–08	Princeton University	Union Theological
Dr. John M. P. Metcalf	1908–16	Oberlin College	Yale University
Dr. Frederick A. Sumner	1916–33	Oberlin College	Union Theological
Dr. Buell Gallagher	1933–43	Carleton College	
Dr. James T. Cater**	1943–45	Atlanta University	
Dr. Adam Daniel Beittel	1945–52	Findlay College	University of Chicago
Dr. Arthur D. Gray	1952–64	Talladega College	Chicago Theological
Dr. Herman Long	1964–76	Talladega College	University of Iowa
Dr. Aaron Brown***	1976–77	Talladega College	University of Chicago
Dr. Joseph Gayles	1977–83	Dillard University	Brown University
Dr. Randolph Bromery***	June–December 1983	Howard University	Johns Hopkins University
Dr. Paul B. Mohr	1984–88	Florida A & M University	Oklahoma State University
Dr. Joseph Thompson***	1988–91	na	na
Dr. Joseph Johnson	1991–98	Grambling State University	Univeristy of Colorado
Dr. Marguerite Archie-Hudson	1998–	Talladega College	University of California–Los Angeles

*Held title of principal.
**Acting president.
***Interim president.

In 1931, the college was among the first admitted to the "approved" list of the Southern Association of Colleges and Secondary Schools. In 1941, it would also be added to the "List of Approved Institutions Whose Qualified Graduates Are Admitted to Graduate Schools of the Association of American Universities."[24] In its 1932 Annual Report, the AMA compared Talladega favorably with four other four-year colleges that it supported.[25] By then, Talladega had the largest number and highest percentage of students in AMA-funded schools graduating from college. It received the largest contribution but the smallest percent of its total income from the AMA.

Before the 1920s, the composition of the faculty and administration fitted the pattern for black schools supported by northern denominational groups. The faculty, which had consisted of a mere two teachers in 1867, stood at forty-one in 1915, including twenty-nine white and twelve black Americans, twenty-nine women and twelve men. Twenty were engaged in academic work, six in industrial education, one in agricultural science, and fourteen in the primary school. By 1925, black Americans made up 66 percent of the faculty, although Talladega had not yet had a black president.

In 1933, Buell G. Gallagher became president at age twenty-nine. He had taught at Doane College in Crete, Nebraska, had never lived in the South, and had no previous contact with black education. The trustees recognized the risk they were taking in appointing a person of such limited experience. But they believed that Gallagher combined scholarship with the best of the spirit of the early missionaries and a thorough, fresh, modern outlook on life. With these qualities, he embodied what they believed to be the raison d'être of the college. The choice proved a brilliant one. During his administration, major changes were implemented that improved the college in all its aspects. In 1938, the American Council on Education elected the college to be one of twenty-two institutions nationwide chosen to take part in a three-year cooperative study of general education. The result was a decisive modernization of the general division (freshman and sophomore year) curriculum. The traditional New England course of study was firmly retired in favor of a range of introductory courses distributed across the main areas of learning: humanities, social sciences, and natural sciences, along with work in mathematics and foreign languages. What followed in the major division (junior and senior year) was work in a field of concentration with a serious intellectual or professional orientation. The fields available were biology, chemistry, economics, elementary education, English, history, mathematics, modern languages, music (a five-year program), physical education, physics, psychology, and sociology. Auxiliary courses were offered in fine arts, philosophy, political science, and religion. In order to qualify for graduation, each senior was required to complete the general requirements and the requirements in a field of concentration. The latter included a research project, an experience that many alumni/ae remember as a highlight of their undergraduate education.[26]

Another major change during Gallagher's tenure was the creation of a college council that involved faculty, students, and administrators in the formulation of college policy. It was, according to a description in the college's 1937 catalog, "composed of six members of the student body elected by the students of the three upper classes, six instructors elected by the college faculty, and six administrative officers serving ex officio. Questions of policy are discussed in the council, and when a consensus is reached, the policy agreed upon goes into effect." Unique for its time, this concept was well received, although a few administrators and faculty members opposed the necessity for consensus and some students objected to the seeming powerlessness of students in a body where their votes were outweighed two to one.

In 1939, the well-known black painter Hale Woodruff was commissioned to do a mural in the new library showing scenes of the slave revolt aboard the ship *Amistad,* the subsequent trial of the Africans, and their return to Africa. Woodruff, who taught at Atlanta University and New York University, had studied at the John Herron Institute in Indianapolis, the Academie Scandinave and Academie Moderne in Paris, and with the painter Henry O. Tanner. The mural was but one of several efforts undertaken during Gallagher's administration to blend traditional academic work, black American cultural concerns, and a greater participation of faculty, students, and administrators in the governance of the college community.

James T. Cater, who was appointed acting president in 1943, had received his baccalaureate degree from Atlanta University in 1909 and earned a second B.A. at Harvard in 1912. After several years at Straight College in New Orleans, he joined the Talladega staff as the college's first black dean during the Sumner presidency, remaining in that position for more than twenty-five years. He received two leaves of absence to work on his doctorate at the University of Chicago and the University of Wisconsin, but did not complete the degree. In their history of Talladega, Maxine Jones and Joe Richardson report that his correspondence, "liberally sprinkled with letters [from other colleges] asking his advice, suggests that he became a well-respected college administrator." According to the 1927 Talladega yearbook, every student either admired or respected Cater or stood in awe of him. Frederick Brownlee, who represented the AMA on the board of trustees, described him "as a man of keen intelligence, prophetic vision and high character" who had "built these qualities" into all his work and relationships at Talladega.[27] After serving as acting president—the first black American in the post—for two years, Cater returned to the deanship under the next president, Adam Daniel Beittel. His rapport with the faculty was an important factor in building support for the revised general division curriculum. It is no accident that his years as dean coincided with the period when the college's record for awarding baccalaureate degrees to students who successfully pursued graduate and professional degrees was at its most impressive.

It took the two years that Cater served as acting president for the institution to find a successor to Gallagher, even though Talladega had attracted some national attention for its successes and was in reasonably sound financial shape. Several factors were at work. The AMA and the school's white trustees were insistent on appointing a white president. Black trustees, a minority on the board, felt strongly that a person's race should not be a prior disqualification for the presidency. They also felt that the time for ending the white-only policy of filling the position of president was long past. It appears, however, that no serious consideration was given in the search to Cater or to any other black candidate. At the same time, the realization that the racial situation in the South would become more complex in the wake of World War II caused some white Americans, whom the trustees considered acceptable, to be unwilling to stand as candidates for the presidency. Although Talladega's next president would be white, the movement toward black presidents was being pushed both by the desire of black Americans to see the position open to candidates of any race and the limited number of strong white candidates interested in being considered for the position.

Beittel came to the college with good qualifications. He had earned a B.A. at Findlay College, an M.A. at Oberlin, and a Ph.D. at the University of Chicago. He had been professor of religion, professor of sociology, and dean of Guilford—a private white college in North Carolina. His administration got off to a good start but trouble was not long in developing. Some black and white faculty were disappointed that Cater had not been offered the position. Under any circumstances, it would have been no easy task to follow the charismatic Gallagher and the highly respected Cater. Criticism of Beittel's administrative style quickly developed and disagreements arose on several issues, the most troublesome of which had to do with the future of the college's elementary and secondary schools. This more than anything else created fissures in a college community that from the early days of the Gallagher administration had enjoyed a broad consensus on most major issues. Beittel's opposition to segregated schools was shared by all in the college community, but his approach to dealing with that issue at the local level provoked major conflicts. The college viewed itself as an interracial community isolated from a surrounding world that was strongly opposed to any mixing of the races. Within such an environment, the presence of interracial elementary and secondary schools, which the children of black and white faculty and staff could attend on a basis of equality, was seen as important and viewed with pride. The existence of these pre-college institutions also made life significantly more comfortable for families within the college community and admission was open to children whose parents had no official connection to the college. The college-run secondary school was the only one in the county from which a black student could earn a high school diploma.

Beittel and a majority of the trustees wanted to close the elementary and secondary schools for two reasons: first, they were expensive to operate and used up funds that the trustees felt the college could better employ; second, Beittel and the trustees believed that the town of Talladega could not be forced to meet its obligation to provide secondary education for all children as long as the campus schools existed. Cater and members of the faculty agreed that the town should support public schools but felt that to end interracial pre-college education on the Talladega campus would force children of faculty and staff into segregated schools for the first time—and, in doing so, weaken the college's ability to hire the faculty it wished. In addition, students leaving local public schools would be less well-prepared for Talladega and other colleges. Nonetheless, in January 1948, the trustees voted to discontinue Sessions Elementary and Drewry High Schools.

When, at the board's Spring 1951 meeting, the college trustees failed to award permanent tenure to an economics professor, it was rumored that President Beittel opposed tenure because Dean Cater supported it and that Cater's support reflected his disappointment at his failure to be appointed as president. There is no firm evidence to back up either rumor, but community division on the school and leadership issues became so heated that intervention by the trustees proved necessary. The charges made by the faculty against the president were reported in an unprecedented June 2, 1952, "Trustee Edition" of *The Talladegan* (the magazine of the campus community):

1. That the President has taken an ambiguous attitude on racial discrimination and racial segregation.
2. That he lacked administrative integrity and efficiency in his relations with the faculty and the Board.
3. That he has failed to give leadership and does not possess the competency required by a College of the standing and prestige of Talladega.
4. That he made financial matters the paramount consideration in every aspect of his administration.[28]

The trustees rejected all the charges as unfounded but nonetheless took the extreme step of dismissing Beittel, his other key administrators, and the professor. It was a story that reached the *New York Times:*

> Trustees of Talladega College in Alabama settled a three-year intramural squabble at the liberal arts biracial college by dismissing the entire administration, including Dr. A. D. Beittel, the college president, it was announced yesterday. . . .
>
> In releasing its decision the board said: . . . "The members of the body believe that Dr. Beittel has been wronged both by the charges made against him and the methods resorted to by those who have attacked him."
>
> However, the statement continued, "circumstances have arisen which make it impossible for him to carry on as president of the college" and the board regretfully requested his resignation effective August 31.[29]

The situation involving the elementary and secondary schools provides a clear example of a problem growing out of institutionalized racism, segregation laws, and customs, for which no solution satisfactory to the college community could be reached without major political, social, and economic changes in the region—changes over which the college had little influence. Thus, the trustees' action had no chance of solving the problem and, in retrospect, their decision in the affair is not surprising. College trustees are generally reluctant to alter positions when under pressure by faculty and students to do so. The evidence in support of the board's exoneration of Beittel with respect to the charge that he had an "ambiguous attitude" on racial discrimination and racial segregation is compelling. No less compelling to the college community was the importance of a nonsegregated educational environment—a microcosm of a better society for the children of black and white parents who were committed opponents of racism. Behind it all was the inevitable dissonance created by prejudice and racial discrimination in a society that claimed and sometimes aspired to be a democracy.

The Beittel crisis and the changing times did lead to one striking transformation at Talladega. When the trustees next met to consider a new president for an institution suddenly in crisis, there was no more talk about whether the selection process should be white-only or racially open. In August 1952, the board announced that it had chosen Arthur D. Gray as the college's first black president eight and a half decades after the school's founding. He did continue an unbroken tradition of ministers appointed to that post (although acting president Cater was not a minister). Unlike all of his predecessors, he was an alumnus of the college, having graduated in 1929. And unlike his immediate predecessor, he was a consensus builder, a talent desperately needed by one who would shepherd the college into a new era marked by civil rights activism, desegregation, and the black power and black consciousness movements. The *New York Times's* report on his inauguration, although inaccurately reporting the extent of integration at Talladega College, does reflect the growing interest in issues related to desegregation in education:

> Dr. Arthur D. Gray was inaugurated today as the eighth president of Talladega College in academic ceremonies on the campus before 500 students, faculty members, visiting educators and delegates from thirty-three colleges and universities.
>
> The new president is an alumnus of Talladega and the first Negro to head the college since the American Missionary Association of the Congregational Church founded it in 1867. He also is a graduate of the Chicago Theological Seminary and prior to accepting the college presidency was pastor of the Church of the Good Shepherd in Chicago.
>
> Talladega has an inter-racial faculty and its doors are open to students of any race. For several years there have been white students enrolled at Talladega as both regular and exchange students from non-Southern areas.[30]

In addition to his position at the Church of the Good Shepherd, Gray also chaired the executive committee of the General Council of Congregational Churches in America. As a result, he was well known and respected both in Talladega alumni/ae and Congregational Church circles. This may in part explain why Talladega College held a special attraction for students living in Chicago whose parents attended the Congregational Church. Chicago, in turn, attracted many Talladega graduates.

Gray's abilities as a consensus builder helped the community recover from the disruptions of the simultaneous departures of President Beittel and Dean Cater. This capacity undoubtedly contributed to the progress made at the college during a difficult period. It is unlikely that any institution could have escaped problems of the sort encountered during the Beittel administration without suffering some disruption and ill effects, but Talladega's ability to stay the course is impressive.

Herman Long, who followed Gray in 1964, was also a graduate of Talladega College (as was his wife) and the first president who was not a minister. He brought to his presidency a commitment to black higher education shared by his predecessors and, like several of them, possessed the ability to adjust to changing circumstances without compromising the basic principles that gave special meaning to the institution. Before becoming president, he had been director of the department of race relations at Fisk University and was frequently sought out to assist in dealing with racial conflicts throughout the country.

As a result of his personality—faculty and students alike loved him— Long's background made him an ideal choice for the era. Since its founding, the college had opposed segregation and discrimination and, from the early twentieth century on, saw itself as the kind of interracial community it hoped the country could become. Until the late 1940s, however, it had been satisfied to model this idea and had shown considerable restraint in its dealings with issues of discrimination in its immediate environment. The usual approaches had involved discrete negotiations between college administrators and local or state Whites who recognized the institution's economic value to the region, and contacts in which students used guile to maintain their dignity and such legal rights as existed in the region while avoiding outright conflict with local white Americans.

Typical of these contacts was the handling of arrangements involving travel to Talladega from northern and western states from which Blacks were able to purchase reservations on interstate trains that did not include the humiliation of Jim Crow seating. However, when their travel originated in Talladega, the same persons would be assigned to seats in coaches based on their perceived race. The challenge then was to secure reserved seats on northbound trains while circumventing local segregation laws and gaining the benefit of the Interstate Commerce Commission rulings against segregation in interstate travel. Two approaches were used. One was for students who were "white" in appearance to secure the required reservations in Birmingham or Anniston for their group. The second, more daring and thus more satisfying, involved making reservations by telephone in which the ticket agent was advised that "Mr. or Mrs. X" was sending a "boy" or "girl" to pick up the tickets. The student then arrived at the station, entered either the black or white waiting room, and passed to the ticket agent an envelope "sent by Mr. X" that contained the reservation description, number, and payment. The student generally left with instructions to deliver the ticket directly to Mr. X.

These restrained approaches began to change in the years following World War II. Unlike at public black colleges, however, where early opposition to segregation came primarily from students, administrators, faculty, and students were all involved at Talladega. Beittel, who became president the year the war ended, was at the time the only president who had lived and worked in the South before being appointed to his post. Because of, or in spite of this background, he was openly critical of segregationist and discriminatory practices in Alabama and in Talladega, condemning them in such areas as public education, recreation, health care, and policing. He urged white ministers in the town to recognize that it was time for a change in race relations, made written protests to the governor of the state, and sought, without much success, to attract white students to the school. His own son attended Talladega and graduated in 1950.

When in 1956 the University of Alabama in Tuscaloosa expelled Autherine Lucy, the first black student admitted, President Arthur Gray invited her to spend some time at Talladega to allow her to get away from the threats and harassment she was encountering in her hometown of Birmingham. This action was not well received by local Whites. Lucy's lawyer, Arthur Shores, was a graduate of Talladega and a member of the college's board of trustees. Students followed the lead of the administration. The student-run campus newspaper, *The Talladega Student,* chose not to run an ad placed by a local business because the employees in the store insisted on calling black customers by their first names. On another occasion, the student body addressed a letter to the governor protesting the 1960 expulsion of students from the black public state college in Montgomery for public but orderly protests against segregation. In January 1961, students conducted a protest march in nearby Anniston following the beating of a student returning from Christmas vacation and of the driver of a college car sent to meet him at the Anniston train station. Later in the year, students established a social action committee and planned a variety of "direct actions" in hopes of bringing about changes in the town.

Until the mid-1960s, the targets of student-initiated protest activities were generally racial prejudice and discrimination and so were supported by the faculty and administration. The changes that followed were of two types. One was the use of techniques of the civil rights movement to secure changes in college rules and the way the school operated. In 1965, for instance, students expressed objections to compulsory chapel and a student sit-in at the administrative building protested actions taken against six students charged with plagiarism on their senior projects. Several issues such as compulsory chapel had been of concern to students several decades earlier, but by the 1960s, it was becoming clearer that, as at colleges throughout the country, Talladega's faculty and administrators would have far less control in setting the parameters of student life than in the past. At the invitation of the student senate, Stokely Carmichael visited Talladega in the fall of 1966. He returned for a second visit in the fall of 1968, by which time there was a significant group on campus supporting his version of black power. Whether this group composed a majority of students is unclear. If it was a minority, the issues and the spirit of the times made it quite a forceful one. In their history of Talladega, Maxine Jones and Joe Richardson report that the demand for a greater voice in campus governance "represented to these students their commitment to the self determination of Black people."[31] Under the leadership of proponents of this view, students regularly presented the administration with lengthy sets of demands concerning the regulation of student social life, food service, and security.

In a second notable change in protest patterns, students focused their efforts on gaining a voice in matters that had generally been decided by faculty. Occasionally a few faculty members joined with students in advocating a greater student voice in college decisionmaking processes. More rarely, individual faculty members supported students whose view of black power included distrust of integrated institutions and organizations. This latter view was obviously at odds with Talladega's long-held vision of itself as an integrated community. On several occasions, President Long spoke of the divisiveness of those who viewed all black organizations as ipso facto preferable to those that were integrated. Long understood the thinking that led people to such positions but saw it as divisive and counterproductive.

In 1968 and 1969, students continued earlier efforts to eliminate social restrictions and gain greater voice in decisionmaking. Initially this process moved along quietly, resulting in a relaxation of some social restrictions on students, although the faculty refused to agree to students' request for an end to senior comprehensive and oral examinations. The peaceful nature of this process came to an end in April 1968, when police from the town arrested two students who had witnessed an accident on a public street running through the campus. They were charged with disorderly conduct for refusing to move away from the spot of the accident when requested to do so by the police. The students claimed they had moved from the street to private college property, placing them beyond police authority. This minor event sparked a protest demonstration and a march on the city jail by more than 200 students, the college president, and the college chaplain. En route they learned that the arrested students had been freed on bond. The charges were dropped several days later. Nonetheless, due to students' desire to have a greater voice in campus affairs, relations between students and the administration remained tense until the school year ended.

At the start of the 1969–70 academic year, the Black Student Association (BSA), an organization composed mainly of freshmen and sophomores, appeared anxious for conflict with the administration. They declared October 15 a day of protest against the war in Vietnam. A second demonstration was organized on October 23 in support of student protests against a teacher in the Thirteen College Curriculum Program who was accused of giving a weekend assignment in retaliation for earlier criticisms.[32] The Faculty Grievance Committee hastily determined that a hearing on the complaint was warranted and that it should follow American Association of University Professors' (AAUP) guidelines. Students described the AAUP procedure to be a needless delay, occupied the administration building, and closed all other academic buildings except one where music students were able to keep their practice schedules. President Long refused to negotiate with students while the academic buildings were occupied and ordered a recess from November 6 to 17, at which time classes resumed without incident. For the next three years there were no other major conflicts.

Student demonstrations in 1972 followed a female student's charge that a white professor of mathematics had forcefully removed her from his office. While a hearing on the charge was being considered, students presented a list of demands, one of which called for the immediate dismissal of the faculty member. The faculty member had admitted engaging in a shouting match with the student and taking her arm in an attempt to get her out of his office. The College Grievance Committee recommended that the faculty member apologize to the student and step down as department chair. The faculty approved the Committee recommendation and voted that no reprisals be taken against the students involved in the protest. The complainant agreed but the BSA leadership did not accept the decision. High levels of tension accompanying rumors of threats to burn the faculty member's house led President Long to place him on paid leave for the rest of the year and assist him in securing a faculty position at another college.

Although the black power movement and an urge for greater student empowerment in campus decisionmaking were crucial factors in these campus upheavals, developments of the post-*Brown* era played a fundamental role in them as well. By the end of the 1960s, a number of the most promising and best prepared students from Alabama and surrounding states who might have attended Talladega were beginning to be siphoned off into selective traditionally white colleges. The student body, in other words, was changing—and so was the campus environment. Students now had more of a sense that there was a wider, more exciting world out there that was opening up to them, and the environs of a small Alabama town, even one where racial restrictions were slowly easing, looked far less inviting. There was little to do off-campus, and the anger and divisiveness on campus corroded much of the traditional closeness that had not so long before characterized student-student and student-faculty relations. There now seemed to be not one but many missions toward which students, faculty, and administrators often seemed to be moving in various confusing and even contradictory ways.

The faculty, too, was affected by changes in the larger world around Talladega. With racial restrictions easing more quickly in Alabama's urban than in rural areas, faculty members who previously would have lived on or near the campus were by the mid-1970s moving en masse to nearby cities. Anniston, Birmingham, and other nearby cities offered a greater choice in housing accommodations and a more interesting lifestyle. Many of the most positive of post-*Brown* changes were, ironically, having an erosive effect on life at Talladega.

Nonetheless, Talladega's success in preparing students for graduate and professional study continued to be impressive. Tables 8.3 and 8.4 provide information on advanced degrees earned by graduates during the nine decades between 1899 and 1988. Although the total number of bachelors degrees is documented by data from the office of the College Registrar and the number of Ph.D. and medical degrees have been well researched, it is highly likely that the list of graduates who earned masters degrees is incomplete, because the records of masters degrees based on the institutions from which recipients received baccalaureate degrees were less well kept.

Throughout most of the college's history, a higher percentage of Talladega graduates earned advanced degrees than at most private black colleges, but the pattern of changes reflects the national pattern for private black colleges. There were small numbers of advanced degrees before the 1920s, reflecting the limited number and poor quality of public secondary schools and the dominance of industrial training in the curricula of public and some private black post-elementary institutions. Approximately one in ten graduates during the decade between 1909

TABLE 8.3

Graduates Who Earned B.A.s in Each Decade from 1889–98 to 1979–88

Decade	Bachelors	Masters	Doctorate	Medical	Dental	Law	Total Advanced
1889–98	5	0	0	0	0	0	0
1899–1908	150	1	na	5	5	4	10
1909–18	68	2	1	4	na	4	7
1919–28	218	4	15	5	1	5	25
1929–38	448	41	34	6	3	3	87
1939–48	436	94	24	10	4	4	140
1949–58	576	146	41	21	3	12	223
1958–68	616	156	15	6	6	14	191
1969–78	948	56	16	8	na	8	88
1979–88	950	138	6	3	2	11	160
Total	**4,415**	**638**	**152**	**68**	**13**	**56**	**931**

Sources: Hill, *Traditionally Black Institutions;* Holmes, *Evolution of the Negro College,* p. 99; Talladega College Office of the Registar, September 24, 1999; 1970 report of Talladega College President Herman H. Long; and United Negro College Fund, *General Statistics 1977–78.*

Note: na indicates that data are not available.

TABLE 8.4

Institutions from Which Advanced Degrees Received by Talladega Graduates

Ph.D. Degrees in Arts and Sciences

University Michigan (25)	Columbia University (9)	New York University (9)
University of Chicago (7)	University of Wisconsin (5)	Nova University (5)
University of Iowa (5)	Howard University (4)	Northwestern University (4)
University of Pittsburgh (4)	Stanford University (4)	Florida State University (3)
Cornell University (3)	University of Alabama (3)	University of Minnesota (3)
Brown University (3)	South Florida University (3)	Washington State University (3)
Other universities (50)		

Medical Degrees

Meharry Medical School (28)	Howard University (11)	Harvard University (4)
University of Illinois (3)	Other medical schools (22)	

Law Degrees

Howard University (9)	Temple University (5)	Harvard University (4)
University of Alabama (3)	University of Indiana (3)	State University of NY (3)
Other law schools (25)		

Note: Number in parentheses is number of Talladega graduates who have earned advanced degrees at the institutions listed.

and 1918 earned an advanced degree, approximately two in ten during the next decade, three in ten in the following, and four in ten during the 1949–1958 decade. In the following three decades, the numbers declined to approximately three in ten and then one in ten, before rising to approximately 1.5 in ten during 1979–1988. These changes reflected rising percentages of black Americans graduating from secondary schools, improvements in the quality of public secondary education (although the quality of schools for black Americans lagged significantly behind that for white Americans) and postsecondary institutions, and the mission and commitment of individual institutions. The rate at which Talladega graduates earned advanced degrees in the 1930s, 1940s, and 1950s was well above the national average. The decline after the 1950s resulted, at least in part, from the enrollment in selective traditionally white colleges of many of the black students who were most likely to pursue graduate and professional degrees.

According to a 1961 U.S. Public Health Service monograph on the "Baccalaureate Origins of 1950–59 Medical Graduates," Talladega ranked eighteenth in the United States in percentage of graduates who received medical degrees, with an index of 13.0 per 1,000 graduates. It was first among black colleges in graduates who later were granted science doctorates (8.2 per 1000 graduates for the period 1950–59), and ranked fifty-fifth among the top one hundred colleges in the country in this area. It tied with Howard University for first place among black colleges in the production of female doctorates (one doctorate per 80.4 female graduates).[33]

What important insights are provided or reinforced by a brief look at the experiences of one private black college over the course of nearly a century? First, although each black college's experiences have been different, the events described in this case history provide a capsule of the history of most private black colleges from their nineteenth-century beginnings. Second, the case history makes clear the importance over a sustained period of time of sound leadership committed to a set of basic, agreed-upon goals. This is typical of most successful institutions and is an absolute necessity for those that operate under the disadvantages faced by black colleges. In the case of Talladega, the college enjoyed sixty-eight years of high quality leadership, during which it held firmly to its mission of giving students the rigorous academic preparation required for succeeding in graduate and professional studies. Third, the intrusion and detrimental consequences of segregation and discrimination in education can be seen in every aspect of black college life—academic, economic, social, and political. Fourth, for black colleges and other institutions with limited resources, commitment to one's primary goals often required that difficult decisions be made with respect to ancillary goals, many of which were also important and attractive. Fifth, it is a constant challenge to maintain an institution's integrity while accommodating changing conditions over which the institution has little or no control. Some of the challenges faced by black colleges in their first century seem hard to believe of a society claiming a commitment to the lofty principles of democracy and equality. Recognizing such situations and developing strategies and tactics for dealing with them has been and continues to be the proving ground of black-college leadership. Finally, the case history reflects both the tenacity and the vulnerability of small private black colleges, the luck reflected in the timing of the extraordinary leadership of a Buell Gallagher or a Herman Long, and the sagacity of a board of trustees willing to take a chance on a twenty-nine-year-old with one year of teaching and no administrative experience. For Talladega as for other private black colleges, it was the quality of leadership, the clarity of its sense of mission, and a focus on its primary goals that sustained it through the difficult times that private black colleges faced.

A close examination of enrollment data, the academic preparation of entering students, and retention rates shows that Talladega in the 1970s shared four problems common to most private black colleges. The first was that of maintaining and improving academic standards as institutions enrolled a declining percentage of the most able black high school graduates. The second was to devise means of increasing enrollment so as to bring in more revenue and make fuller use of the physical facilities and existing faculty. The third was to increase the student retention rate throughout the four years of college work. The fourth was to provide adequate support services for students who possessed considerable intellectual ability and met college admission requirements but whose academic background included poor quality elementary and secondary schooling.

The mid-1970s represent something of a watershed in the development of private black colleges early in their second century of existence. But the events producing this alteration in the flow of things are only part of major societal changes influencing all education in the fourth quarter of the twentieth century. Black colleges found themselves facing old challenges not fully met while, like the rest of higher education, confronted new ones of sizable proportions.

CHAPTER 9

Leadership and Luck

TALLADEGA WAS ONLY one of many private black colleges that passed through the stormy post-*Brown* era. Despite fears for their future, stringent budgets, and aggressive competition from predominantly white colleges, many private black colleges emerged in remarkably healthy shape from the experience, with their missions intact and, if anything, clearer than before. This is powerful, if incomplete testimony to the inherent staying power of these colleges and to the continuing need for them in our society.

We asked ourselves how these strong survivors managed. We compared a number of plausible theories against our observations and those of other witnesses. For example, ambitious strategic plans and high aspirations might seem to be the foundation for success, but in fact do not appear to guarantee it. Distinguished past reputation, reinforced by reasonably sized endowments might seem to be the formula for a strong future, but some private black colleges—like several predominantly white colleges and universities—had these advantages and still suffered noticeable slumps. Our best explanation for institutional vitality in these strong survivors is that a college that enjoys consistent, competent leadership over fifteen or twenty years can achieve surprisingly good results through good times and bad.[1]

This chapter offers three case histories that tell of success, often achieved against difficult odds. They give glimpses of different leadership styles and strategies, shaped more by specific context and personality than by conformity with any textbook standard of how good leaders behave. The three colleges are quite different from each other in purpose and financial strength. Although we rely on reports from the presidents of these colleges, we do not mean to imply that the only significant leadership for these schools is provided by their presidents. In fact, a key conclusion from all three sketches is that the definition of strong institutional leadership—in any sustained sense—must include a strong and supporting board of trustees and dedicated faculty and administrative leadership outside the president's office.

The three cases describe change at Stillman College in Tuscaloosa, Alabama, Spelman College in Atlanta, and Xavier University of Louisiana in New Orleans (see Table 9.1). These are not the only three private

TABLE 9.1

Selected Characteristics of Three Colleges, 1997

Characteristics	Stillman College	Spelman College	Xavier University of Louisiana
Location	Tuscaloosa, Alabama	Atlanta, Georgia	New Orleans, Louisiana
Year founded	1876	1881	1915
Religious affiliation	Presbyterian	Independent	Roman Catholic
Tuition and fees (1996–97)	$5,200	$9,500	$8,200
Enrollment	1,035	1,937	3,506
Percentage of students from in-state	75	17	48
Percentage of students who receive financial aid	90	81	89
Percentage of students who graduate within five years	34	70	49
Percentage of students who enroll in graduate school within a year of graduation from college	15	38	37
Distribution of majors among 1995 graduates (percentages)	Business 42 Social sciences 16 Education 13 Biology/life sciences 9 Communications 6 Other 14	Social sciences 42 Psychology 16 English 13 Physical sciences 9 Biology/life sciences 6 Other 14	Biology/life sciences 30 Business 15 Physical sciences 15 Psychology 10 Social sciences 7 Communications 5 Other 18

Sources: College Entrance Examination Board, *The College Handbook* (New York: College Entrance Examination Board, 1996), pp. 211, 490, 696; United Negro College Fund, *1998 Statistical Report*, p. 28.

black colleges that have prospered in recent years and have enjoyed consistent and capable presidential leadership. One could as well have chosen ten or fifteen others about which the same could be said. And virtually all extant private black colleges have enjoyed some periods of excellent leadership and good luck, or they would not be in business today.

STILLMAN COLLEGE

Stillman College is a coeducational liberal arts college that enrolled fifteen hundred students in 2000. The College was chartered in 1876 by the General Assembly of the Presbyterian Church in the United States as a training school for black Christian ministers. Its hundred-acre campus is located on the western edge of Tuscaloosa, Alabama, a city of about seventy-eight thousand persons, which also contains the nineteen-thousand-student main campus of the University of Alabama. Approximately two-thirds of Stillman students come from Alabama high schools, the largest number coming from a band of counties extending roughly two hundred miles south from Tuscaloosa to the Gulf Coast. The College offers majors in the arts and sciences, and preprofessional programs in engineering, law, medicine, the ministry, and social work. In the first half of this century, Stillman was known for training elementary and secondary schoolteachers, and for sending graduates into the ministry and social-service careers. These traditions survive, but the most popular undergraduate major today is business administration.

In the 1970s, Stillman was shaken by the new competition for black students and faculty coming from northern colleges and universities, as well as from previously all-white southern public universities. Table 9.2 shows, in approximately ten-year intervals, the enrollment numbers and College Board Scholastic Aptitude Test (SAT) verbal score levels for Stillman and Spelman Colleges and for Xavier University. During the difficult early years of the 1970s, Stillman maintained its enrollment numbers in the 650–800 range, but was forced to admit many less well prepared students to maintain the size of its enrollment.

Despite its efforts, Stillman's enrollment began to decline, just as the Presbyterian Church experienced reduced parishioner contributions and began reducing its traditionally substantial contributions to the college's operating budgets. Dr. Harold N. Stinson, Stillman's first black American president, had achieved important improvements in the college's curriculum, particularly in mathematics and science. In the mid-1970s, however, he began to develop health problems, which were not immediately obvious, even though they interfered with memory and

TABLE 9.2

Enrollment, Mean Verbal Aptitude Scores, and Class Rank in Three Colleges,
1966–95 (Selected Years)

	Fall 1966	Fall 1976	Fall 1984	Fall 1995
Stillman College				
Undergraduate enrollment	648	752	696	815
Mean SAT Verbal score for entering freshmen	328	257	342	N.R.
Percentage of U.S. black high school seniors scoring higher than this	25	47	21	—
Percentage of freshmen class who were in top fifth of their high school class	N.R.	25	N.R.	18
Spelman College				
Undergraduate enrollment	794	1,244	1,430	1,708
Mean SAT Verbal score for entering freshmen	374	382	N.R.	490
Percentage of U.S. black high school seniors scoring higher than this	14	12	—	2
Percentage of freshmen class who were in top fifth of their high school class	51	19	N.R.	N.R.
Xavier University of Louisiana				
Undergraduate enrollment	1,006	1,572	1,661	2,886
Mean SAT Verbal score for entering freshmen	377	336	418	453
Percentage of U.S. black high school seniors scoring higher than this	13	23	7	4
Percentage of freshmen class who were in top quarter of their high school class	N.R.	36	36	57

Sources: Cass and Birnbaum, *Comparative Guide to American Colleges,* 1968–69 edition, pp. 66, 676, 696; Cass and Birnbaum, *Comparative Guide to American Colleges,* 1977 edition, pp. 606, 613, 724; Cass and Birnbaum, *Comparative Guide to American Colleges,* 1996 edition, pp. 582, 586, 695.

Note: N.R. indicates that the college did not report that data item that year. Roughly defined, the verbal section of the College Board Scholastic Aptitude Test (SAT) attempts to measure a student's verbal reasoning power. It is a narrow measurement, but one of the few available for large numbers of U.S. high school seniors. In 1966, the SAT was the required admission test for all three colleges. For most of the remaining years in these colleges, either the Scholastic Aptitude Test or the American College Testing Program (ACT) examinations could be chosen by an applicant. This shift meant that the 1976–95 test data represents no more than half of the enrolled students in the freshman class. The extent to which SAT test takers differ from ACT test takers is not known.

concentration. As a result of his failing health, Stinson did not organize a vigorous response to the new financial and enrollment challenges. In 1980, he finally took medical leave and at the end of the next year he retired. On January 1, 1982, Dr. Cordell Wynn, dean of the school of education at Alabama Agricultural and Mechanical University, became Stillman's new president.[2]

Wynn remembers arriving at a college in danger of closing. Enrollment had declined sharply to a mere 523 students, and more were preparing to leave. Operating budget shortfalls were being paid for out of the college's small endowment. Its short-term bank loans were rising dangerously. Faculty morale was low. Unrepaired windows were boarded up in the main women's dormitory, and its roof leaked as did the one on the men's dormitory. The college's central heating system had just failed. George A. LeMaistre, a local banker, lawyer, and chairman of the Stillman board of trustees, told Wynn, "The first thing you have to do is get that place looking as if someone lives there."[3]

Wynn appeared confident as he took office and was everywhere at once. He almost daily inspected the campus, instructing the buildings and grounds crew which window frames should be painted next, which lighting fixtures repaired, and which sagging shutters restored to their proper shape. He recruited a new chief academic officer, but otherwise retained the key administrative staff members from the Stinson administration. "I tried to work with the people who were there," Wynn recalls. "I encouraged them to be good managers, but I remained the leader." He organized a committee of ten with participation from faculty, staff, students, trustees and Tuscaloosa citizens to produce a "vision plan": "a road map, a blueprint for all aspects of the college." It outlined curriculum needs, a fundraising plan, and a restatement of the College's moral and spiritual values.

In 1995, near the end of his presidency, Wynn explained these values in a speech at the Smithsonian Institution:

> From the beginning, historically black colleges and universities knew that their roles would be dual; and, even today, they continue to be more than a place to go to get an education. They must also be oases of culture and richness of heritage in the black experience as well as historical legacies of black achievement. They are committed to academic excellence; and, at the same time, they must be centers for reinforcement, motivation, stimulation, nurturance and assistance. No other institution of higher learning must do so much, for so many, with so little.

Wynn himself joined community and national organizations, including the Chamber of Commerce of West Alabama and several U.S. Department of Education advisory panels, both to help them and to give Stillman College greater visibility. Within six years, he had been named a trustee of the University of Alabama system and was honored as Alabama Administrator of the Year. During the same period, he was also serving as the chair of the presidents of the UNCF and as chairman of the National Association for Equal Opportunity, a Washington-based organization founded to represent the legislative interests of historically black public and private colleges and universities.[4]

He defines his presidential style as "leadership by walking around." Wynn said recently: "Visibility is so important to leadership. You have to be visible on campus, in the community, in the state." He estimates that in many of his years as president, he knew by name at least three-quarters of Stillman's students, and frequently would greet them and talk with them on his campus rounds.

Sue Thompson, a local attorney, Stillman alumna, and trustee recalls the early Wynn years:

> One of the first things Dr. Wynn did was to paint and make things look better. Students started to behave better. His Committee of Ten wrote that long-range plan. The product was broadly inclusive. He really cared about a collective vision. Then, he did take it as a blueprint. He kept bringing the mission statement back and including it in the agenda folders for the trustee meetings. Also he educated us to concentrate on policy and to stay out of implementation."[5]

Stillman College showed remarkable resilience during the 15½ years of Wynn's presidency. By 1997, Wynn's final year as president, enroll-ment had risen to just over a thousand students. The college's annual budget was regularly in balance or had a slight surplus. Its two-million-dollar endowment, one of the smallest among members of the UNCF in 1980, by 1997 was valued at twenty million dollars, one of the group's ten largest. By the end of his tenure, a computer science major was intro-duced, the teacher education program strengthened, and the faculty enlarged. The college had constructed two new buildings and renovated two older dormitories. Wynn left office in good health, but nonetheless described the investment of energy in his presidential years as "sacrificial."[6]

Dr. Ernest McNealey became Stillman's fifth president on July 1, 1997. When selected, he was associate provost and dean of undergraduate academic affairs at the State University of New York at Stony Brook. Prior to that he was professor of art and vice president at Claflin College. McNealey is more quiet and reserved than Wynn. He listens carefully. "Dr. Wynn and I get on famously," he has said, "but I have chosen not to do 'leadership by walking around.' At least for now I have put much of my energy into getting a joint sense of where we all are going."[7]

Probably the most important thing a new president can do is, in McNealey's words, to "get a joint sense of where we all are going." Although there is no sure recipe, the usual ingredients include assessment of the college's already-established momentum and capacity, contribution of whatever the incoming president can offer, and a calling forth of new energy from others on the scene. Serial descriptions of shared vision at Stillman College—when Wynn arrived in 1989, when McNealey took office in 1997, and today, in 2000—show dramatic change. When Cordell Wynn took office, the first task of the college's administration, trustees, and faculty had been to develop enough financial strength and confidence in the future to "get the place looking as if someone lives there" and to keep it that way. Wynn's early "Vision Plan" planning process then raised the sights. Stillman would increase enrollment, offer new subjects, raise academic standards, attract money from new sources, and start to become recognized outside its home region. In fact, these goals were attained.

Building on the success of the Wynn years, McNealey's first strategic planning process in 1998 again raised the sights. This Five-Year Strategic Plan, prepared by McNealey, faculty, and staff, declared that Stillman should continue to grow and aspire to be one of the top three hundred liberal arts colleges in the nation in terms of quality.[8] Such a plan once more required that many changes take place at the same time. The plan calls for an enrollment increase to fifteen hundred students by 2002, a student body with higher entrance and graduation standards, and a more nearly even gender balance. Stillman College in 1997 enrolled 368 male students, or 36 percent of the total. (All UNCF institutions together that year reported 40 percent male enrollment.) McNealey directed the reorganization of the admission office, and announced that, after forty years of going without, Stillman would have a varsity football team and a new football stadium. The college fielded a mostly freshman team in 1999 that achieved a respectable first year record: three wins and six losses. The second-year record was six wins and three losses, including a win over Clark Atlanta University, a much larger school. Stillman College grew to fifteen hundred students by 2000, two years ahead of the strategic plan's target, and has 46 percent male enrollment. Two years after his arrival, McNealey was optimistic. "I think the future is quite bright," he said. "We are enrolling students who would not have considered coming to Stillman two years ago. The general level of our expectations has become geometrically different."[9]

The 1998 strategic plan also recommended establishment of a required thesis project for all seniors in the student's major subject area, and a required departmental exit examination. These have been adopted. McNealey believes academic quality and reputation are likely to improve if the college attempts to achieve distinction in a few areas, even if that means cutting back or eliminating other fields of study. Faculty hiring in biological sciences and teacher education indicate Stillman's intent to make a reputation in these fields, and McNealey hopes for similar emphasis in the arts. Areas to be merged or eliminated were under discussion but have not been identified as this is written.

Some of McNealey's agenda did not wait for adoption of the strategic plan. On arrival, he directed that the completion schedule for the $4.7 million Cordell Wynn Humanities, Communications and Fine Arts Center be accelerated a year, to open in 1999. Within a few months of McNealey's arrival, the Stillman campus buildings were interconnected with fiber optic cable, three microcomputer laboratories were established, and computers provided to faculty who did not already have them. In March 2000, UNCF President William H. Gray III noted in accepting a large gift from Microsoft and IBM that only 15 percent of students in black colleges own a computer, compared with 55 percent of all college students. Stillman's desire to improve its technology was partly to prepare students for the computer requirements of subsequent jobs or graduate study, but also to improve the quality of Stillman's instruction. The Stillman 1998 strategic plan explains: "Students who are exposed to classroom uses of technology tend to become more technologically literate, more attentive in class, and more likely to communicate with faculty and other students outside of class."[10]

There is no question that Stillman's vital life signs are stronger than most observers would have imagined possible twenty years ago and that they are still improving. In September 1997, when we first visited Stillman College, one of us after lunch asked a group of trustees, the dean, the new president, and several administrative officers what a college like Stillman needs to be most concerned about. Without hesitation, Stillman's Board Chairman Moses C. Jones, Jr., replied:

> Historically black colleges are at a critical stage. They're more important than ever. They have more experience than any other kind of college in developing minority potential. Some African Americans will do fine wherever they go. But surely not all. Just look at the production of Ph.D.'s and managerial leadership—a disproportionate share attended private black colleges. Here at Stillman, we need to make sure we stand and prosper. The end of affirmative action makes that even more important. Individuals are not going to get special breaks. We need to train people to succeed in graduate admission competitions, with no favors given.[11]

SPELMAN COLLEGE

In 1881, Sophia B. Packard and Harriet E. Giles, two missionary teachers from the American Baptist Home Mission Society of New England, opened a school for young black women in the basement of the Friendship Baptist Church of Atlanta. Three years later, aided by a donation from the John D. Rockefeller family, land and buildings were purchased, and the school was named Spelman Seminary, in honor of the mother of Mrs. Rockefeller (Laura Spelman Rockefeller).[12] Over the years, Spelman College's reputation among historically black colleges has developed in much the same way as the reputation of Smith College or Wellesley College once grew among traditionally white ones. Ruth J. Simmons, former Spelman provost and recent president of Smith College was appointed president of Brown University in November 2000.[13] Several decades ago, such moves from black college leadership to the presidency of a major private research university did not occur. In the mid-1970s, Spelman was probably the only one of the three colleges discussed in this chapter which most casual observers would have labeled elite. This reputation arose severally from Spelman's ability to attract students from across the nation, the accomplishments of its graduates, the visibility of its administrative and faculty leadership, and its early membership in an Atlanta collegiate consortium, the Atlanta University Center.

From its founding until 1953, four white women led Spelman College: Sophia Packard, Harriet Giles, Lucy Hale Tapley, and Florence Read. Dr. Albert E. Manley, dean of the college of arts and sciences at North Carolina College, Durham, North Carolina, became Spelman's fifth president in July 1953—its first black president and its first male president. Under Manley's presidency, the College achieved regional accreditation from the Southern Association of Colleges and Schools. Spelman graduates were increasingly encouraged to train for professional careers and for work in government and business management.[14]

By 1976, Manley's last year in office, Spelman enrolled over twelve hundred students and was graduating almost two-thirds of all entering freshmen—a high proportion for most colleges, black or white.[15] Responding to pressure to share power, the Spelman board of trustees during the 1970s added to its membership an alumnae representative, a faculty representative and a student representative. Many students and faculty hoped that when Manley retired, the next Spelman president would be one of their own, a Spelman graduate. Instead, the board of trustees chose Dr. Donald M. Stewart, a northern-educated black administrator whose experience included service as a Ford Foundation program officer and as executive assistant to Martin Meyerson, president of the University of Pennsylvania. The immediate reaction of a student group was to lock the board of trustees in the main administration building until, a day later, their release could be negotiated. The board's selection did not change, however, and when Stewart moved into the president's house three months later with his wife and two sons, he was pleased to find that the initial hostility to his appointment seemed to have dissipated.[16] Although his plans would create occasional unease, he pursued an aggressive agenda to raise academic standards, involve larger numbers of faculty in published research and publication, reorganize student recruitment, and further broaden the range of career choice for Spelman women toward graduate study and professional careers.[17]

Stewart organized a comprehensive, large-scale capital fund drive, using a $4.2 million challenge grant from the Rockefeller Brothers Fund as the centerpiece. By its end in 1981, Spelman had raised over $12 million in new funds, including $9 million added to its endowment. Spelman's endowment market value, which stood at $11.4 million in 1978, had risen to $35.3 million in 1983. Successful completion of the drive also improved the College's general credit rating, so that it was able to borrow at more favorable interest rates than previously, thus enabling it to build a new dormitory.[18] In addition, Stewart's personal persuasion convinced DeWitt Wallace, founder of the *Reader's Digest,* to establish within the New York Community Trust a $1 million endowment in 1980 titled the DeWitt Wallace/Spelman College Fund, with its income paid annually to the college. By 1992, when the principal of the Fund was finally transferred to the college, its value was $41.2 million. The college then designated the money as an endowment for scholarship stipends and curriculum development in its honors college.

Stewart's success at soliciting endowment and his decision to raise tuition more rapidly than in the 1970s together strengthened the college's basic financial structure. As these moves succeeded, a larger percentage of the college's operating budget was financed by "hard money"—generally thought to be relatively certain; and a smaller portion came from government and foundation grants, or "soft money"— whose renewal was less subject to the college's control and often more erratic. Fundraising, meanwhile, became an expanded team effort. The president still carried a heavy fundraising schedule, but a much-enlarged staff performed background research on many more corporations, foundations, government agencies, and individuals than was possible earlier. Spelman began to receive the same kind of national fundraising exposure that successful private colleges and universities elsewhere had developed ten and twenty years earlier.

Stewart also reorganized student recruitment. The size of the admissions staff tripled. An honors program was introduced within the curriculum, offering special courses, seminars, and events. To qualify for the honors program, an applicant was required to present a combined verbal and math score of 1,000 or higher on the SAT, and to have a B average or better in high school.[19] The College's expenditure for scholarships (not including government funds), increased from $178,000 in 1978 to nearly $500,000 in 1984, with about one-quarter of the 1984 total going to the honors program. As Table 9.2 shows, Spelman's enrollment increased at the same time that the test scores of entering students also rose. This occurred despite the intense recruitment pressures from predominantly white colleges that affected virtually all the historically black colleges in those years.

By the time Stewart left in late 1986, the proportion of faculty with doctoral degrees had increased from 58 to 70 percent. There was a chemistry department, a computer center, a women's studies program, a program in organization and management, a continuing education program for adult students, stronger humanities and social sciences faculties, and a modernized set of administrative services for admissions, financial affairs, and development. Faculty became eligible for sabbaticals, and a new peer-review process was installed to improve and reduce somewhat the granting of faculty tenure. By 1986, visitors to Spelman College reported that, more frequently than in the past, Spelman students and faculty compared the demands of their work with what would be required at leading traditionally white private colleges, rather than solely at other historically black colleges.[20]

Two years prior to the end of Stewart's presidency, an evaluator for the Rockefeller Brothers Fund reported her general assessment of the effect of the Stewart fund drive and of the College's progress at that time:

> Movement—forward movement—has been the distinguished mark in Spelman's recent history. . . . Spelman strikes today's observers as an uncommonly lively place, energized by a sense of striving, secure in its goals. It should come as no surprise that the institution's ambitions outpace its resources when projected forward in time. Spelman has long since stopped talking about "survival;" the new watchword is "excellence." The pursuit of excellence will inevitably lead the College into another major effort to increase endowment; anything less may be taken as a sign of stagnation, if not failure.[21]

In April 1987, the Spelman board of trustees announced the selection of Dr. Johnnetta B. Cole as the college's seventh president—its first black American female president, and the first career university scholar in the job. Prior to coming to Spelman, Cole was professor of anthropology at Hunter College and director of Latin American and Caribbean Studies at the City University of New York. Cole studied at Fisk University, received her bachelors degree from Oberlin College and a Ph.D. in anthropology from Northwestern University. Both Presidents Cole and Stewart sought expanded leadership opportunities for black American women and believed that a demanding women's college education was the key for many of them. Both encouraged the Spelman faculty to publish and to establish closer peer relationships to excellent faculty everywhere. Both created stronger administrative structure, which in turn helped raise more money more predictably. Stewart's style was cautious and low key. Cole's was electric.

In a recent interview, Cole recalled her initial approach to her job:

I knew I had to give academic leadership *and* raise money. I tried to give academic leadership by keeping up with my field—although perhaps not as much as I should have ideally—by teaching, and by my relationship with faculty. But if I spent all my days on campus there was no way I could raise the money we needed. I was advised to appear on television, in magazines, and present a strong picture for the College. The media really jumped on that presidency: "After 107 years, a black woman president!"[22]

Cole's warmth and energy attracted attention wherever she went. She traveled, lectured, and appeared on national television. Three months after she took office, *Ms. Magazine* featured her in a major article as "Sister Prez," and the label stuck. Coverage followed in *Change Magazine,* the *New York Times,* and continued television appearances. At the college, her message to students was "You can soar even farther than you ever imagined." The message also usually noted that individual aspiration borders on selfishness if it fails to include community service.[23]

Within a year, Camille and Bill Cosby announced a gift of $20 million to build the Camille Olivia Hanks Cosby Academic Center and to endow three faculty chairs at the college. This was by far the largest single private gift ever made to a black college, and the largest by a black American family or individual to any college. It became the centerpiece in a capital fund drive that eventually raised $113.8 million.[24]

Cole believed that both Spelman faculty and students needed a broader range of experience, and so she increased the college's connections to other institutions. Faculty exchanges were established with the University of Wisconsin and Princeton University. Spelman became a charter participant in a project linked to New York University, in which faculty from several historically black colleges came to New York each summer to do research or teach summer courses. Faculty publication rose sharply, along with participation in national faculty networks and associations. A Phi Beta Kappa chapter was established at Spelman in 1997. Meanwhile, an increasing if still small number of Spelman students studied abroad or accepted overseas internships, and more overseas students came to Spelman to study.

On campus, Cole established once-a-month open-office hours, when students could come in and talk to her. Early in her days on campus, she would walk the campus and encourage students to make appointments to walk and talk with her. Of regular monthly breakfast meetings with the student government association, she says, "We spoke candidly with each other, and had an agreement we would not surprise each other—either way."[25]

Observers of Spelman history, including Presidents Stewart and Cole, suggested that although it may be convenient to describe the college's history by referring to individual presidencies, the college could not have developed as it did since 1970 without significant leadership continuity in major administrative offices and in the faculty. Among such key people are Etta Z. Falconer, associate provost for science programs and policy and Calloway professor of mathematics, Lois Moreland, a professor of political science who retired in 1999 and Robert D. (Danny) Flanigan, vice president for business and financial affairs and treasurer. Falconer, a faculty member since 1965, helped build a remarkable level of interest in the natural sciences, raised money for research, and helped ensure that the science curriculum stayed current. When she came to Spelman, mathematics and biology were the only sciences offered. About 10 percent of the college's students majored in science. Falconer recalls: "In those days, the sciences were relatively unimportant at Spelman. This wasn't any one person's fault. It was just the prevailing thought: women didn't do science, particularly African American women. It was very important to change that mindset!" Led by Falconer and her colleagues, Spelman established departments of chemistry and computer science, a physics major, and an environmental sciences program. In 2000, one-third of Spelman students majored in science. The most recent publication of the National Research Council on collegiate origins of Ph.D. recipients reports that Spelman ranked second only to Howard University in the production of Ph.D.s in natural and social sciences for black American women.

Moreland came to Spelman in 1959, founded the political science department in 1964, and served as academic dean from 1970 to 1972. Her encouragement influenced literally hundreds of Spelman graduates to pursue careers in law, diplomacy, and international affairs. Moreland was the program designer and first director of the International Affairs Center, financed by The Ford Foundation to serve Spelman and the other colleges of the Atlanta University Center. The Center's programs provided international affairs internships and research opportunities in Washington, D.C., for students and faculty, and brought diplomats to Spelman both for short visits and longer residencies.

Flanigan was hired in 1970. Eventually he became principal architect of the college's financial policies, and played a key role in placing its endowment management on a professional and high performance basis. He introduced capital budgeting and designed a system for creating annual operating budgets in which faculty members were key participants. Annual budgeting was integrated with long range budget planning.

Johnnetta Cole resigned the Spelman presidency in 1997 to become presidential distinguished professor of anthropology, women's studies, and African American studies at Emory University. Cole was succeeded by Dr. Audrey Forbes Manley, M.D., the first Spelman alumna president. Audrey Forbes graduated from Spelman in 1955, and from Meharry Medical College in 1959. She served on Spelman's board of trustees from 1965 to 1967, and married President Albert E. Manley that year. Prior to her selection as Spelman's president, she was deputy surgeon general and acting surgeon general of the United States.

Although it is too soon to record the specific benchmarks of the Audrey Manley years, the early themes of her presidency are similar to those of the Stewart and Cole years: strong support for women's careers in science, advocacy of leadership opportunities for women, and insistence on giving back to one's neighborhood or to some larger community. These themes are reflected in a new long-range plan for the college, approved by the trustees in 2000. Dr. Manley intends to develop partnerships in Africa and in the Caribbean. She hopes the college will continue to gain strength in the sciences, and in August 2000, finished constructing a new $30 million science building.[26]

Looking back, Spelman College has adapted to difficult times, grown stronger, and achieved a visibility and constant purpose which would have been hard to imagine thirty years ago.

XAVIER UNIVERSITY OF LOUISIANA

In 1997, Xavier University of Louisiana enrolled more than 3,500 men and women, three-quarters of whom were undergraduates. During the past fifteen years, it has been one of the fastest growing and most successful of the historically black private colleges. Xavier ranks first in the nation in the number of black students receiving bachelors degrees in the life sciences and the physical sciences. It has educated almost one-quarter of the nation's black pharmacists, and for several years has produced the largest number of successful black matriculants to medical schools of any undergraduate college in the United States. Seventy percent of Xavier applicants to medical schools are accepted, almost twice the national average for all students from all colleges.

"Xavier is an historically Black university with a unique Catholic character," reads its mission statement. "The University's ultimate purpose is the promotion of a more just and humane society. To this end, Xavier prepares its students to assume leadership roles in society. This preparation takes place in a pluralistic setting environment that incorporates all relevant educational means, including teaching, research, and community service."[27]

Xavier's history begins with Katharine Drexel. She was born in Philadelphia in 1858, the daughter of Francis Anthony Drexel, a banker, and one of the wealthiest Catholics in America. From an early age, Katharine and her stepmother, Emma Bouvier Drexel, were active in local charity work. In her late twenties, Katharine became interested in missionary work among poor black and American Indian children, visited Indian reservations, and with the encouragement of Patrick J. Ryan, archbishop of Philadelphia, founded the Order of the Blessed Sacrament for Indians and Negroes. The order, eventually spending an estimated $15 million from Katherine's inheritance, established a boarding school for Pueblo Indians in Santa Fe and a school for black girls in Rock Castle, Virginia.[28] In 1915, Drexel also founded Xavier Preparatory School for black students in New Orleans, and in 1925, obtained a charter for an undergraduate collegiate program. Mother Katherine Drexel was canonized as a saint in the Roman Catholic Church, in Rome, on October 1, 2000. She was the second American-born saint of the Catholic Church.

The Order of the Blessed Sacrament governed Xavier University until 1970, when control was transferred to a lay board of trustees, one-third of whom were to be representatives of the Sisters of the Blessed Sacrament. In a March 1998 interview, Sister Monica Loughlin, president of the Sisters of the Blessed Sacrament (SBS), at the Mother House in Bensalem, Pennsylvania, described the basic teachings which the order from the beginning hoped to instill in all of the students enrolled in SBS schools: individuals are the major factor in social change; underprivileged people should be helped to develop their own leadership; success breeds success; attractive surroundings are important to successful education; individuals have responsibility to contribute to the welfare of others less fortunate; and helping others become independent is preferable to paternalism.[29]

Norman C. Francis became Xavier's first lay president in 1968. A graduate of Xavier and Loyola University Law School in New Orleans, he served in the Army and returned to Xavier in 1957 as dean of men. Ten years later, he was appointed executive vice president, and the next year, president. He was the instigator of a university-wide governance study that outlined how final governing authority might be transferred from the Sisters of the Blessed Sacrament to a lay board at a time when the Sisters made up about a quarter of the university faculty and staff.

Sister M. Juliana Haynes, SBS, assistant professor of music and one of the first Sisters on Xavier's independent board, gives Francis much credit for the smooth transfer of authority, and for the University's leadership stability since then. "Francis internalized the mission of Xavier," she says. "He believes it and he lives it. And he picked senior people to work with him who were like that."[30] Norman Francis himself gives the Sisters major credit both for recognizing the proper time to move toward independence and for meaning it when they said they were letting go. In this special situation, Francis might have tried merely to replace the control that the Sisters were giving up with his own strong personal control. He did not. He understood that Xavier would fare better in the long run if its real leadership included not only trustees and the president, but also faculty and key administrators. The circumstances then did not require him to be "everywhere at once," as they did for Cordell Wynn at Stillman. Instead, he had time to hire senior administrators with great care and to lay out the terms under which he expected to delegate administrative authority so that, for example, the university could continue to operate smoothly whether he was on campus or away from it. In effect, he accepted some loss of presidential authority in the short run, hoping in the long run to raise the general level of commitment to Xavier's mission. Francis commented:

> I saw to it that nothing came to the board without passing through the staff or the appropriate committees. No blindsiding. When I hired key staff people I told them: "I'll never shame you in public; I'll support you and give you credit for your decisions."
>
> I'm proud of the initiative which faculty have taken in the major academic decisions. Faculty did all the program definition work in designing the new science center, for example. And all the Board meetings start with the question: "Should we fire the President?"[31]

Today, Norman Francis has held the top staff office longer than any of the current presidents of historically black colleges. Like many successful college presidents, he also became a national leader in U.S. higher education. In 1983, he co-authored *A Nation at Risk,* a report by the National Commission on Excellence in Education, which called attention to weaknesses in pre-collegiate education. He has chaired the boards of the College Entrance Examination Board, the Educational Testing Service, the American Association of Higher Education, the Southern Education Foundation, and the Southern Association of Colleges and Schools. Respected in New Orleans political circles, he is also founder of a community development corporation that seeks to improve economic opportunity and housing in Xavier University's urban neighborhood.[32]

In 1970, Xavier University enrolled approximately 1,300 undergraduates, almost half of whom majored in the precareer fields of business and education. Among the liberal arts majors, humanities and social sciences students clearly outnumbered those in the natural sciences.[33] In the early

1970s, no more than ten Xavier graduates each year went on to medical schools. Several of these graduates subsequently complained that their science preparation was not what it should have been. A group of Xavier science faculty members decided to do something about this problem. The group included JW Carmichael, a physical chemist, and three biologists: Jacqueline T. Hunter, Sister Grace Mary Flickinger, and Dierdre Dumas Labat. Beginning in 1977, they obtained federal and private foundation support to improve the science preparation of high school students by offering intensive summer science programs. Many of these students later would enroll at Xavier. Some of the money also went to redesign Xavier's entry-level science courses. New courses and special workbooks were developed. These were meant to ensure that Xavier students who arrived at the university with relatively little mathematics and science preparation and with an interest in science would not be left behind. The workbooks contained plain English definitions of scientific terms, and a review of math concepts needed in science courses. A highly structured freshman-year science and math curriculum was organized that would lead to upper class schedules allowing greater freedom. Finally, Xavier faculty noticed that some students were not being monitored closely enough to ensure timely intervention when they encountered difficulty. So students were required to meet weekly with their academic advisors and report their course grades.[34] Each summer, a letter is now sent to each student's home, containing a chart that compares their grades to those of Xavier students who recently obtained admission to graduate schools. In 1998, ninety-five of its seniors went on to medical school, approximately twice the number of first-year black medical students produced by each of its nearest competitors: Howard University, Morehouse College, Spelman College and Harvard College.[35]

JW Carmichael, the first director of the Xavier summer science program for high school students, believes that ensuring excellent preparation in the early years of science training is crucial. In 1990, he told a *New York Times* reporter: "The typical college faculty member sees his job as weeding out kids who come into a science course, in the interest of maintaining quality. I could always drop people from a helicopter into Lake Ponchartrain and see how many drown. But what we do is start from the shore and teach them how to swim."[36]

Carmichael is irreverent about the emphasis on research for faculty in many university science departments. In casual conversation, he appears irreverent about most things, except perhaps the need for proper curriculum structure, faculty cooperation, and relentless follow-up for his science students.[37]

Another view of Xavier's success in science comes from Sister Grace Mary Flickinger, SBS, professor of biology and chair of the university's committee on athletics, who helped launch the revised science programs. Flickinger taught elementary school and high school biology in several eastern cities before coming to Xavier thirty-two years ago:

> The difference between a true scientist and me is that I'm a teacher at heart. I am thrilled when "our own" go forth and succeed—particularly in doctoral study. I think the secret of Xavier's success is that we have maintained competitive standards in the sciences. Then we are cheerleaders and help our students meet the standards. Some will fail, but a large proportion do not.

Flickinger is a plain spoken, strong person. She gives great credit to Carmichael for the driving, competitive energy he generates to improve science at Xavier. By the mid-1990s, more than half of Xavier undergraduates were majoring in one of the natural sciences. She also gives credit to consistent administrative support. "One of our strengths is that Norman Francis is not on an ego trip. Not everyone would adapt to the curmudgeon behavior of JW Carmichael."[38]

One unusual feature of the Xavier University administration is the length of service and continuity of the president's senior officers. Since Francis became president in 1968, three of his top assistants have together served a total of more than eighty years. Xavier's executive vice president, Anthony Rachal, Jr., and its chief development officer, Clarence J. Jupiter, both joined the Francis cabinet in 1968 and retired in 1997. Both were Xavier graduates, active community volunteers, and leaders in their fields outside the University. Rachal served as chief operating officer, often acting for the president in his absence. Jupiter directed Xavier's first two comprehensive capital campaigns, reorganized alumni/ae relations and giving, and helped raise more than $71 million during his development career. Jupiter was a national leader in promoting ethics in collegiate fundraising and a mentor to new development officers in several of the historically black private colleges. Sister Mary Veronica Drawe joined the Xavier faculty as a chemistry teacher in 1946; at her retirement in 1992 she was dean of the university and dean of arts and sciences.[39] The presence of experienced, trusted senior staff both extended the reach of the board and reinforced presidential leadership, enabling Francis to exert national influence, plan, and raise money off-campus without the administration losing its day-to-day focus.

In the years since Norman Francis became president, Xavier has acquired or constructed four major buildings, completed three major building additions, and renovated several old structures. As of June 30, 1999, the Xavier endowment was $27 million, one of the top ten private black colleges endowments, but far less than Spelman's $181 million, and far less per student than those of the leading predominantly white private universities of comparable size. If one examines Xavier's record of enrollment growth, student successes, curriculum change, and financial achievement, it gets extremely high marks. But its most memorable achievement has been its sustained, delegated style of leadership in which faculty, students, trustees and administration for three decades concentrated together on increasingly ambitious goals.

Xavier's recent growth and change raises questions for the future. Can its original combination of rigor and nurturing spirit be maintained and institutionalized, now that the Sisters of the Blessed Sacrament make up less than 5 percent of the faculty, and now that the total student body exceeds three thousand persons? Can the University's success in raising government, corporation, and foundation money—necessary to finance the science expansion—now be balanced with a higher proportion of hard money—tuition and endowment income—in the budget? Without such a rebalancing, it will be hard to raise faculty salaries to the level Francis sees as necessary. These are tough questions, but at least they are questions that come from success rather than mere survival.[40]

The transformation that Xavier—and a number of other private black colleges with strong leadership—underwent in recent decades often has had subtle effects on college life and on the nature of the colleges themselves. Among the greatest changes that these schools will have to face in coming years undoubtedly will be the makeup of the student body. Most historically black colleges, asked to describe their distinctiveness, will note two strands of their history: their demonstrated record of producing black American leadership in American society, and their willingness to educate young men and women who have relatively weak high school preparation for college. Now that some of these colleges have achieved sufficient recruitment success to become selective, however, their traditional admissions policies are being reconsidered and sometimes redefined. Table 9.3 describes for each of the three case-history colleges the percentage of entering freshmen with less than a 3.0 high school grade average, and also the verbal SAT score marking the boundary between the two bottom quartiles of the freshman class. On these measures, Xavier has proved more open to students who need extra early help with writing and study skills than Spelman College. In turn, both Xavier and Spelman have been much more selective than Stillman College.

Another aspect of selection policy is to determine what balance to seek between homogeneity and diversity of racial and ethnic background. All historically black colleges emphasize that they do not discriminate against any group, but they do not naturally draw many white applicants, and few of the colleges actively solicit them. Of the three colleges in this chapter, Xavier has most actively attracted non-black students. The attraction for white Americans probably began at the professional and gradu-

TABLE 9.3

Risk Tolerance at Spelman, Xavier, and Stillman, 1995

	Spelman College	Xavier University of Louisiana	Stillman College
Percentage of 1995 freshmen with a high school GPA less than 3.0	15	48	84
Verbal Scholastic Aptitude Test score marking the top of the bottom quartile of entering freshmen	410	370	360
Percentage of black high school seniors who took the SAT and scored higher than the bottom quartile	29	37	41
Percentage of applicants admitted	47	84	43

Source: College Entrance Examination Board, *The College Handbook* 1977, pp. 211, 490, 696.

Note: Stillman College provided American College Testing (ACT) data instead of SAT scores; the ACT bottom quartile boundary on the English section of the test was converted to a VSAT equivalent.

*The verbal test score distribution for black senior high-school test takers for 1995 was provided by the College Board. There were 103,872 such test takers that year.

ate level. For example, since 1965, Xavier has been New Orleans' only licensed college of pharmacy. Table 9.4 illustrates the diversity of Xavier enrollment.[41]

What, then, are the important points to take away from these three stories? The most obvious lesson is that they happened and that they are hardly the only such stories that might be recounted. These three colleges illustrate the power of sustained, focused leadership, in a difficult period for all nonprofit institutions. The record is particularly impressive when one remembers that these colleges often were dealing with students who lacked the advantage either of wealth or of excellent prior schooling. Leadership is, of course, easiest to write about if it seems to be one-person leadership. But in all three of these success stories a much broader, not purely presidential definition of initiative and leadership is needed to account for what went so well for so long. Certainly the presidents were at the center of action, but they could not control all of it and they understood that.

TABLE 9.4

Xavier University Enrollment, Classified by Racial and Ethnic Status, Fall 1996

Racial or Ethnic Group	Undergraduate Enrollment	Other*	Total Enrollment	Percentage of Total Enrollment
Black/black American	2,523	610	3,133	88.8
White (non-Hispanic)	16	180	196	5.6
Asian	26	50	76	2.2
Hispanic	9	11	20	0.6
Nonresident alien	41	38	79	2.2
Ethnicity unknown	9	13	22	0.6
Totals	2,624	902	3,526	100.0

Source: Xavier University of Louisiana, *University Profile.*
*Mainly graduate studies and pharmacy.

What about the role of luck in these three cases? Luck is part of the chapter title, but is hard to identify specifically. The three cases were selected partly because they turned out well, aided, obviously, by strong leadership. One can only speculate what their stories might have been in the face of greater misfortune. One obvious feature of these three cases is that all six presidents (Wynn, McNealey, Stewart, Cole, Manley, and Francis) enjoyed constant good health. All lasted through an unbroken succession of long work days. But only in some cases would the existing administrative structures have lasted successfully through prolonged presidential illness. Perhaps the depression-free economy of the 1980s and 1990s could be identified as a large piece of good luck. These decades were characterized by relatively low inflation, favorable capital markets, and despite strong attempts to dismantle it in the early 1980s, a constant flow of federal student aid and targeted subsidies to historically black public and private colleges. The financial climate provided an underpinning for good leadership to achieve good results that was absent, for example, in the 1930s. That said, the most consistent companion of long-term institutional success, however one chooses to measure it, still appears to be sustained, focused, and competent leadership.

CHAPTER 10

The Graduates

RELATIVELY LITTLE has been published that sums up the importance of undergraduate black colleges and other colleges as pathways to black American leadership in business, government, and the professions. As it turns out, historically black colleges have proved to be far more important pathways to leadership than is generally recognized. The record, assembled from a variety of sources, is a remarkable one, and gives powerful evidence for that claim.

This observation in no way overshadows other broad but less favorable observations about the condition of race relations in the United States. Although most racial and ethnic minority group members are found in increasing numbers in the leading professions, as a rule they are still underrepresented in those ranks, and generally in colleges and graduate schools. Asian Americans provide an exception. Minority underrepresentation is even more pronounced in corporate hierarchies, with minorities becoming rarer the higher one moves up the corporate ladder. Minority underrepresentation is all the more troubling because a gap has been growing during the past twenty years in earnings and presumably in economic opportunity between college-educated persons and those with only a high school education or less.[1] One of the nation's most demanding long-term political and economic questions today is what strategy, if any, government should follow to prevent this gap from becoming larger and thus to reduce the distance between the haves and the have nots.

For those who prefer personal anecdotes to columns of figures and percentages, this chapter and the following one may act like speed bumps in a roadway, but those with the patience to sort through the numbers will be rewarded with a fascinating tale. Analysis of the statistical surveys offers a compelling and consistent picture. The tables presented here confirm that black colleges paved the way, when other paths were blocked, for the formation of a college-educated black middle class, and for the training of a larger-than-proportional share of today's top black leadership in American business, government, and the professions.

Two types of national data sources made it possible to examine the careers of graduates of both private and public black colleges. One type of data indicates the undergraduate colleges attended by black Americans who have achieved distinction in their careers. Such individuals are often identified well past the middle of their careers. Typically, recent data show that they received their bachelors degrees during the 1960s, with a smaller but significant number graduating in the two decades immediately before or after that decade. This pattern of college graduation partially overlaps the 1970s, when predominantly white colleges and universities began intense recruitment of the ablest black high school students. Data sources for specific career distinctions include the following:

Measure of Career Distinction	Source[2]
Leaders in ten U.S. cities	Who's Who Among African Americans (1998–99)
Lawyers	Who's Who Among African Americans (1998–99)
Generals and Admirals in the U.S. military services	Who's Who Among African Americans (1998–99)
Senior U.S. officials in the executive branch, 1998	Journal of Blacks in Higher Education, Spring 1998
Recipients of MacArthur Fellowships (1981–98)	Journal of Blacks in Higher Education, Summer 1998

The second type of data show the undergraduate college attended by current recipients of Ph.D.s and also by first-year medical students. These records permit a glimpse of how black American college graduates of the 1980s and 1990s are beginning to contribute to these two professional groups. In the future it may be possible to extend this review to include new graduate degree holders in business, law, and other fields. However, those undergraduate collegiate origins have not yet been recorded by any national data source. No local or statewide sampling was attempted for this study.

CAREER DISTINCTION

The largest single data source for classifying the collegiate origins of distinguished black Americans is *Who's Who Among African Americans (1998–99)*. Because the judgment of who is distinguished and who is not is often subjective, the tables derived from this source should be regarded as rough indicators, even though they show percentage estimates that suggest precision. Most readers of any *Who's Who* listing can think of individuals who should have been included but were not, and this particular list is no exception. But there is no reason to believe that the editors biased their choices in favor of those who attended a particular type of college. As a result, this publicly available listing of black Americans, compiled by a competent black American selection panel, seems well suited for our purposes.[3]

Table 10.1 summarizes the collegiate origins of black Americans in ten selected U.S. cities who appear in *Who's Who Among African Americans*. It indicates that historically black public and private colleges have contributed a substantial proportion of black American leadership in American cities. The percentage of individuals who attended such colleges ranges from 20 percent in New York City to more than 60 percent in Atlanta and Nashville. Private black colleges alone contributed between a quarter and a half of the leadership identified in *Who's Who* for four of the ten selected cities: Charlotte, Atlanta, New Orleans, and Washington, D.C. If we compare the cities in the table with the list of forty private colleges given in Chapter 1, we see that such southern cities as Atlanta,

TABLE 10.1

Black American Leadership in Ten Selected Cities (1998), Classified by Type of Undergraduate College Attended

City	*Percentage Who Received Bachelors Degrees at Historically Black Private Colleges*	*Percentage Who Received Bachelors Degrees at Historically Black Public Colleges*	*Percentage Who Did Not Receive a Bachelors Degree from a Historically Black Private or Public College*
Atlanta, Georgia	46	15	39
Charlotte, North Carolina	26	21	53
Chicago, Illinois	14	10	76
Dallas, Texas	13	20	67
Los Angeles, California	15	9	76
Minneapolis/Saint Paul, Minnesota	15	10	75
Nashville, Tennessee	36	29	35
New Orleans, Louisiana	31	24	45
New York, New York	11	9	80
Washington, D.C.	32	17	51

Source: Shirelle Phelps, ed. *Who's Who Among African Americans (1998–99)* (Detroit: Gale Research, 1998).

Note: The tabulation of graduates in this table includes alumni of Howard University. The percentages represent a tabulation of college origins of all persons in *Who's Who Among Africans* who are included in the city listings for these cities.

Nashville, and Washington, D.C., have at least one well-known private black college. In the northern cities that do not contain any of these colleges, often one or two local institutions contribute a large cadre of local black American leaders: Roosevelt University in Chicago, and City University of New York (CUNY) in New York City.

Although the percentages in Table 10.1 concerning city leadership cadres may speak for themselves, is there any other benchmark to further establish their significance? One approach is to inquire what proportion of all bachelors degrees going to black Americans was awarded at historically black private and public colleges in the appropriate comparison years. The federal government did not record and classify degrees awarded by the race of the recipient until the mid-1970s. The individuals included in Table 10.1, however, typically received bachelors degrees in the mid-1960s. In 1977, when race-specific statistics were first available, 12.3 percent of bachelors degrees granted to black Americans were awarded at historically black private colleges, and 23.7 percent at historically black public colleges. By 1996, the percentages were 10.4 percent and 18.9 percent, respectively. Although the number of bachelors degrees awarded by historically black colleges had actually increased, those awarded to black American graduates at predominantly white colleges had grown at a faster rate.

The percentage of black American bachelors degrees accounted for by historically black colleges in the mid-1960s might reasonably be estimated at about 15 percent for private black colleges, and 30 percent for black public colleges.[4] Because the contribution of historically black colleges to black American urban leadership generally lies above these percentages in cities across the United States, and especially so in southeastern cities where historically black colleges are present or close by, this contribution is disproportionately high.

Table 10.2 shows the collegiate origins for black American lawyers, admirals, and generals. Approximately one-third of the lawyers on the list and two-thirds of the flag-rank military officers received bachelor's degrees at historically black colleges. The private colleges accounted for 20 percent of the lawyers and 30 percent of the admirals and generals.

Table 10.3 indicates the collegiate origins of forty-nine senior black American federal executive-branch appointees in the Clinton administration. Fifteen of these (31 percent) received bachelors degrees from private black colleges, and five individuals (10 percent) graduated from black public colleges. The remaining twenty-nine officials graduated from twenty-four different predominantly white undergraduate colleges —sixteen private and eight public.

Table 10.4 shows that of sixty black American recipients of MacArthur Foundation grants (so-called "genius awards") between 1981 and 1998,

TABLE 10.2

Distinguished Black American Lawyers and U.S. Military Leaders Who
Graduated from Historically Black Colleges

	Percentage Who Received Bachelors Degrees at Historically Black Private Colleges	Percentage Who Received Bachelors Degrees at Historically Black Public Colleges	Percentage Who Graduated from Other Colleges
Lawyers	20	15	65
Admirals and generals	30	33	37

Source: Phelps, ed., *Who's Who Among African Americans.*

eleven, or 18 percent, attended private black colleges, one attended a black public college, thirty-two attended predominantly white colleges, and sixteen did not attend college.[5]

Finally, Table 10.5 summarizes this chapter's five-part survey of the collegiate origins of distinguished mid-career black Americans. In each of the professions listed and in most of the selected cities, the number of private black college graduates equaled or exceeded the share estimated by calculating what percentage of all black American bachelors degrees were awarded in such colleges in the years from just prior to the *Brown* decision to the mid-1970s. We have noted that these black colleges throughout this period paid lower salaries to faculty and staff than did their predominantly white counterparts, and operated on smaller budgets in older and less well-equipped buildings. If one takes into account these operating conditions, the record of their graduates becomes even more remarkable.

MEDICAL STUDENTS AND RESEARCH DOCTORATES

The college enrollment patterns of black students have changed in the past thirty years. A much higher proportion of these students study at predominantly white colleges and universities today than was true in the 1970s. Have not most of the future black professionals, then, decided to go north and west today, to study at flagship public universities and selective private colleges? Certainly some have.

Statistics are available for two major areas of graduate study. The Association of American Medical Colleges tracks the race and collegiate origins of students entering medical school. The Doctorate Records file of the National Academy of Sciences does the same for recipients of

TABLE 10.3

Collegiate Origins of Forty-Nine Senior Black American Officials in the U.S. Federal Executive Branch, 1998

Executive	Position	Undergraduate Degree	Graduate Degree
	Graduates of Historically Black Private Colleges		
Anderson, Bernard E.	Assistant secretary, Employment Standards Administration	A.B., Livingstone College	M.A., Michigan State University; Ph.D., University of Pennsylvania
Argrett, Loretta G.	Assistant attorney general, Tax Division	B.S., Howard University	J.D., Harvard Law School
Baquet III, Charles R.	Deputy director, Peace Corps	B.A., Xavier University of Louisiana	M.S., Syracuse University
Berry, Mary Frances	Chairman, U.S. Commission on Civil Rights	B.A., Howard University	Ph.D., Howard University, J.D., University of Michigan
Coleman, Rodney	Assistant secretary, Manpower Affairs, Department of the Air Force	A.B. Howard University	—
Herman, Alexis M.	Secretary of Labor	B.A., Xavier University of Louisiana	—
Hunt, Jr., Isaac C.	Commissioner, Securities and Exchange Commission	B.A., Fisk University	LL.B., University of Virginia School of Law
Lyles, Lester L.	Director, Ballistic Missile Defense Organization	B.S., Howard University	M.S., New Mexico State University
Mallett, Robert L.	Deputy secretary, Department of Commerce	B.A., Morehouse College	J.D., Harvard Law School

Name	Position	Degrees	
Robinson, June M.	Director, Small Business Programs, Department of Labor	B.S., Howard University	M.S., Southern Illinois University
Satcher, David	Assistant secretary of Health and Surgeon General	B.S., Morehouse College	M.D. and Ph.D., Case Western Reserve University
Stanton, Robert G.	Director, National Parks Service	B.S., Huston-Tillotson College	—
Watkins, Dayton J.	Administrator, Rural Business Cooperative Services	B.A., Howard University; B.A., University of Maryland	M.A., Central Michigan University; MBA, Mount Vernon College
West, Jr., Togo D.	Secretary of the Army	B.S., Howard University	J.D., Howard University
Winston, Judith	General counsel, Department of Education	B.A., Howard University	J.D., Georgetown University

Graduates of Historically Black Public Colleges

Name	Position	Degrees	
Brickhouse, Eugene A.	Assistant secretary for Human Resources, Department of the Army	B.S., Virginia State University	M.A., University of Texas, San Antonio
Holmes, James	Director, Census Bureau	B.A., Albany State College	—
Mastern, Charles C.	Inspector general, Department of Labor	B.S., Albany State College	M.A., University of Arkansas
Nash, Robert J.	Assistant to the president and director of presidential personnel	University of Arkansas, Pine Bluff	M.A., Howard University
Watkins, Shirley R.	Undersecretary of Agriculture	University of Arkansas, Pine Bluff	M.Ed., University of Memphis

(continued on the next page)

TABLE 10.3 *(Continued)*

Collegiate Origins of Forty-Nine Senior Black American Officials in the U.S. Federal Executive Branch, 1998

Executive	Position	Undergraduate Degree	Graduate Degree
	Graduates of Other Undergraduate Colleges*		
	Undergraduate Colleges Represented:		
	University of Arkansas (2)	Oakland University	
	Massachusetts Inst. of Technology (2)	University of Pennsylvania	
	Michigan State University (2)	Rutgers University	
	Northwestern University (2)	Smith College	
	Stanford University (2)	Swarthmore College	
	Amherst College	Syracuse University	
	Baker University	Temple University	
	University of California, Berkeley	University of Virginia	
	University of Colorado	Wellesley College	
	Columbia University	Williams College	
	Harvard University	University of Wisconsin, Madison	
	Eastern Michigan University	Yale University	

Source: Journal of Blacks in Higher Education, Spring 1998, pp. 58, 59.

Note: Due to the difficulty of identifying black Americans in some U.S. government departments and due to personnel turnover, this list should not be considered comprehensive.

*Graduates not listed individually.

TABLE 10.4
Sixty MacArthur Foundation "Genius Grant" Awards to Black Americans
(1981–98)

Grantee	College Attended	Field of Endeavor
Graduates of Historically Black Private Colleges		
Avery, Byllye Y.	Talladega College	Public affairs
Edelman, Marian Wright	Spelman College	Public affairs
Holt, Thomas Cleveland	Howard University	History
Hopkins, Donald	Morehouse College	Medicine
King, Calvin R.	Philander Smith College	Public affairs
McLoyd, Vonnie C.	Talladega College	Psychology
McPherson, James A.	Morris Brown College	Fiction writing
Reagon, Bernice Johnson	Spelman College	Music
Scott, John T.	Xavier University of Louisiana	Visual arts
Shirley, Aaron	Tougaloo College	Medicine
Wilson, William Julius	Wilberforce University	Sociology
Graduates of Historically Black Public Colleges		
Woodson, Robert L.	Cheyney State University	Public Affairs
Graduates of Other Colleges*		

Undergraduate Colleges Represented:

American University (Cairo)	University of Illinois
Antioch	Southern Illinois University
Atlanta College of Art	Judson College
Auburn University	State University of New York (Buffalo)
Brooklyn College	Oberlin College
Beaver College	Otis Art Institute
Bowling Green University	University of Pennsylvania
University of California (Berkeley)	Pepperdine University
University of California (Los Angeles)	University of Pittsburgh
Catholic University	Radcliffe College
Cornell University (2)	University of San Francisco (2)
Eastern College	Swarthmore College
Emerson College	Washburn University
Hamilton College	University of the West Indies
Harvard University	Yale University

Source: *Journal of Blacks in Higher Education,* Summer 1998, New York, p. 31.
Note: Sixteen winners of MacArthur awards did not attend college.
*Graduates not listed individually.

research doctorates. These records show that private black colleges for many years were seedbeds for black physicians-to-be, and that recently they have become even more productive—more productive than they were in the mid-1970s, and consistently more productive than the predominantly white colleges on average. With respect to research docto-

TABLE 10.5
Summary of Collegiate Origins for Selected Careers of Distinguished Black Americans

Achievement or Award	Percentage of Achievers with Bachelors Degrees from Historically Black Private Colleges	Percentage of Achievers with Bachelors Degrees from Historically Black Public Colleges
Bachelors degree recipient:		
Mid-1960s	15	30
Mid-1970s	12–13	24
Mid-1990s	10	19
Listed in *Who's Who Among African Americans* (1998–99) in ten selected cities:		
Atlanta	46	15
Charlotte	26	21
Chicago	14	10
Dallas	13	20
Los Angeles	15	9
Minneapolis/St. Paul	15	10
Nashville	36	29
New Orleans	31	24
New York	11	9
Washington, D.C.	32	17
Lawyers listed in *Who's Who Among African Americans* (1998–99)	20	15
Admirals and generals in *Who's Who Among African Americans* (1998–99)	30	33
Senior officials in the Clinton Administration	31	10
Winners of MacArthur "Genius Grants"	18	2

Note: This table summarizes the separate surveys that were discussed in detail in this chapter, and summarizes Tables 10.1 through 10.4.

rates, however, private black colleges in 1996 accounted for only half as many black Ph.D.s and Ed.D.s per hundred bachelors degrees as was true for predominantly white colleges; this represents a decline by private black colleges from a position of above-average productivity twenty years earlier. We now outline the basic trends in the collegiate origins of black medical students and black doctorate recipients, and then derive the rough productivity indices, mentioned above, for three college sectors: private black colleges, public black colleges, and all students in predominantly white colleges.

Table 10.6 shows the undergraduate college origins of black first-year students in U.S. medical schools for 1978 and 1997. These first-year

TABLE 10.6

Collegiate Origins of Black Entering Students in U.S. Medical Schools, 1997 versus 1978

	1997		1978	
Baccalaureate Sources of Black Entering Students	*Number of Students*	*Percentage of All Black Entrants*	*Number of Students*	*Percentage of All Black Entrants*
Historically black private colleges	222	20	149	16
Historically black public colleges	74	7	78	8
Other colleges	837	73	711	76
Total blacks American entrants	1,133	100	938	100
All other entrants	15,032		15,116	
Total medical school entrants	16,165		16,054	
Black Americans as a percentage of all entering medical school students		7.0		5.8
Graduates of historically black private colleges as a percentage of all entering medical students		1.4		0.9

Source: Association of American Medical Colleges, Student and Applicant Information Management System (SAIMS) database system (Washington, D.C., 1997 and 1978).

Note: SAIMS database shows collegiate origins of matriculants, classified by race/ethnicity of students. Black students who are resident U.S. citizens are grouped with African and other black students. American citizens make up more than 90 percent of the totals.

classes each contained slightly more than 16,000 students of all races. Black students made up 5.8 percent of the total in 1978, and 7.0 percent in 1997. Among black first-year medical students, those from historically black private colleges made up 16 percent of the total in 1978 and 20 percent in 1997—or more than double their proportionate share when compared with the percentage of black bachelors degrees awarded by those colleges. The recent performance of these private colleges is even more impressive if one adjusts for the size of different student population pools. We can create a rough productivity index by dividing the number of bachelors degrees awarded by a particular group of colleges into the number of medical school matriculants from that group of colleges in the following year. Table 10.7 indicates how many medical school matriculants there were per thousand bachelors degrees in 1978 and 1997 from private black colleges, black public colleges, and students of all races in all four-year colleges. Viewed this way, the private black colleges are a particularly productive college sector for health professionals, and during the past twenty years have become more so. In 1997, medical schools enrolled twenty-five graduates of private black colleges per thousand graduates of those colleges, but only fourteen medical students per thousand came from graduates of all races of all four-year undergraduate colleges. It should be remembered that only relatively small numbers of historically black college students are involved, and even smaller numbers of colleges. For example, if we repeat the calculation but omit the largest single-school contribution (from Xavier University), the private black college sector then would yield sixteen medical school entrants per thousand bachelors degrees, a much lower figure that is still slightly above the national average.

In national terms, the annual number of research doctorates awarded to black Americans is not large. Black Americans are less well-represented at the doctoral level than at any other degree level in higher education.[6] In 1996, black Americans received 3.5 percent of doctoral degrees, 6.0 percent of masters degrees, 7.7 percent of bachelors degrees, and 9.2

TABLE 10.7
Collegiate Productivity Index for Medical Students

Year	Black Students from Private Black Colleges	Black Students from Public Black Colleges	All Students from All Four-Year Colleges
1978	21	6	17
1997	25	5	14

Note: Table entries indicate number of students entering medical school per 1,000 B.A. graduates for each collegiate sector listed.

percent of associate degrees. For that year they represented 11.3 percent of full-time, first-time freshmen in four-year colleges and 14.3 percent of the eighteen- to twenty-four-year-old population.

Table 10.8 shows the percentage of black research doctorates in 1977, 1987 and 1996 who earned bachelors degrees at private black and black public colleges. The total number of doctoral degrees received by black Americans declined in the 1980s and then increased in the 1990s. The contribution of historically black private and public colleges, although still significant, declined by the end of this period. In 1978, private black and public colleges together produced 44 percent of all the black graduates who received doctorates that year; in 1996, those colleges produced 21 percent. One obvious reason for this decrease was that a larger percentage of black undergraduates were receiving bachelors degrees from predominantly white institutions.

Table 10.9 shows the same kind of rough productivity index for the production of research doctorates by historically black colleges as did Table 10.7 for medical students. For doctoral studies, the numbers for all four-year colleges have not changed much between 1977 and 1996, whereas those for historically black colleges decreased. In a speech on June 7, 1999, Antoine M. Garibaldi, then provost and chief academic officer of Howard University, noted that although black Americans are underrepresented compared with the general population in terms of receiving Ph.D.s and Ed.D.s, the historically black public and private

TABLE 10.8

Collegiate Origins of Black American Recipients of Research Doctorates, 1977–96, Selected Years

		Number of Black American Doctorates		
Year Doctorate Received	Total Number of Black American Research Doctorates	Who Received Bachelors Degrees at Private Black Colleges (percent)	Who Received Bachelors Degrees at Public Black Colleges (percent)	Who Received Bachelors Degrees at Other Colleges (percent)
1977	1,450	275 (19%)	370 (25%)	805 (56%)
1987	1,221	162 (13%)	195 (16%)	864 (71%)
1996	1,837	169 (9%)	223 (12%)	1,445 (79%)

Source: National Science Foundation Web CASPAR Database System, Doctorate Records File.

Note: Analysis performed by Kimberley C. Edelin, Research Scientist, Frederick D. Patterson Research Institute of the United Negro College Fund, Fairfax, Virginia. Total U.S. research doctorates in these years were: 31,716 (1977), 23,370 (1987), and 42,415 (1996).

TABLE 10.9

Collegiate Productivity Index for Research Doctorates

Year	Black Students from Private Black Colleges	Black Students from Public Black Colleges	All Students from All Four-Year Colleges
1977	38	27	34
1987	27	19	33
1996	18	14	36

Sources: Table 10.8; Nettles, Perna and Freeman, *Two Decades of Progress,* Table 14.

Note: Table entries indicate number of research doctorates per 1,000 B.A. graduates for each collegiate sector listed.

colleges remain a concentrated source of candidates. If we rank U.S. colleges and universities in order of the number of their black bachelor-degree recipients who went on to earn doctorates between 1991 and 1995, nine of the top ten producers in the United States are still historically black institutions.[7]

One of the frustrating results of quantitative analysis is that it usually suggests worthwhile questions that are left unanswered. For example, comparing the tables on medical students and research doctorates, raises the question of why black Americans' pursuit of research doctorates has dropped so sharply during the past two decades, whereas their pursuit of medical degrees increased slightly. Were black students particularly attuned to the nation's economic signals, which for many of these years indicated difficulty in obtaining tenure-track university appointments, compared with continued opportunity and good earnings in medicine? Was the behavior of graduate schools of arts and science different from that of medical schools with respect to admission and retention of minority students? Or were other factors at work?

Why do public black colleges consistently send more students than private black colleges on to research doctoral study, whereas the private colleges consistently send larger delegations to medical school? This might be because historically black public universities offer Ph.D. programs in many fields, but only two private institutions, Howard University and Atlanta University, produced significant numbers of Ph.D.s in many fields in the past twenty years.[8] In contrast, the major historically black medical schools—Howard, Meharry, and Morehouse—are private institutions. However, graduates of both public and private colleges often seek graduate training at predominantly white universities, and so these speculations, even if correct, give only a partial answer.

Whatever may be the full answers to these questions, regional accrediting agencies increasingly ask during their periodic visits: Do the career patterns of your graduates indicate your educational program gave them a worthwhile start? Legislators who consider whether continued institutional subsidy is merited may ask similar questions. For historically black colleges, the answer to such questions is quite clear. Its graduates of past years, and today, create a competitive aggregate record by the most demanding measures in common use.

CHAPTER 11

The Students

WHAT CAN STUDENT opinion and attitude surveys, taken over several decades, tell us about the changing generations of students at private black colleges? How do these opinions and attitudes differ from those of students at other private colleges? Since 1966, Professor Alexander W. Astin and his colleagues at the Higher Education Research Institute (HERI) at the University of California, Los Angeles, have conducted an annual survey of the backgrounds, attitudes, and ambitions of college freshmen. In selected years, HERI also conducted follow-up surveys of freshman cohorts. These Annual Freshman Surveys elicit responses from more than 250,000 freshmen each year. Participating colleges represent the major sectors of postsecondary education, including historically black four-year private colleges and historically black four-year public colleges. The size, design, and continuity of this survey program permits examination of changes in freshman profiles over nearly three decades, and also permits comparisons among the different educational sectors. Dr. Linda J. Sax and William S. Korn separated replies from black freshmen so that responses from three sectors are compared for this chapter: black freshmen at black four-year private colleges, black freshmen at black four-year public colleges, and black freshmen at other (non-black) four-year colleges. These replies, in turn, are compared with those from all entering freshmen at private four-year colleges.[1]

In most respects, black freshmen, no matter what type of college they attend, respond to the Annual Freshman Survey in ways similar to students of other races. Although there are differences, a typical freshman, black or white, is likely to be eighteen or nineteen years old, thinks of herself or himself as politically moderate, plans to major in something, as well as do volunteer or paid work, wants to prepare for a career in business or one of the professions, expects to make at least an adequate living, and eventually to raise a family. That said, there are distinct differences in response patterns. For example, a higher proportion of freshmen at private black colleges, when compared with freshmen at other four-year private colleges, say they intend to pursue advanced degrees, be authorities in their field of choice, be successful in their own businesses, be community leaders, and help others in difficulty. They appear to understand that meeting these goals will demand extra effort. These students also state with greater-than-average frequency that they need remedial college work in mathematics, science, and foreign languages. Rather than describe all the statistical similarities and differences, we highlight the main ones, and then provide summary tables.

Black undergraduates make up about 95 percent of the student body in private black colleges, compared with 83 percent at black public colleges, and 11 percent at all four-year private colleges.[2] Approximately 55 percent of the students in four-year private colleges in the United States are women, compared with 60 percent for historically black public colleges and for private black colleges. Three-quarters of all black freshmen associate themselves with one of the major Protestant religions, Baptists contributing more than half that total. In four-year private colleges generally, less than half of freshmen are Protestant, but more than one-third are Roman Catholic, compared with less than 10 percent of black freshmen.[3]

HIGH SCHOOL GRADES AND TEST SCORES

Based on conventional measures of preparation for college, a higher percentage of Latinos and black Americans come to college with weak preparation than do white Americans and Asian Americans. In 1997, the College Board reported the following percentages of below-median scores for the 1,067,993 high school students taking the Scholastic Assessment Test (SAT):

Percentage of Group Scoring below the National Median (Verbal Score)[4]

White American	45
Asian American	55
Latino	69
Black American	78

Table 11.1 provides self-reported high school grades in the Annual Freshman Surveys of 1975 and 1995. A higher percentage of all students in four-year private colleges reported high school grades of B+ or higher than did black freshmen attending all types of colleges. Reported high school grades in all populations and types of colleges have improved significantly during the past two decades. This is generally attributed to grade inflation in schools and colleges, but other reasons may also contribute. Whatever the reasons for high school grade improvement, there is less difference now than twenty years ago between the high school grades reported by black college freshmen and by all freshmen in four-year private colleges. In the 1995 the Cooperative Institutional Research Program (CIRP) survey, freshmen estimated where they thought they

TABLE 11.1

Annual Freshman Surveys, 1975 versus 1995: Percentage of Students Who
Received Average Grades of B+ or Higher in High School

Year	Percentage Black Freshmen at Black Private Four-Year Colleges	Percentage Black Freshmen at Black Public Four-Year Colleges	Percentage Black Freshmen at Other Four-Year Colleges	Percentage All Freshmen at Four-Year Private Colleges
1975	25	19	37	48
1995	41	25	50	58

Source: Annual Freshman Survey database, 1975 and 1995, Higher Education Research Institute, UCLA.

Note: In the Annual Freshman Survey Reports (see Linda J. Sax, Alexander W. Astin, William S. Korn, Kathryn M. Mahoney, *The American Freshman, National Norms for Fall 1998* [Los Angeles: Cooperative Institutional Research Program, 1998]), Apppendix A discusses research methodology and Appendix E comments on confidence intervals and the precision of the normative data. In this table, for example, the survey authors calculate that the confidence interval for black freshmen at private black four-year colleges is no larger than plus or minus 2.0 percent, if one wihses to be 95 percent confident that the true result is within the stated band. In other words the actual percentage of black freshmen at four-year private black colleges who received average high school grades of B+ or higher in 1995, reported here as 41 percent, should fall between 39 and 43 percent of all such freshmen.

needed remedial work and tended to confirm the pattern described above (Table 11.2).

OCCUPATION AND INCOME OF PARENTS

Tables 11.3 and 11.4 track the recent rapid growth of the black middle class. Occupations and levels of formal education attained by parents of black freshmen were sharply different from those of the parents of white freshmen in 1971. By 1995, the patterns had become quite similar. By 1995, the majority of parents of freshmen in all four-year private colleges had graduated from college or graduate school, and most of the mothers no longer were full-time homemakers. Much greater change occurred between 1971 and 1995 in the education and occupation patterns for the parents of black freshmen. Levels of formal education and professional attainment are reported slightly higher for parents of freshmen at private black colleges than for parents of black freshmen at predominantly white colleges. Both groups reported higher levels of formal education than parents of freshmen at black public colleges.

The private black colleges also attract freshmen who are noticeably more willing to travel a long way to college than most other freshmen.

TABLE 11.2

Freshmen Who Estimate They Need Remedial College Work in Particular Subjects

Remedial Subject	Percentage Black Freshmen at Black Private Four-Year Colleges	Percentage Black Freshmen at Black Public Four-Year Colleges	Percentage Black Freshmen at Other Four-Year Private Colleges	Percentage All Freshmen at Four-Year Private Colleges
English	14	19	17	10
Reading	7	8	7	4
Mathematics	44	48	42	22
Social studies	6	10	7	3
Science	22	20	22	10
Foreign language	27	23	22	11

Source: Annual Freshman Survey database, 1995, Higher Education Research Institute, ULCA.

Table 11.5 indicates that 43 percent of private black college freshmen said they traveled more than five hundred miles to college in 1995, more than twice the percentage reported by other groups. However, these long-distance travelers are not distributed evenly among private black colleges. Morehouse, Spelman, Fisk, and Tuskegee are among those which draw 70 percent or more of their students from outside their home states. In contrast, such colleges as LeMoyne-Owen, Florida Memorial College, and Jarvis Christian concentrate on serving a local or regional clientele, and typically enroll only about 15 percent of their students from outside their home states.[5]

Changing family income patterns among black freshmen appear consistent with the changing occupational and formal education patterns of their parents. Three tables showing family incomes (Tables 11.6 through 11.8) compare the family incomes of black freshmen with those of all black families and of all U.S. families in selected years between 1971 and 1995. Each table records family income comparisons at different percentile levels: median, top 25 percent (75th percentile), and bottom third. Self-reported income levels—such as the CIRP Annual Freshman Survey data—may well be less reliable than national census data. This means that although the reported percentages for black freshmen may not be accurate, any data biases are likely to persist in a consistent way so that the trends illustrated remain valid.

These tables show that all U.S. families, on average, have higher income than black families in the years between 1971 and 1995. However,

TABLE 11.3
Mother's Education and Occupation

	Percentage Black Freshmen at Black Private Four-Year Colleges		Percentage Black Freshmen at Black Public Four-Year Colleges		Percentage Black Freshmen at Other Four-Year Colleges		Percentage All Freshmen at Four-Year Private Colleges	
	1971	1995	1971	1995	1971	1995	1971	1995
Mother's education								
Some high school (or less)	30	7	43	12	34	10	12	7
High school graduate	30	24	32	34	36	30	39	26
Some college	15	22	12	20	16	23	20	15
College degree (and possibly some graduate school)	16	28	10	23	9	24	23	29
Graduate degree	9	19	3	11	5	13	6	23
Mother's occupation								
Business woman	3	16	2	12	3	13	5	13
Business (clerical)	5	7	3	7	6	7	8	8
School teacher	18	19	11	16	9	19	9	17
Homemaker (full time)	30	5	34	4	37	5	54	13
Nurse	6	8	6	10	7	8	5	9
Labor (semiskilled or unskilled)	9	3	14	6	11	3	3	3
Unemployed	5	5	5	8	6	5	3	5
Other	24	37	25	37	21	40	13	32

Source: Annual Freshman Survey database, 1971 and 1975, Higher Education Research Institute, UCLA.

TABLE 11.4
Father's Education and Occupation

	Percentage Black Freshmen at Black Private Four-Year Colleges		Percentage Black Freshmen at Black Public Four-Year Colleges		Percentage Black Freshmen at Other Four-Year Colleges		Percentage All Freshmen at Four-Year Private Colleges	
	1971	1995	1971	1995	1971	1995	1971	1995
Father's education								
Some high school (or less)	39	11	57	15	43	13	16	7
High school graduate	27	28	24	40	29	32	25	26
Some college	11	18	9	19	14	20	17	15
College degree (and possibly some graduate school)	11	24	7	18	9	21	25	29
Graduate degree	10	19	3	8	5	14	17	23
Father's occupation								
Businessman	9	18	7	13	9	16	37	30
College teacher	1	1	–	–	1	1	1	1
Doctor or dentist	2	3	–	–	1	2	4	3
School teacher	6	5	4	5	3	4	3	8
Lawyer	1	2	–	1	1	1	2	3
Engineer	3	6	2	5	3	6	7	7
Career military	3	4	3	5	3	4	1	1
Farmer, forester	3	–	7	1	2	–	4	2
Skilled worker	13	8	13	11	14	9	9	8
Laborer (semiskilled or unskilled)	23	8	32	11	32	10	8	6
Unemployed	4	7	4	7	4	8	1	2
Other	32	38	28	41	27	39	23	29

Source: Annual Freshman Survey database, 1971 and 1995, Higher Education Research Institute, UCLA.

TABLE 11.5

Miles from Home to College

Miles from Home to College:	Percentage Black Freshmen at Black Private Four-Year Colleges		Percentage Black Freshmen at Black Public Four-Year Colleges		Percentage Black Freshmen at Other Four-Year Colleges		Percentage All Freshmen at Four-Year Private Colleges	
	1971	*1995*	*1971*	*1995*	*1971*	*1995*	*1971*	*1995*
10 or less	15	8	18	21	22	13	14	10
11 to 100	20	17	42	26	30	38	31	36
101 to 500	33	32	34	36	31	33	37	38
More than 500	32	43	6	17	17	16	18	16

Source: Annual Freshman Survey databases, 1971 and 1995, Higher Education Research Institute, UCLA.

TABLE 11.6

Percentage of Black Families with Incomes below the U.S. National Median versus Percentage of Families of Black Freshmen with Incomes below the National Median, 1971–95

	1971	*1975*	*1985*	*1995*
National median family income level (current dollars, all families)	14,203	17,349	37,580	55,365
Percentage of black families below national median	73	72	71	69
Percentage of families of black freshmen whose incomes are below national median:				
Black freshmen at private black four-year colleges	77	84	70	64
Black freshmen at public black four-year colleges	89	89	90	80
Black freshmen at other four-year private colleges	84	78	70	70

Sources: U.S. Bureau of the Census, Current Population Reports, *Money Income in the United States, 1995* (P-60-193) (Washington, D.C.: U.S. Government Printing Office, 1996), pp. B-9, B-10; Annual Freshman Survey databases, 1971, 1975, 1985, and 1995, Higher Education Research Institute, UCLA.

TABLE 11.7

Percentage of Black Families with Incomes above the U.S. National Seventy-Fifth Percentile verus Percentage of Black Freshmen with Incomes above the National Seventy-Fifth Percentile

	1971	1975	1985	1995
National seventy-fifth percentile family income level (current dollars, all families)	22,549	27,569	59,292	88,675
Percentage of black families above the seventy-fifth percentile	10	11	11	12
Percentage of families of black freshmen whose incomes are above the national seventy-fifth percentile:				
Black freshmen at private black four-year colleges	8	6	12	17
Black freshmen at public black four-year colleges	3	3	4	7
Black freshmen at other four-year private colleges	4	8	11	12

Sources: U.S. Bureau of the Census, Current Population Reports, *Money Income in the United States, 1995* (P-60-193) (Washington, D.C.: U.S. Government Printing Office, 1996), pp. B-9, B-10; Annual Freshman Survey databases, 1971, 1975, 1985, and 1995, Higher Education Research Institute, UCLA.

the family incomes of black freshmen at private black and public colleges, and at all other private colleges, have improved noticeably over the years compared with black family income generally as well as U.S. family incomes. Within the three sectors of black freshmen, the highest incomes are reported at private black colleges, and the lowest at black public colleges. Perhaps the most striking change is that at private black colleges between 1971 and 1995, the percentage of black freshmen who reported that their family incomes equaled those of the top quarter of U.S. families increased from 8 to 17 percent.

In reviewing the data presented in these tables, it seems clear that the black middle class has not abandoned historically black private and public colleges; otherwise both total enrollment and reported family income levels for students in these schools would be declining. But there may be other significant information not given in the table. For instance, there were probably sizable low-income groups that were represented in the 1970s college data that do not appear in the data for 1995. Federal student aid today often covers a smaller portion of a needy student's college costs than it did in the 1970s. And federal student financial aid

TABLE 11.8

Percentage of Black Families with Incomes below the National Thirty-Third
Percentile versus Percentage of Families of Black Freshmen with Incomes
below the National Thirty-Third Percentile

	1971	1975	1985	1995
National thirty-third percentile family income level (current dollars, all families)	11,263	13,034	28,960	42,166
Percentage of black families below the thirty-third percentile	57	55	56	53
Percentage of families of black freshmen whose incomes are below the national thirty-third percentile:				
Black freshmen at private black four-year colleges	66	74	57	51
Black freshmen at public black four-year colleges	80	79	82	67
Black freshmen at other four-year private colleges	72	64	55	57

Sources: U.S. Bureau of the Census, Current Population Reports, *Money Income in the United States, 1995* (P-60-193) (Washington, D.C.: U.S. Government Printing Office, 1996), pp. B-9, B-10; Annual Freshman Survey databases, 1971, 1975, 1985, and 1995, Higher Education Research Institute, UCLA.

for low-income students in the 1970s was predominantly grant aid; today it is predominantly loans.

Scattered signals from colleges throughout the United States suggest that most colleges are less inclined today than twenty years ago to recruit the very neediest students. Furthermore, now that a few private black colleges have large enough applicant pools to be selective and to expect higher test scores and high school grades, these colleges may find that the students with the best credentials tend to come from middle- and upper-income families, rather than from the lowest-income families. These factors may be part of a pattern that seems to suggest rising prosperity among the families of black freshmen.[6]

HIGH EXPECTATIONS

Table 11.9 summarizes the highest academic degrees planned by freshmen and selected life objectives that they believe are important. All freshmen in 1995 appear more inclined than in 1975 to pursue the most

TABLE 11.9
Freshman Degree Plans and Life Goals

Goals	Percentage Black Freshmen at Black Private Four-Year Colleges		Percentage Black Freshmen at Black Public Four-Year Colleges		Percentage Black Freshmen at Other Four-Year Colleges		Percentage All Freshmen at Four-Year Private Colleges	
	1975	1995	1975	1995	1975	1995	1975	1995
Highest degree planned								
Bachelors	18	11	29	21	21	16	32	23
Masters	38	29	39	39	32	33	30	40
Ph.D. or Ed.D.	20	27	16	22	19	25	11	17
M.D., D.D.S., D.V.M., or D.O.	10	21	3	8	13	17	10	11
LL.B. or J.D. (law)	6	9	3	5	9	7	7	5
Other	8	3	10	5	6	2	10	4
Objectives considered to be important or essential								
Be authority in own field	74	82	75	80	72	76	60	64
Be successful in own business	53	63	56	65	46	55	37	38
Be very well off financially	54	88	60	91	49	86	33	67
Have administrative responsibility	27	51	31	53	26	45	17	36
Raise a family	57	75	53	72	55	70	62	74
Be a community leader	27	57	27	49	27	48	15	34
Promote racial understanding	*	69	*	62	*	73	*	36
Help others in difficulty	74	81	70	74	75	76	69	66

Sources: Annual Freshman Survey databases, 1971, 1975, and 1995, Higher Education Research Institute, UCLA.
*The list of possible objectives offered in the 1975 survey did not include this checkoff option.

demanding graduate programs. Although there were exceptions, black
freshmen generally reported wanting to attain a higher degree than did
all freshmen at four-year private colleges. Such ambitions increased to a
greater extent between 1975 and 1995 for black freshmen than is true for
private college freshmen generally.

One conclusion that can be drawn from the second section of Table
11.9 is that black freshmen at all types of colleges have raised their sights
significantly between 1975 and 1995, and that they intend, along
with enjoying personal success, to be community-minded adults. These
community-minded responses are significantly more frequent from
black freshmen than from private college freshmen generally.

Table 11.10 shows that freshmen of all kinds appeared to be more self-
confident in 1995 than in 1971, but the percentage increases for black
freshmen were noticeably greater than for private college freshmen generally. Freshmen are least confident about their mathematical ability
compared with other areas, and black freshmen at all types of colleges
express even greater doubts on this subject.

What is one to make of the generally high expectations of these freshmen? A skeptic will note that more freshmen aspire to the most advanced
degrees than will achieve them. For example, in any year in the near
future, one might estimate from past trends that there will be a national
total of no more than 25,000 first-year students in medicine, dentistry,
osteopathy, and veterinary medicine and about 1.1 million first-time, full-
time freshmen in four-year colleges and universities. If 10 percent of all
four-year college freshmen persisted in their plans to enter one of these
medical fields (as implied in Table 11.9), there would be about 110,000
first-year medical students, not 25,000. Almost four out of five freshmen,
therefore, are likely to change their plans. At the same time, however,
high expectations almost certainly were an important ingredient in producing the remarkable medical school admissions record achieved by
graduates of private black colleges during the past two decades.[7] In a
more general sense, the Annual Freshman Surveys indicate that most
freshmen come to college with high aims. This is particularly so for black
freshmen. Experience and time will then help to tell them in more
specific terms what aiming high means.

LIBERAL ARTS VERSUS PRECAREER MAJORS

How do the trends in broad areas of study compare in the past three
decades? By 1996, 57 percent of bachelors degrees in private black colleges were awarded in liberal arts subjects, compared with a similar 59
percent for all private colleges. The balance between liberal arts and

TABLE 11.10
Self-Confidence

Percentage of Students Who Rated Themselves above Average or Highest 10 Percent in the Following:	Percentage Black Freshmen at Black Private Four-Year Colleges		Percentage Black Freshmen at Black Public Four-Year Colleges		Percentage Black Freshmen at Other Four-Year Colleges		Percentage All Freshmen at Four-Year Private Colleges	
	1971	1995	1971	1995	1971	1995	1971	1995
Academic ability	32	67	24	44	43	67	63	64
Intellectual self-confidence	38	74	32	66	44	72	42	56
Mathematical ability	16	39	14	30	23	40	37	43
Writing ability	29	51	25	39	31	48	35	45
Drive to achieve	64	83	58	70	68	82	58	71
Social self-confidence	37	65	31	62	42	65	30	47
Understanding of others	68	77	58	67	69	76	68	73

Source: Annual Freshman Survey databases, 1971 and 1995, Higher Education Research Institute, UCLA.

precareer majors at private black colleges was about what it had been twenty-five years earlier, whereas private colleges generally went through a noticeable shift away from liberal arts and toward precareer majors. Table 11.11 illustrates these changes.

Within the liberal arts, Table 11.12 shows that student concentration shifted away from the humanities and toward the natural sciences—both in private black colleges and private colleges generally. Meanwhile, as Table 11.13 shows, student interest at private black colleges grew rapidly in business and declined in school teaching.

ASSESSMENT OF SATISFACTION

When some of the Annual Freshman Survey's respondents were revisited four years later, what did they say about their college experience? Was the testimony of black students similar to the others, or quite different? Most students at historically black colleges and at all other private colleges said they were satisfied or very satisfied with their college experience and with the courses in their major field. Most gave high marks to the quality of instruction they received (Table 11.14). In 1997, HERI located a large sample of 1993 freshman respondents and asked about their academic experience, specific support services in the college they attended, attitudes related to the diversity of faculty and students, and whether they would choose the same college again (see Tables 11.14 through 11.17).

Table 11.15 shows that even though a majority of all private college freshmen and of black freshmen enrolled in their first-choice college, black first-choice percentages were lower than the average for all freshmen at all private colleges. Four years later, the follow-up respondents declared with slightly stronger majorities that they would choose the same college again. Whether enrollment in their college of first choice raises respondents' later ratings of satisfaction has not been tested. However, students at private and public black colleges were more critical of their laboratory facilities and equipment as well as their housing than were students at other colleges. Private black college students were also noticeably more critical of computer facilities, libraries, and financial aid services.[8] The Annual Freshman Survey does not include a full inventory of the specific services a student might rate, so that Table 11.16 reports the available opinions but it is not a sharp diagnostic tool. No sector of college students seems pleased with campus health services.

The data in Table 11.17 resist easy explanation. The table reports student satisfaction with dimensions of campus life that, broadly speaking, affect one's sense of community. Students of all races at predominantly white colleges expressed clear dissatisfaction with the ethnic/

TABLE 11.11

Percentage of Bachelors Degrees Awarded Classified by Major Subject Areas

Year	Private Black Four-Year Colleges		Public Black Four-Year Colleges		All U.S. Private Four-Year Colleges		All U.S. Four-Year Postsecondary Institutions	
	Liberal Arts Majors	Pre-Career Majors	Liberal Arts Majors	Pre-Career Majors	Liberal Arts Majors	Pre-Career Majors	Liberal Arts Majors	Pre-Career Majors
1996	57	43	51	49	59	41	59	41
1991	53	47	44	56	58	42	55	45
1986	50	50	45	55	61	39	56	44
1981	48	52	41	59	61	39	56	44
1976	51	49	38	62	65	35	59	41
1971	59	41	41	59	69	31	60	40

Source: National Science Foundation WebCASPAR database system.

Note: For this table "Liberal Arts Majors" were those with bachelors degrees in engineering, physical sciences, geosciences, math and computer sciences, life sciences, psychology, social sciences, science and engineering technologies, humanities, religion and theology, art and music, and architecture and environmental design. "Pre-Career Majors" include degrees in education, business and management, communication and librarianship, law, social service professions, and vocational services and home economics.

TABLE 11.12

Percentage of Liberal Arts Bachelors Degrees Awarded to Students Majoring in
the Natural Sciences, 1966–96

Year	Private Black Four-Year Colleges	All Four-Year Private Colleges
1966	41	38
1976	34	38
1986	59	51
1996	49	44

Source: National Science Foundation WebCASPAR System.

Note: Subject areas classified here as "Natural Sciences" are engineering, physical sciences, geosciences, mathematics and computer sciences, and life sciences. "Liberal Arts" subjects are defined in the source note to Table 11.11. Example of interpretation: In 1996, 49 percent of the bachelors degree recipients (in private black four-year colleges) classified as "liberal arts" majors in Table 11.11 were natural science majors.

racial diversity of their faculty, which on average is almost 90 percent white. Sixty-five percent of students at historically black private colleges said they were satisfied or very satisfied with the faculty diversity they encountered. The faculty racial mix at these colleges includes about 60 percent black and 25 percent white.[9] Although more than half of all students were satisfied or very satisfied with their contact with faculty and administration, students at black colleges were less enthusiastic about this aspect of their college experience.

Students at historically black colleges also seem comfortable with the student mix they encounter, even though, unlike the faculty, the racial

TABLE 11.13

Percentage of All Bachelors Degrees Awarded to Students Majoring in
Education and in Business and Management

	Education Majors		Business and Management Majors	
Year	Private Black Four-Year Colleges	All Four-Year Private Colleges	Private Black Four-Year Colleges	All Four-Year Private Colleges
1966	37	16	4	13
1976	24	13	20	16
1986	19	7	31	26
1996	9	9	23	24

Source: National Science Foundation WebCASPAR Database System.

Note: The percentages in this table are percentages of all degree recipients in each type of college, not percentages of "liberal arts" graduates, as were calculated in Table 11.12.

TABLE 11.14

Satisfaction with Academic Experience

	Percentage Black Freshmen at Black Private Four-Year Colleges	Percentage Black Freshmen at Black Public Four-Year Colleges	Percentage Black Freshmen at Other Four-Year Colleges	Percentage All Freshmen at Four-Year Private Colleges
Was satisfied or very satisfied with overall college experience	82	75	73	90
Was satisfied or very satisfied with the overall quality of instruction	77	70	82	88
Was satisfied or very satisfied with the courses in (my) major field	84	80	85	90
Was satisfied or very satisfied with science and mathematics courses	68	67	68	62
Was satisfied or very satisfied with social science courses	72	59	70	69
Was satisfied or very satisfied with humanities courses	72	60	72	72

Source: College Student Survey database, Higher Education Research Institute, UCLA.

Note: Replies come from 12,205 respondents, 10,898 of whom took the Annual Freshman Survey in 1993, and 1,307 of whom took it prior to 1993. Private black colleges participating in the 1993 survey were Claflin, Dillard, Morehouse, Shaw, Spelman, Tuskegee, and Xavier. Although response numbers vary slightly for each question, the black student response numbers in the left-hand three columns were approximately 290 (private four-year colleges), 210 (public four-year colleges), 300 (other four-year colleges). Approximately 7,300 students form the population for all freshmen in all four-year colleges. HERI estimates that sampling error will be largest in the first three columns and may be as large as plus or minus 6.8 percent for black freshmen in public black colleges and 5.7 percent for other black freshmen. This estimated sampling error means that one may have 95 percent confidence that the true percentage for line 6, column 2 (reported as 60 percent) lies somewhere between 53.2 percent and 66.8 percent.

TABLE 11.15

College Choice: 1993 Black Freshmen in Four-Year Colleges Followed up in 1997, Compared with 1993 Freshmen of All Races in All Four-Year Private Colleges

	Private Black Four-Year Colleges	Public Black Four-Year Colleges	Black Students Attending Other Four-Year Colleges	Students (All Races) Attending Four-Year Private Colleges
Percentage of 1993 freshmen who attended their first choice college	61	57	65	76
Percentage of 1993 freshmen who in 1997 would choose the same college again	72	67	70	80

Source: College Student Survey database, 1997, Higher Education Research Institute, UCLA.
Note: Private black colleges participating in the 1993 survey and 1997 follow-up were Claflin, Dillard, Morehouse, Shaw, Spelman, Tuskegee, and Xavier.

TABLE 11.16

Satisfaction with Facilities, Housing, and Support Services

Item Related	Percentage Black Freshmen at Black Private Four-Year Colleges	Percentage Black Freshmen at Black Public Four-Year Colleges	Percentage Black Freshmen at Other Four-Year Colleges	Percentage All Freshmen at Four-Year Private Colleges
Laboratory facilities and equipment	38	51	58	52
	(25)	(21)	(6)	(10)
Library facilities	35	61	53	55
	(47)	(17)	(29)	(26)
Computer facilities	54	64	63	61
	(29)	(15)	(20)	(19)
Student housing	29	21	41	51
	(32)	(34)	(24)	(19)
Financial aid services	34	34	47	44
	(36)	(37)	(23)	(16)
Campus health services	38	40	44	42
	(23)	(11)	(27)	(20)

Source: College Student Survey database, Higher Education Research Institute, UCLA.

Note: 1997 Follow-up responses are shown from 1993 freshmen. Percentages are shown for students saying they were satisfied or very satisfied. Students answering "dissatisfied" are in parentheses. Other possible ratings, not shown here, were "neutral" and "can't rate."

TABLE 11.17
Community and Diversity

Item Rated	Percentage Black Freshmen at Black Private Four-Year Colleges	Percentage Black Freshmen at Black Public Four-Year Colleges	Percentage Black Freshmen at Other Four-Year Colleges	Percentage All Freshmen at Four-Year Private Colleges
Contact with faculty and administration	65	55	77	86
	(11)	(10)	(6)	(2)
Ethnic/racial diversity of faculty	65	60	25	35
	(11)	(10)	(50)	(23)
Ethnic/racial diversity of students	64	66	33	35
	(7)	(4)	(37)	(25)
Opportunity for community service	65	53	71	64
	(6)	(6)	(1)	(3)
Sense of community on campus	58	58	47	58
	(19)	(13)	(30)	(17)

Source: College Student Survey database, Higher Education Research Institute, UCLA.
Note: 1997 follow-up response from 1993 freshmen. Percentages are shown for students saying they were satisfied or very satisfied. (Students answering "dissatisfied" are in parentheses.) Other possible ratings were "neutral" and "can't rate."

mixture (95 percent Black) is relatively homogeneous. Students at other colleges express less satisfaction but were not asked why. When asked about satisfaction with "sense of community on campus," more than half of the respondents said they were satisfied or very satisfied. The only exception was black students who did not attend historically black colleges. Almost one-third of these students said they were dissatisfied with the sense of community on campus. Again, the signal of dissatisfaction is clear, but the precise reasons are not.

GRADUATION RATES

The graduation rate of black freshmen—the percentage of full-time degree students who graduate within six years of entering college—in all National Collegiate Athletic Association (NCAA) member colleges is about the same as for freshmen at private black colleges. Table 11.18 summarizes the performance of NCAA member colleges, which include about half the historically black private and public colleges. Possible reasons for not graduating include transfer to another institution, death, withdrawal, and dismissal. Colleges in Divisions I and II offer athletic scholarships; Division III colleges do not. The graduation rate for private black colleges in Division I is 53 percent and in Division II, 38 percent—close to the graduation rates for all black freshmen in those divisions.

What can we make of this? Highly selective four-year colleges tend to believe that the higher the graduation rate, the better the institutional performance. But segments of American higher education have at different times valued the open-door idea: students who attend college for a time and then decide to leave may be conducting a valid educational experiment for themselves. A high completion rate need not be everyone's ambition. But if a graduation rate of 40 percent to 50 percent seems too low, what should be done about it? Should institutions groom their student bodies by denying admission to those with ambivalent goals or weak academic preparation? This could be done, but one of the important national contributions of historically black colleges is that, for the most part, they have avoided such exclusivity. Should they pay greater attention to the financial capability of their students to attend full time for four consecutive years without undue borrowing? A more predictable and better-financed program of grant aid for low-income students would not only help bring more students into postsecondary education but would also help maintain them through degree completion. Should the schools concentrate on improving such college functions as academic advising, course placement, and the provision of financial aid information to boost completion rates? These are only a few of the considerations

TABLE 11.18
Percentage of 1991–92 Freshmen Who Graduated Six Years Later

Division	Historically Black Private Colleges*	Historically Black Public Colleges*	Black Freshmen at All NCAA Colleges in Each Division	
			Private	Public
Division I	53	30	51	37
	(3)	(18)		
Division II	38	32	36	29
	(12)	(15)		
Division III	43	49	45	30
	(3)	(1)		

Source: Marty Benson, ed., *1998 NCAA Graduation Rates Report* (Overland Park, Kan.: National Collegiate Athletic Association, 1998).

Note: Among private black colleges, the Division I colleges included here are Bethune-Cookman, Hampton, and Howard. Division II private colleges are Lane, Johnson C. Smith, LeMoyne-Owen, Livingstone, Miles, Morehouse, Morris Brown, Paine, Shaw, St. Augustine's, St. Paul's, Tuskegee, and Virginia Union. Division III private colleges are Bennett, Fisk, and Stillman. Among public black colleges, the Division I colleges included here are Alabama State, Alcorn State, University of Arkansas–Pine Bluff, Coppin State, Delaware State, Florida A. & M., Grambling State, Jackson State, University of Maryland–Eastern Shore, Mississippi Valley State, Morgan State, North Carolina A. & T., Norfolk State, Prairie View A. & M., South Carolina State, Southern University (Baton Rouge), Tennessee State, and Texas Southern. Division II public colleges are Alabama A. & M., Bluefield State, Bowie State, Cheyney, University of District of Columbia, Elizabeth City State, Fayetteville State, Fort Valley State, Kentucky State, Lincoln (Missouri), North Carolina Central, Savannah State, Virginia State, and Winston Salem State. The Divisions III public college is Lincoln University (Pennsylvania). The graduation rates for freshmen of all races in private NCAA member institutions are: Division I, 68 percent; Division II, 47 percent; Division III, 66 percent. In public NCAA member institutions, the graduation rates for all students are: Division I, 53 percent; Division II, 40 percent; Division III, 50 percent.
*Number of colleges is given in parenthesis.

that face institutions addressing the issue of graduation rate. The variety of plausible questions about graduation rate makes simple arguments and simple treatments unlikely to yield a useful general strategy for change.

Are other important, unresolved questions suggested when the freshman surveys and follow-up studies are considered together? We think there are. First, in the follow-up responses, students at black colleges were notably critical of some of their colleges' physical assets (libraries, laboratories, and housing) and yet they said they would be more inclined to choose their particular college again than they had been at the time of freshman admission. Is this an early warning of a shift in college preferences at historically black colleges, and thus an indicator of a shift in enrollment patterns if those physical conditions are not quickly improved? Or is it reasonable for policymakers to continue their reliance on the other indicators of general satisfaction and loyalty seen in the survey responses? The question is a difficult one for black college administrators, because major investments in construction cost large sums in an environment where capital funds already are in short supply.

Second, it is unclear from the CIRP data whether there are growing numbers of qualified, low-income black students who fail to attend these colleges (or any other kind) solely because they cannot afford it. The trends shown in Table 11.8 indicate that this might be the case. If so, should college, state, or federal student-aid policy be changed to increase enrollment of low-income students? It is neither easy nor tidy work to judge who "should" participate in higher education. Yet this kind of assessment has been important in the nation's recent past. Certainly the federal assistance provided by the postwar G.I. Bill of Rights and the grants authorized by the Higher Education Act of 1965 played important roles in the great educational success of black college graduates, as well as of the World War II generation more generally. Whether more need-based grant aid, not merely extra loans, should be made available to college students is an uncomfortable question for taxpayers today because a satisfactory answer may cost real money. This question of public support for broad access, treated in greater detail, will be the subject of Chapter 15.

CHAPTER 12

Faculty: Challenge and Response

BETWEEN 1975 AND 1985, black enrollment declined slightly in all colleges, including the private black colleges. During the 1970s, black colleges also experienced a sharp drop in the number of well-prepared black enrollees. Aggressive recruitment and generous student aid offers from predominantly white colleges and universities proved extremely effective in attracting many of these students away from black colleges. Beginning in 1985, however, black collegiate enrollment increased in all types of colleges, exceeding the 1975 levels by the mid-1990s. Over the next decade, enrollment at private black colleges increased even more rapidly than at other private colleges. Once again significant numbers of well-prepared black freshmen with high test scores were enrolling at private black colleges.[1]

What caused the turnaround in enrollment in the late 1980s and 1990s? With so many forces in play, it is hard to establish cause and effect. Several demographic and economic trends affected all U.S. colleges during those years in ways that tended to increase college enrollment. Black and white family incomes were rising, as was the number of both black and white high school graduates. Meanwhile, after a period of inflation and budget stringency, many colleges launched building and renovation programs to make their campuses more attractive to prospective students. This chapter speculates that the growth of faculty development activity in the 1980s and 1990s also was important in producing the new enrollment pattern. "Faculty development" is an old term, whose meaning keeps changing. Forty or fifty years ago, it generally referred to ways by which individual faculty members might improve their skills or restore their vitality after years of teaching. Examples included sabbatical leaves, individual research projects, and advanced degree study. During the past two or three decades, the term has broadened to include efforts to change or improve subject matter and to tailor teaching methods to the different learning styles of students. Such efforts, strictly speaking, are not new; but they are now more often planned and carried out under the direction of faculty committees representing many departments and academic specialties on campus. This approach typically does not substitute for the work of such traditional academic departments as physics or history or English, but it does provide new flexibility to achieve change when the task at hand is one which transcends departmental lines. For

TABLE 12.1

Opening Fall Enrollment, Private and Public Black Colleges versus All
Postsecondary Institutions, 1970–95 (in Thousands)

Year	Private Black Four-Year Colleges	Public Black Four-Year Colleges	All U.S. Private Four-Year Colleges	All U.S. Postsecondary Institutions
1970	54	122	1,877	8,649
1975	62	163	2,040	11,291
1980	63	155	2,270	12,235
1985	61	150	2,329	12,412
1990	68	173	2,485	13,872
1995	73	187	2,610	14,445
Percentage change				
1975 to 1985	−1	−8	14	10
1985 to 1995	20	25	12	16
1970 to 1995	34	53	39	67

Source: National Science Foundation WebCASPAR database system.
Note: Enrollments in each cell are rounded to thousands.

example, a college concerned that its graduates lack adequate writing skills may decide that all departments, not just the English department, should help to teach writing and that faculty drawn from many departments should be trained to provide this instruction. The effort to introduce new information technology into all areas of teaching is another task that often proceeds more efficiently when organized across a whole faculty, rather than merely department by department. At many colleges during the first part of the twentieth century, the standard form of instruction required that a teacher lecture, and that students take notes and subsequently take examinations on how much they retained. More recently, faculty-wide workshops have accelerated adoption of many different ways of learning: discussion groups, research projects, off-campus internships, and many other options. For our discussion of the past thirty years in private black colleges, the most important faculty development activities were those which accelerated change in what was taught and how it was taught, as these colleges adapted to the new student mix and to the broad national shifts in curriculum.

Readers who are familiar with assessments of teaching and learning understand that although a few areas of this work can be reliably measured, many important areas cannot. No single number or table is offered here to measure the contribution of faculty development activity to the improved fortunes of private black colleges in the 1980s and 1990s. Although any given qualitative answer to this broad question might be dismissed as "soft," it is difficult to dismiss consistent indicators from four independent sources: the observations of three long-service faculty members; an external review of two foundations' fifteen years of faculty development projects in private black colleges; the record of increased spending for faculty development by foundations, corporations, and colleges; and the authors' own observations beginning in 1980.

THE STUDENT RECRUITMENT CHALLENGE OF THE 1970s

The student recruitment challenge of the 1970s was very serious indeed, as shown by the case studies of Spelman, Stillman, and Xavier presented in Chapter 9. Of the three, only Spelman moved sufficiently quickly and effectively to offset the effect of the new post-*Brown* competition. Scholars David S. Webster, Russell L. Stockard, and James W. Henson have reported that, between 1970 and 1978, black freshmen who had been in the top quartile of their high school classes and who only a few years earlier would have attended black colleges, more frequently chose predominantly white ones. Correspondingly, the proportion of top-quartile black high school seniors who enrolled in black colleges in 1978 had dropped to 31 percent, a decline of ten percentage points since 1970.[2]

There appears to have been no comprehensive study of admission trends or of the skills of students enrolled in historically black colleges during the 1970s. A few memos and letters survive, however, from observers who were only indirectly involved with student recruitment, and who were writing for other purposes. When, for example, the president of Johnson C. Smith University asked for alumni recommendations about how to strengthen the college's alumni association in 1971, Bryant George, an alumnus, wrote to the newly created alumni advisory committee, calling for a much greater sense of urgency and for fundamental institutional reform. George was then a program officer on the national staff of The Ford Foundation, and his memo to the committee was entitled "Johnson C. Smith University: An Endangered Species":

> Open enrollment (admission without respect to your high school grades) in the northern state schools, extensive scholarships in northern and western private schools, the desegregation of cheap and accessible southern state colleges and the massive rise of junior colleges could by itself finish off all of the black colleges. The cost of private education is rising. So far the private black colleges have absorbed this cost by holding down faculty salaries, limiting library acquisitions and other cost cutting devices. Black faculty of quality will not much longer agree to subsidize the private education of other peoples' children. Many have left already and others are poised to go. . . .

We will not be able to raise money or keep the school open by being what we are today. We are today about what all black schools are—uncertain of direction, underfinanced and losing students and faculty. We will have to do today something different and better. In the absence of this, there will continue to be just enough money available for us to die slowly.[3]

In 1979, a private black college, not one of the best endowed, sought a grant from the Andrew W. Mellon Foundation to improve humanities instruction and to teach communication skills. The proposal described what seemed to be increasingly urgent needs:

Few [of our entering] students have ever attended a professional concert. Few have read a literary masterpiece. Even fewer have heard of or can define the term humanities. . . . Entering students also suffer from grossly inadequate academic preparation and skills development. Most require intensive training in reading and writing skills before they can begin to appreciate the subject matter of courses in the humanities.[4]

Observers in some southern states began to note in the 1970s that the manner in which elementary and secondary school desegregation was carried out was often less advantageous to black students than to white ones, leaving even more black students than before ill prepared for further study. William E. Sims, a member of the Department of Education at Colorado State University, wrote in an editorial for the *Journal of Negro Education* that "In many southern states dreams faded as Black communities lost their high schools which could have been saved and integrated. The center of culture, the academic community, was destroyed. . . . This is one-sided racial desegregation at its best from a white perspective, at its worst from a Black perspective."[5] The special difficulties introduced by desegregation in some communities included transfer of the ablest black teachers to predominantly white schools and increased tracking of black students away from college preparatory courses.

FACULTY RESPONSE

The energy and urgency of the response of many faculty in the private black colleges to the new circumstances played a relatively unpublicized but crucial role in the recovery of these colleges. The faculty development movement arrived in the private black colleges in the 1980s and flourished. Aided by federal Title III funds, private gifts, and foundation and corporate grants, most private black colleges stepped up their assessments of curriculum and teaching methods and experimented broadly to see what might work better under the new conditions. Many colleges redefined their general education offerings, offered more emphasis on basic writing and mathematical skills, and attempted to introduce a larger variety of teaching methods to match the varied learning styles and capacities in the new student mix. A full financial record of this heightened activity is not available, but information from eight national foundations that supported private black colleges throughout the 1980s and 1990s indicates that their grant authorizations for faculty development were more than four times higher in the 1990s than in the 1970s.

We asked three respected faculty members, each of whom had taught at a private black college for more than thirty years, to write short essays on their memories of the student recruitment challenge of the 1970s and the various faculty responses to it. They were asked to describe what they saw at their own institutions and to assess the main trends of the period as they experienced them. Their accounts, offered below in italic type, corroborate the importance of heightened faculty development activity during the 1980s and 1990s to the revitalization of black college life, but suggest that the timing and effect of some of the enrollment challenges varied from one college to the next. In the next three sections, these three faculty members speak in their own words.

Ann D. Taylor is a mathematician, vice president for academic affairs, and dean of the faculty at Bethune-Cookman College in Daytona Beach, Florida. Dr. Taylor received her bachelors degree from Talladega College, a masters degree in mathematics education from North Carolina A & T State University, and a Ph.D. in educational administration from American University. She has held faculty and administrative positions at Bethune-Cookman for more than thirty years:

My experiences of working in higher education began in 1968. For six years prior to that, I was an instructor of mathematics on the secondary school level. I had the opportunity to teach in a public high school as well as a private college-prep school. This was during the height of the Civil Rights Movement and both teaching experiences were in all-black schools. My change to higher education came just when black students were beginning to look at majority institutions as a choice for college, although this was still not the norm. I chose to begin my career in higher education at a historically black college, Bethune-Cookman College, because of my private school experience as a college student and as a teacher.

In the 1960s, students came to HBCUs with stronger backgrounds in mathematics and other basic college prep courses.[6] I attribute this to the fact that black students had not begun to go to the majority institutions in great numbers. Since the Civil Rights Act of 1964 had not yet had a great effect, black college-bound students still considered the HBCUs first among their college choices. Indeed in most cases, their list of choices included only HBCUs. Thus, the "prestigious" black colleges at that time, such as Howard, Spelman, Morehouse, Fisk, Talladega, Hampton, garnered a fair share of the talented black students. Most of these students had graduated from segregated public schools, mainly in the South, along with newly integrated schools where they had proven themselves to be good students. They had to be in order to survive.

The Seventies ushered in a time of choice, when students began to become very much aware of the fact that the HBCU was not their only option. Also, majority institutions began to seek out and actively recruit black students. However, only the best were recruited with attractive scholarships and grant offers. There was a noticeable change in the student populations of the HBCUs: the decrease of students "prepped" for college was drastic.

This brought on the dilemma of how to best serve these students' needs (or deficiencies) and yet retain them and ultimately graduate them. It was during the seventies decade that remedial programs (sometimes referred to as developmental programs) began to find a prominent place in college offerings. These programs included courses in English, mathematics, and reading, which were designed to bridge the gap between what should have been learned in high school (and perhaps elementary school) and what was actually learned or retained. In many cases, the gaps were extremely wide. Faculty had to become accustomed to extreme variations in the ability and preparation of entering students, and also had to be prepared to teach and reach those students. For after all, the HBCUs found themselves in the position of having to accept what was left in the recruitment pool after most of the better students had removed themselves, having opted for majority institutions.

Faculty institutes that addressed ways of reaching these students became popular. Foremost among them, in my opinion, was the Institute for Services to Education (ISE) which held summer institutes from 1970–80 for faculty from HBCUs and which presented methods of teaching and of curriculum development. The effect of ISE in terms of faculty development was and is tremendous. Many of the faculty members in that program remain in service and occupy top administrative positions in higher education institutions throughout the nation.

During the 1980s, majority institutions seemed to be especially interested in minority students because of certain government grants that were available to the institutions based on the number of minority students enrolled. Thus, affirmative action plans were built into admissions processes and there was the continued loss of the better minority students to majority institutions. Additionally, there was a major effort to recruit minority faculty. To be able to say that the institution had a few minority faculty was a means of recruiting minority students. The competition to hire minority, particularly black, faculty became crucial for the HBCUs because majority institutions were able to offer higher salaries, lighter teaching loads, and more opportunities for research. This trend continued into the nineties.

But around 1993, the trend began to turn around. Government grants became fewer based on minority enrollment and Black students found the climate uncomfortable at many majority institutions. As a result, black students (and their parents) began to take another look at the HBCUs. In general, student enrollments started taking an upward turn for the HBCUs in the mid-nineties. Many students returning to our colleges expressed their need for more "nurturing" than had been received at the majority institutions. Certainly, HBCUs have been traditionally noted for the kind of atmospheres that allow[s] a student to enter "where they are" and be nurtured to "where they should be." And as the decade of the Nineties ends, my experience in higher education in general, and the HBCUs, specifically, affords me with a bright outlook on the future of these institutions that have survived for so long and have produced so many leaders and good citizens that others may have not given a chance. Although securing Black faculty remains a problem for the HBCUs because of the opportunities available at other institutions, the future is bright for all who have dedicated their careers to educating a population of people who deserve the chance to succeed.

Carrell P. Horton, a professor of psychology and dean of academic affairs at Fisk University, joined the faculty there in 1966 and retired in 1999. Dr. Horton received a bachelors degree from Fisk, a masters degree in sociology from Cornell University, and a Ph.D. in human development (developmental psychology) from the University of Chicago:

During the last three decades, Fisk experienced serious enrollment swings, serious financial difficulties, and—to a lesser extent—increased tension between liberal arts and career-focused education and speculation about the quality of its student body. For a time, Fisk's problems were chronicled almost daily in the local press and frequently in the national press. By the middle 1970s, it was clear that the institution would have to be proactive in meeting the challenges it was facing.

One aspect of Fisk's initial response was to drop temporarily the requirement of standardized test scores for admission, stating only that they were strongly recommended. This action caused serious faculty concern, primarily in terms of at least the perception that the quality of students would decline. This perception was and is difficult to document conclusively, given the many variables that can mediate between ability and achievement. The concern, however, along with knowledge of financial difficulties, was among the likely contributors to a number of faculty resignations in the mid- to late-1970s.

For a while, Fisk did seem to fall heir to an increasing proportion of students whose primary motivation may have been a search for the "black experience," having graduated from predominantly white secondary schools. Student questionnaires and the geographical distribution of the student body supported this belief. The 1970s saw a shift in student hometowns, with an increasing proportion of students drawn from outside the South.

The steps that Fisk took initially to remedy its situation covered virtually every aspect of its operations. After study and evaluation by outside consultants and representatives of all University constituencies, the following other actions stand out in memory: temporary "abatements" in faculty and staff salaries; streamlining of all curricula, dropping of some majors, development of cooperative and dual degree programs, and a revamped general education program; greater emphasis on shared university governance; and overhaul of administrative functions, including academic management.

In all of the steps Fisk took, it was understood that the mission of providing a liberal arts education of excellence was not to be compromised. Fisk did not undertake major changes in the characteristics of its student body, although a carefully planned recruitment and admissions strategy evolved over time. Some special, time-limited programs for adult learners were and are offered, but traditional college-age students continued to be the primary recruitment targets. Neither was there a major shift from traditional liberal arts majors to more applied programs. A program in business and a computer science major were added, but majors such as biology and psychology have not been displaced, although there has been a decline in some majors, paralleling a national trend.

Steps taken on the road to recovery have had effects on both the curriculum and the faculty. During the extremely lean years, institutional funds for faculty development declined at the same time that already below-average faculty salaries were not keeping pace with inflation. The need for faculty development, however, was greater than ever. The faculty responded to their need by instituting their own development programs as they sought to respond to changes in curriculum, staffing, tighter course and course-load regulations, sometimes gloomy perceptions of the student mix, and an overall increase in faculty responsibilities; the institution responded by addressing ever more carefully its criteria for and expectations of new faculty hires, and by strengthening its commitment to faculty development.

The last three decades at Fisk were years of anxiety, forward planning, and change, but change undertaken with a backdrop of the institution's purpose and mission. Over the years, strategies have been added, revised, and dropped in response to specific internal and external challenges and the changing face of higher education. The institution's constituencies have been at various times either or both change agents and adapters to change.

Ben E. Bailey is professor of music and chairman of the music department at Tougaloo College; he is also director of institutional research, assessment, and planning. Dr. Bailey received a bachelors degree at Jackson College, now Jackson State University. He received a masters degree and Ph.D. in music education at Northwestern University:

Faculty development has been important to Tougaloo College during the last thirty years, but the student enrollment trends are different from Bethune-Cookman College and Fisk University. Enrollment at Tougaloo increased from less than 1,000 students in the fall of 1979 to a peak of 1,153 in the fall of 1993, but then declined steadily to a low of 890 in 1998. Throughout this period, Tougaloo students have been, for the most part, first generation students from families of modest economic status. Tougaloo's low tuition and fees are still out of reach of many students and their families. At any one time, more than 85 percent of students receive substantial financial aid. Federal financial aid programs and privately endowed scholarships enable a significant number of students to remain and receive their degrees. Still, there is never enough. George A. Owens, a retired Tougaloo president, often said that during his tenure the College had always had hard times or worse.

If you go back to the 1960s, our students were very idealistic. Many were active in the Civil Rights Movement and all felt the world could be greatly improved. They believed that the economically deprived and the socially outcast would prevail, and they challenged any threat to their ideals. Then the militancy which had been directed to the controlling white society outside the gates began to turn inward. Students began to challenge the authority of the college administration and faculty. Several class boycotts were held, and the college authorities held hostage. Wisely, the president did not act hastily and throw students out. He thought students should be allowed to challenge authority if they were to become leaders, and he tolerated much of their youthful rebellion.

In the late 1970s and 1980s, some of our enrollment increase came from the admission of part-time non-traditional adult students who wanted to qualify for jobs in child care and Headstart centers, but most came from growth in numbers of traditional, college-aged students. Many of these chose Tougaloo because of its reputation as a center of Civil Rights activity during the 1960s. The state NAACP was founded here in the 1930s, and the Mississippi chapter of the American Civil Liberties Union was established here in 1969. Many students also were attracted by the record of Tougaloo alumni who entered professions like law, medicine and college teaching—where Blacks have been underrepresented for many years. These students intended from the beginning to attend graduate school and thought a Tougaloo degree would help their chances of being admitted to a good one.

The recent enrollment decline began in 1993, and we think we know why. Tougaloo College is located on the Northern edge of Jackson, Mississippi, and is close to a state university, two four-year colleges, and the largest community college in the state. All these institutions have newer and more aesthetically pleasing facilities than Tougaloo, and the university and the community college have much lower tuition rates. This competition hurts our admission effort, along with the continued strong recruitment of the more able African American students by white institutions. There are instances when students who initially chose white institutions later transferred to Tougaloo, but their number is not large enough to offset the total enrollment decline.

At the same time that enrollment decreased, some of the faculty felt that the new generations of students were less well prepared for college study than previous generations. It is true that many had been short changed by the integrated schools, where unsympathetic counselors and teachers had little faith in their abilities and channeled them away from college preparatory courses. Many of the brighter students were told that the historically black colleges had nothing to offer and were directed toward the white colleges which, if they had to accept Blacks, wanted only the more able. Yet, test data suggested that the students did not differ significantly from earlier students in their level of achievement. The mean composite American College Testing score hovered around 18 throughout the decade. In fact, the College continued to attract a good number of students of exceptional ability.

In order to address the under preparedness of entering students, Tougaloo College offered a pre-freshman summer program which evolved into a Division of Basic Studies and later into the Comprehensive Academic Resources Division, which oversees social and academic adjustment of freshmen and promotes the retention of students. Under a grant from the National Endowment for the Humanities, the Interdisciplinary Career Oriented Humanities Major was established. "Writing Across the Curriculum" was instituted as a program designed to improve critical thinking and quality of learning as well as students' writing ability. Experiments with learning styles and case studies were also conducted. Community service was added as a degree requirement, and while interest in the sciences remained strong, students began to gravitate toward the business administration and accounting emphases in economics as well as mathematics/computer science. Student interest in education as a major also resurged. These trends reflected the shift of student interest toward more direct career preparation.

These moves were supported by a faculty of great diversity in ethnicity, educational background, and geographic origin. This group includes many young white and Asian, as well as newly minted African American doctorates. Some are Tougaloo College graduates who have obtained degrees from the most prestigious universities: Harvard, the University of Virginia, Princeton, Syracuse and the Sorbonne. Recently a number of retirees from the public schools also have joined the faculty. Many of our new programs required rethinking of what it means to teach and learn. Grants from such foundations as the Lilly Endowment, The Ford Foundation, the Mellon Foundation, the Bush and Hewlett Foundations and others supported faculty workshops to understand the changes in our work, to launch the programs, and to design ways to assess their results. We remain convinced that Tougaloo College has a mission to fulfill, and that we will carry it forward.

A FOUNDATION VIEW

An outside view of recent changes in teaching and learning at private black colleges was offered in 1994 by Dr. Dean K. Whitla, former director of the office of instructional research and evaluation at Harvard University, and Dr. Asa Grant Hilliard III, professor of education studies at Georgia State University. They visited twenty-three private black colleges to evaluate faculty development grants made to them under a 1986 ten-year grant program sponsored jointly by the Bush Foundation and the William and Flora Hewlett Foundation. Although different foundations operate under different requirements and guidelines, the Bush-Hewlett grants nonetheless are similar in many ways to others supported by the Lilly, Kellogg, and Mellon Foundations, as well as the Howard Hughes Medical Institute. These two evaluators found that most of the grants touched the professional lives of many of the faculty in the participating colleges, and that the project activities helped to improve the quality of teaching. Despite tight budgets, most of the colleges planned to continue many of the projects using their own funds after foundation-grant payments ceased. In their interim evaluation report they state, in summary:

> Virtually all the projects concentrated ultimately on meeting student needs, rather than concentrating on other outcomes such as research or faculty sabbaticals. . . . Following is a sample list of project activities.

- Workshops to improve the computer skills of the faculty.
- Development of writing-across-the-curriculum materials.
- Individual and group faculty travel to conferences on how to teach critical thinking.
- Development of general education curricula.
- Mini-grants to individual faculty members or groups to develop new courses.
- Development of "learning communities" which reflect different learning styles.
- Development of collaborative learning experiences.
- Development of teaching strategies to improve student competence in reading, writing, and mathematics.
- Programs to improve faculty productivity.
- Assisting students to pass standardized examinations for entry to graduate school or for teacher certification.
- Computer literacy programs.

A number of colleges analyzed student records and polled faculty about student needs, to establish the first priorities of their faculty development programs. Money was then allocated according to need, usually by a central faculty committee established for this purpose. The colleges are accustomed to stretching a dollar, and did so in designing these programs as well. . . . The Bush-Hewlett faculty development programs helped many UNCF colleges to reposition themselves vis-à-vis the new student body. While there is a trend for more African American students to choose UNCF colleges, the changes which have been made in pedagogical style still represent important improvements.

Financial reports from eight national grantmaking foundations provide a partial index of the increase in faculty development activity that occurred in private black colleges over the past twenty years. Most of these foundations supported private black colleges throughout this period; they also supported faculty development projects in other colleges. Table 12.2 shows that the aggregate amount these foundations spent for faculty development in the 1990s was more than four times the amount spent on similar projects in the 1970s. The purposes of faculty development under these grants included curriculum change, shifts in teaching methods, computer literacy, faculty professional development, and assessment of outcomes and processes.[7]

In the 1970s, this group of foundations authorized approximately $12 million for the abovementioned purposes, with relatively unspecific faculty-development support the predominant emphasis during the first five years, and curriculum assessment and change the main emphasis in the last half-decade. In the 1980s, the same foundations authorized $21 million for faculty development in these colleges. Curriculum change was still the main focus, but introduction of new technology and additional teaching methods were now close behind. The total for the 1990s will be more than $51 million, with curriculum content again in first place.

The aggregate dollar figures in Table 12.2 sound substantial. By all testimony, they certainly heightened faculty and administration interest in faculty development. But they never have been large enough directly to relieve the severe budget limitations faced by most private black colleges. For example, suppose a college set as its top priority the improvement of its faculty and staff salary scales to be competitive with other private colleges. A rough calculation indicates that an average-sized UNCF institution in 1997 would have needed an additional $3.8 million per year simply to achieve a 25 percent increase in faculty and staff salaries.[8] Similarly desirable but prohibitively expensive goals—even for most large foundations—might include a major increase in student aid funds or elimination of deferred building-maintenance program. Typically, that kind of money must come from elsewhere than private gifts and grants.

Applying such average-institution calculations to the gross trends in Table 12.2, and assuming that the $51 million in major-foundation spending for faculty development in private black colleges in the 1990s was spread equally across the forty private black colleges, each institution

TABLE 12.2

National Private Foundation Grant Authorizations for Faculty Development in Historically Black Private Colleges, 1970–99
(in Thousands)

Foundation or Administering Organization	1970–74	1975–79	1980–84	1985–89	1990–94	1995–99
Current use grants						
Bush and Hewlett	–	–	–	3,347	2,730	1,539
Howard Hughes	–	–	–	6,780	7,900	4,600
Kellogg	205	691	75	–	22,616	–
Lilly	460	2,641	1,600	7,519	440	3,858
Mellon	6,350	1,305	990	–	890	2,297
Packard	–	–	–	990	2,546	1,492
Current use subtotal	7,015	4,637	2,665	18,636	37,122	13,786
Endowment grants						
Mellon	–	–	6,150	350	–	–
Mott	–	–	–	2,900	500	–
Endowment subtotal	–	–	6,150	3,250	500	–
Grand total	7,015	4,637	8,815	21,886	37,622	13,786

Source: Data were provided by the individual foundations.

Note: Most of these funds were granted directly to colleges and universities. Within the total of Mellon grants, however, $4.5 million was administered by the UNCF, and $2.3 million by the Southern Education Foundation. Within the total of Lilly grants, $4.0 million was administered by UNCF. The foundations in Table 12.2 are: Bush Foundation, St. Paul, Minnesota, in cooperation with the William and Flora Hewlett Foundation, Menlo Park, California; Howard Hughes Medical Institute, Chevy Chase, Maryland; W. K. Kellogg Foundation, Battle Creek, Michigan; Lilly Endowment, Indianapolis, Indiana; Andrew W. Mellon Foundation, Flint, Michigan; and David and Lucile Packard Foundation, Los Altos, California.

would have received about $125,000 per year. (Title III and other govern-
ment funds and corporate and private gifts also are used for faculty
development; and the colleges themselves subsidize faculty development
projects in a significant way by freeing up faculty time for them. These
contributions are not included in the calculations discussed here.) This
amount could, at best, finance the sponsoring of extra workshops, the
hiring of consultants, the planning of course revisions, and perhaps the
dispatch of faculty members to other campuses to observe model practice
elsewhere. Such activities can be powerful stimulants to improving the
climate for teaching and learning. But $125,000 a year or even three
times that amount cannot support such yearly budgeting burdens as
provision for general salary increases or for student aid to all students
with demonstrated financial need.

Much of the faculty development activity described in this chapter was,
in fact, low-budget activity. For the most part it was accomplished by
volunteers or faculty working with small stipends and was guided by
temporary committees organized to make a specific plan, oversee a particular pilot project, or implement a desired change.

This nomadic mode of task organization to achieve college-wide reform has drawbacks as well as important benefits. For example, since
most faculty service of this kind is voluntary, it is seldom that calls for help
elicit complete faculty participation. Some observers also say that those
whose teaching might benefit most from working on a project typically
are the most reluctant to participate. In addition, it is often difficult for
outsiders to learn just what was done in a faculty development project or
what effect it had upon student learning. This is hardly surprising. With
scarce hours available to do the actual project work, many faculty members prefer to spend their time on project design and implementation
rather than on devising measures to determine the effectiveness of the
project that would ultimately lead to scholarly publication.

However, the benefits of this flexible organizational style often out-
weigh the shortcomings. The use of volunteer effort allows the startup, at
least, of reasonably ambitious tasks without upsetting the college's core
operating budget. This is a tremendous advantage for private black colleges. Projects requiring college-wide design can give faculty the chance
to establish collegial ties outside their home departments and thus
broaden their perspectives. For a few, this experience provides a training
ground for subsequent academic leadership roles, such as dean or
provost or president. Many colleges of all kinds have suffered from the
on-the-job-training mistakes of newly appointed senior officers who
lacked such prior experience and who initially assumed that being
provost would be about the same as being department chair. Finally, in
private black colleges that in their early years were accustomed to a

strong top-down leadership style, the recent faculty development movement may have helped faculty to take the initiative and responsibility for
planning that is already assumed by faculty in many other colleges. This
initiative includes such matters as taking active part in forming budget
policy and helping design long-range academic and student admissions
strategy.

CHAPTER 13

The Small Colleges

BOOKS, MAGAZINE articles, and scholarly commentaries about private black colleges in the past half century have had little to say about the smallest colleges, except when reporting on their occasional financial failures or noting the limited choice within their academic programs. The more favorable notice given to larger colleges and universities should come as no surprise. Larger institutions receive the major gifts that attract media fanfare. And larger institutions can better afford to sponsor research that is published and widely read. The success of an economic enterprise is often judged by its rate of growth: to remain small is not generally seen as a sign of success. But when the smallest colleges are observed carefully, although their difficulties are evident, their strengths come into focus. These strengths deserve respectful attention.

DIFFERENT VIEWS OF "SMALL"

What do we mean when we say "small"? In 1970, Earl Cheit studied the budgets of forty-one public and private colleges and universities for the Carnegie Commission on Higher Education. At a time when the financial climate appeared to be worsening, Cheit found that more than two-thirds of the colleges in his study were either "headed for financial trouble" or "in financial difficulty," and that private liberal arts colleges and private universities were the most likely to be in difficulty.[1] In this climate, fortunately a temporary one, the Carnegie Commission sought to help planners and trustees in all sectors of higher education to understand the definition of optimum size for different types of institutions. The Commission suggested the following minimum and maximum full-time enrollments:

Type of Institution	Minimum Enrollment	Maximum Enrollment
Liberal arts college	1,000	2,500
Community college	2,000	5,000
Comprehensive college	5,000	10,000
University	5,000	20,000

The Commission emphasized that these numbers are only rough guides based on observation and not on economic laws. In fact, the Commission pointed out that with careful program design, excellent liberal arts colleges can exist with fewer than a thousand students; and owing to the political difficulty of limiting growth, many public universities might grow above the suggested limit.[2]

The Commission addressed the issue of minimum enrollment with, "All things considered, we suggest that colleges will run a risk of failing to take advantage of economies of scale and/or of not offering their students an adequate choice of programs if they do not reach [these] minimum enrollments."[3] But it also cautioned against a reflexive growth mentality, and by implication endorsed some aspects of smallness:

> Many state finance agencies assume that bigger is at least cheaper. We find this is not the case beyond relatively modest size. We also find no evidence that academic quality necessarily increases beyond a modest size. We ask that there be consideration for the costs of size as well as the advantages. Such costs include:

> Loss of attention to students
> Loss of personal acquaintance among faculty members
> Inrease in administrative complexity
> Increase in disruptive events on campus.[4]

Small size, as the Commission recognized, may bring special problems. In his 1986 Charles H. Thompson Lecture at Howard University, Luther H. Foster, president emeritus of Tuskegee University, called for improved strategic planning and management at historically black colleges. But he acknowledged how difficult this is, especially for presidents of small colleges. In his vivid words: "There is little time for planning while fires rage daily." Foster then suggested that a college needed at least eight hundred students to be efficient, basing his estimate upon a minimum-sized model in which there are fifteen departments, each with at least three professors, and a faculty-to-student ratio of one to eighteen.[5]

Table 13.1 shows that all of the ten smallest member-colleges of the United Negro College Fund in 1976 and 1997 had far fewer students than recommended by the Carnegie or the Foster minimum-sized guidelines, averaging about six hundred students in both periods. Nine of the ten smallest member-colleges in 1997 were also among the ten smallest member-colleges in 1976.

In 1976, The Ford Foundation published a study that questioned whether the earlier Carnegie-recommended minimum size for liberal arts colleges might have been set too high. Joseph A. Kershaw, professor of economics and provost of Williams College, examined the financial condition of three New England liberal arts colleges enrolling two hundred, three hundred, and six hundred fifty students each. He also looked

TABLE 13.1
Ten Lowest-Enrollment UNCF Colleges, 1976 and 1997

1997		*1976*	
College	*Head-Count Enrollment*	*College*	*Head-Count Enrollment*
Barber-Scotia	500	Barber-Scotia	526
Bennett	617	Bennett	618
Edward Waters*	482	Florida Memorial**	402
Huston-Tillotson	696	Huston-Tillotson	677
Jarvis Christian	472	Jarvis Christian	526
Lane	673	Lane	701
Paul Quinn	641	Paul Quinn	537
St. Paul's	658	St. Paul's	626
Talladega	650	Talladega	620
Wiley	651	Wiley	589
Size range	472–696	Size range	402–701
Mean size	604	Mean size	582

Sources: United Negro College Fund, *1976 Statistical Report* (New York: United Negro College Fund, 1977); United Negro College Fund, *1997 Statistical Report.*

*Edward Waters College, Jacksonville, Florida, was not accredited in the 1970s, and was not a UNCF member then.

**Florida Memorial College, Miami, Florida, increased its enrollment to 1,643 students by 1997.

at colleges enrolling fewer than seven hundred fifty students, which at the time accounted for about 5 percent of all undergraduate enrollment:

> We conclude that these three institutions are in much the same sort of difficulty that afflicts much of unendowed private higher education. They need more capital, and if they find it and manage things well, they will stay alive. . . . The small college has supplied a special type of education to a special type of student and still does. It does this at a cost per student that is not very different from that incurred elsewhere. . . . An initially skeptical observer [he is referring to himself] who believes in the merits of a diversified higher educational system has to hope that these institutions, and at least some of the other small ones, find their way through the troubles of the present and the next few years.[6]

What are the special attributes of the small historically black private colleges that deserve attention? As implied in Table 13.1, these colleges are resilient. They are survivors. Many of their students come from small and mid-sized communities. In 1997, 63 percent of the students in the ten smallest colleges came from the college's home state. They often had

below-average college preparation, achieved relatively low scores in national aptitude tests, and did not have college-educated parents. For
these students, unlike those attending more cosmopolitan black colleges,
the choice is often between the college they chose and no college at all.
Although these small colleges produce professional leaders and the occasional national star, they concentrate on developing basic skills and on
giving ill-prepared black youth a real chance for success in an urban
white-collar or professional work culture. Small size and the tradition of
nurturing that often goes with it can produce close personal support that
is particularly valuable for unsophisticated students who may have much
to absorb if they hope to establish middle-class lives and careers.

VALUE ADDED AT TEXAS COLLEGE

One of the authors of this book, a former college admissions officer,
visited Texas College in 1979 to review a foundation proposal. As one part
of his general orientation, he was invited to review high school transcripts
and to scan whatever aptitude test scores were available. These documents suggested that many Texas College freshmen arrived on campus
with skills comparable to those of tenth-, ninth-, or even eighth-graders
from an adequately financed suburban high school. Also on file was a list
of where the college's 1976 graduates were employed. The list, compiled
by the college alumni office, displayed questionnaire replies of seventy-
four of the ninety-six bachelors degree recipients for that year. Forty-five
women and twenty-nine men reported the following occupations and
employers six months after graduation:

Job Title	Number
Public school teacher	30
Graduate student	9
Business college teacher	1
City inspector	1
Funeral home director	1
J.C. Penney merchandise manager	1
Southwestern Bell Telephone manager	1
Distributorship manager	1
Department store branch manager	1
Drug store assistant manager	1
Clerical worker	3
Social worker	1
Bookkeeper	1
Service technician	1
Mail clerk	1

Hospital orderly	1
Fireman	1
Employer Name (job title not listed):	
Texaco Oil Company	2
Dial Chemical Company	1
U.S. Army	1
No employer or job title reported	13
Total respondents, Class of 1976	74

If a similar questionnaire had been sent to the Class of 2000, the pattern probably would be less concentrated in public school teaching, and a larger proportion would have reported jobs in business and government. We do not know the extent to which the twenty-two nonrespondents from the class of 1976 were employed similarly to the graduates that year who did reply. Although Texas College in the mid-1970s drew about 40 percent of its students from Texas high schools, 61 percent of the class of 1976 graduates reported first jobs or graduate study within Texas. More than half of these, in turn, resided within 100 miles of the college.

The foundation visitor twenty-one years ago—this book's co-author—thought the Texas College graduates list was an exceptional one. No precise scales have ever been developed to measure exactly how much a college contributes in four or five years to prepare a graduate for further work and learning. But even though other post-college employment lists might appear similar to this one, most of the people on the Texas College list—in academic and social terms—had come an unusually long distance in a very short time. The value added by their college experience had to have been high. Texas College contributed to those students in a variety of ways not likely to be found anywhere except perhaps at another small and specialized college. Texas College will appear later in this chapter as a case study in leadership. This vignette illustrates the kind of institutional value added that several of the smallest private black colleges frequently achieve.

When things go well, the small black colleges accomplish a great deal with little money. Their reserves are too thin, however, to cushion for long either mistakes or misdirection. The June 30, 1997, market value of the endowments of the ten smallest colleges in Table 13.1 ranged from $1,057,000 (Edward Waters College) to $13,051,000 (Jarvis Christian College). The mean value for the ten was $5,851,000 or, on average, enough to pay for about seven months of their operating expenses in 1996–97. For comparison, the Morehouse College endowment was equal to two years of its current expenses, and Spelman's—the best-endowed of the private black colleges—was equal to three.[7] (The endowment at Williams

College as of June 30, 1999, was equal to seventeen years of its current operating expenses.) Between 1988 and 1999, seven private black colleges, most with small enrollments, encountered sufficient difficulty to generate a public record—either in bankruptcy court or assigned by a regional accrediting agency. Bishop College in Dallas declared bankruptcy in 1988 and closed. The private black colleges that lost full accreditation status with the Southern Association of Colleges and Schools (SACS) during that eleven years are Barber-Scotia College, Edward Waters College, Knoxville College, Morris Brown College, Paul Quinn College, and Texas College. (Of these, all but Knoxville and Texas had been restored to full accreditation by July 1999.)

Although each had particular circumstances, the difficulties of each of these colleges became obvious at times when the presidency or board leadership was weak, and when financial reserves were inadequate to finance a turnaround. All but Bishop and Morris Brown were small colleges at the time their difficulties became public knowledge.

TURNAROUND AT TEXAS COLLEGE

Texas College provides a glimpse of how easily an apparently stable, small-scale operation can destabilize. It also demonstrates the restorative power of determined leadership and the importance of the roles played by the major peer networks, SACS, and UNCF.

Texas College was founded in Tyler, Texas, in 1894 by a group of ministers of the Christian Methodist Episcopal (CME) Church. Tyler lies one hundred miles east of Dallas, and about ninety miles west of Shreveport, Louisiana. Texas College is a coeducational liberal arts college with majors in humanities and education, business and social sciences, and natural and computational sciences, and enjoys a good reputation in teacher preparation. Two-thirds of the faculty hold doctorates or professional degrees in their fields, which is about average for private black colleges. Faculty salaries are in the lowest quartile for the UNCF group. The college follows an open admissions policy and identifies its mission as "providing access and opportunity to educationally, socially, and/or economically underprepared students."[8] The family incomes of Texas College students typically are low; most students require financial aid to attend. Enrollment has varied from about 400 to 600 students over the past two decades—until 1993, when it dropped to between 200 and 300.

The recent history of Texas College can be divided into three periods. The period from 1990 to 1994 was a time of growing difficulties in leadership and financial management that elicited repeated expressions of concern from SACS. From 1994 to 1996, a new leadership team mounted a comprehensive attempt to avoid loss of accreditation. The attempt didn't quite succeed. From 1996 to 2000, a series of blows struck the college, including loss of regional accreditation, federal funds, and UNCF membership. At the same time, a major recovery effort directed by the college administration continued to push the school toward healthy operation and reinstatement of regional accreditation.

The difficulties the college faced in the mid-1990s were summarized by Bishop Marshall Gilmore, presiding prelate of the Eighth District of the CME Church and chairman of the Texas College board of trustees, and by Haywood L. Strickland, the college's president who had been recruited by Gilmore:

In recent years the College has suffered from instability and weakness in its administrative leadership. In fact, since 1986, the College has had four presidents [two died in office] and three interim presidents, and witnessed ongoing turnover in other administrative offices. This discontinuity in leadership, unstable, and often ineffective management resulted in poor oversight and operational breakdowns in critical areas of the College. The problems created as a result of the breakdowns in operations led the Southern Association of Colleges and Schools (the regional accrediting body) to notify the College that it was in serious jeopardy of losing its accredited status. Administrators of the College at that time failed to respond to these warnings.[9]

The troubles that had accumulated by late 1994 included a $2.1 million claim against Texas College by the U.S. Department of Education for mismanagement of federal student financial aid programs from 1992 to 1994, a dispute over loan funds management with the Texas Guaranteed Student Loan Corporation, and a claim by the Internal Revenue Service that the salaries reported on W-2 forms understated the amounts paid. Enrollment sank to 267 students. Bills from local suppliers were not paid on time. In an October 1994 visit, a team from SACS recommended seventy-four changes in virtually every aspect of the college's operation. The college was given one year on probationary status in which to carry out the recommendations or face the possible loss of regional accreditation.

Such a sharp downhill pitch for any college is not pleasant. An initial failure to respond adequately to a regional accrediting body's recommendations for improvement usually results in the school being placed on notice. Continued noncompliance leads to a warning and a visit to assess compliance. If noncompliance persists, the SACS Committee on Criteria and Reports makes a recommendation to the full membership on whether probation, the last step before loss of accreditation, is warranted. If a college then loses its accreditation, it immediately becomes ineligible for federal student aid programs and for institutional aid under Title III B of the Higher Education Act of 1965. Full accreditation status is also a requirement for membership in UNCF and for the chance to benefit from UNCF's distributions of annual unrestricted funds, and receipts from occasional capital drives. Major foundation gifts often are contingent upon satisfactory accreditation status. Late in 1994, in short, Texas College was within a year or so of losing more than one-third of its ordinary sources of revenue, unless accreditation could be preserved or a totally new support system quickly invented.

In mid-1994, Bishop Marshall Gilmore was elected chairman of the Texas College board of trustees. He was an experienced college trustee, having served on the boards of Paine College, the Interdenominational Theological Center, and Mississippi Industrial College. The president of the college at that time was a temporary, interim appointee. Bishop Gilmore understood that only a new president of unusual background and determination stood a chance of setting Texas College on a path to recovery. Gilmore was acquainted with Haywood Strickland, then a corporate officer of UNCF, and concentrated on recruiting him. Strickland's experience almost uniquely fitted him for the job. He knew firsthand about reviving small, troubled colleges. A graduate of Stillman College in 1960, he had taught history there during the presidency of Harold N. Stinson. Strickland later became president of Stillman's National Alumni Association and chairman of its board of trustees. Strickland's professional experience included service as president of Kittrell College in North Carolina, assistant executive secretary of the SACS; and vice president of UNCF and national director of its most recent capital fund drive. At first Strickland refused Gilmore's invitation to come to Texas College. But three telephone calls and one month of reflection led him to accept. Strickland became president of the college on November 1, 1994.[10]

Just as President Cordell Wynn did on arriving at deteriorating Stillman College in 1982 (see Chapter 9), Strickland tried immediately to generate both obvious short-term successes and sensible long-range strategic plans. Given the looming threat of loss of accreditation, Strickland's starting position was even more demanding than Wynn's.

He immediately informed major creditors of the College's shaky financial condition and his plans for improving it, agreeing to pay what he could when he could. Like Wynn, he directed the repair of leaking roofs and the elimination of especially severe building and grounds problems. He hired strong academic and financial administrators and reorganized the accounting, student aid, and financial administration of the college. He invited the faculty to create a formal organization of its own, and asked it to help develop strategic plans for which areas of study the college should emphasize. He directed a comprehensive review of all academic programs and reassigned or replaced faculty to ensure that fields of study were covered by teachers with credentials in those fields. An academic advising system for students and a performance evaluation system for faculty were launched.[11] He arranged for forgiveness or payment of the Department of Education and Internal Revenue Service claims against the college. Fundraising improved significantly. For the first time in several years, the year-end operating budget showed a positive balance.

A follow-up visiting team from SACS reduced by more than half the number of recommendations that required attention, but the visitors were still dubious about the college's long-term financial viability and so did not change the earlier recommendation that Texas College lose accreditation. The team's recommendation to remove accreditation, upheld at a December 1995 SACS meeting, was appealed by the college. On May 10, 1996, despite further financial and administrative improvements, the appeal was denied. Federal funds and UNCF membership were immediately withdrawn. The bad news did not, however, mean loss of degree-granting authority. Earlier, as Strickland attempted to avoid negative action by SACS, he also applied to the Texas Higher Education Coordinating Board for temporary authority to grant degrees in the state of Texas. This was granted early in 1997.[12] After fifteen months of remedial work, Strickland and his colleagues had almost rescued the college from the effects of eight years of prior administrative turmoil and neglect. By mid-1996 the college was alive, coherently managed, but stripped of many of the financial supports that sustain most other private colleges. To survive, the Texas College urgently needed to invent an emergency financial structure. Strickland and the board of trustees estimated that outside of tuition, few sources of revenue could conceivably replace the lost income, even on a temporary basis. The best prospects for help seemed to be the CME Church, local and community foundations, alumni, and perhaps a few individual donors. The Texas College planners understood that virtually all of their students needed continued grants and loans if they were to remain enrolled. Therefore, any additional gifts should be directed into a locally designed version of the missing federal student aid programs. Strickland calculated that such an emergency financial structure might support perhaps 250 to 300 students. He estimated that the college could remain open at that level and retain enough faculty to be able subsequently to serve an expanded enrollment if federal and UNCF funds started to flow in again.[13]

While working out its emergency operating plan, Texas College also applied for candidacy status in SACS, the first formal step toward full reaccreditation. SACS approved candidacy status in December 1997.

This permitted application to the Department of Education for restoration of Title III funds and student aid eligibility. Unresolved accounting problems from early in the decade delayed until January 1999 the renewal of this federal income to the college.

Between 1997 and mid-1999, a key element in saving the college was the support of the CME Church. The Church borrowed $7.3 million on behalf of the college and is currently engaged in a capital fund drive largely intended to retire this debt. The Church also reduced its annual gifts to three other CME-related colleges, Lane, Miles, and Paine, so it could give more to Texas College. Surprisingly, the college was able to balance its budget during those years, eliminating $1.7 million of accumulated debt, improving the appearance and technology infrastructure of the campus, and providing better academic opportunities for its small student body.

Six years after accepting the Texas College presidency, Haywood Strickland felt he had given his best effort to the college's drive for reaccreditation. However, final approval, if it were to come, was taking much longer than expected. During the fall of the year 2000 he accepted the presidency of Wiley College, a small private black college in Marshall, Texas. "I needed some new energy, some new challenges, and the chance to start a new venture," he said a few months after arriving at Wiley.[14]

The Texas College board of trustees quickly replaced Strickland. On December 1, 2000, Dr. Billy C. Hawkins, former provost and academic vice president at Mississippi Valley State University, became Texas College's new president. With only twelve months to present the College's final case for SACS reaccreditation, Hawkins made plans to raise additional unrestricted money in a new fund drive, and to try to increase enrollment of both recent high school graduates and older adults. SACS is scheduled to consider the school's application for reaccreditation in December 2001. If approved, Texas College would be eligible to reapply for membership in UNCF and to request grants from national foundations with some chance of serious consideration. Dr. Glenda F. Carter, until 2000 the college's executive vice president and professor of education, said of the future: "We'll always stay open to those who need the opportunity. We want to have an even mix of needy and of stars. Right now we're a little overweighted towards the needy."[15]

REFLECTION

What can be learned from the Texas College experience that applies more generally to small private black colleges? Sustained, competent leadership appears to be crucial for a small and financially vulnerable college. This was true for all of the colleges we examined. In the smallest colleges, the role of the president seems particularly important, but even then, he or she cannot succeed without a strong supporting team.

More generally, there are at least two broad criteria that can be used to judge the performance of a college or university. The easiest to use as a measure is the importance of an institution's research and publication record and the recorded distinctions of its graduates. Harder to quantify but surely as important is the value added for students by the college experience. Many small second-chance colleges excel in providing this value, even if the statistical proof remains elusive.

A critical observer may ask: Even if these smallest colleges are capable of surviving, should they? And do these colleges (and the larger black colleges as well) merit special, targeted federal subsidy of the kind they receive today under Title III of the Higher Education Act of 1965? We answer yes to both questions.

The latter question will be dealt with in Chapter 16. As to the former, two distinctive features of the American system of higher education are that it educates an unusually large portion of the nation's population and that it does so with an unusually diverse array of institutions. Both of these characteristics help make the system expensive. The American system includes both public and private institutions, large and small, single-gender and coeducational, often with historic ties to particular races, religions, or regions. The educational scene includes competition and duplication, tradition and experiment, obvious success and signs of impending failure. The nation's traditional respect for local institutional autonomy permits all these things to occur so long as the institutions themselves are able to survive. If the past is any guide, some of the small black colleges will close or merge, but others will continue and will prove to be incubators for future growth and improvement.

Are there circumstances for which it is best for a small college to close? There are indeed such circumstances. For instance, colleges that offer poor, irrelevant, or fraudulent programs are good candidates for closure. But just as the founding charter of any college should not be treated as a ticket to eternal life, so the smallness of a college should not be treated as sufficient cause for closure. Texas College is one of several small institutions that provide significant added educational value to an important group that is often underserved by the rest of the educational system. Texas College also is a small institution where strong leadership revealed surprising resilience under the most difficult circumstances.

CHAPTER 14

Student Aid

EVER SINCE THE G.I. Bill of Rights gave World War II veterans enough money to attend college, fueling the greatest collegiate expansion in history, public aid for college students has helped sustain American colleges and universities. Because much of this aid is targeted toward those with little wealth or financial help from family, its availability is especially important to such students and to colleges, such as the private black colleges, that attract a disproportionate share of low-income students. Although the past record is generally counted as a national success, Michael S. McPherson, president of Macalester College, and Morton Owen Schapiro, president of Williams College offer good reasons to be concerned about the future:

> For more than 30 years, the U.S. system for financing undergraduate education has been based on the principle that colleges and universities, together with federal and state governments, should help financially needy students to pay for their education. Now . . . [the federal and state] governments are shifting resources from lower-income students to the children of middle-class taxpayers, who have more political clout. Those changes threaten the educational prospects of our neediest young people, and the health and stability of U.S. higher education in general.[1]

Thomas R. Wolanin, research professor of education policy and of political science at George Washington University, explains in financial terms why federal student aid policy is so important:

> Of all federal programs, those that provide for student financial assistance have the most pervasive affect on American higher education. Federal support for research affects a couple hundred major research universities; Title IX [1972 Amendments to the Higher Education Act of 1965] has its principal impact on approximately 300 institutions with Division I athletic programs; affirmative action in admissions is, of course, primarily relevant only to the 300 or 400 selective colleges and universities. Institutions in these three categories—research universities, Division I athletics, and competitive admissions—tend to be an overlapping group. . . for example, Duke, Georgetown, Stanford, the University of Michigan.
>
> The point is that while relatively small subsets of institutions feel the brunt of federal policy in these and other areas, all 3,880 of them—with a handful

of exceptions—are significantly impacted by federal student aid policy. In the coming academic year (1998–99), federal student aid programs will make available nearly $50 billion in aid, about 75 per cent of the aid available from all sources. Approximately 40 per cent of all students in American higher education will receive federal financial assistance.[2]

Although there are times when it looks better at a distance than up close, the U.S. system of postsecondary education has been the envy of many other countries since World War II. This is because it serves a relatively high proportion of the population, provides varied training throughout life, and thus permits individuals to pursue almost any career their talent allows. It is of enormous practical importance that, although expensive, the system is flexible enough to allow an individual a second chance in his or her educational career if the first misfires or is of poor quality.

The shift from elite to mass higher education after World War II was made possible by a political compromise, which sought to achieve an expensive goal while spending as few taxpayer dollars as possible. The goal was to remove economic barriers to postsecondary education for any student who was able to maintain satisfactory academic standing at any accredited college. Congress could have set up a universal entitlement program like those offered only to top students in several European countries—essentially paying the whole bill, including living costs, for every eligible student. But the price for doing this in the United States seemed unrealistic on a mass scale. Instead, Congress insisted that all the existing players continue to contribute as before: parents (from income, savings, and other assets), students (from work, savings, or loans), and the colleges (from endowment income or current funds). Federal and state taxpayers would then remove the remaining financial barriers for the neediest students by contributing the difference between what was available and what was needed to cover the annual cost of college attendance. Although the aid formulas tended to cover a smaller percentage of the costs at the most expensive colleges than at the least expensive ones, the calculations took most costs into account, and ensured that reasonable choice, as well as broad access, was incorporated into the congressional strategy.

To work, such a plan requires a data system in which each prospective student could enter an account of his or her earnings and negotiable assets, as well as the details of parental earnings, assets, and liabilities. A number of selective colleges that wanted to stretch their scholarship budgets to aid as many students as possible devised such a reporting system in the 1950s. It provided the colleges' financial aid officers with the necessary data to estimate how much a student's family might be expected to contribute toward his or her education. In 1954, these colleges established the College Scholarship Service, a subsidiary of the New York-based College Entrance Examination Board. The College Scholarship Service conducted a "need analysis" on each student's application for aid. The scholarship stipends and loan amounts calculated this way were called "need-based student aid." The federal government then adopted these need-based principles in designing the Higher Education Act of 1965, the nation's first mass system of postsecondary student grants, jobs, and loans. Ideally in such a system, if everyone plays their proper part, students and families do as much as they can and the federal government (and states, if they have similar supplementary plans) spends grant funds only where needed in approximately the amount needed. If families refuse to do their part, or if the government program is underfunded, students may find themselves forced to work or borrow more than expected, and so may opt for a lower-priced education, or may decide not to go to college at all.

Whether such a student-aid system does indeed pay for reasonable postsecondary access and choice for low-income students depends on a number of guideline details that turn out to be very important. A key question is whether the formula for calculating how much a needy student may receive in grants, loans, and work will cover most of the attendance costs for expensive colleges. Related to this, of course, is whether the appropriation for the program is large enough so that, in the end, eligible students may receive the calculated amounts of grants and loans. Generous funding would permit low-income students to attend any college or university where they could gain admission and maintain satisfactory standing. This, in turn, would mean that the nation's array of colleges could afford to display diversity of family incomes and occupations, as well as racial and ethnic backgrounds in its student mix. If through underfunding or restrictive rules the system does not permit needy students to attend expensive colleges, economic pressures shape the collegiate scene, concentrating prosperous students at the expensive colleges and leaving low-income students principally attending local, low-cost colleges. In the extreme case, a stratified collegiate caste system is established in place of a universal access system.

Depending on the way one calculates expected family contribution for a student, similar disparities can result. If money must be rationed tightly but is to promote broad access, the formula should be more stringent for families with upper-middle incomes and large assets, on the theory that those families—although they might welcome aid—will probably pay the college bills if they have to, whereas low-income families cannot pay. But if the goal is not broad access but popular appeal to the middle class, the formula can be more generous to the mildly prosperous. With the same total appropriation, less money will then go to low-income students, greater income stratification will occur across different types of colleges, and a smaller number of students will participate in postsecondary education.

Because student aid usually comes in a package offer that includes a student job, a loan, and an outright grant, it is possible to vary the balance among these forms of aid and so vary the amount of long-term debt that poorer families must carry. A public strategy of meeting calculated need by requiring only a few hours of student work per week and taking out only small loans not surprisingly turns out to be an expensive public strategy, although an attractive one for students. The long-term cost to the taxpayer can be reduced, and in recent years has been, by shifting the mix toward loans. But the student loan burden then rises, changing some college and enrollment choices and eventually affecting career plans.

The Washington office of the College Board estimates that federal need-based aid made up about 50 percent of all such student aid in 1971, rose to a high of more than 80 percent in 1986, and by 1999 dropped to about 60 percent. Need-based aid has been the predominant form of aid from federal programs, many state programs, and from private and public colleges. It is a well-conceived system, but one that can slip out of adjustment when one or more of its major participants acts independently. The remainder of student aid, sometimes called "merit aid," is awarded to students at any income level without passing through need analysis, and may be awarded to attract students with high test scores or high class rank, or with special characteristics such as alumni parentage, geographic or racial origin, or particular talent.[3]

From the late 1940s to 1978, federal aid to postsecondary students expanded sharply through the G.I. Bill of Rights for veterans, the Higher Education Act of 1965, its 1972 amendments that created Pell Grants, and the establishment of need-based aid student aid programs in about half of the states.[4] Most observers would say that the nation in this period came as close as it ever has to achieving, by any reasonable definition, universal access to and choice in college attendance. These were also the years when many colleges discovered that they could afford to recruit and shape their student mix—and that this was an advantageous move. Many of them drew larger numbers of students from across the nation and from a wider variety of religious, ethnic, and racial backgrounds than was possible before. It was this reshuffling of the student population that so drastically affected private black colleges.

In the years from about 1980 to the present, although need-based aid has survived, the principle has been challenged and eroded. The relatively generous student aid program gradually became less generous, particularly for low-income students. This in turn raises the question of whether the original goals of broad access to and choice in postsecondary education are still part of the national vision.

VANTAGE POINT: THE LOW-INCOME STUDENT

At first glance, the general trends in student aid expenditures seem impressive. In constant dollars (adjusted for inflation), total available postsecondary student aid approximately doubled between 1980 and 1998, while total annual costs of attending public or private four-year colleges (also inflation-adjusted) rose between one-third and one-half. Total enrollment in the nation's colleges and universities increased about one-third. The college participation rate for unmarried eighteen- to twenty-four-year-old high school graduates increased at all levels of income, although the participation rate for the prosperous remained consistently higher than for the poor. In 1997, 89 percent of high school graduates from the top family-income quintile (family incomes of about $74,584) participated in postsecondary education, compared with 53 percent from the lowest family income quintile (family income below $25,063).[5] The introduction in 1998 of federal tuition tax credits, it is estimated, will eventually be worth another eight billion dollars per year to students whose families have incomes large enough to pay a significant income tax. Plenty of student aid money thus has been added to higher education budgets in the past two decades. But most of the new money smoothed the way for students who were college-bound anyway, rather than creating new opportunity for low-income students.

Only from the vantage point of low-income students can the erosion of effective student aid be clearly seen. In 1981, more than half of all student aid was in the form of grants, mostly need-based; by 1999, such grants made up only 40 percent of federal student aid; the system had shifted toward loans, many of which were available to middle and upper-middle-income students. Although Pell Grants (the largest program of need-based federal grants for low-income students) grew over the years, their purchasing power per student did not keep pace with inflation. In 1981, the maximum Pell Grant covered about 80 percent of the cost of attending a public four-year college; by 1999, it covered about 40 percent.[6] The Annual Freshman Survey of the UCLA Higher Education Research Institute confirms that students feel growing concern about their ability to pay for their college education. Students at private black colleges, whose family incomes are typically below the national average, show greater-than-average concern (Table 14.1).

In any attempt to assess the financial condition of low-income college students and would-be college students, however, there is a problem of

TABLE 14.1

Percentage of Freshmen Reporting "Major Concern" about Ability to Finance
Their Educations, 1985 and 1995

	1985	*1995*
All U.S. Four-Year Private Colleges	15	20
Historically Black Private Colleges	20	27

Source: Annual Freshmen Survey, database, 1985 and 1995, Higher Education Research Institute, UCLA.

Note: The preparation of separate data for private black colleges is described in Chapter 11.

availability of evidence and data. The Department of Education, the College Board, the UNCF, and many state agencies collect a great deal of information about enrolled students, but very little about potential students who are not enrolled. Some people lack the desire to enroll in college, have better things to do, or have disabilities that make most college programs inaccessible to them. But some with ability and desire are stopped solely for lack of money. If we are to assess how well or poorly the nation has provided a reasonable approximation of broad access to postsecondary education, we should be able to estimate whether this latter group is large or small, growing or shrinking. The College Board published a national study in 1978 which estimated that about 5 percent of high school graduating seniors in the mid-1970s were in this group, or approximately 12 percent of those who did not go on to postsecondary education soon after completing high school. A panel of about 2,600 high school guidance counselors and youth workers made these estimates based on the number of students in their two most recent graduating classes who, they thought, should have gone directly into postsecondary education but who failed to do so solely because they lacked the money.[7] However, the survey has not been replicated, nor, to our knowledge, has any public or nonprofit agency again attempted to measure the size of this group.

In a previous chapter, we speculated on why the family incomes of students attending private black colleges seemed to be increasing compared with black family incomes in general. Are growing numbers of low-income potential students failing either to apply or to remain in college simply because they are less and less able to afford the cost?[8] No one seems to have a reliable answer.

A report by a 1994 Minnesota legislative task force assessing that state's postsecondary student aid programs took note of this information gap: "It seems odd to operate a program to lower the barriers to postsecondary education without occasionally assessing who is on the other side of the barriers."[9] One circumstance that had stimulated the Minnesota legislature to seek a review of the Minnesota State Grant Program had been an apparent drop in state scholarship applicants from low-income families. Between 1985 and 1992, the number of Minnesota state financial-aid applications (for need-based state grant aid) from families earning $60,000 or more increased by nearly five thousand, or 80 percent, but declined by seven thousand applications, or 27 percent, from families with incomes of $30,000 or less. The task force also observed that the number of Minnesota high school graduates dropped slightly in those years, but not enough to explain the drop in financial aid applications.[10] Neither the task force nor anyone else ever found out with certainty what lies behind those trends.

TIME FOR A THOROUGH REVIEW?

The key developments in student financial aid since 1980 can be summarized as follows. The good news is that the basic federal commitment to aid low-income students has persisted for more than forty years, despite occasional political assaults and internal dissent. Because need-based aid at best has always been a supplementary system placed on top of pre-existing structures, its survival for four decades is no small achievement. However, the formulas to calculate financial need have changed in a direction that offers greater benefits to middle-income and occasionally upper-income families than to low-income groups. New public money for college financial aid has been appropriated predominantly for loans and tax credits for middle-income families. At the same time, changes have occurred in the collegiate institutional environment. Many private colleges and some public ones, seeking to maximize net tuition revenue (tuition minus student aid) have increasingly responded to the truth that three small scholarships to three middle-income students will generate more net tuition than one big scholarship to someone from a very low-income family. In addition, "merit" aid—awarded without regard to the recipient's financial circumstances—has increased in total amount much faster in recent years than has need-based aid. The result of such trends has been a restratification of the college student population, so that high-income students increasingly cluster at flagship private and public universities, and low-income students are concentrated at two-year colleges and lower-cost four-year colleges.[11]

If one imagines need-based student aid for a moment as an automobile, one could say that when it was designed, it appeared to be a reliable, energy-efficient, shiny, new family car. Today, after forty-plus years and two hundred thousand miles on rough roads without a major overhaul, it is showing its age. No time for an overhaul of the public student aid vehicle is likely to be a convenient time. And responsibility for the different aspects of the system is so decentralized and yet interrelated that it is difficult to identify manageable repairs. However, the coming decade may provide a better opportunity to reexamine and repair our student aid system than this country has experienced for some time. The original postwar purposes of student financial aid have enjoyed consistent and strong public support. The Roper Center for Public Opinion Research at the University of Connecticut has collected ninety-three large-scale surveys concerning student aid since the 1950s. The surveys were conducted by Louis Harris and Associates, the Gallup Organization, the Roper Organization, Yankelovich, Skelly and White, Opinion Research Corporation, and by major newspapers, magazines, and television networks. Only three of the surveys indicated a public preference for reducing or abandoning public grants or loans for needy college students, even when it might mean lower priority to other major areas in the federal budget or might result in tax increases. The other ninety surveys indicated generally strong support for public student aid that enables people to attend college who cannot otherwise afford it.[12]

The present moment in the nation's economic history would seem to favor such a reexamination. In the next few decades, the nation's economy will demand larger numbers of highly trained workers with at least a college education, but many elementary and secondary school students today live in families without the money to pay for college expenses. If the polls are right and if the public generally still hopes to take further steps to remove the economic barriers to postsecondary education, the federal budget probably could tolerate noticeably larger appropriations for need-based grants.

If an overhaul proves politically possible, what should be repaired? Certainly a first step might be a national discussion of how far voters wish to go in trying to remove the financial barriers for all postsecondary students through aid that is truly need-based—aid that makes the difference between attending or not attending college and that offers reasonable choice between different types of colleges. If the original purposes of federal student aid are affirmed, the next step might be to increase appropriations for grants targeted mainly at low-income students and to curtail sharply, if economies are needed, income tax credits that do not help low-income families. The methods now used to calculate expected family contributions could be evaluated to see if they are fair and efficient. Finally, a mechanism could be established for periodically assessing how many prospective students there are who do not participate in postsecondary education solely because they lack the money.

TABLE 14.2

Selected Federal Money Flows to Colleges as a Percentage of Total Current
Fund Revenues, 1984 and 1996

	Private Black Colleges		All U.S. Private Colleges	
	1984	1996	1984	1996
Government grants and contracts as a percentage of total current fund revenue	18.2	21.3	3.5	2.8
Pell Grants and other federal scholarships as a percentage of total current fund revenue	11.7	9.3	3.7	3.5
Totals	29.9	30.6	7.2	6.3

Source: NSF WebCASPAR database system.

Note: "Private black colleges" are four-year accredited historically black private institutions, including Howard University. "U.S. private colleges" include Baccalaureate (Liberal
Arts) Colleges I and Baccalaureate (Liberal Arts) Colleges II in the Carnegie Classification
System. Within private black colleges the principal grants are Title III grants, although
some research contracts and grants also are included. Most U.S. private colleges do not receive Title III grants unless they serve large hispanic populations or are tribally controlled
colleges or HBCUs.

In a book primarily concerned with private black colleges, this discussion about public financial aid for college students may seem like a
detour. Student aid, after all, is the broadest kind of public-spending
issue, affecting virtually all colleges and universities. Its rules affect
equally persons of all races. Yet we choose to highlight this question
because of the relatively high concentration of low-income students attending private black colleges. Changes in this particular area of public
policy will have exceptionally strong impact on these colleges: on who
they can enroll, and on the quality of education they provide. Federal
support provides a significantly larger proportion of total current fund
revenue in private black colleges than in private colleges generally. The
most important sources of federal support are need-based Pell Grants for
low-income students and government grants. Private black colleges receive institutional support grants under Title III B of the Higher Education Act of 1965 (amended), but most colleges do not. Table 14.2 shows
that if these two types of federal supports—need-based student aid and
general support grants—are compared with total current fund revenue,
nearly one-third of the current income of private black colleges derives
from these federal sources, whereas the same figure for private colleges

as a whole is only 6 percent. At the same time, UNCF reports that federal scholarships and fellowships make up a much higher proportion of the total scholarship funds of private black colleges (49 percent) than of private colleges generally (17 percent).[13]

This plea for reexamination of public policy in postsecondary student aid is not made in the belief that it will be easy. But we are confident that if it does not occur, historians thirty or forty years from now will identify failure to reexamine and overhaul as one of the significant missed opportunities of our time.

CHAPTER 15

External Sources of Support

Spending decisions made by external organizations—not by individual donors—shape the fate of private black colleges to a greater degree than is true for most private colleges. Most other private colleges derive a higher percentage of their income from tuition, paid by many individual students and their families, and from gifts by individual alumni/ae. The different pattern experienced by private black colleges arises from their history of serving low-income families who cannot afford high tuition, and from having to live within extremely lean operating budgets. In the language of investment counselors, the portfolio of income sources for private black colleges is not only smaller but also less diversified than for most private colleges. Its performance is relatively dependent on a few large potential sources of money, many of which may have other primary loyalties than supporting private black colleges. The good news is that during the past three decades, rising support from these large sources— government, corporations, and foundations—has fueled not only survival but improvement for many private black colleges. In the short term, this must count as a major success. The bad news, the investment counselor might say, is that in the long run, dependence on this particular cluster of sources looks riskier and more vulnerable to unexpected adversity than do the more diversified sources of income.

Table 15.1 compares revenue patterns for UNCF member colleges and all private colleges and universities in 1995–96. Government support and private gifts together accounted for 45 percent of the revenue of these private black colleges, compared with 26 percent for all private colleges. In that year, thirty-nine private black colleges were members of UNCF. (The forty-five private black colleges listed in Chapter 1 as the basic population for this study included, in addition to the UNCF members, Howard and Hampton Universities, and four smaller colleges.) Private gifts include, in order of magnitude, gifts from corporations, foundations, and individuals. This table understates the importance of government support to both black and other private colleges. Part of their tuition income, although indeed paid by students to the colleges and counted as their income, began as public student aid that was awarded to students to make their attendance and tuition payments possible.

Table 15.2 provides a ten-year comparison of the same revenue items for UNCF colleges as were shown in Table 15.1 for 1995–96 for UNCF

TABLE 15.1

Percentage Distribution of Revenue Sources in UNCF Member Colleges and in
U.S. Private Colleges and Universities, 1995–96

Source of Revenue	UNCF Member Colleges (Percentage of Total Revenue)	U.S. Private Colleges and Universities (Percentage of Total Revenue)
Tuition and fees	37	42
Government support	26	17
Private gifts	19	9
Endowment income	3	5
Auxiliary enterprises and other	15	27

Source: The United Negro College Fund, *Statistical Report 1998*, pp. 21, 22.

Note: Auxiliary enterprises, such as dormitories and food service, usually operate close to breakeven and are separate from a college's core education budget. "Private gifts" include foundation, corporate, and individual gifts.

colleges. Table 15.2 shows that the dependence of UNCF college on government support and private gifts actually increased from 38 percent to 45 percent between 1986 and 1996. The largest component of this change was the growth of corporate gifts, particularly those directed to particular colleges and for specific, restricted purposes. Among these private gifts, less than 2 percent of total revenue came from individual alumni/ae gifts.

The major external sources of revenue—those in addition to tuition—have different growth patterns and different reasons for appearing predictable or unpredictable today. Here we discuss Title III of the Higher Education Act (amended), the major federal source of revenue after

TABLE 15.2

Percentage Distribution of Revenue Sources in UNCF Colleges, 1985–86 and
1995–96

Source of Revenue	Percentage of Total Revenue 1985–86	Percentage of Total Revenue 1995–96
Tuition and fees	39	37
Government support	21	26
Private gifts	17	19
Endowment income	4	3
Auxiliary enterprises	19	15

Sources: Table 15.1; United Negro College Fund, *Statistical Report 1987* (New York: UNCF, 1988), p. 20.

student aid, and the recent patterns in gifts from corporations and large foundations.

TITLE III

The Higher Education Act of 1965 not only launched a large need-based student-aid program for low-income postsecondary students, it also began direct-support institutional grants to historically black private and public colleges. In its first eleven years, Title III lacked any race-specific language, referring to the eligible colleges only as "developing institutions." Yet the earliest of its grants went to historically black colleges, which was consistent with the purpose of the legislation as Congress understood it when it was passed. By the mid-1980s, however, more than half the grant funds were being awarded to predominantly white institutions that also served large numbers of low-income students and that declared that they too were "developing." In 1986, Title III was amended to contain separate sections providing support not only for historically black colleges, but also for Hispanic-serving institutions and tribally controlled colleges.

Thomas Wolanin, the political scientist at George Washington University, provides a useful general perspective on the special reasons for providing recurring federal operating support to minority-serving colleges:

> The direct federal grants for institutional support provided to the minority-serving institutions are clearly an exception to the main direction of federal policy for higher education. Where minority-serving institutions—the HBCUs, the tribally controlled community colleges, and the HSIs (Hispanic Serving Institutions)—do a uniquely effective job in serving populations for which the federal government has a special responsibility or in which it has a special interest, and where these institutions lack the resources to carry out their mission, the federal government has adopted programs to directly support these institutions. This is far, however, from a policy of across-the-board direct federal support to all higher education institutions.[1]

Title III allocations in the federal budget for 2000 included a targeted institutional subsidy of $179 million for historically black colleges, $42 million for Hispanic-serving institutions, and $6 million for aid to tribally controlled Native American colleges.[2] In contrast, the federal student aid budget (for all undergraduate colleges and universities) for 2000 is more than a hundred times larger than the Title III budget for minority-serving institutions: $50.6 billion, the largest part of which is for new student loans. Such targeted assistance to historically black public and private colleges was justified in two principal ways. First, federal responsibility was asserted in the Thirteenth, Fourteenth, and Fifteenth Amendments to the Constitution to protect the rights of freed slaves and promote their effective full citizenship; second the Congress wished to attempt to remedy the effects of past federal and state discrimination against these colleges. A statement of "Findings and Purposes" in the 1986 legislation reads:

> States and the federal government have discriminated in the allocation of land and financial resources to support public black institutions under the Morrill Act of 1862 and its progeny, and against public and private Black colleges in the award of Federal grants and contracts under this Act and other Federal programs which benefit institutions of higher education. . . . The current state of Black colleges and universities is partly attributable to the discriminatory action of the States and the Federal Government and this discriminatory action requires the remedy of enhancement of Black postsecondary institutions to ensure their continuation and participation in fulfilling the Federal mission of equality of educational opportunity.[3]

Historically black colleges in this legislation are defined as colleges founded prior to 1964 (the year in which major civil rights legislation passed), whose founding purpose was the education of black students. The list of eligible schools changes slowly over the years as eligible colleges merge or lose accreditation or close. Roughly speaking, there are about a hundred two- and four-year historically black colleges, about half of which are public. Their student bodies are predominantly but usually not exclusively black. A few, mostly public schools, started as completely black but now have white student majorities: Kentucky State University, Lincoln University (Missouri), Bluefield State College (West Virginia), West Virginia College, Alabama A & M, Albany State College (Georgia), and the University of Arkansas (Pine Bluff).

Title III funds for a black college are rationed according to the number of low-income students enrolled, the total number of graduates, and the number of graduates who attend graduate schools in fields where black Americans are underrepresented. Grant amounts today range upward from a statutory minimum of $500,000; few exceed $1.5 million. Although colleges must propose specific purposes for their grants, the statutory list of possible purposes is so broad that Title III money is virtually unrestricted money. Because $500,000 is the smallest grant a college may receive, Title III grants make up a more significant portion of total revenue in small-budget colleges than they do in large ones. Such colleges as Clark Atlanta University, Xavier University, Hampton University, and Morehouse College, which have led the black college enrollment expansion of the past fifteen years, have seen their Title III funds diminish as a percentage of total revenue.

Danny Flanigan, treasurer and vice president for business and financial affairs at Spelman College, remembers the impact of Title III funds when they first started flowing into the college treasury in the late 1960s and early 1970s. At that time private black colleges were not in a good position to raise tuition in any significant way, yet they urgently needed money for student recruitment, faculty salaries, program improvement, administrative reform, and the maintenance and improvement of their physical plants. Flanigan explained in a recent interview:

> Title III was the only major infusion of new flexible money which came to Spelman College in those years. The money was used to launch some of the natural science programs which have proved important since then. It was used selectively to improve faculty salaries. Spelman was one of five or six colleges then which used Title III funds to hire a full-time development officer and create an embryonic development office. And in other important ways we used it to shore up the budget. Title III typically would have brought in about $600,000 a year in a $5 million total budget—or about 12 percent of the total. Today the percentage is not as significant—slightly over a million of Title III funds in a $52 million budget—but the flexibility to initiate and to strengthen what is most important still is very significant.[4]

Norman Francis, president of Xavier University, has similar memories. Xavier used its early Title III money to renovate critical classrooms, buy equipment, and launch some of the natural sciences programs that would later help to build the University's record of success in science. Student retention at that time was a problem. Some of the Title III money was spent for computer-equipped centers to teach writing. Some of it established an academic counseling service. Title III money also helped to create both a development office and a planning office for the University.

"Title III complemented the need-based funds which went to students and which stimulated our expansion," Francis recalls. "Title III enabled the black colleges to fill in when something important couldn't be financed from other sources. It was the best kind of money. It still serves that important flexible function—even if the proportional size of the grants for some of us is smaller now."[5]

One would think that, after thirty-five years, the main arguments would have crystallized on the fate of Title III subsidies. But particular aspects of the issue have changed significantly over the years. These changes emerge every few years, when the Higher Education Act goes through its periodic reauthorization process.

The most powerful early arguments in favor of Title III support for historically black colleges looked to the past—to the constitutional amendments establishing federal responsibility for the full citizenship of former slaves and the importance of remedying years of federal and state discrimination. During the 1980s, however, the desire of the Reagan administration to shrink government played into the debates about Title III's renewal. The administration did not directly challenge the desirability of strengthening black colleges, but the label "developing" in the developing institutions portion of the act was seen by the administration and some in Congress as a way to bring Title III to an end. All that was needed (the reasoning went) was to establish criteria that would signal, before too many more years had passed, that these black colleges had indeed "developed"—and so presumably could be deprived of their Title III subsidies. Partly to resist the introduction of a deadline, and partly to insulate these colleges from increased competition with predominantly white colleges, which more frequently were claiming that they, too, were "developing" and thus eligible for Title III funds, the 1986 reauthorization of the Higher Education Act created separate sections for historically black colleges and for other colleges that also served large proportions of low-income students.

Favoring the idea of long-term continuity of Title III support, Christopher F. Edley, Sr., president and chief executive officer of UNCF wrote to the *Washington Post* prior to the 1986 reauthorization: "Accounting for 5 to 10 percent of the operating budgets of these institutions, Title III makes possible on black college campuses the growth and development experienced by majority white campuses."[6]

Today, proponents of Title III subsidies for private black colleges advance other primary reasons for continuance. First, they argue, these colleges have worked successfully with minority students who have had deficient pre-college education. In the coming years, the workforce will require that larger numbers of such students be educated if they are to perform well in our fast-changing economy. Helping to maintain and strengthen this record through direct support of black colleges has become an increasingly important national responsibility. Second, these colleges are important roots for black Americans, having preserved significant parts of their cultural history and nurtured a significant proportion of their political, spiritual, and professional leadership.

The principal arguments against Title III do not appear to have changed as much. Opponents still feel that institutional subsidy of any kind is bad policy, and that continuing subsidy is worse. Some are skeptical about federal investment in black colleges, having interpreted the *Brown* decision to mean that these colleges should no longer exist. Some dislike affirmative action, whether applied to individuals or to institutions. Finally, a few favor continuing Title III, but changing the distribution formula to provide more money to the larger and more prosperous minority-serving colleges and less to the smaller, more vulnerable ones. These arguments opposing Title III have not prevailed, in part because they have not coalesced into any clear opposition bloc and because the money at stake is so small compared with the size of student aid and other major federal programs. In addition, Title III advocates have been well positioned in Congress and are frequently aided by advocates with key positions in the federal administration.

We believe that there is a historic federal responsibility to assist historically black private and public colleges, only made stronger by their track record of effective performance, and by the emerging need to educate larger numbers of low-income persons to at least the baccalaureate level. Some day such a subsidy may indeed not be needed, but we think it is needed now and should not be viewed as a short-term commitment. As to the Title III distribution formula, one could argue for any number of changes, although we do not.

We have discussed the importance of Title III of the Higher Education Act because it is the largest single long-term program of federal institutional aid to help black colleges directly, but it is not the only form of federal assistance to private black colleges. Several other kinds of help deserve mention. In 1980, President Jimmy Carter launched a White House Initiative on Historically Black Colleges and Universities that established an office responsible for helping black public and private colleges participate more fully in existing federal higher education research and assistance programs. Located in the Department of Education, the office has been sustained and strengthened by executive orders issued by each president since Carter. The office monitors compliance in twenty-seven federal departments and agencies, publishes periodic reports, and through its national advisory board, recommends federal policy with respect to these colleges and universities.[7]

In addition, private black colleges are eligible for matching grants under the Omnibus Parks and Public Lands Management Act of 1996 to restore selected old buildings that have been placed on the National Register of Historic Places.[8] Finally, in the 1980s and early 1990s, a small number of the larger private black colleges received special congressional appropriations to construct single buildings, such as a center for health sciences at Tuskegee University, and a health and fitness center at Bethune-Cookman College.

Today the call for ending Title III support for historically black colleges is less insistent. Perhaps that is because the accomplishments of these colleges are more widely accepted, or perhaps because Title III now encompasses several minority-serving groups of colleges—not just one— and thus appeals directly to more voters. Whatever the answer may be, it is clear that Title III, along with the generally available federal student-aid programs, has been extremely important to the substantial accomplishments and improvements of private black colleges in the past two decades.

CORPORATIONS AND FOUNDATIONS

Gifts and grants from corporate foundations provide the majority of private gifts, which in turn make up nearly a fifth of the typical private black college's annual income.[9] The other big source of private gifts is private foundations, including such familiar names as Ford, Kellogg, Kresge, or, more recently, Hewlett, Packard, and Gates. The large foundations usually are named after a founder or founding couple, and were endowed at the time of founding with corporate stock of a major corporation. Following the passage of the Tax Reform Act of 1969, private foundations were encouraged to diversify investments to avoid holding only the securities of the founder's corporation. The foundations are required each year to pay out a minimum percentage—currently 5 percent—of the current market value of their endowment assets.

Unlike private foundations, corporations may donate not only money, but also goods manufactured by the corporation or the skills and time of its employees. Several of the private black colleges were introduced to information technology by shipments of computers from IBM, Hewlett-Packard, and other computer manufacturers. The 3M company has provided copiers. IBM and others loaned scientists to teach in colleges with few or no faculty members knowledgeable about computers. Companies for many years offered undergraduate scholarships, with the hope that the scholarship holder might accept a summer internship and then become a candidate for employment after graduation.

One of the main shifts that UNCF officials see in the grant-making scene is the increasing frequency with which both corporation and foundation gifts are restricted to particular purposes. Corporations, particularly in the late 1990s, moved away from making recurring unrestricted gifts either to individual colleges or to UNCF for formula-based distribution to the members. Instead, gifts are for purposes that are more directly business-related, and that can be justified to shareholders as related to corporate profitability. "A science-based company might have given UNCF repeated unrestricted gifts of fifty thousand dollars a year," says William Gray, UNCF president, "but in high-profit years may also be willing to give two or three hundred thousand if we can put together a program to stimulate the training of more minority engineers."[10]

The annual volume of charitable giving by major corporations is more unpredictable than that for most foundations. A survey conducted by the

Chronicle of Philanthropy, comparing 1999 corporate giving with that for 1998, showed that Ford, Microsoft, Phillip Morris, Prudential Insurance Company of America, and Wal-Mart Stores all increased the volume of corporate gifts more than 40 percent in that single year, while Citigroup, Chevron, and Texaco decreased their gifts by more than 10 percent each.[11] Large foundations also vary their total payments from year to year, but the percentage variation usually is much smaller.

Prior to 1953, many corporate gifts to colleges were restricted, to those directly related to their business, such as corporate scholarships for relatives of employees. Until that time, existing legal precedents made a corporation vulnerable to shareholder lawsuits if its gifts were not demonstrably business related. A 1953 New Jersey court decision, however, ruled against shareholder objections, saying that an unrestricted contribution to Princeton University by a New Jersey fireplug manufacturer was not an illegal contribution, and by implication that a broader standard of corporate citizenship was permissible. Over the next decades, unrestricted corporate giving became much more common. A report to the UNCF board of directors in 1979 estimated that by then more than 95 percent of corporate gifts to UNCF were unrestricted, whereas this could be said of only two-thirds of its foundation gifts.[12] Then, coming full circle in the late 1990s, restricted gifts once more become the largest portion of annual UNCF receipts. Table 15.3 shows that between 1995 and 2000, total private gifts to UNCF increased by a factor of almost 2.5, but during the same period restricted gifts increased fivefold. A recent and comprehensive summary of private gift receipts in all private black

TABLE 15.3
Private Gifts to the United Negro College Fund, 1995 and 2000

Type of Gift	1995	2000
Unrestricted gifts	$44,100,000	$ 63,800,000
Percentage of total gifts	75	44
Five-year percentage increase	—	45
Restricted gifts	$15,000,000	$ 81,000,000
Percentage of total gifts	25	56
Five-year percentage increase	—	440
Total private gifts	$59,100,000	$144,800,000
Percent of total gifts	100	100
Five-year percentage increase	—	145

Source: United Negro College Fund.

Note: The table excludes capital campaign receipts and government contract grants. The private gifts summarized here probably account for between one-quarter and one-third of all private gifts to UNCF member colleges in these years.

colleges is not available. However, the main trends illustrated in this UNCF summary appear to provide a reasonable proxy, even though the UNCF receipts include a higher proportion of gifts from large national corporations than is true for private gifts going directly (not through UNCF) to the member colleges.

The terms "unrestricted" and "restricted" indicate roughly how much freedom a gift recipient has to determine the final purpose for which the money will be spent. A restricted gift must be spent for a previously specified purpose or returned to the donor, while an unrestricted gift gives college trustees virtually total discretion in deciding on its use. It is not necessarily true, however, that a restricted gift is less important to a college's main purposes than an unrestricted one. This might be the case if the gift were, say, a soft drink machine contributed by its manufacturer. But the computer technology grants that many colleges received in the 1980s and 1990s were probably directed toward needs that were deemed close to top priority by the recipient colleges. If the donor and recipient communicate clearly before the gift is made, the restrictions need not be onerous. Without such communication, however, the usefulness of restricted gifts may be much less than that of unrestricted ones.

The trustees of large foundations have no shareholder interest to consider, other than what they perceive to be community interest, or, in relatively few instances, the preferred fields of interest stated by the founder. Many large foundations believe they should promote social change, and have a persistent desire "to make a difference." Typically, the large foundations hire more staff per grant dollar than do the corporate giving programs, allowing foundation staff more time to travel, visit grant applicants, and plan long-term grant sequences in some detail. An example of this increased attention to planning comes from a staff paper mailed in preparation for the September 1971 board of trustees meeting at The Ford Foundation. Ford became the single largest supporter of historically black colleges in the 1970s, shortly after board discussion and endorsement of this staff memo:

> The missing element in this effort [to improve minority education]—and the one we propose to add—is a grant program that asserts our conviction that a selected group of black colleges not only should survive, but should be reaching for better levels of quality and the certainty of purpose that will open new options for them and demonstrate the potential for vitality of black higher education and scholarship. . . .
>
> It is unlikely that all the private black colleges can succeed. Some are too poor, too small, or too ill-administered to survive the growing competition of public institutions including the low-cost community colleges. But some, perhaps a dozen or so, have strong prospects for robust growth and qualita-

tive competitiveness. These are the institutions that should be the special target of our program.[13]

The $50 million that Ford eventually granted to twenty-five private black colleges represented an electrifying endorsement of the performance and potential of these colleges. The Foundation's actions would leave for later discussion among the colleges and other donors whether there were indeed only a few of these colleges with a prospect for "robust growth" and whether the Foundation's by-invitation-only manner of identifying prospective recipients of its largest grants was the appropriate method. By contrast, for example, the organizing principle of the UNCF is that all of its members (approximately forty in recent years) merit support and have potential for long and worthwhile service. Our own conclusion from earlier chapters is that even the most financially vulnerable private black colleges can succeed if they enjoy consistently good leadership, and that since grantmakers inevitably take a chance on the future, most foundations and corporations should include a larger pool of potential grant candidates than merely the most promising ten or fifteen institutions. If more of these colleges received serious consideration, we think it would promote a greater sense of fairness throughout the system and create a greater possibility that a few well-led but vulnerable colleges will have a chance for sustained financial improvement. Many, although not all of the foundation's faculty-development grants described in an earlier chapter resulted from the inclusive process advocated here, and these grants generally produced very good results.

Uncertainty about the total amount available from foundation grants each year is probably not greater than that for corporate giving, although some of the determinants differ. Both corporate and foundation grants to these colleges vary depending on how the key boards judge the relative importance of grants to private black colleges compared with other worthwhile social and cultural purposes. Both sources of grants grow when business conditions are favorable, as has occurred almost without precedent since the early 1980s. Corporate giving volume tends to move relatively quickly in response to corporate profits; whereas foundations, calculating 5 percent of endowment market value and paying out at least that amount within two years, are responding to similar pressures, but typically have longer to smooth out large fluctuations in revenue. Occasionally, a large new foundation is endowed and subsequently develops a strong interest in private black colleges, which enlarges the colleges' stream of grants. This occurred when the Hewlett, Bush, and Packard foundations were founded or reorganized in the 1970s, and also with the Annenberg and Gates foundations in the late 1990s. But even if the total of foundation grants holds steady or grows, these colleges still may encounter sharp discontinuity in funds if several key donors, planning independently, coincidentally act in a way that significantly lowers their donations to a single college or purpose. For example, a 1991 survey conducted by the Pew Charitable Trusts of Philadelphia identified the ten largest foundations that supported private colleges for the years 1987–90. A poll of these ten by Bush Foundation staff in 1992 indicated that seven of them had made building or endowment grants to those colleges throughout the 1980s. Between 1990 and 1992, however, five of those seven foundations conducted program reviews and separately decided to cease making such capital grants. Even though UNCF was about to begin a multi-year capital fund drive, the withdrawal of five major foundations from capital grant-making more or less at once must have been a blow to long-term planning in crucial if unglamorous areas of the colleges' operation. We think this danger of several foundations inadvertently distorting a generally sensible pattern of large-foundation grants has increased, now that fewer of these foundations seem inclined to make the unrestricted or multi-purpose grants that in earlier decades acted as a shock absorber to the system.

UNCF

Although not, strictly speaking, an original source of external funds for individual institutions and not inclusive of all private black colleges, UNCF is crucial in gathering these funds. The origin and development of UNCF, the first effective collegiate fundraising consortium in the United States, is described in Chapters 6 and 12. In recent years, between one-quarter and one-third of private giving, mainly corporation and foundation gifts, received by UNCF member colleges was initially solicited by UNCF and granted to UNCF en route to the colleges. In 1999 and 2000, this amounted to more than $100 million a year.

As its founder Frederick Patterson predicted, a disciplined, cooperative effort, endorsed by national political and corporate leaders, can generate a basic public awareness of a group of colleges, many of which otherwise would continue to remain hidden from public view. This, in turn, makes possible annual direct mail and television appeals to individuals with no other direct links to those colleges. In short, UNCF provides a public platform from which successful individual colleges have an improved chance to make their own public case. Finally, the existence of national, public support for this group of colleges strengthens their federal lobbying efforts to help define or maintain direct support through such programs as Title III or need-based student aid for all of postsecondary education.

Meanwhile, on a per-student basis, the formula by which UNCF distributes unrestricted annual fund gifts to its members favors the smaller institutions, even though the larger colleges individually receive larger total amounts. Because the smaller schools often lack access to major foundations and national corporations, UNCF distributions are particularly important to them.

Given credible leadership and the cooperation of the member-college presidents, UNCF occupies a strategic fundraising position for those major gifts that even the larger private black colleges would find hard to duplicate. If the desired purpose for a large gift does not fit sensibly with the usual UNCF formula distribution for unrestricted gifts, UNCF can design an administrative process that does fit. Several foundations, for example, want to help UNCF college faculty complete doctoral studies, but do not wish to set up their own separate selection process to choose among individual candidates. UNCF provides selection committees and administrative staff. As more and more large donors wish to make targeted grants for specific purposes, UNCF has enlarged the size of its program administrative staff. Examples of sector-wide programs launched by grants between 1995 and 2000 and administered centrally are a $130 million program to improve technology infrastructure in UNCF colleges, financed principally by Microsoft, IBM, and AT&T; UNCF staff also provide central administration for a $42 million Lilly Endowment grant, which distributes single, major block grants to each UNCF member college for major building and equipment improvements, faculty development, and scholarships. The Bill and Melinda Gates Foundation recognized the central staff capacity of UNCF in 1999 when UNCF was granted a billion dollars—the largest single private gift in the history of higher education—to allow at least a thousand black American, hispanic, Native American, and Asian American students of high achievement to attend the college their choice. Graduate students are also eligible for support, based on demonstrated financial need, in fields where minorities are underrepresented: mathematics, science, engineering, education, and library science.[14]

Initiative for some UNCF-administered programs comes from within the member colleges. One such effort, started in 1995 with Mott Foundation support, is the Fiscal and Strategic Technical Assistance Program (FASTAP). This program established an assessment and consulting service that helps member colleges improve financial management, business and financial aid office procedures, and institutional planning. Among other things, FASTAP is designed to help the most vulnerable institutions avoid the kind of trouble that nearly closed Texas College in the early 1990s. First priority for FASTAP consultants goes to colleges with the most urgent problems. By unanimous consent of member-college presidents, each college must participate in the program if it encounters one or more of the following difficulties: sanction by a regional, state, or federal funding authority; an operating deficit for two consecutive years; a need to seek emergency financial assistance from UNCF, such as an advance against anticipated fund distributions; or other operating or financial deficiencies evident on review of the college's audited financial statement. During its first year of operation, five of the six colleges that were under accreditation sanctions have, with FASTAP assistance, had full accreditation restored. Only one member college since 1995 has posted two consecutive years of deficit. Knoxville College and Texas College are seeking to have full accreditation restored.[15]

Another important UNCF service is research and periodic collection of statistics about member colleges and about black education generally. This is provided by the Frederick D. Patterson Institute of UNCF. Its output not only improves UNCF current fundraising, but also provides a database for scholars that extends back to the 1970s.

Although UNCF is the largest and perhaps most visible of the organizations that provide assessments of private black colleges and administer external grants on their behalf, it is not the only significant one. The Southern Education Foundation, based in Atlanta, is another such organization. It administers foundation grants for the benefit of private and public black colleges, and produces major reports on the progress of elementary, secondary, and postsecondary education in the southern states. Important data and assessment also come from government sources: the Department of Education and the President's Board of Advisors on Historically Black Colleges and Universities.

If the presidents and trustees of private black colleges were to review their collective performance in dealing with major sources of external support during the past three decades, there is much reason for pride. Funds received from Title III, corporations, and foundations have all increased substantially. Private black colleges retained the loyalty of major supporters and attracted significant new contributions from others, such as companies in the information technology and pharmaceutical industries. Most of the political challenges to reduce or dilute federal program support were successfully resisted. Still, much remains to be done. Most of these colleges still lack financial reserves in proportion to the scope and current expense of their programs. Most of the colleges thus remain vulnerable to any prolonged economic downturn or political sea change. A task remains, then, to consider strategies that permit more of these colleges to improve their chances for independent, long-term growth and financial health.

CHAPTER 16

Leadership and Financial Independence

"HERE AT STILLMAN, we need to make sure we stand and prosper," Moses Jones, chairman of the college's board of trustees, told the authors at the end of our 1997 visit to the school. As we wrote the book, we too, were concerned with how in the coming decades private black colleges will "stand and prosper." One of our goals was to identify operational tasks that their leaders might control, or at least influence in ways that are important for their colleges' futures. Our sketches of Xavier University, and Stillman, Spelman, and Texas Colleges indicate that sustained, competent leadership itself is the single most significant ingredient in maintaining or strengthening any of these colleges. Leadership is a particularly important issue for private black colleges because their financial reserves are so much slimmer than those of their white college counterparts, however one chooses to define such reserves. Circumstances require that black college leaders be more consistently surefooted, or be prepared to suffer more severe consequences when missteps occur.

Perhaps the most important lesson we learned from the experience of successful private black colleges was that, although one man or woman can make a powerful difference in such an environment, the strength of his or her leadership also must be measured by the cohesion of the educational community that underlies it. Heroic single-person leadership is not enough. The nature of the community's support is crucial. The successful presidents we interviewed did not deny their own importance, but also emphasized key contributions made by faculty trustees and members of their administrative cabinets. We do not think they were merely being politic.

Our impression is that the organized role of faculty is different in many black colleges than that in other colleges. In all schools, the faculty is responsible for the front-line teaching, advising, and nurturing of students. Given the financial realities, faculty in historically black private colleges have accepted these responsibilities with less pay and heavier teaching loads. Although there are signs of change, the voice of the faculty in governing the typical private black colleges has long seemed weaker than at predominantly white colleges. Unsurprisingly then, the faculty culture in many private black colleges has permitted a greater presidential range of action than one might otherwise expect, but has also left the faculty less able to oppose a poor president or steer a college through periods of administrative ineffectiveness. For example, there was no organized faculty intervention to help deal with the consequences of President Stinson's illness at Stillman College, but there was quick faculty acceptance of President Wynn's curriculum initiatives—acceptance of a kind hard to imagine at Williams or Wellesley. The organized faculty role in governance has grown stronger in many predominantly white colleges and universities. The same trend can now be detected at many private black colleges. Little has been written about this or the effects of the growing faculty development movement on institutional self-definition and institutional leadership patterns. Decentralized faculty initiative was crucial to the survival and adaptation of many private black colleges in the 1970s and subsequently to their increasing strength.

At the same time, the trustees are at the top of any college or university organization chart. They are the legal owners of the institution's assets and the stewards of its educational programs. They choose each new president. Despite the importance of trustees and the availability of minutes of their meetings, however, much of the evidence needed for a diagnostic assessment of the performance of trusteeship today is not available.

Two benchmark studies of trusteeship of private black colleges were financed by The Ford Foundation about thirty years ago. In 1967–68, Samuel M. Nabrit and Julius S. Scott, Jr., both respected educators, administered questionnaires and visited with trustees at fifty private black colleges to assess quality and vitality of governance. At that time those boards had 1,255 members, of whom 730 were black and 525 white. Colleges supported by the African Methodist Episcopal Church, the Christian Methodist Episcopal Church, and the American Baptist Convention were governed by boards with black trustee majorities; institutions independent of church support or supported by the Protestant Episcopal Church, the Presbyterian Church, the United Church of Christ, and the United Methodist Church had white trustee majorities.[1] No trustee was under twenty years old, few between twenty and thirty, and many were over seventy. The 222 clergymen made up the largest single occupational group. Only 11 percent of all trustees were women. Nabrit and Scott found that many boards of trustees presented opportunities for significant improvement. Problems included poor attendance at meetings, weak contribution to a school's financial support, lack of understanding of the curriculum philosophy and objectives, minimal oversight of plant maintenance and restoration, and insufficient attention to town-gown community relations. Nabrit and Scott also noted that "The perceptions and performances of the board members of the institutions we studied are characteristic of institutions across the nation."[2]

In 1970–71, Professor Daniel C. Thompson of Dillard University conducted a large survey of students and faculty published as *Private Black Colleges at the Crossroads*. Thompson also interviewed more than three hundred administrators and trustees. The conclusions he drew from these interviews are generally consistent with the Nabrit and Scott findings:

> Because many trustees have very limited knowledge of their colleges and lack the time to better acquaint themselves, their committees seem to do little more than listen to reports dealing with specific areas of concern, then recommend that matters be handled by applying existing policies. From what we could learn, such trustees are not often prepared to recommend and push for creative innovations.[3]

When we visited the three case-study colleges described in Chapter 9, we usually met with trustees. Although we did not concentrate our attention on governing-board operations, we heard much anecdotal evidence to suggest a more encouraging general impression than the one suggested by the 1968 Nabrit and Scott study. For example, Spelman's board had helped the college achieve impressive fundraising results. Stillman's presidents and board chairpersons appeared to enjoy close and mutually supportive relationships. At Xavier University, many people observed in different ways that the Sisters of the Blessed Sacrament and the university administration had been closely intertwined and that the Sisters were an important part of Xavier's successful growth. The Texas College board chairman Bishop Marshall Gilmore recruited an able president during a crisis and persuaded the C.M.E. Church body to contribute unprecedented financial support to help save the college. Julius Scott estimates today that if he conducted a general study similar to his Ford-financed 1968 survey, it would probably inspire greater confidence in the boards of trustees than did the original. Other observers of trustee and director performance, on nonprofit and for-profit boards, believe there is an improved involvement and competence in all types of boards. This improvement includes execution of specific tasks such as selection of new board members, avoidance of conflict of interest, and acquiring information about the activity being governed.[4]

We have said that the single most important factor affecting the future of private black colleges is whether they will attract and hold excellent leadership—by which we mean the president and key administrators, faculty, and trustees. Although many anecdotal accounts exist, reliable public or published analyses of faculty-administration relationships and trustee-administration performance are surprisingly rare. Perhaps these topics are deemed too sensitive for a public forum. Nonetheless, our optimism for the future would improve if such subjects were more openly discussed.

FINANCIAL ENVIRONMENT AND INSTITUTIONAL STRATEGY

Whoever fills the key leadership roles in whatever working relationships during the next twenty or thirty years, the higher education marketplace does not make for an easy environment. When major trends in private black colleges and in four-year private colleges are compared (Table 16.1), the following past relationships are highlighted. Tuition and fees at private black colleges are roughly two-thirds those at four-year private colleges, although the per-student annual educational and general expenditure is roughly comparable. This approximate relationship has been true for the past twenty years. Looking more closely, however, expenditure per student was greater in private black colleges than in U.S.

TABLE 16.1

Educational and General Expenditure per FTE Student at U.S. Private Colleges and at Private Black Colleges (in Constant 1992 Dollars), 1976, 1988, and 1996

	1976	*1988*	*1996*	*Percentage Increase (1976 to 1996)*
Private black colleges				
Educational and general expenditure per FTE student	9,228	9,969	13,556	47
Tuition and fees per FTE student	(3,516)	(4,679)	(6,347)	60
U.S. four-year private colleges				
Educational and general expenditure per FTE student	7,959	10,987	14,491	82
Tuition and fees per FTE student	(5,055)	(7,382)	(10,165)	101

Source: National Science Foundation WebCASPAR database system.

Note: The expenditure category is adjusted total educational and general expenditures and transfers (excluding Pell Grants and nonmandatory transfers). Tuition and fees also are in 1992 constant dollars. "FTE" is the abbreviation for full-time equivalent.

private colleges in 1976. The curves crossed in the mid-1980s. Private black colleges now spend a little less per student. Because both types of colleges presumably would prefer to minimize the deficit between tuition/fees and expenditure per student, it is hard to escape the conclusion that cost pressures are and have been relatively hard on private black colleges, and show no sign of easing. Private black colleges that wish to continue to provide relatively favorable faculty-to-student ratios—and so must at least maintain a salary schedule already competitively lower than it should be—do not have obvious management strategies to improve the situation. Cost per student at these schools have been under pressure for some time: tuition and fees, which have risen in inflation-adjusted terms, have nonetheless proven more difficult to increase at private black colleges than at private colleges generally. While further tests of tuition elasticity or creative attempts at reorganizing and controlling expenses are possible, this particular group of colleges probably will not be able to improve their financial strength significantly in these ways.

Is there, then, no way to break out of this gloomy scenario defined by sticky tuition prices and the constant need to economize? Perhaps, but it is not an easy way. The college hoping for a breakout must first develop a specific vision of one or more niches in the student marketplace in which it might reasonably aspire to be a leader if it is to be especially attractive. In pursuing that vision, its leaders must always be aware of the tension between short-term imperatives and long run considerations for allocating resources when trying simultaneously to raise money for both. Easy for us to suggest, you may say, since we are sufficiently removed from the everyday struggles of black college leaders. The voice of Luther Foster echoes from an earlier chapter: "There is little time for planning while fires rage daily."[5]

Developing a strategic vision is an art—one difficult to design reliably from a distance. Good visions arise from an intimate understanding of a college's existing and potential strengths, and some sense of what its future students, not yet present, might find particularly valuable. Stillman College appears to have displayed such vision in its decision to re-emphasize its role in the preparation of elementary and secondary school teachers, as well as to strengthen the sciences and the arts. Xavier University's insistence that its science graduates be at a competitive level for graduate study has become a valuable signature for that institution. The successful vision must not only make sense in itself, but also seem promising and important enough so that those parts of the college outside of the spotlight will support—or at least tolerate—that extra concentration of effort. Without a consensus among administration, trustees, and faculty, it will be difficult to convince outside donors that one college's desire for contributions should rise above that of others who are also competing for funds. In addition, without such an internally generated consensus, trustees and presidents will find it almost impossible to resist or redirect occasional well-intentioned, unplanned gifts and grants that may initially seem worthwhile, but may distract the college from its basic plans for development in destructive ways.

For example, if a college about to seek major gifts and grants for a new science center is unexpectedly offered half the cost of a $10 million gymnasium and indoor sports and fitness center—providing the remaining costs of the sports center can be raised within the next two years— what should the president and trustees do? The answer may not be clear, unless the college's long-term needs and possibilities have already been discussed, and some consensus achieved as to what are the best paths for growth and change. Concentrating on raising money for and building a sports center may look pretty attractive if there are no other serious plans afoot. But if concentrating upon the sports center now means putting off a plan that could redefine the college's main strengths, the sports center should probably wait. Although a dollar raised for almost any legitimate purpose may count as a dollar, the same amount raised for a college's strategic, top-priority work by comparison counts as two or three dollars.

According to a recent survey of presidential tenure by the American Council on Education, the average tenure of a president of a four-year private college as of 1995 was seven years. Based on the same survey methodology, the average presidential tenure in private black colleges for 1998 also turns out to be seven years. If one eliminated from these calculation a few long-serving presidents such as Norman Francis of Xavier with his thirty-two years on the job, average service would be closer to five or six years.[6] A survey by Ayers and Associates, Inc. conducted for the Kresge Foundation in 1998 calculates the average tenure of chief development or fundraising officers in private black colleges at 7.1 years.[7] We define "long view" asset-building strategies as those that yield their greatest and most visible benefit some years after the initiator of the strategy has left office. One does not need to favor the long view to ensure meeting this year's deadline for applying for Title III funds, or that tuition and student fees are collected promptly. It does require the long view to spend scarce time and money planting oak saplings, or cultivating an individual donor whose likelihood of rewriting his or her will is small, or providing extra staff to try to increase by one or two thousand the number of alumni/ae donors—most of whom today can only give small annual gifts, but at least a few of whom may some day offer the college much greater sums.

Top leadership can probably function more effectively, other things equal, if its practitioners hold office eight or nine years rather than four or five. Any disadvantage largely disappears, however, if the incumbents—

whatever their length of service—can manage to devote energy to the long-term imperatives, while at the same time trying to put out the daily fires.

PLANT AND ENDOWMENT ASSETS

Without trying to prescribe comprehensive changes in fundraising strategy for private black colleges, we call attention to two asset classes: physical plant and endowment. In many private black colleges, these need more attention and more money than they now receive. We also advocate heightened, better organized efforts to solicit gifts from individual donors, even though that may involve relatively high expense for low immediate returns.

Richard P. Dober, a planning and design consultant at Dober, Lidsky, Craig and Associates, has reviewed the history of black college campus growth in the 1960s and 1970s. Campuses throughout the United States coped with the enrollment expansion of those years, he reports, by taking advantage of government loans to finance the needed construction. But he notes that there was a price for this quick building splurge: a large number of buildings that now must be replaced or remodeled:

> The federal government recognized the need for colleges generally to expand, and recognized they would need capital funds to do it. But there was never enough to meet the rising enrollment demands, so several kinds of informal rationing occurred. Colleges had to compete for public money, and under most public guidelines the most competitive proposals were those which promised the largest number of square feet per construction dollar. Rarely was landscaping money made available. So all across the country there were a lot of raw looking sites. The federally financed campus construction of the 1960s, for the most part, doesn't compare all that well with what was built before or since. In the historically black colleges the 1960s dormitory buildings were devoted more to shelter than to some of the collegiate purposes—meeting spaces, study spaces, recreation spaces— which are insisted upon today.[8]

A 1989 Joint Report of the Association of Physical Plant Administrators and the National Association of College and University Business Officers (NACUBO), "The Decaying American Campus: A Ticking Time Bomb,"[9] notes that physical plant management encountered a series of unusual challenges in recent years:

> Between 1950 and 1975, higher education's physical space tripled in size. More college and university space was constructed during this 25 year

period than in the prior 200 years. . . . By the late 1970s and 1980s the situation had changed. The baby boom of the 1950s and 1960s had declined, resulting in fewer traditional aged students. Inflation and soaring energy costs . . . squeezed college and university operating budgets. Although many new facilities had been built during the 1960s, their construction was at the expense of older buildings which were deteriorating and accumulating backlogs of undone maintenance. In addition, many of the buildings constructed during the 1960s were not of optimal quality in terms of longevity. . . . The facilities were functional in the near term, but not likely to hold up over time.[10]

A follow-up survey in 1996 estimated that the nation's colleges and universities as a group had accumulated deferred maintenance work which, if performed in that year would cost $26 billion, or about 9 percent of the estimated replacement cost of the total physical plant. By far the largest amount of this backlog was in public and private research universities. The median black college had an estimated backlog of accumulated deferred maintenance of $2.8 million, of which about one-third was estimated by participating colleges to be urgent. Since on average public black colleges have greater enrollment than private black colleges, the estimated backlog was probably overstated when applied only to private black colleges.[11]

The National Trust for Historic Preservation in 1998 placed all 103 historically black public and private colleges on its annual roster of America's Most Endangered Historic Places, calling national attention to deferred maintenance on their still-standing early buildings. Eleven million dollars of federal assistance for restoration projects was awarded in a public parks appropriation in 1996. Other projects were assisted by a portion of the recent $42 million Lilly Endowment grant. But much of the work remains to be done.[12] The challenges of physical plant management will require careful planning and sustained leadership. One of these challenges is to stabilize and eventually restore early historic buildings that mark the beginning of black higher education in the United States. Another challenge, described by Richard Dober, is to make up for the standards of building that characterized the 1960s; many of these structures are now showing their age, and, because construction standards have changed, are no longer code-compliant.

Endowment is a flexible asset if not unduly restricted by its donor. Even a small endowment can function like the family savings account—a hedge against unexpected distress. If the endowment is much larger than those of its competitors, the college's leaders are in a position to consider such long-term strategies as charging less tuition, paying better salaries, offering more special programs, reducing average class size, or some combination of these things. A college with much less endowment than its close competitors experiences the reverse of those advantages. No college, to our knowledge, ever asserted it had enough endowment.

For many years, private black colleges lived hand to mouth. Capital funds often were solicited to meet a crisis: a major classroom building having burned down; or the chapel roof needing replacement. Meanwhile, the most fortunate predominantly white private colleges had been raising endowment funds for several generations. Private black colleges are aware of the eventual desirability of achieving significant endowments and many are working at it.

By June 1997, seven of the thirty-nine UNCF colleges reported endowment with market value in excess of $25 million:[13] Clark Atlanta University, Dillard University, Johnson C. Smith University, Morehouse College, Spelman College, Tuskegee University, and Xavier University of Louisiana. The average 1997 market value of the seven endowments was $61 million per college. If each of these colleges followed a policy of spending 5 percent of their endowments' market value each year (a common policy among foundations and colleges with large endowments), this would provide an amount equal to approximately 5 percent of those operating budgets. Although this would be useful, it offers nothing like the possibility for profound change yielded by the more-than-$700-million endowments of such colleges as Wellesley or Smith.[14]

The leadership of private black colleges also must find a long-term way to pay for the extra expense of more extensive cultivation of individual donors, if endowment is to play a significantly larger role in the finances of private black colleges in the next decades. A few graduates of these colleges and other wealthy individuals now give endowment funds to these colleges, as do some foundations and corporations. Periodically both the federal government and UNCF have operated matching programs to stimulate interest in endowment-building. The main gamble, however, is whether enough alumni/ae have accumulated sufficient wealth and are willing to share it with their college to make an intense effort to cultivate such gifts worthwhile. One fundraising consultant familiar with many private black colleges said that as of 1999, only two of them employed a full-time planned-giving officer (someone who helps wealthy donors plan mutually advantageous ways to transfer some of their assets to the college before or after their deaths). Not more than half the private black colleges are even believed to attempt to classify the financial giving capacities of their graduates.

Here, and in the case histories of Spelman College and Xavier University of Louisiana (Chapter 9), we pointed out that once a college commits itself to raising endowment money, its administration takes on extensive fundraising obligations. The development office must then have the capacity to learn about a large number of major donor prospects and to work with them. The president and at least some trustees also must add the work of courting potential donors to their calendars.

If the effort begins to be successful, as is the case for the seven UNCF colleges with the largest endowments, the requirements of endowment management become quite different from those of managing an annual operating budget. These new requirements change both who is needed for trustee service and the president's relationship with the board of trustees. Large and small endowments have different management requirements. Colleges with relatively small endowments of, say, one to five million dollars may feel they should treat these funds like an emergency savings account. If so, the funds must be accessible when needed and not subject to volatile changes in value. A college business manager or chief financial officer can manage such investments simply by dealing in fixed-income securities with local or regional bankers, without much direct involvement of the president or trustees. In 1997, ten UNCF colleges had endowments of this size. In 1991, Alan H. Kirschner wrote in a paper for the Association of Governing Boards that two-thirds of the investment portfolios of UNCF college endowments were conservatively invested in interest-bearing securities, whereas one-third of the portfolios of other private colleges (often with larger endowments) were so invested.

In 1997, the largest nine endowments of private black colleges (those which exceeded $25 million in market value) included mainly funds that were not required for current expenditure, and that could be invested for relatively high return, necessarily accepting some risk of market volatility and even temporary loss of value. Endowments of this size usually require that the institution officers develop the capacity to judge what asset mix makes sense, and to select and monitor outside professional managers, including equity managers. Under these circumstances, a board of trustees must have the sophistication and discipline to develop objective selection processes for optimal choice of outside fund managers and to avoid the fact or appearance of conflict of interest. Most boards that oversee a large endowment also adopt written asset-allocation policies and guidelines prescribing the maximum percentage of endowment asset value that may be drawn down in any year to support operating expenses. The adherence to such policies is often viewed as a threshold requirement by foundations, corporations, or individuals when they consider whether to make an endowment gift to a college. Those requirements, in turn, force the president and board of trustees to seek different qualities when examining potential trustees who will be expected to help solicit or manage endowment funds.

Alice Green Burnette, one of the most respected career fundraisers for private black colleges, recently interviewed more than a hundred college presidents, trustees, and observers of black colleges and selected non-profit organizations. These interviews highlight the importance of increasing the number of trustees who will help raise major gifts, and improving the ability of presidents and fundraisers to make use of this talent. In her draft manuscript of a handbook for black American fundraising professionals, she remarks:

> One of the questions I posed to all interviewees was this one: "Please consider the fund raising food chain as one that has three primary links: the Board of Trustees, the President, and the fund raiser. Which do you think is the weakest link in that chain?"
>
> Of the 113 people I interviewed, all but three (one Trustee and two fund raisers) responded that the Trustees were the weakest link. Of all my findings, this is the one of greatest concern to me.[15]

INDIVIDUAL GIVING

Experienced fundraisers usually estimate that, per dollar eventually received, one of the most expensive ways to raise money is soliciting large numbers of individuals, each one of whom might give a small amount out of current income. In contrast, much less professional time is needed (per dollar eventually received) to apply successfully for Title III funds, or for a large foundation or corporation grant.

Yet growing numbers of private colleges do invest increasing amounts of time, energy, and money cultivating individual gifts—particularly from parents and alumni/ae. The Council for Aid to Education (CFAE) reports that alumni/ae donations are the fastest-growing and also the largest single source of voluntary giving for higher education.[16] More and more predominantly white colleges are now hiring extra staff to coordinate sponsored social occasions, special publications, and special reunions. Why do they do this? The successful colleges say that the search for regular small gifts is also a search for alumni/ae involvement, without which larger gifts from current income, or bequests of lifetime assets are less likely to be secured. True, the alumni/ae of such colleges, on average, have larger assets and have held them longer than the graduates of most black colleges. It is also true, however, that black college graduates today participate in high-earnings careers far more frequently than thirty years ago and have accumulated more discretionary wealth. The prospects for long-term growth of endowment gifts now merit a more generous budget to develop more sustained and sophisticated approaches to cultivating individual gifts than are currently used in most black colleges.

At present, in fact, the measurable vital signs for individual giving in private black colleges appear to be headed in the wrong direction. The UNCF *Statistical Report 1998* indicates that for thirty-eight of its thirty-nine members, 11.9 percent of living alumni gave a smaller percentage to their colleges in 1996–97 than they did twenty years ago. In contrast, a CFAE report on voluntary support of higher education shows that 28.6 percent of living alumni/ae of 292 private liberal arts colleges contributed in 1998, a rising percentage compared with twenty years earlier.[17]

It is easy to understand easily why more attention has not been given to cultivating individual donations at private black colleges. The reasons include small institutional size (therefore relatively small alumni/ae lists), lack of accumulated alumni/ae wealth, and lack of money in the college budget to invest in staff and programs that in turn might involve large numbers of persons in college affairs. But the private black colleges that did make such an investment some years ago, and have maintained it, appear to have been well rewarded. Those that attempted this in the 1970s are generally the most competitive with predominantly white colleges today for the best-prepared black high school graduates, and have moved furthest from dependency on government financial support.

This chapter and the preceding ones on student aid and external sources of support, when taken together, offer an arms-length view of the financial aspect of private black colleges. The view gives roughly equal attention to the environment for private black colleges during the past thirty years and to those needs and functions, common to most of the colleges, over which institutional leadership has some control. Major environmental influences include the amount, predictability, and fairness of student aid, the evolution of Title III, and the general health of the national economy and its capital markets. Major concerns of any individual institution, large or small, are the quality and consistency of its leadership, the adequacy of its current income sources, and the stewardship of its long-term assets.

Such a view, however, gives only passing attention to the central fact that, viewed individually, private black colleges are developing in ways that increasingly diverge in purpose, clientele, financial strength, and prospects for future viability. Although it is impossible to predict with certainty the changes that may occur in the environment for these colleges, the final chapter will assess key background variables, and will speculate about the increasingly varied purposes that different private black colleges might emphasize in the next ten or twenty years.

CHAPTER 17

Stand and Prosper

IN AMERICA TODAY, there is a larger black middle class than ever before. There are now more racially mixed marriages and far more people recognizing their mixed racial identities. We have a black American U.S. secretary of state, U.S. Supreme Court justice, and Nobel Prize winner for literature. There are black quarterbacks in football and coaches in baseball, and increasing numbers of black doctors, lawyers, and stockbrokers. There are more black students in once traditionally white colleges as well as more black Americans in law and business schools. There are increased numbers of personal computers in black homes. There is, in short, enough information at hand about what once would have been called "racial progress" to imagine a United States of America in which the very idea of a college serving only black or only white students might seem at best outdated.

Certainly, in recent decades a number of educators have suggested just that. And yet every now and then, some seemingly trivial event exposes a pattern that reminds us of stark racial realities arising from a long, painful history and showing little sign of going away any time soon. It may be a New Jersey roadside incident that leads to a revelation of widespread racial profiling by the highway patrol; it may be figures released by a research institute on resegregation in housing in Chicago or in education in Mississippi; or a *New York Times* investigation of the way the apportionment of new and old ballot machines in Florida unequally affected black and white voters in a presidential election.

For the world of higher education, *Cheryl J. Hopwood v. The State of Texas* was such an event. Although the case itself involved a predominantly white public university, it reminds us of some of the reasons for the continuing existence of black colleges. Hopwood, a young white woman, was denied admission to the University of Texas Law School, while minority students with lower test scores and grades were admitted. She brought suit in 1992. In 1996, the Fifth Circuit Court of Appeals ruled that she be admitted to the school. In their ruling, the judges decided that the university had been wrong to use race as any kind of factor in its admission process. In doing so, they overturned, at least within the three-state jurisdiction of the Court (Texas, Louisiana, and Mississippi), a precedent set almost twenty years earlier in *The Regents of the University of California v.*

Bakke. In that case, Supreme Court Justice Lewis F. Powell, Jr., in a tie-breaking opinion for the majority, wrote that racial preferences were indeed permissible in a selective admissions process if their purpose was to improve racial diversity in the student body and if they did not arise from fixed minority quotas.[1] The inconsistency in law between the *Hopwood* decision, which in the year 2000 still affects only the Fifth Circuit states, and the *Bakke* decision has yet to be dealt with at the Supreme Court level. Voter initiatives with similar effect to *Hopwood* were passed in the states of California (1996) and Washington (1998). Thus, although these new laws regulate public universities in only five of the fifty states, like the proverbial canary in the mine, they may both signal what is to come and remind us of the deeper currents of racial resentment that continue to flow through the American social landscape.

One can begin to follow *Hopwood's* storm track as it moves out of the Fifth Circuit. Fearing future litigation, such public institutions as the University of Virginia, the University of Massachusetts, and the University of Florida have already voluntarily ceased to use race as a selection variable in admissions. The effect of such decisions—and so of *Hopwood*—on traditionally white colleges and universities may at worst be to undermine, if not devastate the very concept of racial diversity in higher education. Where schools, either to comply with *Hopwood* or preemptively, have abandoned their diversity and affirmative action programs and emphasized selection solely based on SAT and other test scores and high school grades, a sharp drop in minority enrollment has almost always resulted. This partly because underrepresented minorities in postsecondary education, principally black, Latino, and Native American students, on average score lower on standardized admissions tests than Asian and white Americans, but also because such policies are often viewed as hostile by minority students who avoid applying in the first place.[2] Does the future have to turn out this way? Of course not. We and many others would welcome a Supreme Court ruling overturning *Hopwood* and sustaining the earlier *Bakke* decision or something like it.

Another possibility is that *Hopwood* becomes the law of the land, but the colleges and universities that value student diversity discover ways to avoid explicit consideration of race and yet preserve student diversity. Texas was the first state to experiment with this at the undergraduate level, guaranteeing admission to the University of Texas at Austin for any student who graduated from high school with grades in the top tenth of his or her class.[3] Because the racial distribution of students among Texas high schools is such that many student bodies are either predominately white or non-white, it was possible for the University of Texas to regain in its freshman class, in the first year of the experiment, about the same racial diversity that had prevailed before the *Hopwood* decision. Critics of the experimental Texas "percentage plan" note that, perversely, the University of Texas would be able to achieve its diversity goals only by enrolling black students from highly segregated high schools. Black students with stronger academic preparation who attend well integrated high schools would see their admission chances reduced under this arrangement. Critics also worry that this orchestrated result might be used as a basis for reducing or even dismissing efforts to address the major issues of quality and equity in higher education. Thus far, the experiments to adhere to *Hopwood* and still preserve the goal of student diversity do not appear to be good solutions for future national policy.

The U.S. Commission on Civil Rights was even more critical of *Hopwood* and of the Texas percentage-plan experiment because of their effect on diversity and minority opportunity in major national graduate schools:

> The major problem with the percentage plans is their inattention to law schools, medical schools, and other graduate and professional schools, where ending affirmative action is devastating. At the law school of the University of Texas at Austin, the University of California at Berkeley, and the University of California at Los Angeles, African American and Latino enrollments remain well below 1990 figures, which needed increasing, not decreasing. . . . The percentage plans are experimental responses to the attacks on affirmative action. But they are no substitute for strong race-conscious affirmative action in higher education. What is required is a Supreme Court decision reaffirming *Bakke.*

If the *Hopwood* decision were to apply in all states, the admissions policies of most black colleges would not be directly affected, but the colleges themselves would. In fact, some undoubtedly already are. Once belittled or ignored as outcast institutions without significant funding or resources, struggling to stay alive and offer a needed service to belittled or ignored Americans, black colleges, public and private, have over the past century and a half been transformed. As we have shown, they are now recognized for what they have been for the better part of a century: an integral part of the American system of higher education that has not been fully understood. The future of black colleges is inseparable from the future of that system. They are part of the pond in which *Hopwood's* ripples are already being felt.

The white resentment and backlash embodied in the *Hopwood* case serves as a reminder why some graduating black American high school students like Jason Coleman (mentioned in our preface), when facing a choice between better funded, better equipped predominantly white colleges and a black college may choose the black institution. Sensing that at a traditionally white college, they may never be judged on their merits and guessing that an unwelcoming campus atmosphere with half-hidden racial tensions may not be conducive to learning (not to speak of pleasure), more black American high school graduates may opt for black colleges.

In addition, if *Hopwood* determines the models for undergraduate college admissions, more black American high school students who might previously have chosen flagship private or public traditionally white colleges or universities may find themselves shut out. This may already be the case in Texas. Although the figures are not yet conclusive, between 1996 and 1998, when the first effects of *Hopwood* should have been noticeable, total enrollment rose only 3 percent at the black college member-institutions of UNCF, whereas the enrollment of Texas students in UNCF colleges increased a startling 11 percent. If one selects from among the UNCF colleges such nationally known institutions as Clark Atlanta, Dillard and Xavier Universities, or Spellman and Morehouse Colleges, whose academic standards most frequently overlap those at selective colleges, the Texas-origin student delegation increased even more steeply.[4]

The *Hopwood* case is a reminder to the faculties, administrators, and trustees of black colleges that their missions and decisions are inextricably tied to the ongoing story of race and resentment in America. Norman C. Francis of Xavier sums up the feelings of many black college presidents and administrators:

> I know I speak for my colleagues when I say these recent efforts to dissolve affirmative action are wrong. It's a matter of principle. Every youngster ought to have a full range of choice. It is clear that graduates of historically black colleges, as applicants to graduate school at University of Texas, or at Berkeley, are adversely affected. There is both a selection effect, if tests are overvalued, and a climate effect if minority students receive a signal they are not valued.[5]

Take for instance, the seemingly technical issue of admission criteria to medical schools. Dr. Herbert W. Nickens has worked out a statistical model for estimating the racial makeup of the nation's 1996 medical school freshman class, assuming affirmative action had been abolished that year and students had been chosen solely on the basis of grades and standardized test scores. The effect of such a change would have been huge:

> We have modeled what would happen to minority medical school enrollment if minority students were required to have the same level of MCAT [Medical College Admission Test] scores and grades as white students (assuming the scores and grades of Whites were held constant). Overall, under-

represented minority acceptances in 1996 would have dropped nationally
about 80% from almost 2,000 to less than 400, in a no affirmative action
scenario. (This percentage drop is virtually the same percentage drop obtained in a similar projection done for law school admission.) Under this
scenario, only about 2% of all medical students would be minorities, approximately the same as entered medical school in 1966 prior to the start of
affirmative action. Do opponents of affirmative action really want to resegre-
gate medical schools? That is a real possibility, whether or not it is their
intention.

We can also project backward and extend this scenario to estimate how
many minority physicians we would have in the United States if affirmative
action never had been practiced in U.S. medical schools. We estimate that
we would have about 17,000 fewer minority physicians than we actually do,
an astonishing 40% reduction of the approximately 40,000 U.S. trained
underrepresented minority physicians in the nation.[6]

To our knowledge, no statistical models have been created to show the
effect of such a policy change upon individual black colleges. But we can
guess. In recent years, Xavier University of Louisiana, for example, has
been the nation's largest supplier of new black medical students. If *Hopwood* became the national pattern, how many of Xavier's graduates would
be denied admission (because of good but not stellar test scores) to such
selective medical schools as Case Western Reserve, Johns Hopkins, and
Northwestern, and bumped into less selective medical schools? How
many of them would not enter medical school at all? There is no way to
know, but it is clear that the overall effect could be significant. It might be
enough to tarnish Xavier's reputation among black Americans as a pre-
mier place to launch a science or medical career. More than 90 percent
of Xavier's graduates in medical school now complete their M.D. degree.
If medical school admission were to shift to a grades-and-test-scores-only
basis, the loss of diversity in the nation's medical leadership in time
would be significant, as would be the effect on Xavier's ability to attract
top students. Similar arguments pertain to admission to study for other
professions whose apprenticeship begins in university graduate schools,
and to the private black colleges that now send many of their students on
to these graduate schools.

For black colleges, then, the prospect that a pipeline to graduate and
professional education, already too small, might be further constricted,
has to give pause. It is a final reminder that black colleges, which have
never breathed easy in America, cannot afford to be complacent in the
current environment, where the very question of equitable allocation of
educational opportunity is still up for grabs.

THE FUTURE OF PRIVATE BLACK COLLEGES

In the 1970s, when the new force of competitive recruitment of black students and faculty by traditionally white colleges became evident, few observers would have predicted how healthy so many of the private black colleges would be in 2000. We hesitate now, at what may be another critical moment for such colleges, to project their state of health twenty years from now. But what might safely be said? Although there is still the possibility that some of the smaller colleges may merge or even disappear, for private black colleges in general, mere survival is no longer at stake. Instead, these colleges face the challenge of differentiating their missions in an era of rapid technological change.

The 59,000 students enrolled in the forty-five institutions included in this study represent 1 percent of enrollment in all four-year colleges and 26 percent of all black Americans attending four-year private colleges in the United States.[7] And yet, as we have argued, their influence on the rise of a black middle class and the development of black professionals has been an extremely large one. There is no reason to believe that this will not continue to be the case.

We know that students enroll in these institutions for a variety of reasons, including proximity to home, family tradition, affordability, and the presence of a significant number of black faculty with a reputation for working with students who exhibit a wide range of intellectual abilities and pre-college levels of preparation. We also know that on black campuses, race, ethnicity, and family income levels appear to have less influence on student relationships than frequently appears to be the case in institutions where black Americans are a modest minority of the student population.

However, this by no means indicates that private black colleges have a single common future in store. Most observers with whom we spoke felt that differentiation was one of the most significant developments in these schools over the past half-century. In some ways, women's colleges in their experimentation with mission, their general health, and their differentiation offer clues to the future development of the private black college. In the 1970s, women's colleges, too, faced gloomy predictions of their impending demise and severe market pressures as a number of formerly men's colleges became coeducational and began to compete for their prospective students. Some women's colleges such as Vassar followed the path of the former men's colleges and went coeducational. Yet two decades later, the strongest of the women's colleges are flourishing. Most observers would say, for example, that Smith and Wellesley are stronger institutions in 2000 than they were in 1970, and have achieved that success by emphasizing their existing strengths. Like the private black colleges, these women's colleges are far more different from one another than they were in 1970. Some, like Vassar, retained essentially their prior academic program but offered it to a broader student clientele. Others, also reaching for new kinds of students, made substantial program changes. For example, the College of Saint Catherine in Saint Paul, Minnesota—today the nation's largest Catholic women's college—in the 1980s established a weekend college, launched eight new masters degree programs, and acquired the campus, programs, and clientele of Saint Mary's Junior College in Minneapolis. The neighboring University of Saint Thomas, then an undergraduate Catholic college for men in Saint Paul, had decided to admit women, thus creating major new competition in the College of Saint Catherine's traditional market. Finally, a few colleges have recognized that their resources did not permit them to serve their students well and so they have merged or closed. In all of these women's colleges, as at many private black colleges, an intense period of self-examination of mission and governance structure had to precede the final decisions about how to adapt to changed circumstances.

Observers of higher education generally describe the tasks facing the leadership of any college today in similar ways, but the presidents of private black colleges still bear a special burden. Most college leaders now understand, for instance, that the unprecedented demands that the new information technologies make on teaching, curricula, and financial resources are not temporary dislocations: they are not about to go away. They create new patterns in how students learn, and require changes in how colleges make their academic and financial plans. College administrators now understand that their graduates will be part not just of a local or national economy and community but of a global one. At most colleges, the financial pressures of the new economy are forcing reassessments of which students to enroll and, specifically, whether to continue to try as hard as in the past to meet the expensive financial needs of the lowest-income students. Private black colleges, which have traditionally enrolled many such students, must also operate on lean budgets. They face extra difficulties with no easy answers in sight when it comes to the allocation of resources.

They also face other challenges, which, although not perhaps unique to them, are especially important to their mission and existence. In a college admission scene in which the ablest and best prepared students increasingly cluster at the most selective colleges and universities, black colleges must either make significant efforts to preserve and broaden the pathways for their students to achieve satisfying postgraduate careers and community leadership roles, or else relinquish an important aspect of their historic mission. Those that are able to recruit their share of able students and send them on to major graduate and professional schools are likely to focus more on rigorous academic work and leadership. Others will concentrate on the development skills necessary for their students' advancement. At the same time, black colleges must sort out how, simultaneously, to best fulfill their historic purposes: producing literate, humane individuals and helping motivated but less well-prepared students overcome earlier education deficits. Serious attention to improving the state of their finances will be a necessary and universal concern of even those private black colleges with the largest endowments.

We believe that with thoughtful planning, strong leadership, and a bit of luck, many of the private black colleges will remain crucial foundational blocks in the American system of higher education for a predominantly black American clientele. For some young black Americans, they will provide a brief refuge from a tense and difficult world; for others, the first bright opening into that world. They will be a place of convocation and of memory, but also a place for black faculty and students as well as a modestly increasing number of nonblack students and a significant number of nonblack faculty and administrators to build futures of every sort. All of these colleges will need to reassess their competitive strengths and the possible missions that lie ahead of them. All must remain aware of the history that lies behind them. All, whether they want to or not, will have to change.

The story of the private black colleges is a story of success against extremely high odds. This success has helped to advance the still unfinished business of leveling the nation's political and economic playing field, and was crucial both to the emergence of a stronger black middle class and to developing black leadership in government, business, and the professions. This particular group of colleges adds to the rich diversity of origins, purposes, and governance that characterizes U.S. higher education. Private black colleges incur slightly lower expenditures per student compared with other private four-year colleges and also consistently provide significant new opportunities to minority students whose elementary and secondary school education is frequently not among the nations strongest. Such students are likely to make up an increasing proportion of the total U.S. adult workforce in the decades ahead. Continued success will require both strong institutional leadership within these colleges and also public policies that bring predictability and good sense to such issues as federal financial aid for students, direct institutional support for minority-serving institutions, and how the matter of race is used as an explicit factor in admissions decisions made by selective colleges.

Some of the private black colleges will undoubtedly deal better than others with the challenges that new information technologies, the globalization of the economy, and the ever-shifting patterns of financial support impose on them. Some will continue to grow stronger. Some may have difficulty surviving in their present state. But in 2020, it is reasonable to assume that, just as in 1896, 1915, 1954, and 1964, the private black college will be part of the American landscape.

Our final thoughts return to Board Chairman Moses Jones of Stillman College. That these private black colleges stand and prosper is important, not just for Stillman and its sister institutions, but for all of us.

Notes

Preface

1. Tamar Lewin, "Growing Up, Growing Apart," *New York Times,* June 25, 2000, p. 1.

2. For a fuller discussion of published materials on black colleges, see our bibliographical note at the end of the book.

3. John Rawls, *A Theory of Justice* (Cambridge, Mass.: Harvard University Press, 1971), pp. 100–101.

Chapter 1   Panorama

1. U.S. Bureau of the Census, *Statistical Abstract of the United States* (Washington, D.C.: Government Printing Office, 1975), Tables 228 and 231; Susan T. Hill, *The Traditionally Black Institutions of Higher Education, 1860 to 1982* (Washington, D.C.: Government Printing Office, 1984), p. 18. In 1970, total U.S. postsecondary undergraduate enrollment was 6.3 million students; by the mid-1990s it exceeded 12 million students. See National Center for Education Statistics, *Digest of Education Statistics* (Washington, D.C.: Government Printing Office, 1972), Table 82, p. 70, and 1996, Table 172, p. 179.

2. Daniel C. Thompson, *Private Black Colleges at the Crossroads* (Westport, Conn.: Greenwood Press, 1973), p. 269.

3. Vivian W. Henderson, "Negro Colleges Face the Future," *Daedalus* Summer 1971, p. 643.

4. William J. Trent, Jr., "Negro Colleges Face the Future," *Daedalus* Summer 1971, p. 649.

5. United Negro College Fund *Statistical Report 1997* (Fairfax, Va.: United Negro College Fund, 1998), pp. 28, 61–64.

6. This three-part grouping of historically black private colleges is classified by enrollment size. The list is derived from 1995 enrollment statistics from the National Science Foundation WebCASPAR database system, for historically black four-year private colleges. Data for one college came from the United Negro College Fund *Statistical Report 1996* (Fairfax, Va.: United Negro College Fund, 1997), p. 26.

7. United Negro College Fund *Statistical Report 1997,* pp. 14, 31, and Appendixes G and DD. These statistics exclude Howard, Hampton, and Allen Universities, and Texas and Knoxville Colleges.

8. Interview with Richard P. Dober, senior consultant with Dober, Lidsky, Craig and Associates, Belmont, Mass., March 23, 1998.

9. National Science Foundation WebCASPAR database system.

10. United Negro College Fund *Statistical Report 1998* (Fairfax, Va.: United Negro College Fund, 1999), p. 14. National data are derived from U.S. Department of Education IPEDS Fall Faculty Survey, 1996.

11. Andrew Young, *An Easy Burden* (New York: HarperCollins, 1996), p. 41.

12. William H. Gray III, letter to Humphrey Doermann, November 9, 1998, p. 2.

13. Interview with Professor Lois Moreland, Department of Political Science, Spelman College, February 13, 1998. Moreland was the first Spelman faculty representative on the board of trustees.

14. Judith Block McLaughlin and David Riesman, *Choosing a College President: Opportunities and Constraints* (Princeton, N.J.: Carnegie Foundation for the Advancement of Teaching, 1990), pp. xxi–xxxiii.

15. United Negro College Fund *Statistical Report 1997,* pp. 1–20. See also United Negro College Fund annual statistical reports of member institutions, 1971–72 through 1993.

16. Interview with William H. Gray III, president and chief executive officer, United Negro College Fund, March 2, 1999.

17. Enrollment data are reported in Sherman Jones, "Difficult Times for Black Colleges," *Change,* March 1984, p. 29. College Board scores and class rank data for Fisk are compiled from James Cass and Max Birnbaum, *Comparative Guide to American Colleges* (New York: Harper and Row, 1968, 1969, 1975, 1983).

18. Ellis Close, "Teaching Kids to be Smart," *Newsweek,* August 21, 1995, pp. 58–60; Michael A. Fletcher, "Xavier's Desk-Side Manner Is Prescription for Medical School," *Washington Post,* May 10, 1997, pp. 1, 12; "Student Profiled in Journal Says 'No' to Berkeley Spot," *Wall Street Journal,* May 21, 1998, p. A6.

19. Interviews with Robert D. Flanigan, vice president for business and financial affairs, Spelman College, February 2, 1998; Clarence J. Jupiter, vice president for development, Xavier University of Louisiana, October 22, 1997; William H. Gray III, March 2, 1999.

20. Richard Kluger, *Simple Justice* (New York: Random House, 1975), p. ix.

Chapter 2   Major Historical Factors Influencing Black Higher Education

1. William W. Hening (ed.), *Statutes at Large; Being a Collection of All Laws of Virginia, From the First Session of the Legislature in the Year 1619* (Charlottesville: University of Virginia Press, 1969), Statutes 2:170 and 2:260 (1819–23).

2. William Hand Browne (ed.), *Archives of Maryland: Proceedings and Acts of the General Assembly of Maryland* (Baltimore: Maryland Historical Society, 1883), pp. 533–34.

3. Henry Steele Commager, *Documents in American History* (New York: Appleton-Century-Crofts, 1963), p. 100.

4. Alexis de Tocqueville, *Democracy in America* (New York: Vintage Books, 1945), p. 373.

5. Article 1, Section 2 of the Constitution mandated that five slaves were to be counted as three individuals when determining the number of members of the House of Representatives to be allotted to a state.

6. The eleventh Confederate State, Tennessee, had rejoined the Union in 1865.

7. Richard Bardolph (ed.), *The Civil Rights Record: Black Americans and the Law 1849–1970* (New York: Crowell, 1970). Records for years before 1882 are unreliable.

8. C. Vann Woodward, *The Strange Career of Jim Crow* (New York: Oxford University Press, 1966), pp. 67–69.

9. *Hall Strauder v. West Virginia* 100 U.S. 303 (1877) and *Virginia v. Rives* 100 U.S. 303 (1880).

10. "Asking" was not typical of the manner in which compliance with segregation laws was normally sought in the South. In this instance, it may have reflected the objection of the railroad company to the added cost of providing separate coaches, its welcoming of the test, perhaps even its complicity in the test and desire to see the Louisiana law declared unconstitutional.

11. R. L. Desdunes, "Legislation and Legislators," *Daily Crusader,* June 11, 1892, p. 1.

12. *Plessy v. Ferguson,* 163 U.S. 537 (1896).

13. Ibid.

14. Kluger, *Simple Justice,* p. 87.

15. Otto H. Olsen, *The Negro Question: From Slavery to Caste, 1663–1910* (New York: Pitman Publishing, 1971), p. 53.

16. Samuel Eliot Morison and Henry Steele Commager, *The Growth of the American Republic* (New York: Oxford University Press,1937), p. 433.

17. Studies of Nazi Germany concentration camps provided a catalyst for serious examination of this topic. Two sources that provide a starting point for those who wish to explore this topic are Bruno Bettelheim, "Individual and Mass Behavior in Extreme Situations," *Journal of Abnormal Psychology,* October 1943; and Samuel A. Stouffer et al., *The American Soldier: Adjustment During Army Life,* 4 vols. (New York: Arno Press, 1949).

18. Samuel E. Wallace (ed.), *Total Institutions* (Chicago: Aldine Publishing, 1971), pp. 1–2.

19. See John Elliott Cairnes, *The Slave Power* (London: Parker and Sons, 1862); Allan Nevins, *The Ordeal of the Union* (New York: Scribner, 1947); and James M. McPherson, *Battle Cry of Freedom: The Civil War Era* (New York: Oxford University Press, 1988).

20. See Leon F. Litwack, *The Negro in the Free States 1790–1870* (Chicago: University of Chicago Press, 1961). As late as 1868 the second plank of the Republican Platform for the upcoming election supported a guarantee of suffrage to black Americans in the former Confederate states but not in Border States that had remained in the Union.

21. The United States Civil War Center, Louisiana State University (http://www.cwc.lsu.edu/). Union casualties, numbering 335,524 dead and 275,175 wounded were 2 percent of the population and 23 percent of the military.

22. Hatwood J. Perce, Jr. "Civil War: Economic Consequences in the South," *Dictionary of American History,* vol. II (New York: Charles Scribner's Sons, 1976), p. 69.

23. U.S. Bureau of the Census, *A Statistical Abstract Supplement: Historical Statistics of the United States. Colonial Times to 1957* (Washington, D.C.: Government Printing Office, 1960), pp. 123–24.

24. Thomas D. Snyder (ed.), *120 Years of American Education: A Statistical Portrait* (Washington, D.C.: Government Printing Office, 1993), p. 21.

Chapter 3   The Beginnings of Black Higher Education

1. *New England's First Fruits,* reprinted in *Sabin's Reprints,* Quarto Series, No. VII (New York: Joseph Sabin, 1865), p. 23.

2. Colleges established for white women before 1860 included Mount Holyoke in 1837, Judson in 1838, Mary Baldwin in 1842, St. Mary's in 1843, and Mills in 1852. Like black colleges, the best known women's colleges (Barnard, Bryn Mawr, Smith, Vassar, and Wellesley) were established between the Civil War and the 1880s.

3. Of these five institutions, only Wilberforce still exists as a private institution. Avery College closed down. Cheyney and Lincoln are now supported by the state of Pennsylvania. Miner Teacher's College operated for years as a private institution before passing to public control and eventually being merged into Federal City College, which became the University of the District of Columbia.

4. Snyder, *120 Years,* p. 14.

5. U.S. Bureau of the Census, *Social and Economic Status of the Black Population of the United States: An Historical View 1790–1978* (Washington, D.C.: Government Printing Office, 1994), p. 92.

6. Elizabeth Hyde Botume, *First Days Amongst the Contrabands* (Boston: Lee and Shepard, 1893), p. 17.

7. An act to establish a bureau for the relief of freedmen and refugees, 13 Stat. 507 (1865).

8. John W. Alvord, "Fifth Semi-Annual Report," January 1, 1870, reprinted in *Freedmen's Schools and Textbooks* (New York: AMS Press, 1980), p. 8.

9. Ibid., pp. 3–6.

10. This view is also expressed by contemporary opponents of affirmative action in college admission. See Abigail Thernstrom and Stephan Thernstrom, *America in Black and White: One Nation Indivisible* (New York: Simon and Schuster, 1997).

11. John William De Forest, *A Union Officer in the Reconstruction* (New Haven: Yale University Press, 1948), pp. 116–17.

12. John W. Alvord, "Eighth Semi-Annual Report," July 1869, reprinted in *Freedmen's Schools and Textbooks* (New York: AMS Press, 1980), p. 41.

13. Hortense Powdermaker, *After Freedom: A Cultural Study in the Deep South* (New York: Atheneum, 1968), p. 299.

14. U.S. Bureau of the Census, *Historical Statistics of the United States: Colonial Times to 1970* (Washington, D.C.: Government Printing Office, 1976), p. 370.

15. John W. Alvord, "Tenth Semi-Annual Report," July 1870, reprinted in *Freedmen's Schools and Textbooks* (New York: AMS Press, 1980), pp. 3–4.

Chapter 4   Public Schools, High Schools, Normal Schools, and Colleges

1. William Loren Katz, *Eyewitness: The Negro in American History* (New York: Pitman Publishing, 1967), p. 278.

2. Ibid.

3. Walter L. Fleming, *Documentary History of Reconstruction*, vol. 2 (Cleveland: Arthur H. Clark, 1907), pp. 183–84.

4. Peter Bergman, *The Chronological History of the Negro in America* (New York: New American Library, 1969), p. 241; U.S. Bureau of the Census, *Statistical Abstract Supplement*, 1960; U.S. Bureau of the Census, *A Compendium of the Ninth Census* (Washington, D.C.: Government Printing Office, 1872).

5. Bureau of Education, *Biennial Survey of Education, 1916–18* (Washington, D.C.: Government Printing Office, 1919), p. 694.

6. John W. Alvord, "Ninth Semi-Annual Report," January 1, 1870, and "Tenth Semi-Annual Report," July 1, 1870, reprinted in *Freedmen's Schools and Textbooks* (New York: AMS Press, 1980), pp. 64, 52–54. The additional institutions established before 1870 are identified in T. J. Jones, *Negro Education*. The term "advanced institutions," as used in the Freedmen's Bureau reports, and the term "high and normal schools and colleges," as used in the 1917 report, refer to the same group of institutions.

7. Alvord, *Freedmen's Schools*, pp. 49–50, 61–62.

8. W. E. B. Du Bois, *The Souls of Black Folk* (Millwood, N.Y.: Kraus-Thomson Organization, 1973), pp. 83–84.

9. Horace Mann Bond, *The Education of the Negro in the American Social Order* (New York: Prentice-Hall, 1934), p. 36.

10. Alvord, *Freedmen's Schools*, p. 75.

11. Howard University maintained a preparatory school for several years but did not include an elementary division.

12. T. J. Jones, *Negro Education*. All institutions are rated as either "large or important" or "small or less important."

13. Such overexpansion existed solely in relation to available resources, not in terms of need. Approximately one-third of black five- to nineteen-year-olds was not enrolled in school in 1915. The earliest available census data on black higher education are for 1940. At that time, less than 2 percent of black Americans had completed four years of college.

14. T. J. Jones, *Negro Education*, pp. 1–6.

15. Ibid., pp. 9–11.

16. U.S. Bureau of the Census, *Historical Statistics*.

17. Howard University, which received an annual appropriation from the federal government, was controlled by an independent board of Trustees and classified in the study as a private institution.

18. Brenda Stevenson (ed.), *The Journals of Charlotte Forten Grimke* (New York: Oxford University Press, 1988), pp. 394, 410–11, 477–78.

19. James M. McPherson, "What Yankee 'Schoolmarms' Taught Post-Civil War Blacks," *University: A Princeton Quarterly* 57(4) (1973): 3.

20. Table 4.1 lists a total of ninety-five schools. Information on numbers of teachers and students is available on only seventy-five of these. The term "advanced schools and colleges," as used in the Freedmen's Bureau reports, refers to post-elementary schools. Later reports use the term "normal and high schools and colleges" to refer to the same group of institutions.

21. Alvord, *Freedmen's Schools*, pp. 52–54, 64.

22. T. J. Jones, *Negro Education,* pp. 321–56.

23. James M. McPherson, "White Liberals and Black Power in Negro Education, 1865–1915," *American Historical Review* 75(5) (1970): 1380–86.

24. W.E.B. Du Bois, *Dusk of Dawn* (Millwood, N.Y.: Kraus-Thomson Organization, 1975), pp. 30–31.

Chapter 5   Curriculum

1. McPherson, "What Yankee Schoolmarms Taught," p. 4.

2. Dwight Oliver Wendell Holmes, *The Evolution of the Negro College* (New York: Teacher's College, Columbia University, 1934), p. 54.

3. Bond, *Education of the Negro,* pp. 360–61.

4. Ibid., pp. 361–62. Mark Hopkins (1802–87) was a Williams College graduate who taught philosophy, theology, and education at that institution. His fame rested on his skill as a teacher. Theodore Woolseley (1852–1929) was professor of international law at Yale University from 1878 to 1911. Charles Finney (1792–1875) was a lawyer before studying theology and serving as pastor of the First Congregational Church in Oberlin, Ohio, as well as president of Oberlin College. The Henry Fairchild mentioned in the quotation is probably a typographical error and was meant to be James Harris Fairchild. James Harris Fairchild (1817–1902) taught theology at Oberlin College from 1841 to 1898 and served as Oberlin's president from 1866 to 1889. All were well-respected academics at northern colleges and universities at which small numbers of black Americans studied as graduate or undergraduate students in the late nineteenth and early twentieth centuries.

5. W.E.B. Du Bois, "Striving of the Negro People," *Atlantic Monthly* 80 (1897): 194–95.

6. Howard University, *Howard University Catalogue 1918–1919* (Washington, D.C.: Howard University, 1918), pp. 116, 126.

7. Tougaloo College, *Tougaloo College Catalog* (Tougaloo, Miss.: Tougaloo College, 1904), p. 13.

8. From a speech entitled "Talladega Yesterday and Tomorrow," delivered by George Williamson Crawford on the occasion of conferring on him the honorary degree of doctor of laws by Talladega College. George Williamson Crawford, *The Talladegan,* May 1950, pp. 2–3.

9. Holmes, *Evolution of the Negro College,* p. 86.

10. From the 1868 American Missionary Association *Annual Report,* p. 35, as cited in Holmes, *Evolution of the Negro College,* p. 86.

11. Booker T. Washington, *Up From Slavery* (New York: Doubleday, Page, and Co., 1901), pp. 217–23.

12. Henry Allen Bullock, *A History of Negro Education in the South from 1619 to the Present* (New York: Praeger, 1970), p. 88.

13. *Colored American Magazine,* November 1907, p. 333.

14. T. J. Jones, *Negro Education,* p. 5.

15. Holmes, *Evolution of the Negro College,* pp. 165–72.

16. T. J. Jones, *Negro Education,* vol. I, p. xi.

17. Ibid., vol. I, p. 22.

Chapter 6   Higher Education in a New Century

1. T. J. Jones, *Negro Education,* pp. ix–x.

2. Ibid., p. 303. Not included were ninety-four schools offering some secondary-level courses that were operated by city and county governments.

3. There were also two public institutions in the South in 1915 serving black Americans that offered college courses leading to a baccalaureate degree.

4. Institutions offering college courses in 1942 included fifty-eight four-year and thirty-three two-year colleges.

5. Tuskegee Normal and Industrial Institute, *Annual Catalog, 1927–1928* (Tuskegee, Ala.: Tuskegee Normal and Industrial Institute, 1927), p. 14.

6. U.S. Bureau of the Census, *A Statistical Abstract Supplement,* p. 10.

7. U.S. Bureau of Education, *Survey of Negro Colleges and Universities,* Bulletin 7 (New York: Negro Universities Press, 1969), p. 2.

8. U.S. Office of Education, *Statistics of the Education of Negroes,* 1933–34 (Washington, D.C.: Government Printing Office, 1939), pp. 4, 8.

9. U.S. Office of Education, *National Survey of the Higher Education of Negroes* (Washington, D.C.: Government Printing Office, 1942).

10. Hill, *Traditionally Black Institutions,* p. 12.

11. One of the remaining two institutions, Clark Atlanta University came into existence in 1989 as a result of the merger of Atlanta University and Clark College. The other, Oakwood College, was not ranked in the top fifteen in any of the categories and years included in the table.

12. W.E.B. Du Bois, collector, "Documents of the War," *Crisis* 18 (May 1919): 16–21.

13. From *Bulletin of Atlanta University,* October 1907, quoted in Clarence A. Bacote, *The Story of Atlanta University* (Princeton, N.J.: Princeton University Press), pp. 216–17.

14. Ibid., p. 263.

15. Horace Mann Bond, *Education for Freedom* (Princeton, N.J.: Princeton University Press, 1976), pp. 388–89.

16. Joe M. Richardson, *A History of Fisk University,* 1865–1946 (University, Ala.: University of Alabama Press, 1980), pp. 85–100.

17. Howard University, *Catalogue,* pp. 50–51.

18. Nathan I. Huggins, Martin Kilson, and Daniel Fox, *Key Issues in the African-American Experience* (New York: Vintage, 1971); Bullock, *History of Negro Education,* p. 200.

19. See Harry Washington Greene, *Holders of Doctorates Among American Negroes: An Educational and Social Study of Negroes Who Have Earned Doctoral Degrees in Course, 1876-1943* (Boston: Meador Publishing Company).

20. Claude McKay, *Harlem Shadows* (New York: Harcourt Brace, 1922), p. 6.

21. Holmes, *Evolution of the Negro College,* p. 209.

22. U.S. Office of Education, *National Survey,* pp. 103–4.

23. In 1995, the United Negro College Fund changed its public name to "The College Fund/UNCF" for its annual fund drive, and on its business stationary. Its tax exemption title remained United Negro College Fund, however, and many of its programs retained the UNCF title. For editorial convenience, we use United Negro College Fund (UNCF) in this book without intending to imply author preference for particular titles one way or the other.

24. Alma Rene Williams, *A Research History of the United Negro College Fund, Inc., 1944–1987* (New York: United Negro College Fund, 1988 [unpublished manuscript]), pp. 335–98.

25. Ibid., p. 390.

26. Ibid. During the decade, $12.8 million was raised in annual campaigns and $1.2 million in a capital campaign. The cumulative raised by March 1999 was $1.4 billion ($1.1 in annual campaigns and $298 million in capital campaigns).

27. T. J. Jones, *Negro Education,* p. 233.

28. Ridgely Torrence, *The Story of John Hope* (New York: Macmillan, 1948), p. 146.

Chapter 7   Two Decades of Desegregation

1. *Brown v. Board of Education,* 484.

2. *Hodge v. United States,* 203 U.S. 1 (1905).

3. *Missouri ex rel. Gaines v. Canada,* 305 U.S. 637 (1938); and *Sipuel v. Board of Regents,* 339 U.S. 631 (1938). Gaines did not enroll in the University of Missouri and the state quickly established a separate school for black Americans. Sipuel found it necessary to appeal to the Supreme Court a second time before she was eventually admitted to and graduated from the University of Oklahoma law school and was admitted to the bar. Oklahoma did not establish a separate school for black Americans.

4. Loren Miller, *The Petitioners: The Story of the Supreme Court of the United States and the Negro* (Cleveland: World Publishing, 1967), pp. 335–36.

5. *McLauren v. Oklahoma State Regents,* 339 U.S. 637 (1950); and *Sweatt v. Painter,* 339 U.S. 629 (1950) (involving the University of Texas). Both contributed to the emerging interpretation of *Plessy.*

6. W.E.B. Du Bois, "Does the Negro Need Separate Schools?" *Journal of Negro Education* 4 (1935): 335.

7. Christopher Jencks and David Riesman, "The American Negro College," *Harvard Educational Review* 37 (1967): 25–26.

8. National Science Foundation WebCASPAR database system.

9. Small numbers of Blacks had taught in traditionally white colleges before the 1960s, but the impact on college going and job opportunities was relatively insignificant.

10. U.S. Bureau of the Census, *Social and Economic Status of the Black Population,* pp. 22–26.

11. Data from 1955 from United Negro College Fund, *Statistics of Member Colleges 1955–56 School Year* (Fairfax, Va.: United Negro College Fund, 1957); and National Science Foundation WebCASPAR database system.

12. U.S. Bureau of the Census, *Social and Economic Status of the Black Population*, pp. 24–26.

13. Ibid., pp. 28–29.

14. These data were obtained from information provided by each of the Foundations. Other national and regional foundations made grants to private black colleges but information on annual appropriations was not readily available.

15. Bacote, *Story of Atlanta University*, p. 139. The list of monographs published include the following: *Mortality Among Negroes in Cities*, 1896; *Social and Physical Conditions of Negroes in Cities*, 1897; *Some Efforts of American Negroes for Their Own Social Betterment*, 1898; *The Negro in Business*, 1899; *The College-Bred Negro*, 1900; *The Negro Common School*, 1901; *The Negro Artisan*, 1902; *The Negro Church*, 1903; *Some Notes on Negro Crime Particularly in Georgia*, 1904; *A Selected Bibliography of the Negro American*, 1905; *Health and Physique of the Negro American*, 1906; *Economic Cooperation Among Negro Americans*, 1907; *The Negro American Family*, 1908; *Efforts for Social Betterment among Negro Americans*, 1909; *The College-Bred Negro American*, 1910; *The Common School and the Negro American*, 1911; *The Negro American Artisan*, 1912; *Morals and Manners among Negro Americans*, 1914; *Select Discussions of Negro Problems*, 1916; and *Economic Cooperation among Negroes of Georgia*, 1917.

16. M. O. Chandler and M. C. Rice, *Opening Fall Enrollment in Higher Education, 1967* (Washington, D.C.: U.S. Office of Education, 1968), pp. 52–134; Frank Bowles and Frank A. DeCosta, *Between Two Worlds* (New York: McGraw-Hill, 1971), pp. 83–85; and C. H. Thompson, "The Relative Enrollment of Negroes in Higher Educational Institutions in the United States," *Journal of Negro Education* 22(3): 432–41.

17. Leslie Dominits, professor of German at Talladega College; discussion with Henry N. Drewry, June 1980.

18. Franklin & Marshall College, *Baccalaureate Origins of Doctoral Recipients* 6th ed. and 8th ed. (Lancaster, Penn.: Franklin and Marshall College, 1996, 1998) provide lists showing the number of undergraduates from each college who received doctorates. One covered the period 1986 to 1995, the other 1920 to 1995.

19. Robert Goodwin, "Roots and Wings," *Journal of Negro Education* 60(2): 123.

20. A. Bartlett Giamatti, *A Free and Ordered Space: The Real World of the University* (New York: W. W. Norton, 1979), p. 36.

21. The United Negro College Fund, *Statistics on Member Colleges* for the 1958–59, 1963–64, 1968–69, and 1974–75 school years.

22. Included were Oakwood and Stillman Colleges in Alabama, Bethune-Cookman and Edward Waters Colleges in Florida, Barber-Scotia in North Carolina, Voorhees College in South Carolina, and St. Paul's in Virginia.

23. Some of these degrees were earned before 1954 and some after 1975. Although precise information is not available, the low rate at which black Americans earned Ph.D. degrees before the 1950s suggests that most were earned after the *Brown* decision.

24. The traditionally white colleges included in the comparison are Carrol, Central (Pennsylvania), Geneva, Lebanon, Lenoir Rhyne, Morningside, Pacific, and Wartburg Colleges and Nebraska Wesleyan University. The black colleges

included are Benedict, Bennett (North Carolina), Bethune-Cookman, Jarvis, LeMoyne-Owen, Rust, St. Augustine, Stillman, and Tougaloo Colleges and Johnson C. Smith and Virginia Union Universities.

Chapter 8   Talladega College: A Case History (1867 to 1975)

1. Leonard E. Drewry, a graduate of Oberlin College, joined the Talladega faculty in 1926 after teaching at Virginia Theological Seminary and College and at Kansas Vocational College. He was thirty-three at the time of the anniversary pageant.

2. Frederick Sumner, the grandson of U.S. Senator Charles Sumner, a native of Massachusetts, attended Harvard College and Law School. His grandfather had been elected to the Senate in 1851, where he served during the presidential administrations of Lincoln, Johnson, and Grant. He had few peers in the Congress in his opposition to slavery and his commitment to full and equal rights for freedmen. In 1856, he was brutally beaten and seriously injured while seated at his desk in the Senate. His attacker was Preston S. Brooks, a South Carolina relative of Senator Andrew P. Butler, whom Sumner had criticized in a Senate speech two days earlier. After recuperating for three and a half years, Sumner returned to the Senate, to which he had been almost unanimously reelected during his absence.

3. McPherson, "What Yankee 'Schoolmarms' Taught," p. 4.

4. Talladega College, *Alumni Directory* (White Plains, N.Y.: Charles C. Harris Publishing, 1997).

5. American Missionary Association, *Annual Report* (New York: American Missionary Association, 1871), pp. 45, 46.

6. Alvord, *Freedmen's Schools and Textbooks,* pp. 31, 34.

7. Augustus Field Beard, *A Crusade of Brotherhood: A History of the American Missionary Association* (Boston: Pilgrim Press, 1909), pp. 173–74.

8. Ibid., pp. 178–79.

9. The speech was delivered in 1950 on the occasion of the presentation by the college of an honorary degree of doctor of laws to George Williamson Crawford. Crawford graduated from Yale Law School and spent much of his professional career as counsel for the city of New Haven, Connecticut. He was also a long-time member of the board of trustees of Talladega College.

10. The term "black belt" is used to refer to sections of southern states having black soil and traditionally having a large percentage of black Americans in the population. Both of these reasons have been cited as the origin of the term.

11. Maxine D. Jones and Joe M. Richardson, *Talladega College: The First Century* (Tuscaloosa: University of Alabama Press, 1990), p. 40.

12. Talladega College, *Talladega College Catalogue* (Talladega, Ala.: Talladega College, 1896), pp. 4, 28, 39.

13. T. J. Jones, *Negro Education,* p. 84.

14. Ibid., p. 85.

15. Ibid., pp. 22, 23.

16. Ibid., pp. 85, 86.

17. U.S. Bureau of Education, *Survey of Negro Colleges and Universities,* p. 59.

18. The pipe organ was in service until 1952, when it was replaced by a gift from an alumnus, T. K. Lawless 1909, a dermatologist and graduate of Northwestern Medical School.

19. Information provided September 24, 1999, by the Talladega College Office of Institutional Research.

20. Only a few students entering the college in 1927 had attended racially mixed schools, as Talladega operated the only racially mixed four-year secondary school in Alabama.

21. Excerpts from October 1999 letter from Anne Laurie Derricotte Tucker.

22. Gloria Williams Gleason, teacher in Chicago Public Schools (retired), comments in response to questions regarding her recollections of her experiences as a student at Talladega College, recorded in 1998.

23. *The Talladegan,* January 1931, p. 1.

24. From the *Report of the Committee on the Classification of Universities and Colleges,* given at the 45th meeting of the Association of American Universities at the University of Toronto, October, p. 80.

25. American Missionary Association, *Annual Report* (New York: American Missionary Association, 1932), pp. 57–59. The other AMA institutions were LeMoyne, Memphis, Tennessee; Straight, New Orleans, Louisiana; Tillotson, Austin, Texas; and Tougaloo, Tougaloo, Mississippi.

26. Talladega College, *Talladega College Catalog* (Talladega, Ala.: Tallageda College, 1936), pp. 26–27. A minimum of fifteen units (each representing a year's work in a secondary school subject meeting five times each week) were needed for admission to the college. Required were: 3 units in English, 1 in history, and 1 in science; a minimum of 6 from the fields of agriculture (1), biology (1), chemistry (1), civics (½), economics (½), English (1), French or German (2), history (1), hygiene (½), mathematics (3), Latin (4), physical geography (1), physics (1), and psychology (1); and a maximum of 4 from commercial subjects cooking, mechanics drawing, iron work, music, and sewing. General division students were required to give evidence through examination of a grasp of knowledge secured in three first-year college survey courses in social science, natural science, and humanities and two second-year survey courses selected from the fields of humanities, physical sciences, biological sciences, and social sciences. In the field of concentration, students pursued a program of work arranged in consultation with their advisors and approved by the dean. This included six courses, each pursued for a period of 36 weeks. Successful completion of a comprehensive examination in the field of concentration was required.

27. Jones and Richardson, *Talladega College,* p. 144.

28. *The Talladegan,* June 2, 1952, "Trustees Dismiss College Officials."

29. *New York Times,* June 9, 1952, p. 18.

30. "Elected as the President of College at Talladega," *New York Times,* August 20, 1952, p. 18; "Gray Heads Talladega," *New York Times,* April 11, 1953, p. 15.

31. Jones and Richardson, *Talladega College,* p. 223.

32. The Thirteen College Curriculum Program (TCCP) was collaboratively planned by thirteen black colleges to help weaker students improve their academic skills.

33. Herman H. Long, *A Note on the Production of Doctorates among the Graduates of Talladega College* (Talladega, Ala.: Talladega College, 1972). From a study by William A. Manuel and Marion E. Altenderfer, "Baccalaureate Origins of 1950–59 Medical Graduates," Public Health Service Monograph No. 66. (Washington, D.C.: U.S. Government Printing Office, 1961).

Chapter 9   Leadership and Luck

1. The authors acknowledge that this assertion about the association between success and sustained good leadership looks better as a piece of street common sense than as the result of a controlled scientific experiment. And in this case, causation runs both ways. Good leadership promotes institutional success; institutional success makes it easier to attract wise and energetic new leadership.

2. The events of the mid-1970s at Stillman College were reported to us in interviews with Dr. Cordell Wynn, March 16, 1999; Mrs. Sarah Davis, vice president for administration, March 17, 1999; and Dr. Haywood L. Strickland, president of Texas College and former Stillman faculty member, July 7, 1999. Wynn received an A.A. degree at Boston University, a B.S. from Fort Valley State College in Georgia, and a Ph.D. from Georgia State University. Positions held prior to Alabama A & M included assistant dean and professor at the School of Education, Alabama State University, and assistant superintendent of the Bibb County school system in Macon, Georgia.

3. Cordell Wynn interview, March 16, 1999.

4. Cordell Wynn interview, March 16, 1999.

5. Sue Thompson interview, September 19, 1997.

6. Cordell Wynn interview, March 16, 1999; and Stillman College, *Stillman College Catalog, 1998–2000* (Tuscaloosa, Ala.: Stillman College, 1998), pp. 6–10.

7. Ernest McNealey interviews, September 18, 1997 and March 15, 1999.

8. Stillman College, *Strategic Plan: July 1, 1988–June 30, 2003* (Tuscaloosa, Ala.: Stillman College).

9. Ernest McNealey interviews, March 15, 1999, and December 8, 2000.

10. Stillman College, *Strategic Plan*, p. 13.

11. Notes from a luncheon conversation, September 18, 1997.

12. Spelman College, *Spelman College 1997–98 Bulletin* (Atlanta: Spelman College, 1998), p. 2.

13. Simmons, a black American, is the daughter of a Texas sharecropper. She attended Dillard University in New Orleans and earned her Ph.D. at Harvard University. Spelman and Dillard are private black colleges; Smith, Brown and Harvard are elite, predominantly white ones.

14. Spelman College, *1997–98 Bulletin*, pp. 2–7.

15. Cass and Birnbaum, *Comparative Guide*, 8th ed., p. 606.

16. Donald M. Stewart interview, March 15, 1999; Robert D. Flanigan interview, February 13, 1998. Stewart received a bachelors degree from Grinnell College and a doctorate in public administration from Harvard University.

17. Donald Stewart interview, March 15, 1999; Robert D. Flanigan interview, February 13, 1998; Norman M. Rates, professor of religion interview, February 13, 1998.

18. The description of income sources as "hard" or "soft" is an administrator's shorthand for the likelihood that a particular source is reliable over a long period. Tuition and endowment income are usually considered hard sources, even though one could imagine circumstances under which either might unexpectedly cease. Individual gifts for current use and government grants are usually called soft, even though they might recur many times.

19. Rockefeller Brothers Fund, "Sound Futures: Initial Evaluation Report on Creel Committee Grants," unpublished staff paper, November 1984, pp. A26–A35. The paper assessed the impact of grants, totaling nearly $100 million, made to institutions to which the Rockefeller family had given significant support in the past. The grants were intended to promote institutional independence. Spelman's challenge grant was one in this group of nineteen.

20. Donald M. Stewart, Robert D. Flanigan, Lois Moreland, and Norman M. Rates interviews, February 13, 1998. Visitor observations are those of the authors, in periodic foundation site visits between 1978 and 1986. In 1986, Stewart became president of the College Board, a New York-based national membership organization that deals primarily with the transition from high school to college, and that sponsors the Scholastic Assessment Test, the Advanced Placement Program, and other programs and publications.

21. Rockefeller Brothers Fund, "Sound Futures," p. A37.

22. Johnnetta M. Cole interview, March 31, 1999.

23. Johnnetta M. Cole interview, March 31, 1999.

24. Spelman College, *1997–98 Bulletin,* p. 4.

25. Johnnetta M. Cole interview, March 31, 1999.

26. Dr. Audrey Forbes Manley interview, April 1, 1999; and Robert D. Flanigan interview, December 7, 2000.

27. Xavier University of Louisiana, *1996–98 Catalog* (New Orleans: Xavier University of Louisiana, 1996), pp. 6–7.

28. Daniel F. McSheffery, "A 20th Century Example," *Xavier Gold,* Summer 1998, pp. 38–43.

29. Sister Monica Loughlin interview by Henry N. Drewry, Bensalem, Pennsylvania, March 3, 1998.

30. Sister M. Juliana Haynes interview, Xavier University, October 22, 1997.

31. Norman C. Francis interview, October 22, 1997.

32. Presidential tenure information was provided by The College Fund/UNCF in 1998. Biographical information is from Dr. Francis's 1998 resume. The assessment of his role in regional politics was provided on October 23, 1997, by Ashton Phelps, Jr., president and publisher, *The Times Picayune,* New Orleans.

33. College Entrance Examination Board, *The College Handbook* (New York: College Entrance Examination Board, 1972), p. 441.

34. Continuing support for the summer science program for high school students and for strengthening science at Xavier has been provided by the Howard Hughes Medical Institute since 1989. Carmichael believes that the Hughes support, which is sustained and relatively flexible, played a big part in Xavier's ability to increase the number of graduates admitted to medical schools.

35. Fletcher, "Xavier's Desk-Side Manner," pp. A1, A12–A13.

36. Susan Chira, "Tiny Black College Takes High Road in Sciences," *New York Times*, March 28, 1990, p. B8.

37. JW Carmichael interview, October 24, 1997. Carmichael believes that the periods which would ordinarily follow his first two initials represent unnecessary frills. He prefers not to use the periods.

38. Sister Grace Mary Flickinger interview, October 23, 1997; and Xavier University of Louisiana, *University Profile 1996–97* (New Orleans: Xavier University, 1997), pp. 18, 19.

39. *Xavier Gold* 1998, pp. 1, 44, 45. Comment provided by Norman C. Francis, April 19, 1999.

40. Norman Francis and Calvin S. Tregre, vice president for fiscal affairs, interviews, October 24, 1997. These questions were raised by both Francis and Tregre.

41. Xavier University of Louisiana, *University Profile*, p. 15.

Chapter 10   The Graduates

1. Thomas M. Smith and others, *The Condition of Education 1996* (Washington, D.C.: Government Printing Office, 1996), pp. 115–16. This report from the Office of Educational Research and Improvement shows the earnings of those holding bachelors and graduate degrees to be consistently more than 50 percent higher than the earnings of high school graduates, which in turn are about 50 percent higher than the earnings of those who complete only nine to eleven grades of school.

2. For the first three measures see Shirelle Phelps, ed., *Who's Who Among African Americans (1998–99)* (Detroit: Gale Research, 1997). Data for senior U.S. officials in the executive branch are from *Journal of Blacks in Higher Education*, Spring 1998, pp. 58, 59. Data for MacArthur Fellowships are from *Journal of Blacks in Higher Education*, Summer 1998, p. 31.

3. The advisory board for *Who's Who among African Americans (1998–99)* was William C. Matney, Jr., founding editor of this *Who's Who* series; Lerone Bennett, Jr., executive editor of *Ebony* magazine; Vivian D. Hewitt, former librarian, Carnegie Endowment for International Peace; Jean Blackwell Hutson, former curator, Schomburg Center for Research in Black Culture; and Jessie Carney Smith, university librarian, Fisk University.

4. U.S. Department of Education, National Center for Education Statistics, Integrated Postsecondary Education Data System (IPEDS) provides data on enrollment and degrees attained, by race, since 1977. The percentages for the mid-1960s are estimated by linear projection of the 1977–96 rate of change back to 1965, and then doubling that rate for the years 1965–77. For private black colleges, this creates a range from 13.5 percent to 15.0 percent for the 1965 estimates. For the black public colleges, the same method produces a range from 26.7 percent to 30.0 percent for the 1965 estimates.

5. These awards, officially entitled MacArthur Fellowships, range in size from $160,000 to $375,000, payable over five years. According to the program guidelines, the awards are for "talented persons who have shown extraordinary originality and dedication in their creative pursuits, and a marked capacity for self-direction." Occupations of recipients include writers, scientists, social scientists,

humanists, artists, and teachers. The program is described in "The Work Ahead: New Guidelines for Grantmaking" (Chicago: John D. and Catharine T. MacArthur Foundation, 1998).

6. Michael T. Nettles, Laura W. Perna, and Kimberley Edelin Freeman, *Two Decades of Progress: African Americans Moving Forward in Higher Education* (Fairfax, Va.: Frederick D. Patterson Institute of the United Negro College Fund, 1999), pp. 91, 92.

7. The nine historically black institutions are: Howard, Spelman, Hampton, Tuskegee, Southern A & M (Baton Rouge), Florida A & M, North Carolina Central, North Carolina A & T, and Jackson State. Wayne State University, the fourth most productive institution, is not an historically black college or university (HBCU). The basic data source is P. H. Henderson, J. E. Clarke, and C.M.A. Reynolds, *Doctorate Recipients from United States Universities, Summary Report 1995* (Washington, D.C.: National Academy Press, 1996).

8. In 1989, Atlanta University merged with Clark College to become Clark Atlanta University and retained its doctoral research degree programs.

Chapter 11   The Students

1. Linda J. Sax et al., *The American Freshman: National Norms for 1996* (Los Angeles: Higher Education Research Institute, UCLA, 1996). Appendix D lists the following four-year private black colleges as having participated in the survey in the years indicated. Although the participants represent all sizes of private black colleges, a majority of them in most years come from the top third of the total list, ranked by enrollment size:

1971	1975	1985	1995
Hampton	Clark Atlanta	Morehouse	Dillard
Morris Brown	Dillard	St. Paul's	Hampton
Philander Smith	Livingstone	Spelman	Morehouse
Spelman	St. Paul's	Tuskegee	Philander Smith
Talladega	Shaw		Spelman
Virginia Union	Spelman		Talladega
	Virginia Union		Tougaloo
	Xavier		Tuskegee
			Xavier

Linda Sax is assistant professor and director of the Cooperative Institution Research Program (CIRP) at the Higher Education Research Institute. William Korn is associate director for operations.

2. Nettles, Perna, and Freeman, *Two Decades of Progress*, pp. 20–23.

3. *1995 Annual Freshman Survey* database.

4. This data was provided by Frederick H. Dietrich, vice president for operations, the College Board, in June 1998, for 1995 test-taking high school seniors. The national median verbal score for that year was V427. These scores are not recentered. Recentering occurred in 1996, with the effect that scores at most

percentile levels were raised slightly. One might present instead the score distribution from both verbal and mathematical sections of the test, or from the mathematical section only, but the percentiles would not change significantly.

5. United Negro College Fund, *Statistical Report 1998,* pp. 34–40.

6. Michael S. McPherson and Morton Owen Schapiro, *The Student Aid Game: Meeting Need and Rewarding Talent in American Higher Education* (Princeton, N.J.: Princeton University Press, 1998), pp. 49–51, 135–143. This is the most comprehensive recent description of the financial incentives affecting college enrollment at all income levels and of their policy implications.

7. First-year enrollments in medicine, veterinary medicine, osteopathic medicine, and dentistry were provided to the authors by the Association of American Medical Colleges, the Association of American Veterinary Medical Colleges, the American Osteopathic Association and the American Dental Association. First year, full-time freshmen enrollment in four-year colleges is shown in Nettles, Perna, and Freeman, *Two Decades of Progress,* pp. 8–11.

8. In March 2000, The United Negro College Fund announced receipt of three corporate gifts of money and equipment, the total valued at $101 million, to provide new computer hardware, software, and training to member colleges. The donations came from Microsoft, IBM, and AT&T. UNCF President William H. Gray III at that time estimated that "15 per cent of students at historically black colleges own computers, compared with 55 per cent of students nationally." This report is from Scott Carlson, "3 Companies Give $101-Million for Computing at Black Colleges," *Chronicle of Higher Education,* March 24, 2000, p. A52.

9. Nettles, Perna, and Freeman, *Two Decades of Progress,* p. 85.

Chapter 12   Faculty: Challenge and Response

1. The shorthand term "well prepared" is clearly an approximation and assumes quite different meanings from one college to the next. However, in many of our site visits, experienced faculty recalled vividly the change in the student mix they had observed during the 1970s. Self-reported student data in the HERI Annual Freshman Surveys reinforced these faculty observations: in the 1970s, and to a lesser extent in the mid-1990s, the high school grades of black college freshmen were lower than those of freshmen generally. Freshmen at black private and public colleges also reported more frequently than all freshmen at private colleges that they needed remedial work, particularly in mathematics, science, and languages. Nationwide standardized test results, in turn, reinforce the observations of these faculty and freshmen.

2. David S. Webster, Russell L. Stockard, and James W. Henson, "Black Student Elite: Enrollment Shifts in High-Achieving, High Socioeconomic Status Black Students from Black to White Colleges during the 1970s," *College and University: Journal of the American Association of Collegiate Registrars,* Spring 1981, p. 286. The percentages cited are from self-reported student responses to the HERI Annual Freshman Surveys in 1970 and 1978.

3. Unpublished memorandum to the Johnson C. Smith University Alumni Advisory Committee, Teaneck, New Jersey, April 20, 1971, pp. 2, 3.

4. Excerpt from a proposal to the Andrew W. Mellon Foundation, New York, quoted in the Foundation's trustee docket dated March 28, 1979.

5. William E. Sims Jr., "Black Colleges—Bicentennial Offers Little Hope," *Journal of Negro Education* 45(1976): 219–22.

6. The term "HBCUs" is a common shorthand for "historically black colleges and universities."

7. Kenneth E. Eble and Wilbert J. McKeachie, *Improving Undergraduate Education through Faculty Development* (San Francisco: Jossey-Bass, 1986). Eble and McKeachie trace the history of faculty development and describe a Bush Foundation program for colleges in the Upper Midwest with operating guidelines similar to those used for private black colleges. The authors assess which strategies for change worked well and which seemed less effective.

8. The United Negro College Fund *1998 Statistical Report*, Appendix Y, reports that the 1997 current expenditure of undergraduate UNCF colleges was $878,507,000. If one assumes that about 65 percent of current expenditure is for faculty and staff salaries, and that this segment of the total should increase by 25 percent, this creates a total requirement of $142 million, or $3.8 million per year for each of the thirty-eight member undergraduate colleges.

Chapter 13   The Small Colleges

1. Carnegie Commission on Higher Education, *The More Effective Use of Resources* (New York: McGraw Hill, 1972), p. 27.

2. Carnegie Commission on Higher Education, *New Students and New Places* (New York: McGraw Hill, 1971), pp. 5–7, 65–95. The comment that public universities might grow above these suggested limits was a huge understatement. The largest U.S. public campuses now enroll more than 50,000 students each.

3. Carnegie Commission on Higher Education, *New Students and New Places*, p. 82.

4. Ibid., p. 6.

5. Luther H. Foster, "The Hazards in Black Higher Education: Institutional Management," *Journal of Negro Education* 56(1987), pp. 141, 142.

6. Joseph A. Kershaw, *The Very Small College: A Report to The Ford Foundation* (New York: The Ford Foundation, 1976), p. 21.

7. United Negro College Fund, *1998 Statistical Report*, pp. 74, 79.

8. Texas College, *1998–2000 Catalog* (Tyler, Tex.: Texas College, 1998), p. 5; Haywood L. Strickland, Glenda Carter, and Marshall Gilmore, "Perpetuation of the Legacy: A Case for the Survival of Texas College" (August 1996), p. 1.

9. Haywood L. Strickland and Marshall Gilmore, "Shaping the Future of Texas College: An Update" (July 1997), p. 1.

10. Haywood L. Strickland interview, July 7, 1999; "Omega Psi Fraternity Honors Strickland, Carter," *Tyler Morning Telegraph*, November 20, 1997, Section 2, p. 11.

11. Strickland, Carter, and Gilmore, "Perpetuation," pp. 5, 6.

12. Strickland, Carter, and Gilmore, "Perpetuation," pp. 4–6.

13. Haywood L. Strickland interview, July 7, 1999.

14. Haywood L. Strickland interview, December 7, 2000.

15. Glenda Carter interview, July 7, 1999.

Chapter 14 Student Aid

1. Michael S. McPherson and Morton Owen Schapiro, "Gaining Control of the Free-for-All in Financial Aid," *Chronicle of Higher Education,* July 2, 1999, p. A48. The omitted portion of this quotation notes the increased use of student financial aid to recruit highly desirable students. This assessment is particularly pertinent to black colleges, whose students often come from families with low incomes.

2. Thomas R. Wolanin, "Lobbying for Higher Education in Washington," *Change,* September/October 1998, p. 58. For a summary of student aid trends, classified by source and type of aid (grants, loans, jobs), see Lawrence E. Gladieux, Watson Scott Swail, and Alicia Dorsey, *Trends in Student Aid* (New York: College Entrance Examination Board, 1999a).

3. Gladieux, Swail and Dorsey, *Trends in Student Aid 1999,* pp. 4, 16. Gladieux notes that virtually all the change in proportion in the past ten years (toward increased federal student aid that is not based on need) is due to growth in unsubsidized, market-rate loans, an option introduced for federal loans in 1992–93.

4. The early establishment of need-based state systems of grants and loans was concentrated in the Northeast, Midwest and far West, and operated for the benefit of state residents attending in-state colleges. Less than half of the southern states, as of 2000, have significant need-based aid plans. In general, however, students attending private black colleges depended relatively heavily on the federal programs, not state ones.

5. Lawrence E. Gladieux, Watson Scott Swail, and Alicia Dorsey, *Trends in College Pricing* (New York: College Entrance Examination Board, 1999), p. 17.

6. Gladieux, Swail, and Dorsey, *Trends in Student Aid,* p. 16.

7. Humphrey Doermann, *Towards Equal Access* (New York: College Entrance Examination Board, 1978), pp. 61–79 and 122–43.

8. See Chapter 11.

9. *Report of the Minnesota Financial Aid Task Force* (St. Paul, Minn.: Minnesota Higher Education Coordinating Board, 1994), p. 15. Estimating who should participate in postsecondary education but does not solely because of lack of money is admittedly an exercise in approximation. Counselors and youth workers, if asked, must make subjective judgments. One could ask the potential students themselves, but would need to make some adjustments to their replies. When given a choice of a variety of reasons why they drop out or fail to enroll, students in earlier, small studies have consistently overreported financial concerns and underreported dislike or incapacity for college work. Finally, whatever the difficulty of monitoring eighteen-year-olds, the difficulty probably increases when trying to estimate educational and financial needs of adults entering college later in life.

10. Ibid., p. 12.

11. McPherson and Schapiro, *The Student Aid Game,* pp. 42–48.

12. This database search was conducted by the Roper Center for Public Opinion Research in July 1998. The following is a summary of the three surveys in which college student aid financed by taxes did not win at least a plurality of respondent approval. In 1981, 47 percent of respondents to a Roper Poll favored tightening eligibility for college student loans, compared with 37 percent opposed. In 1985, 56 percent of respondents told a *Los Angeles Times* survey that they favored ending college loans to students with family incomes of $30,000 or more. In 1995, 73 percent of respondents to an American Viewpoint survey said they favored reallocating public expenditures away from college programs and toward elementary and secondary education.

13. United Negro College Fund, *Statistical Report 1997,* pp. 70, 72, 73.

Chapter 15　External Sources of Support

1. Thomas R. Wolanin, "The Federal Investment in Minority-Serving Institutions," in *Minority-Serving Institutions: Distinct Purposes, Common Goals,* Jamie R. Merisotis, Colleen T. O'Brien eds., vol. XXVI, no. 2 of *New Directions for Higher Education* (San Francisco: Jossey-Bass, 1998), p. 30.

2. Since 1978, Native American colleges also receive support, calculated on a per-student basis, under the Tribally Controlled Community College Assistance Act. The original legislation authorized payments of $4,000 per student, but recent appropriations permitted actual payments of roughly half that amount. The tribally controlled colleges typically are located near Indian reservations, in rural areas, and usually enroll less than a thousand students each. Enrollment is predominantly tribal members, although others may attend. Hispanic-serving colleges usually are larger, located in urban areas, and also serve many students of non-hispanic backgrounds.

3. Quoted in Wolanin, "The Federal Investment in Minority-Serving Institutions," pp. 23–24.

4. Robert D. (Danny) Flanigan interview, December 3, 1999.

5. Norman C. Francis interview, December 8, 1999.

6. Christopher F. Edley Sr., "For Black Colleges," *Washington Post,* December 2, 1985, p. A23.

7. President's Board of Advisors on Historically Black Colleges and Universities, *1995–96 Annual Report* (Washington, D.C.: U.S. Department of Education, 1996), pp. 2, 3.

8. General Accounting Office, *Historic Preservation: Cost to Restore Historic Properties at Historically Black Colleges and Universities,* GAO/RCED-98-51 (Washington, D.C.: Government Printing Office, 1998), p. 3.

9. A corporate foundation is sometimes endowed, but usually financed annually by the earnings of a single corporation; this kind of foundation is a separate legal entity, but usually a majority of its directors also are employees of the parent corporation.

10. William H. Gray III interview, July 11, 2000.

11. Debra E. Blum, "Corporate Giving Rises Again," *Chronicle of Philanthropy,* July 13, 2000, p. 1.

12. Williams, *A Research History of the UNCF,* pp. 761–69.

13. The Ford Foundation, "Toward a Revised Program Emphasis for the Division of Education and Research of The Ford Foundation," unpublished memorandum to the board of trustees, September, 1971, pp. 30, 34.

14. United Negro College Fund, *A Mind Is . . . ,* Fall 1999, (6)2: 23–28.

15. Information provided by Adrienne L. Powell, director of FASTAP; Marshal L. Ausberry, pastor, Antioch Baptist Church, Fairfax, Virginia, and former FASTAP director; and Adib A. Shakir, senior education consultant, Cassidy and Associates, Washington D.C., on May 20, 1999.

Chapter 16   Leadership and Financial Independence

1. Samuel M. Nabrit and Julius S. Scott Jr., *Inventory of Academic Leadership: An Analysis of the Boards of Trustees of Fifty Predominantly Negro Institutions* (Atlanta: Southern Fellowships Fund, 1968), pp. 41–47.

2. Ibid., p. 18.

3. Thompson, *Private Black Colleges,* p. 232.

4. Thomas E. Holloran interview, February 9, 2000; William G. Bowen interview, January 8, 2000. Holloran is consultant and professor of management, University of St. Thomas. Bowen is the author of *Inside the Boardroom* (New York: John Wiley & Sons, 1994).

5. Luther H. Foster, "The Hazards in Black Higher Education Institutional Management," *Journal of Negro Education* 56(1987): 141.

6. Information provided by the American Council on Education and UNCF. In both cases the question is asked of sitting presidents: How long have you been in office? The average of those answers equals average tenure.

7. Joye Mercer, "New Survey of College Presidents Finds They Are a Little Older and Staying Longer," *Chronicle of Higher Education,* April 10, 1998, p. A49. The UNCF presidential data is from a letter from William H. Gray III to Humphrey Doermann dated April 8, 1998. Development officer data is from Ayers and Associates, Inc., *Institutional Advancement and Development at Historically Black Colleges and Universities: A Report Prepared for the Kresge Foundation* (Washington, D.C., 1998), p. 17.

8. Richard P. Dober interview, March 23, 1998.

9. Association of Physical Plant Administrators of Universities and Colleges, *The Decaying American Campus: A Ticking Time Bomb* (Alexandria, Va.: Association of Physical Plant Administrators of Universities and Colleges, 1989).

10. Ibid., p. 6.

11. Harvey H. Kaiser, *A Foundation to Uphold: A Study of Facilities Conditions at U.S. Colleges and Universities* (Alexandria, Va.: Association of Higher Education Facilities Officers, 1996), pp. 53–65. "Accumulated Deferred Maintenance" is maintenance projects from prior years that were not included in the maintenance process because of perceived lower priority status than those funded. Deferred maintenance includes postponed renewal and replacement maintenance and unperformed unscheduled major maintenance.

12. Arnold Berke, "A Terrible Thing to Waste," *Preservation,* March/April 1999, pp. 60–68.

13. The United Negro College Fund, *1998 Statistical Report,* pp. 23–25, 79. Howard University and Hampton University, not UNCF members, also have among the largest private black college endowments.

14. Ibid., p. 25.

15. Alice Green Burnette, *The Privilege to Ask: A Handbook for African American Fund Raising Professionals* (Atlanta, Ga.: Interdenominational Theological Center, 2000), pp. 16–17, Chapter 9, pp. 1–20. (The numbering starts fresh at the beginning of each chapter.)

16. Council for Aid to Education, *1998 Voluntary Support of Education* (New York: Council for Aid to Education, 1998), p. 40.

17. The United Negro College Fund, *1998 Statistical Report,* p. 76. Also Council for Aid to Education, *1998 Voluntary Support of Education,* p. 38.

Chapter 17 Stand and Prosper

1. Ronald Dworkin, "Is Affirmative Action Doomed?" *New York Review,* November 1998, p. 56; also see *The Regents of the University of California v. Bakke,* 438 U.S. 299 (1978).

2. The year-by-year changes since 1996 in minority enrollment at flagship public colleges and professional schools in Texas and California are chronicled in the national press, probably most fully in the *Journal of Blacks in Higher Education.* Racial group differences have persisted in standardized test results for at least the past forty years. Discussion of this question and further bibliography can be found in Arie L. Nettles and Michael T. Nettles, eds., *Measuring Up: Challenges Minorities Face in Educational Assessment* (Boston: Kluwer Academic, 1999); Robert G. Cameron, *The Common Yardstick: A Case for the SAT* (New York: The College Board, 1989); and Doermann, *Crosscurrents in College Admissions.*

3. Similar plans guaranteeing admission to a stated portion of the state's high school graduating classes have been adopted more recently in California and Florida. It may be too soon to characterize the results, other than to note they contain the same flaw that the critics decry in the new Texas top-10-percent plan.

4. These UNCF enrollment statistics for black Texas freshmen represent an interesting coincidence with the timing of the *Hopwood* decision, but probably cannot be interpreted in a strict cause-and-effect way. For one thing, this particular enrollment curve began rising at least five years prior to *Hopwood.* Also, in California, where a similar successful attack on affirmative action took place in 1996, the enrollment of black students at UNCF colleges actually declined between 1996 and 1998. See Tazewell V. Hurst III, *The College Fund/UNCF Statistical Report 1999.*

5. Norman C. Francis interview, January 13, 2000.

6. Herbert W. Nickens, *Questions and Answers on Affirmative Action in Medical Education* (Washington, D.C.: American Association of Medical Colleges, 1998), p. 7. See also Linda Wightman, "The Threat of Diversity in Legal Education: An Empirical Analysis of the Consequences of Abandoning Race as a Factor in Law School Admission Decisions," *New York University Law Review* 72 (1997), pp. 1–53.

7. Nettles, Perna, and Freeman, *Two Decades of Progress,* pp. 20, 21.

References

Alvord, John W. 1980. *Freedmen's Schools and Textbooks*. New York: AMS Press.
American Missionary Association. 1871. *Annual Report*. New York: American Missionary Association.
———. 1932. *Annual Report*. New York: American Missionary Association.
Annual Freshmen Survey database printouts. 1971, 1975, and 1995. Los Angeles: Higher Education Research Institute, UCLA.
Association of American Medical Colleges. 1997 and 1978. Student and Applicant Information Management System (SAIMS). Washington, D.C.: Association of American Medical Colleges.
Association of Physical Plant Administrators of Universities and Colleges. 1989. *The Decaying American Campus: A Ticking Time Bomb*. Alexandria, Va.: Association of Physical Plant Administrators of Universities and Colleges.
Ayers and Associates. 1998. *Institutional Advancement and Development at Historically Black Colleges and Universities: A Report Prepared for the Kresge Foundation*. Washington, D.C. Typescript.
Bacote, Clarence A. 1969. *The Story of Atlanta University*. Princeton, N.J.: Princeton University Press.
Bardolph, Richard, ed. 1970. *The Civil Rights Record: Black Americans and the Law 1849–1970*. New York: Crowell.
Beard, Augustus Field. 1909. *A Crusade of Brotherhood: A History of the American Missionary Association*. Boston: Pilgrim Press.
Benson, Marty, ed. 1998. *1998 NCAA Graduation Rates Report*. Overland Park, Kan.: National Collegiate Athletic Association.
Bergman, Peter. 1969. *The Chronological History of the Negro in America*. New York: New American Library.
Berke, Arnold. 1999. "A Terrible Thing to Waste." *Preservation*, March/April, pp. 60–68.
Bettelheim, Bruno. 1943. "Individual and Mass Behavior in Extreme Situations." *Journal of Abnormal Psychology*, October, p. 38.
Blum, Debra E. 2000. "Corporate Giving Rises Again." *Chronicle of Philanthropy*, July 13, p. 1.
Bond, Horace Mann. 1934. *The Education of the Negro in the American Social Order*. New York: Prentice-Hall.
———. 1969. *Negro Education in Alabama*. New York: Atheneum.
———. 1976. *Education for Freedom*. Princeton, N.J.: Princeton University Press.
Botume, Elizabeth Hyde. 1893. *First Days Amongst the Contrabands*. Boston: Lee and Shepard Publishers.
Bowen, William G. 1994. *Inside the Boardroom*. New York: John Wiley & Sons.
Bowles, Frank, and Frank A. DeCosta. 1971. *Between Two Worlds*. New York: McGraw Hill.
Browne, William Hand, ed. 1883. *Archives of Maryland: Proceedings and Acts of the General Assembly of Maryland*. Baltimore: Maryland Historical Society.

Bullock, Henry Allen. 1970. *A History of Negro Education in the South from 1619 to the Present.* New York: Praeger.

Bureau of Education. 1919. *Biennial Survey of Education, 1916–18.* Washington, D.C.: Government Printing Office.

———. 1969. *Survey of Negro Colleges and Universities.* Bulletin No. 7, 1928. New York: Negro Universities Press.

Bureau of Refugees, Freedmen, and Abandoned Lands. 1980. *Semi-Annual Reports.* Numbers 1–10, January 1866–July 1870. New York: AMS Press.

Burnette, Alice Green. 2000. *The Privilege to Ask: A Handbook for African American Fund Raising Professionals.* Atlanta: Interdenominational Theological Center. Typescript.

Cairnes, John Elliott. 1862. *The Slave Power.* London: Parker and Sons.

Cameron, Robert G. 1989. *The Common Yardstick: A Case for the SAT.* New York: The College Board.

Carlson, Scott. 2000. "3 Companies Give $101-Million for Computing at Black Colleges." *Chronicle of Higher Education,* March 24, p. A52.

Carmichael, Stokely, and Charles Hamilton. 1967. *Black Power and the Politics of Liberation in America.* New York: Random House.

Carnegie Commission on Higher Education. 1971. *New Students and New Places.* New York: McGraw Hill.

———. 1972. *The More Effective Use of Resources.* New York: McGraw Hill.

Cass, James, and Max Birnbaum. 1968, 1969, 1975, 1977, 1983, and 1996. *Comparative Guide to American Colleges.* 3rd, 4th, 7th, 8th, 11th, and 17th eds. New York: Harper and Row.

Chandler, M. O., and M. C. Rice. 1968. *Opening Fall Enrollment in Higher Education, 1967.* Washington, D.C.: U.S. Office of Education.

Chira, Susan. 1990. "Tiny Black College Takes High Road in Sciences." *New York Times,* March 28, p. B8.

Close, Ellis. 1995. "Teaching Kids to be Smart." *Newsweek,* August 21.

College Entrance Examination Board. 1972 and 1996. *The College Handbook.* New York: College Entrance Examination Board.

Colored American Magazine. 1907. "What Is the Matter with the Atlanta Schools?" 13 (November): 333.

Commager, Henry Steele. 1963. *Documents in American History.* New York: Appleton-Century-Crofts.

Council for Aid to Education. 1998. *1998 Voluntary Support of Education.* New York: Council for Aid to Education.

Crawford, George Williamson. 1950. "Talladega Yesterday and Tomorrow." *Talladegan,* Talladega College. May, pp. 2–3.

Crisis. 1919. "Documents of the War." 18 (May): 16–21.

De Forest, John William. 1948. *A Union Officer in the Reconstruction.* New Haven: Yale University Press.

Desdunes, R. L. 1892. "Legislation and Legislators." *Daily Crusader,* June 11, p. 1.

Doermann, Humphrey. 1970. *Crosscurrents in College Admissions.* New York: Teachers College Press.

———. 1978. *Toward Equal Access.* New York: College Entrance Examination Board.

Du Bois, W.E.B. 1897. "Striving of the Negro People." *Atlantic Monthly* 80:194–95.

———. 1935. "Does the Negro Need Separate Schools?" *Journal of Negro Education*. 4(3): 328–35.

———. 1973. *The Souls of Black Folk*. Millwood, N.Y.: Kraus-Thomson Organization.

———. 1975. *Dusk of Dawn*. Millwood, N.Y.: Kraus-Thomson Organization.

Dworkin, Ronald. 1998. "Is Affirmative Action Doomed?" *New York Review*, November, p. 56.

Eble, Kenneth E., and Wilbert J. McKeachie. 1986. *Improving Undergraduate Education through Faculty Development*. San Francisco: Jossey-Bass.

Edley, Christopher F. Sr. 1985. "For Black Colleges." *Washington Post*, December 2, p. A23.

Embree, Edwin R., and Julia Waxman. 1949. *Investment in People: The Story of the Julius Rosenwald Fund*. New York: Harper and Brothers.

Fleming, Walter L. 1907. *Documentary History of Reconstruction*, vol. II. Cleveland: Arthur H. Clark.

Fletcher, Michael A. 1997. "Xavier's Desk-Side Manner Is Prescription for Medical School." *Washington Post*, May 10, p. A1.

The Ford Foundation. 1971. "Toward a Revised Program Emphasis for the Division of Education and Research of The Ford Foundation." Unpublished memorandum to the Board of Trustees.

Foster, Luther H. 1987. "The Hazards in Black Higher Education: Institutional Management." *Journal of Negro Education* 56(2):141–42.

Franklin & Marshall College. 1996 and 1998. *Baccalaureate Origins of Doctoral Recipients*. 6th and 8th eds. Lancaster, Penn.: Franklin & Marshall College.

Franklin, John Hope, and Alfred A. Moss, Jr. 1988. *From Slavery to Freedom*. New York: Alfred A. Knopf.

General Accounting Office. 1998. *Historic Preservation: Cost to Restore Historic Properties at Historically Black Colleges and Universities*. GAO/RCED-98-51. Washington, D.C.: Government Printing Office.

Giamatti, A. Bartlett. 1979. *A Free and Ordered Space: The Real World of the University*. New York: W. W. Norton.

Gladieux, Lawrence E., Watson Scott Swail, and Alicia Dorsey. 1999. *Trends in Student Aid, 1999*. New York: College Entrance Examination Board.

———. 1999. *Trends in College Pricing, 1999*. New York: College Entrance Examination Board.

Goodwin, Robert. 1991. "Roots and Wings." *Journal of Negro Education* 60(2): 126–32.

Greene, Harry W. 1946. *Holders of Doctorates among American Negroes*. Boston: Meador Publishing.

Henderson, P. H., J. E. Clarke, and C.M.A. Reynolds. 1996. *Doctorate Recipients from United States Universities, Summary Report 1995*. Washington, D.C.: National Academy Press.

Henderson, Vivian W. 1971. "Negro Colleges Face the Future." *Daedalus*, Summer, p. 643.

Hening, William W., ed. 1969. *The Statutes at Large: Being a Collection of all the Laws of Virginia, from the First Session of the Legislature in the Year 1619.* Charlottesville: University of Virginia Press.

Hill, Susan T. 1984. *The Traditionally Black Institutions of Higher Education, 1860 to 1982.* Washington, D.C.: Government Printing Office.

Holmes, Dwight Oliver Wendell. 1934. *The Evolution of the Negro College.* New York: Teachers College, Columbia University.

Howard University. 1918. *Howard University Catalogue 1918–1919.* Washington, D.C.: Howard University.

Huggins, Nathan I., Martin Kilson, and Daniel Fox. 1971. *Key Issues in the African-American Experience.* New York: Vintage.

Jencks, Christopher, and David Riesman. 1967. "The American Negro College." *Harvard Educational Review* 37:25–26.

Jones, Maxine D., and Joe M. Richardson. 1990. *Talladega College: The First Century.* Tuscaloosa: University of Alabama Press.

Jones, Sherman. 1984. "Difficult Times for Black Colleges." *Change*, March, p. 29.

Jones, Thomas Jesse. 1917. *Negro Education: A Study of the Private and Higher Schools for Colored People in the United States.* Washington, D.C.: Bureau of Education.

Kaiser, Harvey H. 1996. *A Foundation to Uphold: A Study of Facilities Conditions at U.S. Colleges and Universities.* Alexandria, Va.: The Association of Higher Education Facilities Officers.

Katz, William Loren. 1967. *Eyewitness: The Negro in American History.* New York: Pitman Publishing.

Kershaw, Joseph A. 1976. *The Very Small College: A Report to The Ford Foundation.* New York: The Ford Foundation.

Kluger, Richard. 1975. *Simple Justice.* New York: Random House.

Lewin, Tamar. 2000. "Growing Up, Growing Apart." *New York Times,* June 25, p. 1.

Litwack, Leon F. 1961. *The Negro in the Free States 1790–1870.* Chicago: University of Chicago Press.

MacArthur, The John D. and Catharine T. Foundation. 1998. "The Work Ahead: New Guidelines for Grantmaking." Chicago: The John D. and Catharine T. MacArthur Foundation.

Manuel, William A., and Marion E. Altenderfer. 1961. "Baccalaureate Origins of 1950–59 Medical Graduates." Public Health Service Monograph no. 66. Washington, D.C.: Government Printing Office.

McKay, Claude. 1922. *Harlem Shadows.* New York: Harcourt Brace.

McLaughlin, Judith Block, and David Riesman. 1990. *Choosing a College President: Opportunities and Constraints.* Princeton, N.J.: Carnegie Foundation for the Advancement of Teaching.

McPherson, James M. 1970. "White Liberals and Black Power in Negro Education, 1865–1915." *American Historical Review* 75(5): 1380–86.

———. 1973. "What Yankee 'Schoolmarms' Taught Post-Civil War Blacks." *University: A Princeton Quarterly.* 57(4):3.

———. 1988. *Battle Cry of Freedom: The Civil War Era.* New York: Oxford University Press.

McPherson, Michael S., and Morton Owen Schapiro. 1998. *The Student Aid Game: Meeting Need and Rewarding Talent in American Higher Education*. Princeton, N.J.: Princeton University Press.

———. 1999. "Gaining Control of the Free-for-All in Financial Aid." *Chronicle of Higher Education*. July 2, p. A48.

McSheffery, Daniel F. 1998. "A 20th Century Example." *Xavier Gold*. Summer, pp. 38–43.

Mercer, Joye. 1998. "New Survey of College Presidents Finds They Are a Little Older and Staying Longer." *Chronicle of Higher Education*. April 10, p. A49.

Miller, Loren. 1967. *The Petitioners: The Story of the Supreme Court of the United States and the Negro*. Cleveland: World Publishing.

Minnesota Financial Aid Task Force. *Report of the Minnesota Financial Aid Task Force*. 1994. St. Paul, Minn.: Minnesota Higher Education Coordinating Board.

Morison, Samuel Eliot, and Henry Steele Commager. 1937. *The Growth of the American Republic*. New York: Oxford University Press.

Nabrit, Samuel M., and Julius S. Scott, Jr. 1968. *Inventory of Academic Leadership: An Analysis of the Boards of Trustees of Fifty Predominantly Negro Institutions*. Atlanta: Southern Fellowships Fund.

National Center for Education Statistics. 1972 and 1996. *Digest of Education Statistics*. Washington, D.C.: Government Printing Office.

National Science Foundation WebCASPAR database system.

Nettles, Arie L., and Michael T. Nettles, eds. 1999. *Measuring Up: Challenges Minorities Face in Educational Assessment*. Boston: Kluwer Academic.

Nettles, Michael T., Laura W. Perna, and Kimberley Edelin Freeman. 1999. *Two Decades of Progress: African Americans Moving Forward in Higher Education*. Fairfax, Va.: Frederick D. Patterson Institute of the United Negro College Fund.

Nevins, Alan. 1947. *The Ordeal of the Union*. New York: Scribner.

New York Times. 1952. "Trustees Dismiss College Officials." June 9, p. 18.

———. 1953. "Gray Heads Talladega." April 11, p. 15.

Nickens, Herbert W. 1998. *Questions and Answers on Affirmative Action in Medical Education*. Washington, D.C.: American Association of Medical Colleges.

Olsen, Otto H. 1971. *The Negro Question: From Slavery to Caste, 1663–1910*. New York: Pitman Publishing.

Phelps, Shirelle, ed. 1998. *Who's Who Among African Americans (1998–99)*. Detroit: Gale Research.

Powdermaker, Hortense. 1968. *After Freedom: A Cultural Study in the Deep South*. New York: Atheneum. Reprint of 1939 edition.

President's Board of Advisors on Historically Black Colleges and Universities. 1996. *1995–96 Annual Report*. Washington, D.C.: U.S. Department of Education.

Rawls, John. 1971. *A Theory of Justice*, Cambridge, Mass.: Harvard University Press.

Richardson, Joe M. 1980. *A History of Fisk University, 1865–1946*. University, Ala.: University of Alabama Press.

Rockefeller Brothers Fund. 1984. "Sound Futures: Initial Evaluation Report on Creel Committee Grants." Staff paper.

Roper Center for Public Opinion Research. Various poll results. Storrs, Conn.: Roper Center for Public Opinion Research.

Sax, Linda J., Alexander W. Astin, William S. Korn, and Kathryn M. Mahoney. 1996. *The American Freshman: National Norms for 1996.* Los Angeles: Higher Education Research Institute, UCLA.

Sims, William E., Jr. 1976. "Black Colleges—Bicentennial Offers Little Hope." *Journal of Negro Education* 45(3): 219–24.

Smith, Thomas M., and others. 1996. *The Condition of Education, 1996.* Washington, D.C.: Government Printing Office.

Snyder, Thomas D., ed. 1993. *120 Years of American Education: A Statistical Portrait.* Washington, D.C.: Government Printing Office.

Spelman College. 1998. *Spelman College 1997–98 Bulletin.* Atlanta: Spelman College.

Stevenson, Brenda, ed. 1988. *The Journals of Charlotte Forten Grimke.* New York: Oxford University Press.

Stillman College. 1998. *Strategic Plan: July 1, 1988–June 30, 2003.* Tuscaloosa, Ala.: Stillman College.

———. 1998. *Stillman College Catalog, 1998–2000.* Tuscaloosa, Ala.: Stillman College.

Stouffer, Samuel A., Edwin A. Suchman, Leland C. DeVinney, Shirley A. Starr, and Robin M. Williams, 1974. *The American Soldier: Adjustment During Army Life.* 4 vols. New York: Arno Press.

Strickland, Haywood L., Glenda Carter, and Marshall Gilmore. 1996. "Perpetuation of the Legacy: A Case for the Survival of Texas College." Typescript.

Strickland, Haywood L. and Marshall Gilmore. 1997. "Shaping the Future of Texas College: An Update." Typescript.

Talladega College. 1896 and 1936. *Talladega College Catalog.* Talladega, Ala.: Talladega College.

———. 1997. *Alumni Directory.* White Plains, N.Y.: Charles C. Harris.

Talladegan. 1931. Talladega College. January, p. 1.

———. 1952. Talladega College. June, p. 1.

Texas College. 1998. *1998–2000 Catalog.* Tyler, Tx.: Texas College.

Thernstrom, Stephan, and Abigail Thernstrom. 1997. *America in Black and White: One Nation Indivisible.* New York: Simon and Schuster.

Thompson, C. H. 1953. "The Relative Enrollment of Negroes in Higher Educational Institutions in the United States." *Journal of Negro Education* 22(3): 432–41.

Thompson, Daniel C. 1973. *Private Black Colleges at the Crossroads.* Westport, Conn.: Greenwood Press.

Tocqueville, Alexis de. 1945. *Democracy in America.* New York: Vintage Books. Reprint of 1840 edition.

Torrence, Ridgely. 1948. *The Story of John Hope.* New York: Macmillan.

Tougaloo College. 1904. *Tougaloo College Catalog.* Tougaloo, Miss.: Tougaloo College.

Trent, William J., Jr. 1971. "Negro Colleges Face the Future." *Daedalus,* Summer, p. 649.

Tuskegee Normal and Industrial Institute. 1927. *Annual Catalog, 1927–1928.* Tuskegee, Ala.: Tuskegee Normal and Industrial Institute.

Tyler Morning Telegraph. 1997. "Omega Psi Fraternity Honors Strickland, Carter." November 20, section 2, p. 11.

United Negro College Fund. *General Statistics of UNCF Member Institutions, 1977–78.*

———. 1957. *Statistics of Member Colleges 1955–56 School Year.* Fairfax, Va.: United Negro College Fund.

———. 1960. *Statistics of Member Colleges 1958–59 School Year.* Fairfax, Va.: United Negro College Fund.

———. 1965. *Statistics of Member Colleges 1963–64 School Year.* Fairfax, Va.: United Negro College Fund.

———. 1970. *Statistics of Member Colleges 1968–69 School Year.* Fairfax, Va.: United Negro College Fund.

———. 1977. *Statistics of Member Colleges 1974–75 School Year.* Fairfax, Va.: United Negro College Fund.

———. 1997. *1996 Statistical Report.* Fairfax, Va.: United Negro College Fund.

———. 1997. *African American Education Data Book.* Fairfax, Va.: United Negro College Fund.

———. 1998. *1997 Statistical Report.* Fairfax, Va.: United Negro College Fund.

———. 1999. *1998 Statistical Report.* Fairfax, Va.: United Negro College Fund.

———. 1999. "A Mind Is . . . ." Fairfax, Va.: United Negro College Fund.

———. 2000. *1999 Statistical Report.* Fairfax, Va.: United Negro College Fund.

U.S. Bureau of the Census. 1872. *A Compendium of the Ninth Census.* Washington, D.C.: Government Printing Office.

———. 1960. *A Statistical Abstract Supplement: Historical Statistics of the United States. Colonial Times to 1957.* Washington, D.C.: Government Printing Office.

———. 1968. *Negro Population in the United States, 1790–1915.* Washington, D.C.: Government Printing Office.

———. 1975. *Statistical Abstract of the United States.* Washington, D.C.: Government Printing Office.

———. 1976. *Historical Statistics of the United States: Colonial Times to 1970.* Washington, D.C.: Government Printing Office.

———. 1994. *The Social and Economic Status of the Black Population in the United States: An Historical View, 1790–1978.* Washington, D.C.: Government Printing Office.

———. 1996. *Money Income in the United States, 1995.* P-60-193. Washington D.C.: Government Printing Office.

U.S. Civil War Center, Louisiana State University, http://www.cwc.lsu.edu.

U.S. Department of Education. 1996. *IPEDS Fall Faculty Survey.* Washington, D.C.: U.S. Department of Education.

———. 1996. *President's Board of Advisors on Historically Black Colleges and Universities. 1995–96 Annual Report.* Washington, D.C.: Government Printing Office.

U.S. Office of Education. 1939. *Statistics of the Education of Negroes, 1933–34.* Washington, D.C.: Government Printing Office.

———. 1942. *National Survey of the Higher Education of Negroes.* Washington, D.C.: Government Printing Office.

Wall Street Journal. 1998. "Student Profiled in Journal Says 'No' to Berkeley Spot." May 21, p. A6.

Wallace, Samuel E., ed. 1971. *Total Institutions.* Transaction Books.

Washington, Booker T. 1901. *Up From Slavery.* New York: Doubleday, Page and Company.

Webster, David S., Russell L. Stockard, and James W. Henson. 1981. "Black Student Elite: Enrollment Shifts of High-Achieving, High Socioeconomic Status Black Students from Black to White Colleges During the 1970s." *College and University: Journal of the American Association of Collegiate Registrars,* Spring, p. 286.

Wightman, Linda. 1997. "The Threat of Diversity in Legal Education: An Empirical Analysis of the Consequences of Abandoning Race as a Factor in Law School Admission Decisions." *New York University Law Review* 72(1):1–53.

Williams, Alma Rene. 1988. *A Research History of the United Negro College Fund, Inc., 1944–1987.* Typescript.

Wolanin, Thomas R. 1998. "Lobbying for Higher Education in Washington." *Change,* September/October, p. 58.

———. 1998. "The Federal Investment in Minority-Serving Institutions." In *Minority Serving Institutions: Distinct Purposes, Common Goals.* Jamie R. Merisotis and Colleen T. O'Brien, eds. New Directions for Higher Education, vol. 26, no. 2. San Francisco: Jossey-Bass.

Woodward, C. Vann. 1966. *The Strange Career of Jim Crow.* New York: Oxford University Press.

Xavier Gold. 1998. Xavier University of Louisiana, pp. 1, 44, 45.

Xavier University of Louisiana. 1996. *1996–98 Catalog.* New Orleans: Xavier University of Louisiana.

———. 1997. *University Profile, 1996–97.* New Orleans: Xavier University of Louisiana.

Young, Andrew. 1996. *An Easy Burden.* New York: HarperCollins.

CASES CITED

Berea College v. Commonwealth of Kentucky, 211 U.S. 45 (1908).

Brown v. Board of Education, 347 U.S. 484 (1954).

Hall Strauder v. West Virginia, 100 U.S. 303 (1877).

Hodge v. United States, 203 U.S. 1 (1905).

Missouri ex rel. Gaines v. Canada, 305 U.S. 637 (1938).

McLauren v. Oklahoma State Regents, 339 U.S. 637 (1950).

Regents of the University of California v. Bakke, 438 U.S. 299 (1978).

Plessy v. Ferguson, 163 U.S. 537 (1896).

Sipuel v. Board of Regents, 339 U.S. 631 (1938).

Sweatt v. Painter, 339 U.S. 629 (1950).

Virginia v. Rives, 100 U.S. 303 (1880).

Index

Page numbers for entries occurring in figures are suffixed by an f; those for entries in notes, by an n, with the number of the note following; and those for entries in tables, by a t.

AAUP (American Association of University Professors), 154

Abolitionists, 14, 24, 28, 33

Academic education, 61–66, 138–39. *See also* Liberal arts

Accreditation, 123; desegregation and, 104; early attempts to obtain, 91–93; FASTAP assistance and, 267; loss of, 238; of Spelman, 168; Texas College and, 238, 239–40, 241–42, 267. *See also* Southern Association of Colleges and Schools

ACNY. (Association of Colleges for Negro Youth), 92–93, 138

Adams, John Quincy, 37

Adams, Myron Winslow, 85

Administration: early appointment of Blacks to, 80; historical perspective on, 53–56; of Xavier, 177

Admirals, 182t, 184, 185t, 190t

Advanced degrees, 156–58, 206. *See also* Doctorates; Masters degrees

Affirmative action, 105, 223, 259, 281, 283–84, 309n4

African Methodist Episcopal Church, 37, 56, 96, 269

African Methodist Episcopal Church Zion, 37, 56

Alabama, 15, 23, 72, 115

Alabama A & M, 257

Alabama Federation of German Clubs, 116

Albany State College, 257

Alcorn College, 50

Alexander, Will W., 85

Allen University, 4

Altenderfer, Marion E., 300n33

Alumni/ae, 85–87, 220, 254, 255, 276, 278–79

Alvord, John W., 36, 38–39, 45, 292nn8,12,15, 293nn6,7,10,21, 298n6

AMA. *See* American Missionary Association of the Congregational Church

American Association of University Professors (AAUP), 154

American Baptist Convention, 269

American Baptist Home Mission Society, 36, 167

American Church Institute and Episcopal Board, 37

American Civil Liberties Union, 226

American College Testing scores, 227

American Council on Education, 146, 273

American Expeditionary Force, 81–82

American Medical Association, 92

American Missionary Association of the Congregational Church (AMA), 34, 36, 37, 56, 98; Straight and, 97; Talladega and, 128, 132, 133, 134, 136, 148

American Revolution, 14, 32

America's Most Endangered Historic Places, 275

Amherst College, 32

Amistad (ship), 37, 147

Amnesty Act of 1872, 17

Anderson, Bernard E., 186t

Andover Townsman, 83

Andrews, George W., 145t

Andrew W. Mellon Foundation, 108, 221, 227, 228, 230t

Anna T. Jeanes Fund, 97

Annenberg Foundation, 264

Annual Freshman Surveys, 196, 197, 198t, 199, 206, 208, 248, 304n1

Archie-Hudson, Marguerite, 145t

Argrett, Loretta G., 186t

Arkansas Baptist College, 4

Armstrong, Samuel Chapman, 49, 58, 62–63, 64

Ashmun Institute, 33

Asian Americans, 181, 197

Associate degrees, 193

Association for the Study of Negro Life and History, 90, 112

Association of American Medical Colleges, 185

Association of American Universities, 146

Association of Colleges and Secondary Schools for Negroes, 77, 93

Association of Colleges for Negro Youth (ACNY), 92–93, 138

Association of Governing Boards, 277

Association of Physical Plant Administrators, 274–75

Astin, Alexander W., 196, 198n

Athletic scholarships, 215

Atlanta Constitution, 85

Atlanta University, 65, 89, 97, 112, 138, 303n7; collaboration with other schools, 95, 96; doctorate program in, 194; first black presidents of, 84, 85; graduate programs in, 78; leadership in, 122; non-black students in, 53. *See also* Clark Atlanta University

Atlanta University Center (AUC), 96–97, 168, 172

Atlanta University Press, 112

Atlantic Monthly, 59

AT&T, 266, 304n8

Auburn University, 116

AUC (Atlanta University Center), 96–97, 168, 172

Ausberry, Marshal L., 307n15

Avery, Byllye Y., 189t

Avery College, 33, 292n3

Bachelors degrees, 117, 124, 156, 173, 206–8. *See also* Graduates

Bacote, Clarence A., 85, 295n12, 297n15

Bailey, Ben E., 225–27

Baptist Church/religion, 37, 56, 87, 96, 197

Baptist Home Mission Society, 57

Baquet, Charles R., III, 186t

Barber Memorial Seminary, 97. *See also* Barber-Scotia College

Barber-Scotia College, 98, 297n22; accreditation loss, 238; enrollment size, 235t; establishment of, 97; faculty size, 122; rank by enrollment, 4; tuition in, 106

Bardolph, Richard, 291n7

Barnard College, 11t, 292n2

Basic education opportunity grants (BEOGs), 107

Beard, Augustus Field, 134, 298n7

Beittel, Adam Daniel, 56, 145t, 148–50, 151, 152

Benedict College, 3, 79, 298n24

Bennett, Lerone, 302n2

Bennett College, 4, 93, 98, 235t, 298n24

Berea College v. Commonwealth of Kentucky, 21

Bergman, Peter, 293n4

Berke, Arnold, 308n12

Berry, Mary Frances, 186t

Bethune-Cookman College, 5, 79, 297n22, 298n24; Congressional appropriations for, 260; endowments in, 11; establishment of, 98; faculty of, 222–24, 226; rank by enrollment, 3

Bettelheim, Bruno, 291n17

Bill and Melinda Gates Foundation, 261, 264

Birnbaum, Max, 290n17, 300n15

Bishop College, 79, 112, 123, 238

Black Codes, 15

Black consciousness, 111, 112

Black power movement, 110–11, 112, 154, 155

Black Student Association (BSA), at Talladega, 154–55

Black studies, 59–60, 111–14

Bluefield State College, 53, 104, 257

Blum, Debra E., 307n11

Board of Missions for Freedmen of the Presbyterian Church, 37

Boards of trustees, 80, 85–86, 269–70

Bond, Horace Mann, 58, 59, 60, 84, 85–86, 293n9, 294n3, 295n14

Botume, Elizabeth Hyde, 292nn6

Bowdoin College, 32

Bowen, William G., 308n4

Bowie State College, 50

Bowles, Frank, 297n16

Braithwaite, William Stanley, 60

Brawley, Benjamin, 89, 112

Brewer, David, 99

Brickhouse, Eugene A., 187t

Bromery, Randolph, 145t

Brooks, Preston S., 298n2

Brown, Aaron, 145t

Brown, Henry Billings, 20, 21

Brown, Henry E., 133, 136, 145t

Brown, Oliver, 100

Browne, William Hand, 290n2

Brownlee, Frederick, 147

Brown University, 32, 168
Brown v. Board of Education, 1, 11, 71, 79, 99–104, 110, 119, 155, 185, 296n1; background of, 100; degrees earned following, 117, 118; enforcement of, 101–2; impact on accreditation, 104; impact on black higher education, 114–15; impact on leadership, 120; impact on recruitment, 220; impact on student aid, 259
Bruce, Blanche K., 33–34
Bryn Mawr College, 6, 292n2
Budgets. *See* Operating budgets
Bullock, Henry Allen, 63, 88, 294n12, 295n17
Bunche, Ralph, 112
Bureau of Education, U.S., 45, 48, 64, 66, 80, 84, 138–39; *Negro Education,* 68, 70; *Survey of Negro Colleges and Universities,* 76–77, 140. *See also* Department of Education, U.S.
Bureau of Refugees, Freedmen, and Abandoned Land. *See* Freedmen's Bureau
Burleigh, Harry T., 129
Burnette, Alice Green, 277–78, 308n15
Bus boycott, 109
Bush Foundation, 5, 227, 228, 230t, 264, 265, 305n7
Business and management majors, 208, 210t
Butler, Andrew P., 298n2

Cairnes, John Elliott, 28, 291n19
California, 281, 309nn2,3,4
Cameron, Robert G., 309n2
Cane (Toomer), 88
Capon Springs conferences, 62, 64
Cardoza, Francis, 32
Carmichael, JW, 176, 177, 301n34, 302n37
Carmichael, Stokely, 110, 111, 153
Carnegie, Andrew, 138, 141
Carnegie Commission on Higher Education, 233–34
Carnegie Library, Talladega College, 138
Carnegie Mellon University, 11t
Carpetbaggers, 37–38
Carrol College, 297n24
Carter, Glenda F., 242, 305nn8,11,12,15
Carter, Jimmy, 260
Cass, James, 290n17, 300n15
Cassedy building, Talladega College, 137

Cater, James T., 145t, 147–48, 149, 150, 151
Catholic Church/religion, 173–74, 197, 286
Census data, 23–24, 39–40, 51, 107
Central College, 297n24
CFAE (Council for Aid to Education), 278, 279
Chandler, M. O., 297n16
Change Magazine, 171
Charles H. Moson Theological Seminary, 96
Chavis, John, 32
Cheit, Earl, 233
Cheryl J. Hopwood v. The State of Texas, 280–84, 309n4
Chevron, 262
Cheyney Training School for Teachers, 33, 127, 292n3
Childs, James E., 136
Chira, Susan, 302n36
Christian Methodist Episcopal (CME) Church, 96, 238, 239, 241, 242, 269, 270
Chronicle, 44
Chronicle of Philanthropy, The, 261–62
Church of God in Christ, 96
CIRP (Cooperative Institutional Research Program), 197, 199, 217
Citizenship rights, 16, 23
City University of New York (CUNY), 184
Civil Rights Act of 1964, 1, 108, 109, 115, 222–23
Civil Rights Enforcement Act of 1870, 19
Civil rights movement, 108–11, 153, 226, 227
Civil War, 14, 15, 28, 32, 34–35, 48, 50
Claflin College, 3, 122
Clark Atlanta University, 166, 283; endowments in, 276; establishment of, 97, 303n7; faculty size, 122; graduate programs of, 3; operating budget of, 10; rank by enrollment, 4, 303n1; Title III funds for, 257
Clark College, 2, 92, 96, 97, 303n7. *See also* Clark Atlanta University
Class rank. *See* High school class rank
Clinton administration, 184
Close, Ellis, 290n18
Closing of institutions, 91, 123, 238
Colby, Abram, 43

Cole, Johnnetta B., 170–73, 180, 301nn22,23,25
Coleman, Jason, 282
Coleman, Rodney, 186t
College Board. *See* College Entrance Examination Board
College Entrance Examination Board, 246, 247, 249
College Fund Drive, 93
College of New Jersey, 32
College of Saint Catherine, 286
Colleges, historical perspective on, 45–50, 292–94nn1–24
College Scholarship Service, 246
Colored American Magazine, 65
Colored Methodist Church, 56
Colored Methodist Episcopal Church, 37
Columbia University, 32
Commager, Henry Steele, 26, 27, 291n16
Commission on Civil Rights, U.S., 282
Community, sense of, 214t, 215
Compromise of 1877, 17
Confederacy, 15, 24, 34, 38, 41, 50, 70
Congregational Church, 137, 151. *See also* American Missionary Association
Congressional appropriations, 260
Congress of Racial Equality (CORE), 110–11
Consolidation and collaboration, 90–98
Constitution, U.S., 14; Thirteenth Amendment, 12, 15, 20, 28, 257; Fourteenth Amendment, 12, 16, 19, 20, 23, 28, 257; Fifteenth Amendment, 12, 16, 23, 257
Cookman College, 98
Cooperative Institutional Research Program (CIRP), 197, 199, 217
CORE (Congress of Racial Equality), 110–11
Cornell University, 113
Corporate gifts, 254, 255, 261–65, 267, 304n8
Cosby, Bill, 171
Cosby, Camille, 171
Cotton, 28–29, 77
Cotton depression, 30
Cotton States Exposition, 62, 63
Council for Aid to Education (CFAE), 278, 279
Crawford, George Williamson, 134–35, 294n8, 298n9
Creek War, 131

Crisis, 65, 81
Curriculum, 57–66, 294–95nn1–17

DaCosta, Frank A., 297n16
Daily Crusader, 20
Daniel, William A., 89
Dartmouth College, 32
Davis, Jackson, 85
Davis, John W., 100
Davis, Sarah, 300n2
Daytona Normal and Industrial Institute, 98
Debating triangle, 60, 138
De Bose, Tourgee, 129
De Bow's Review, 26
Declarational Resolves of First Continental Congress, 14
Declaration of Independence, 12, 14, 26
DeForest, Henry S., 145t
De Forest, John William, 292n11
Degrees: awarded by Talladega, 118, 156–58; desegregation and, 116–18, 122–24; highest planned, 205t, 206. *See also* Bachelors degrees; Doctorates; Masters degrees
Delaware, 50, 100
Democracy in America (Tocqueville), 15
Democratic Party, 16, 17
Denominational groups, 36–40, 66. *See also specific groups*
Department of Education, U.S., 91, 239, 241, 249, 260, 267. *See also* Bureau of Education, U.S.
Department of Health, Education, and Welfare (HEW), U.S., 115
Desdunes, R. L., 20, 291n11
Desegregation, 99–126, 221, 296–98nn1–24; accreditation and, 104; degrees earned following, 116–18, 122–24; impact on leadership, 119–22; process of, 114–16. *See also* School segregation; Segregation
Detroit riots, 110
DeWitt Wallace/Spelman College Fund, 169
Dietrich, Frederick H., 303n4
Dillard, James H., 67, 96–97
Dillard University, 2, 79, 123, 270, 283; curriculum of, 58; endowments in, 276; environment of, 5; establishment of, 97–98; rank by enrollment, 4, 303n1

Dirksen, Everett, 109
Distance from home to college, 198–99, 202t
District of Columbia, 70, 100
Division I colleges, 215, 216t
Division II colleges, 215, 216t
Division III colleges, 215, 216t
Dober, Lidsky, Craig and Associates, 274
Dober, Richard P., 5–6, 274, 275, 289n8, 308n8
Doctorates, 3; awarded to Talladega graduates, 158; collegiate origins of black recipients, 193; collegiate productivity index for, 194t; held by faculty, 122, 123, 170; profiles of recipients, 185–95. *See also* Ed.D. degrees; Ph.D. degrees
Doermann, Humphrey, 306n7, 308n7, 309n2
Dolphus E. Milligan Science Research Institute, 96
Dominits, Leslie, 116, 297n17
Donald, Henderson H., 89
Dorsey, Alicia, 306nn2,3,5,6
Douglass, Frederick, 65
Draft riots, 15
Drawe, Mary Veronica, 177
Dred Scott v. Sanford, 14
Drewry, Henry N., 297n17, 301n29
Drewry, Leonard E., 127, 298n1
Drewry High School, 149–50
Drexel, Emma Bouvier, 174
Drexel, Francis Anthony, 174
Drexel, Katharine, 174
Du Bois, W. E. B., 30, 46, 56, 59, 62, 101, 112, 119, 293n8, 294nn5,24, 295n11, 296n6; academic education encouraged by, 65; degrees attained by, 89; intellectual contributions of, 90
Dunbar High School, 54
Durkee, J. Stanley, 85
Dusk of Dawn (Du Bois), 56
Dworkin, Ronald, 309n1

Eble, Kenneth E., 304–5n7
Ed.D. degrees, 191, 193
Edelman, Marian Wright, 189t
Edley, Christopher F., Sr., 259, 307n6
Education majors, 208, 210t. *See also* Teacher education programs
Edward Waters College, 4, 235t, 237, 238, 297n22

Eliot, Charles, 46
Emancipation Proclamation, 28
Endowments, 8, 10–11, 64–65, 105, 121, 274, 275–78; in selected years, 122t; at Spelman, 11, 144, 169, 172, 177, 237, 276; at Stillman, 165; at Talladega, 144; at Texas College, 237–38; at Xavier, 177–78, 276
Enrollment: between 1950 and 1979, 106f; between 1970 and 1985, 219t; declines in, 9, 218, 226; desegregation impact on, 105; percentage increase/decrease in, 75t; percentage male, 166; by racial and ethnic status, 180t; rank by, 2–5, 303n1; in small colleges, 233–34, 235t; at Spelman, 163t, 168, 169–70, 303n1; at Stillman, 162, 163t; at Talladega, 141–42, 235t, 303n1; at Texas College, 238; at Xavier, 163t, 173, 175, 180t, 303n1
Evolution of the Negro College (Holmes), 90
Executive branch officials, 182t, 184, 186–88t

Faculty, 218–32, 304–5nn1–8; black studies and, 112; challenge of maintaining, 121–23; early appointment of Blacks to, 81, 84, 86; hiring of black in white schools, 105; historical perspective on, 53–56; organized role of, 268–69; racial diversity in, 208–10; response to changing student needs, 221–28; salaries of. *See* Salaries of faculty and staff; of Spelman, 170; of Talladega, 122, 144, 146, 154, 155–56; of Texas College, 238
Faculty development, 218–20, 221–22, 225–226, 269; decline in, 225; grants for, 222, 228–32, 264; ISE effect on, 223
Fairchild, James Harris, 294n4
Falconer, Etta Z., 172
Family income, 105–6, 199–204; above national 75th percentile, 203t; below national median, 202t; below national 33rd percentile, 204t; in early twentieth century, 77; student aid and, 248–50; of Texas College students, 238
FASTAP (Fiscal and Strategic Technical Assistance Program), 266–67
Fathers' education and occupation, 201t
Federal City College, 292n3

Federal Negro Manpower Commission, 112

Federal student aid, 8–10. *See also specific programs;* decreased coverage provided by, 203–4; expansion of, 106–8, 247; importance of policies, 244–45; need for review of, 250–53; as percentage of total revenues, 252t; at Texas College, 239

Ferguson, John H., 20

Fifteenth Amendment, 12, 16, 23, 257

Financial aid. *See* Student financial aid

Financial environment, 271–74

Financial independence, 268–79, 308–9nn1–17

Finney, Charles, 294n4

First-choice college, 208, 212t

First Continental Congress, 14

Fiscal and Strategic Technical Assistance Program (FASTAP), 266–67

Fisk University, 46, 56, 79, 123, 138, 151; curriculum of, 58, 66; degrees awarded by, 118; distance traveled to, 199; endowments in, 144; enrollment size, 9; faculty of, 224–25; first black presidents of, 84; graduate programs of, 78; leadership in, 122; rank by enrollment, 3; recruitment by, 223; student strike at, 87

Fitzhugh, George, 26, 27

Flanigan, Robert D. (Danny), 172–73, 258, 290n19, 300n16, 301nn20,26, 307n4

Fleming, Walter L., 293n3

Fletcher, Michael, 290n18, 301n35

Flickinger, Grace Mary, 176–77, 302n38

Florida, 17, 41, 72, 115, 309n3

Florida Agricultural and Mechanical College, 51–53, 303n6

Florida Memorial College, 4, 98, 199, 235t

Ford Foundation, 5, 108, 172, 220, 227, 261, 262; amount of support from, 263–64; small colleges and, 234; trusteeship study of, 269, 270

Foreman, Clark, 85

Forten, Charlotte, 53–54

Foster, Laurence, 89

Foster, Luther H., 234, 272, 305n5, 308n5

Foundation gifts, 254, 261–65, 267. *See also specific foundations;* accreditation and, 240; for faculty development, 228–32, 264; restrictions on, 261–63; uncertainty about amount from, 264–65

Fourteenth Amendment, 12, 16, 19, 20, 23, 28, 257

Fox, Daniel, 295n17

Francis, Norman C., 174–75, 177, 178, 258, 273, 283, 301n31,32, 302nn39,40, 307n5, 309n5

Fraternities, 88

Frazier, Edward Franklin, 89, 112

Frederick D. Patterson Research Institute, 94, 267

Freedmen: condition of, 23–28; schools for, 34–40

Freedmen's Aid societies, 34, 36–40

Freedmen's Aid Society of the Methodist Church, 36–37, 97

Freedmen's Bureau, 37, 38, 40, 45, 47–48, 54–55, 62, 66, 132, 133; contributions of, 35–36; demise of, 17; investment in education, 39

Freedmen's Bureau Inquiry Commission, 35

Freedmen's Bureau Report, 33

Freeman, Kimberley Edelin, 302n5, 303n2, 304nn7,9, 309n7

"From an Andover Window" (column), 83

Fundraising, 10, 125–26, 169, 171, 276–77

Gallagher, Buell G., 145t, 146–47, 148, 159

Gardner, Anna, 44

Garibaldi, Antoine M., 193

Garvey, Marcus, 30, 90, 111

Gates Foundation. *See* Bill and Melinda Gates Foundation

Gayles, Joseph, 145t

General Education Board, 66, 68, 98, 108, 144

General Education Fund, 85

Generals, 182t, 184, 185t

Geneva College, 297n24

George Washington University, 244, 256

Georgia, 13, 14, 39, 115

Georgia State University, 228

G.I. Bill of Rights, 107, 217, 244, 247

Giamatti, A. Bartlett, 120, 297n20

Giles, Harriet E., 167, 168

Gilmore, Marshall, 239, 240, 270, 305nn8,9,11,12

Gladdings, R. H., 43

Gladieux, Lawrence E., 306nn2,3,5,6

Gleason, Gloria Williams, 299n22

Goodwin, Robert, 120, 297n19
Graduate programs, 3, 78, 88, 117; demand for, 206; at Talladega, 140; Title III funds for, 257; UNCF support for, 266
Graduates, 181–95, 302–3nn1–7; career distinction in, 182–85, 190t; in executive branch, 182t, 184, 186–88t; Mac-Arthur Fellowships awarded to, 182t, 184–85, 189t, 190t, 302n4; medical degrees and doctorates in. *See* Doctorates; Medical schools; of Talladega, 142
Graduation rates, 215–17
Grants, 108, 204, 223, 248, 251, 252; for faculty development, 222, 228–32, 264; problems caused by, 273
Gray, Arthur D., 145t, 150–51
Gray, William H., III, 7, 167, 261, 290nn12,16,19, 304n8, 307n10, 308n7
Great Depression, 30, 74, 76, 77, 86, 112
Great Detour, 63
Greenway, Walter, 86
Growth of higher education, 70–79
Growth of the American Republic, The, 26

Hall Strauder v. West Virginia, 291n9
Hampton Institute: curriculum of, 61, 62–63, 66; donations to, 67; endowments in, 11, 64–65, 144; introduction of college-level program, 74; non-black students in, 53
Hampton University, 79, 123, 254, 303n6; degrees awarded by, 118; graduate programs of, 3; leadership in, 122; rank by enrollment, 4, 303n1; recruitment by, 223; Title III funds for, 257
Hard money, 169
Harlan, John Marshall, 20–21
Harlem Renaissance, 83, 88, 114
Harlem riots, 110
Harlem Shadows, 90
Harris, Abram Lincoln, 89
Hartshorn Memorial College, 91, 98
Harvard College, 32, 176
Harvard Educational Review, 102
Harvard University, 46, 227
Hastie, William, 112
Hawkins, Billy C., 242
Hayes, Rutherford B., 17, 67
Haynes, George E., 89
Haynes, M. Juliana, 174–75, 301n30

Henderson, Vivian W., 2, 289n3
Hening, William W., 290n1
Henson, James W., 220, 304n2
HERI (Higher Education Research Institute), 196, 208, 304n1
Herman, Alexis M., 186t
HEW (Department of Health, Education, and Welfare), 115
Hewitt, Vivian D., 302n2
Hewlett Foundation. *See* William and Flora Hewlett Foundation
Hewlett-Packard, 261
Higher Education Act of 1965, 1, 8–9, 107–8, 217, 246, 247. *See also* Title III of Higher Education Act; Title IX of Higher Education Act
Higher Education Research Institute (HERI), 196, 208, 304n1
High school class rank, 163t, 178, 179t, 197–98, 304n1
High schools, 70–71, 72, 77; historical perspective on, 45–50, 292–94nn1–24; private black, 74
Hill, Susan T., 289n1, 295n10
Hilliard, Asa Grant, 228
Hispanics/Latinos, 197, 256
History of Negro Education in the South, A (Bullock), 63
Hodge v. United States, 296n2
Holloran, Thomas E., 308n4
Holmes, Dwight Oliver Wendell, 58, 89, 91, 294nn2,9,15, 295n20
Holmes, James, 187t
Holt, Thomas Cleveland, 189t
Hope, John, 84, 85, 95, 96
Hopkins, Donald, 189t
Hopkins, Mark, 294n4
Hopson, Mrs. C. M., 132, 133
Horton, Carrell P., 9, 224–26
Houston, Charles, 89
Howard, Oliver Otis, 35
Howard Hughes Medical Institute, 228, 230t, 301n34
Howard School, 48
Howard University, 7, 48, 55, 74, 79, 91, 138, 158, 172, 176, 193, 234, 254, 293nn11,17, 303n6; black studies at, 112; curriculum of, 58, 59–60, 66; degrees earned at, 118; doctorate program in, 194; in early twentieth century, 51, 53; endowments in, 11, 144; first

Howard University (*continued*)
  black presidents of, 84, 85; graduate
  programs of, 3, 78; leadership in, 122;
  in mid-nineteenth century, 45–46, 47;
  non-black students in, 53, 104; rank by
  enrollment, 4; recruitment by, 223; stu-
  dent strike at, 87
Huggins, Nathan I., 88, 295n17
Hughes, Langston, 60, 86, 88
Hunt, Isaac C., Jr., 186t
Hunter, Jacqueline T., 176
Hurst, Tazewell V., III, 309n4
Huston-Tillotson College, 4, 98, 104, 235t
Hutson, Jean Blackwell, 302n2

IBM, 167, 261, 266, 304n8
Ickes, Harold L., 94
Illiteracy. *See* Literacy
Individual gifts, 278–79
Industrial education, 48–49, 50, 53; aca-
  demic education vs., 61–66; decline in,
  88, 92; at Talladega, 134, 139
Institute for Colored Youth, 33
Institute for Services to Education (ISE),
  223
Institutional strategy, 271–74
Interdenominational Theological Center
  (ITC), 96
International Affairs Center, 172
ISE (Institute for Services to Education),
  223
ITC (Interdenominational Theological
  Center), 96

Jackson, Andrew, 131
Jacksonian democracy, 15
Jackson State, 303n6
Jarvis Christian College, 4, 199, 235t, 237,
  298n24
Jayhawkers, 17
Jeanes, Anna T., 97
Jeffersonian Democracy, 131
Jencks, Christopher, 102, 296n7
Jim Crow laws, 15, 18, 152
John F. Slater Fund, 66, 67, 98, 108, 135
Johnson, Andrew, 16, 35
Johnson, Charles S., 84, 112
Johnson, Joseph, 145t
Johnson, Leonard, 132
Johnson, Mordecai, 84
Johnson, Sargent, 88

Johnson, William Hallock, 86
Johnson C. Smith Seminary, 96
Johnson C. Smith University, 4, 98, 144,
  220–21, 276, 298n24
Jones, Edward A., 32, 33
Jones, Maxine D., 147, 153, 298n11
Jones, Moses C., Jr., 167, 268, 288
Jones, Sherman, 290n17
Jones, T. J., 293nn6,12,14, 294nn1,14,22,
  295nn1,16, 296n26, 298n13, 299nn27,32
Jones, Zachariah, 137
Journal of Negro Education, The, 221
Judson College, 292n2
Julius Rosenwald Fund, 108
Jupiter, Clarence J., 177, 290n19
Jury service, 19
Just, Ernest E., 89

Kaiser, Harvey H., 308n11
Kansas, 50
Katz, William Loren, 292n1
Kellogg Foundation, 108, 228, 230t, 261
Kentucky, 21, 50
Kentucky State University, 257
Kershaw, Joseph A., 234–35, 305n6
Kilson, Martin, 295n17
King, Calvin R., 189t
King, Martin Luther, 109, 110
Kirschner, Alan H., 277
Kittrel College, 91
Kluger, Richard, 11–12, 290n20, 291n14
Knoxville College, 4, 60, 138, 238, 267
Korn, William S., 196, 198n
Kresge Foundation, 108, 261, 273
Ku Klux Klan, 16–17, 38, 43, 86, 137

Labat, Dierdre Dumas, 176
Land Grant Act of 1862, 50
Land Grant Act of 1890, 50
Lane College, 4, 87, 235t, 242
Latinos/Hispanics, 197, 256
Laura Spelman Rockefeller Fund, 85
Law degrees, 157t
Lawless, T. K., 299n18
Lawyers, 182t, 184, 185t, 190t
Leadership, 160–80, 300–302nn1–41;
  cohesion of underlying community in,
  268; desegregation impact on, 119–22;
  financial independence and, 268–79,
  308–9nn1–17; by graduates, 182t, 183–
  84; in small colleges, 242–43; in Spel-

man, 160, 167–73; in Stillman, 160, 162–67, 300n2; in Texas College, 238–39; by trustees, 269–70; in Xavier, 160, 173–80, 270
Lebanon College, 297n24
LeMaistre, George A., 164
LeMoyne Normal Institute, 97
LeMoyne-Owen College, 4, 97, 298n24
Lenoir Rhyne College, 297n24
Lewin, Tamar, 289n1
Lewis, Edwin E., 112
Liberal arts, 125, 206–8, 209t. *See also* Academic education
Liberia, 32
Life goals, 205t
Lilly Endowment, 227, 266, 275
Lincoln, Abraham, 16, 28
Lincoln Institute (Kentucky), 91
Lincoln University (Missouri), 91, 257
Lincoln University (Pennsylvania), 33, 51, 98, 100, 292n3; first black presidents of, 84, 85–86; state takeover of, 91
Lips, Julius, 112
Literacy, 24, 31, 34, 45, 57, 103
Litwack, Leon F., 291n20
Livingstone College, 4, 93, 303n1
Loans. *See* Student loans
Locke, Alain, 89, 90, 129
Long, Herman H., 145t, 151–52, 154, 155, 159, 300n33
Lord, Edward P., 136, 145t
Loughlin, Monica, 174, 301n29
Louisiana, 17, 19–20, 39, 115, 280
Low-income students, 248–50, 257
Lucy, Autherine, 153
Luke, William, 136–37
Lutheran Church/religion, 37
Lyles, Lester L., 186t
Lynchings, 15, 17–18, 29, 82, 136–37

Macalester College, 244
MacArthur Fellowships, 182t, 184–85, 189t, 190t, 302n4
McKay, Claude, 89, 295n19
McKeachie, Wilbert J., 304–5n7
McKenzie, Fayette, 87
McLaughlin, Judith Block, 290n14
McLoyd, Vonnie C., 189t
McLuren v. Oklahoma State Regents, 296n5
McNealey, Ernest, 165–67, 180, 300nn7,9
McPherson, James A., 189t

McPherson, James M., 28, 54, 130, 291n19, 293n19, 294nn1,23, 298n3
McPherson, Michael S., 244, 303n6, 305n1, 306n11
McSheffery, Daniel F., 301n28
Mahoney, Kathryn M., 198n
Majors: business and management, 208, 210t; education, 208, 210t; liberal arts vs. precareer, 206–8, 209t; natural science, 208, 210t; at Spelman, 172; at Stillman, 162; at Xavier, 175
Mallett, Robert L., 186t
Manley, Albert E., 84, 168, 173, 180
Manley, Audrey Forbes, 173, 301n26
Manuel, William A., 300n33
Marshall, Thurgood, 100
Mary Allen Seminary, 98
Mary Baldwin College, 292n2
Maryland, 13, 50
Mastern, Charles C., 187t
Masters degrees, 3, 156, 192
Matney, William C., Jr., 302n2
Medical schools, 182; affirmative action and, 283–84; collegiate origins of black students, 191t; collegiate productivity index for students, 192t; number of undergraduates planning for, 206; patterns of attendance, 185–95; Talladega graduates in, 156, 157t, 158; Xavier graduates in, 173, 176, 284
Meharry Medical College, 194
Mellon Foundation (Andrew W. Mellon Foundation), 108, 221, 227, 228, 230t
Mercer, Joye, 308n7
Meredith, 110
Merisotis, Jamie R., 307n1
Merit aid, 247, 250
Metcalf, John M. P., 136, 144, 145t
Methodist Church/religion, 56
Meyerson, Martin, 168
Microsoft, 167, 262, 266, 304n8
Migration, 76
Miles College, 4, 242
Miller, Loren, 99–100, 296n4
Mills College, 292n2
Miner Teacher's College, 33, 98, 292n3
Minnesota, 249–50
Minnesota State Grant Program, 250
Mis-Education of the Negro, The (Woodson), 90
Mission statements, 60–61

Mississippi, 50, 72, 115, 280
Mississippi Industrial College, 123
Missouri, 50
Missouri ex rel. Gaines v. Canada, 99, 296n3
Mohr, Paul B., 145t
Montgomery, Alabama bus boycott, 109
Moore, Lewis B., 89
Morehouse College, 79, 85, 98, 176, 283;
    changes in early twentieth century, 92;
    collaboration with other colleges, 95,
    96; curriculum of, 60; in debating tri-
    angle, 60, 138; distance traveled to, 199;
    endowments in, 237, 276; environment
    of, 5; faculty size, 122; first black presi-
    dents of, 84; rank by enrollment, 4,
    303n1; recruitment by, 223; Title III
    funds for, 257
Morehouse School of Medicine, 96, 194
Moreland, Lois, 172, 290n13, 301n20
Morgan, Thomas J., 57
Morgan College, 98
Morison, Samuel Eliot, 26, 27, 291n16
Morningside College, 297n24
Morris Brown College, 91, 95, 96, 238; fac-
    ulty size, 122; rank by enrollment, 4,
    303n1
Morristown Normal and Industrial Col-
    lege, 91
Mothers' education and occupation, 198,
    200t
Mott Foundation, 108, 230t, 266
Mount Holyoke Female Seminary, 33,
    292n2
Ms. Magazine, 171

NAACP. *See* National Association for the
    Advancement of Colored People
Nabrit, Samuel M., 269, 270, 308n1
NACUBO (National Association of Col-
    lege and University Business Officers),
    274–75
Nash, Robert J., 187t
National Academy of Sciences Doctorate
    Records file, 185
National Association for Equal Oppor-
    tunity, 165
National Association for the Advancement
    of Colored People (NAACP), 65, 81,
    100, 227; black power movement and,
    110; creation of, 29–30; HEW sued by,
    115

National Association of College and Uni-
    versity Business Officers (NACUBO),
    274–75
National Collegiate Athletic Association
    (NCAA), 215, 216t
National Commission on Excellence in
    Education, 175
National Defense Education Act (NDEA),
    106–7, 116
National Education Association, 62
National Endowment for the Humanities,
    227
National Register of Historic Places, 260
National Research Council, 172
*National Survey of the Higher Education of
    Negroes,* 77, 91, 92
National Trust for Historic Preservation,
    275
National Urban League, 30, 110
Nation At Risk, A (report), 175
Native American Indian Fund, 95
Native Americans, 53, 130–31, 256
Natural science majors, 208, 210t
NCAA (National Collegiate Athletic Asso-
    ciation), 215, 216t
NDEA (National Defense Education Act),
    106–7, 116
Need analysis, 246
Need-based student aid, 246, 247, 248,
    250–51, 252, 306n4
Negro Education (study), 68, 70
"Negro Speaks of Rivers, The" (Hughes),
    88
Nettles, Arie L., 309n2
Nettles, Michael T., 302n5, 303n2,
    304nn7,9, 309n2, 309n7
Nevins, Allan, 28, 291n19
New England, 53, 54, 57–58, 80, 101,
    130, 146
New Jersey, 50
New Negro, The (Locke), 89
New Orleans College, 97
Newsweek, 10
New York City Draft Riots, 15
New York Community Trust, 169
New York Times, 10, 150, 151, 171,
    176
New York University, 11t
Niagara Movement, 29–30
Nickens, Herbert W., 283–84, 309n6
Nixon administration, 115

Normal schools, 70, 72, 77; historical perspective on, 45–50, 292–94nn1–24; impact of Depression on, 74
North Carolina, 23, 41, 72, 115
North Carolina Agricultural and Technical College, 109, 303n6
North Carolina Central, 303n6
North Carolina College, 84
Northern states, 26, 34, 76
Nyce, Benjamin M., 145t

Oakwood College, 4, 297n22
Oakwood Manual Training School, 74
Oberlin College, 33, 129, 133, 144, 148, 294n4, 298n1
O'Brien, Colleen T., 307n1
Office of Education, 77
Ohio, 50, 51, 70
Oklahoma, 50
Olsen, Otto H., 291n15
Omnibus Parks and Public Lands Management Act of 1996, 260
Operating budgets, 6, 8–11, 172–73, 286. *See also* Student financial aid
Opinion Research Corporation, 251
Order of the Blessed Sacrament for Indians and Negroes, 174
Owen College, 98
Owens, George A., 226

Pacific College, 297n24
Packard, Sophia B., 167, 168
Packard Foundation, 230t, 261, 264
Paine College, 4, 242
Patterson, Frederick D., 93, 265
Paul Quinn College, 4, 235t, 238
Pauper-school clause of state constitutions, 41
Peabody Education Fund, 67
Pell Grants, 247, 248, 252
Pennsylvania, 70
Perce, Hatwood J., Jr., 291n22
Perna, Laura W., 302n5, 303n2, 304nn7,9, 309n7
Per-student expenditures, 22–23, 271–72, 287
Pew Charitable Trust, 108, 265
Pharmacist training, 173, 179
Ph.D. degrees, 3, 117–18, 182, 191, 193, 194; awarded to Howard graduates, 172; awarded to Spelman graduates, 172;

awarded to Talladega graduates, 156, 157t
Phelps, Ashton, Jr., 301n32
Phelps-Stokes, Caroline, 48
Phelps-Stokes Fund, 48, 66, 68
Philander Smith College, 4, 303n1
Philanthropy, 66–69, 108
Phillip Morris, 262
Phillips School of Theology, 96
Physical plant, 5–6, 274–75
Plessy, Homer, 19–20
Plessy v. Ferguson, 20–21, 64, 99, 291n12, 296n5
Population, black, 25t, 32–33
Populist era, 15
Poverty, 107
Powdermaker, Hortense, 39, 292n13
Powell, Adrienne L., 307n15
Powell, Lewis F., 281
Practical High School, 127
Precareer majors, 206–8, 209t
Presbyterian Church, 96, 162, 269
Presidents, 270; average tenure of, 273–74; early appointment of Blacks as, 84–86, 150–51; faculty relationship with, 268–69; of Spelman, 168–73; of Stillman, 162–67; of Talladega, 144–53; of Xavier, 174–75. *See also* Leadership
President's Board of Advisors on Historically Black Colleges and Universities, 267
Princeton University, 11t, 32, 171, 262
Private black colleges: comparative view of white colleges and, 124–25; data from selected years, 73t; desegregation impact on, 105; distance from home to, 202t; education/occupation of students' fathers, 201t; education/occupation of students' mothers, 200t; endowments in selected years, 122t; enrollment between 1950 and 1979, 106f; enrollment between 1970 and 1985, 219t; faculty development at, 228–32; family income of students, 202t, 203, 204t; as first choice, 212t; future of, 285–88; graduates of, 183, 184, 185, 186–87, 189t, 190t, 191, 192, 193–94; graduation rates in, 215, 216t; growth of, 75–76; high school rank of students, 198t; leadership in, 121; majors in, 208, 209t, 210t; percentage change in enrollment, 75t;

Private black colleges (*continued*)
percentage of degrees awarded by, 123–24; per-student expenditure in, 271–72; remedial work needed by students, 199t; salary comparison with public colleges, 122; satisfaction assessment in, 208, 210, 211t, 213t, 214t; self-confidence of students, 207t; student aid in, 248, 252–53; student degree plans and life goals, 205t

Private Black Colleges at the Crossroads (survey), 270

Progressive era, 15

Protestant Episcopal Church, 269

Protestant religions, 197

Prudential Insurance Company of America, 262

Public black colleges, 114; data from selected years, 73t; desegregation impact on, 105; education/occupation of students' fathers, 201t; education/occupation of students' mothers, 200t; enrollment between 1970 and 1985, 219t; family income of students, 202t, 203, 204t; as first choice, 212t; graduates of, 183t, 184, 185, 187t, 189t, 190t, 191, 192, 193–94; graduation rates in, 216t; growth of, 75–76; high school rank of students, 198t; leadership in, 121; majors in, 209t; miles from home to, 202t; as percentage of all black colleges, 257; post-World War II growth of, 122; remedial work needed by students, 199t; salary comparison with private colleges, 122; satisfaction assessment in, 208, 211t, 213t, 214t; self-confidence of students, 207t; student degree plans and life goals, 205t

Public schools, 15, 41–45, 292–94nn1–24

Quakers, 33, 37

Race progress, 60–61, 64, 76, 88, 115, 128, 280

Race riots, 29, 83, 110

Rachal, Anthony, Jr., 177

Racial/ethnic diversity, 208–10, 214t, 215

Racism: after slavery, 15–23; during slavery, 13–15

Rates, Norman M., 300n17, 301n20

Rawls, John, 289n3

Read, Florence, 168

Reader's Digest, 169

Reagan administration, 259

Reagon, Bernice Johnson, 189t

Reconstruction, 15–16, 17, 19, 23, 24, 37–38, 41, 43

Recruitment: challenge of the 1970s, 220–21; faculty response to changes in, 221–28; at Spelman, 169; by traditionally white colleges, 9, 119, 170, 218, 285

Regents of the University of California v. Bakke, 280–81, 282

Regulators, 17

Remedial college work, 198, 199t, 223

Republican Party, 15–16, 17, 28, 109

Rhoads, Joseph, 112

Rice, M. C., 297n16

Richardson, Joe M., 147, 153, 295n15, 298n11, 299nn27,32

Riesman, David, 102, 290n14, 296n7

Rifle Clubs of South Carolina, 17

Rights of man concept, 14

Risk tolerance, 179t

Roberts, Eugene P., 86

Robert W. Woodruff Library, 96

Robinson, June M., 187t

Rockefeller, John D., 68, 144, 168

Rockefeller, John D., Jr., 93, 94

Rockefeller, Laura Spelman, 168

Rockefeller Brothers Fund, 169, 170, 301n19

Rockefeller University, 11t

Roger Williams University, 91

Roosevelt, Franklin D., 93

Roosevelt University, 184

Roper Center for Public Opinion, 251, 306n12

Ruml, Beasley, 85

Russworm, John, 32, 33

Rust College, 4, 106, 298n24

Rutgers University, 32

Ryan, Patrick J., 174

SACS. *See* Southern Association of Colleges and Schools

Saffort, Albert A., 145t

Saint Augustine College, 4, 298n24

Saint Augustine School, 74

Saint Mary's College, 292n2

Saint Mary's Junior College, 286

Saint Paul Normal and Industrial School, 74

Saint Paul's College, 4, 122, 235t, 297n22, 303n1

Salaries of faculty and staff, 6, 10, 185, 231, 238; historic inequality in, 22–23; minimum, median, and maximum, 123t; in public vs. private colleges, 122

SAT. See Scholastic Aptitude Test

Satcher, David, 187t

Satisfaction assessment, 208–15

Savage, John R., 137

Savery, William, 132

Sax, Linda J., 196, 198n, 303n1

Schapiro, Morton Owen, 244, 303n6, 305n1, 306n11

Scholars, 88–90, 112, 114

Scholastic Aptitude Test (SAT), 9, 162, 163t, 179t, 197, 281

School segregation, 21–23, 42, 63–64; Beittel's opposition to, 148–50; Berea case and, 21; Talladega opposition to, 151–53. See also Brown v. Board of Education; Desegregation; Segregation

Scotia Seminary, 74, 97. See also Barber-Scotia College

Scott, Dred, 12

Scott, John T., 189t

Scott, Julius S., Jr., 269, 270, 308n1

Secondary schools, 77; in early twentieth century, 51, 52t; for freedmen, 34; growth of, 71–74

Segregation, 19–23. See also Desegregation; School segregation

Self-confidence, 206, 207t

Seminaries, 92, 96–97

Separate but equal doctrine, 63–64, 99

Sessions Elementary School, 149–50

Sessions Practice School, 140

Shakir, Adib A., 307n15

Shaw Memorial School, 54

Shaw University, 4, 5, 92, 303n1

Sherman, william Tecumseh, 34–35

Shirley, Aaron, 189t

Shores, Arthur, 153

Silsby, Edwin, 136

Simmons, Ruth J., 168, 300n13

Simmons University, 91, 123

Sims, William E., 221, 304n5

Sipuel v. Board of Regents, 99, 296n3

Sisters of the Blessed Sacrament (SBS), 53, 174, 178, 270

Sit-ins, 109–10, 113

Sixty Yesteryears (play), 128–32, 140

Slater, John F., 67

Slater Fund (John F. Slater Fund), 66, 67, 97, 108, 135

Slave Codes, 15

Slavery, 12, 37; long-term effects of, 24–28; racism after, 15–23; racism during, 13–15. See also Freedmen

Small colleges, 233–43, 305nn1–15; different views of, 233–36; leadership in, 242–43; special attributes of, 235–36

Smith, Jessie Carney, 302n2

Smith, Thomas M., 302n1

Smith College, 168, 285, 292n2

SNCC (Student Non-Violence Coordinating Committee), 110

Snyder, Thomas D., 292nn3,24

Social Darwinism, 19, 64

Soft money, 169

Sororities, 88

Souls of Black Folk, The (Du Bois), 46, 62, 65, 89

Southall, James C., 44

South Carolina, 16, 17, 42, 72, 100, 115

Southern A & M, 303n6

Southern Association of Colleges and Schools (SACS), 123; desegregation and, 104; rejection of black colleges, 70, 92–93; Spelman and, 168; Talladega and, 140, 146; Texas College and, 238, 239, 241–42. See also Accreditation

Southern Christian Leadership Conference, 110

Southern Education Board, 68

Southern Education Foundation, 267

Southern states, 221; condition of freedmen in, 23–26; desegregation impact on education, 114–15; freedmen's schools in, 34–36; history of black higher education in, 32, 51–53; industrial education in, 48–49, 62–63; northern teachers in, 54–55; political and economic instability in, 28–31; post-slavery, 15–21; public schools in, 41–44; school system in early twentieth century, 72–74, 77–78. See also Civil War; Confederacy; Reconstruction; Slavery

Southwestern Christian College, 4

Soviet Union, 106–7

Spelman College, 79, 98, 123, 176, 178, 268, 283, 303n6; changes in, 8; collaboration with other colleges, 95–96, 97; degrees awarded by, 118; distance traveled to, 199; endowments in, 11, 144, 169, 172, 177, 237, 276; enrollment size, 163t, 168, 169–70; environment of, 6; first black presidents of, 85; high school rank of students, 163t, 179t; leadership in, 160, 167–73; operating budget in, 9–10, 172–73; Phi Beta Kappa chapter at, 171; rank by enrollment, 4, 303n1; recruitment by, 220, 223; risk tolerance at, 179t; SAT scores of students, 162, 163t, 179t; selected characteristics of, 161t; Title III funds for, 258; trustees of, 270

Sputnik, 106–7

Stanton, Robert G., 187t

State financial aid, 247

Steele, Henry Commager, 290n3

Stevenson, Brenda, 293n18

Stewart, Donald M., 168–71, 172, 180, 300nn16,17, 301n20

Stillman College, 123, 175, 178, 240, 268, 269, 288, 297n22, 298n24; date of charter, 162; enrollment size, 162, 163t; Five-Year Strategic Plan, 166; high school rank of students, 163t, 179t; institutional strategy in, 272; leadership in, 160, 162–67, 300n2; rank by enrollment, 4; recruitment by, 220; risk tolerance at, 179t; SAT scores of students, 162, 163t, 179t; selected characteristics of, 161t; Vision Plan, 166

Stillman Institute, 74

Stinson, Harold N., 162–64, 240, 269

Stockard, Russell L., 220, 304n2

Stock market crash, 30, 77

Storer College, 87

Story, Joseph, 37

Stouffer, Samuel A., 291n17

Straight College, 97

Strange Career of Jim Crow, The (Woodward), 18

Strickland, Haywood L., 239, 240–41, 242, 300n2, 305nn8–14

Student financial aid, 10, 244–53, 305–7nn1–13; external sources of, 254–67, 307nn1–15; impact on low-income students, 248–50; merit, 247, 250; need-based, 246, 247, 248, 250–51, 252, 306n4; need for review of, 250–53. *See also* Corporate gifts; Federal student aid; Foundation gifts; Fundraising; Grants; Individual gifts; Philanthropy; Student loans

Student government, 86–87

Student loans, 204, 247, 248, 250

Student Non-Violence Coordinating Committee (SNCC), 110

Student protests, 8, 84, 85, 87, 153–55, 226

Students, 196–217, 303–4nn1–9; assessment of satisfaction, 208–15; distance from home to college, 198–99; education of nineteenth century, 51–53; family income. *See* Family income; graduation rates of, 215–17; high expectations of, 204–6; high school rank of. *See* High school class rank; low-income, 248–50, 257; majors of. See Majors; parental occupation, 198–99; SAT scores of. *See* Scholastic Aptitude Test; white. *See* White students

Sumner, Charles, 298n2

Sumner, Frederick A., 128–29, 144, 145t, 298n2

Supreme Court, Kentucky, 21

Supreme Court, U.S., 19, 37, 63–64, 93, 115; *Brown v. Board of Education. See* Brown v. Board of Education; *Cheryl J. Hopwood v. The State of Texas,* 280–84, 309n4; *Dred Scott v. Sanford,* 14; *Hodge v. United States,* 296n2; *McLuren v. Oklahoma State Regents,* 296n5; *Missouri ex rel. Gaines v. Canada,* 99, 296n3; *Plessy v. Ferguson,* 20–21, 64, 99, 291n12, 296n5; *Regents of the University of California v. Bakke,* 280–81, 282; *Sipuel v. Board of Regents,* 99, 296n3; *Sweatt v. Painter,* 296n5

Survey of Negro Colleges and Universities, 76–77, 140

Swail, Watson Scott, 306nn2,3,5,6

Swayne, Wager, 133

Sweatt v. Painter, 296n5

Talented tenth, 65, 119

Talladega (town), 130–31

Talladega College, 5, 127–59, 298–300nn1–33; academic standing of, 140; buildings, 133, 134, 137, 139, 140, 141;

changes in early twentieth century, 92; commitment to academic program, 138–39; curriculum of, 60, 61; in debating triangle, 60, 138; degrees awarded by, 118, 156–58; Drewry High School, 149–50; early community involvement, 137; early relations with white community, 135–37; early rules and regulations, 137–38; early selection process, 133–34; in early twentieth century, 53; endowments in, 144; enrollment size, 141–42, 235t; faculty of, 122, 144, 146, 154, 155–56; federal funds for, 108; first black president of, 150–51; German Club of, 116; modernization of curriculum, 146–47; non-black students in, 53; origin of, 128, 132–33; presidents of, 144–53; rank by enrollment, 4, 303n1; recruitment by, 223; SACS approval of, 146; Sessions Elementary School, 149–50; Sessions Practice School, 140; student protests at, 153–55; tax-exempt status of, 136

Talladega College Little Theatre, 128, 141

Talladegan, The, 144, 149

Talladega Student, The, 153

Tanner, Henry O., 147

Tapley, Lucy Hale, 168

Tarrant, Thomas, 132

Tax credits. *See* Tuition tax credits

Tax Reform Act of 1969, 261

Taylor, Ann D., 222–24

Teacher education programs, 46–47, 50, 72, 162. *See also* Education majors

Tenant farmers, 17

Tennessee, 38, 39, 115

Tennessee Baptist Missionary and Educational Convention, 98

Texaco, 262

Texas, 48, 115, 280, 281–82, 283, 309nn2,3,4

Texas College, 266, 267, 268; enrollment size, 238; rank by enrollment, 4; trustees of, 270; turnaround at, 238–42; value added at, 236–38

Texas Guaranteed Student Loan Corporation, 239

Texas Higher Education Coordinating Board, 241

Thernstrom, Abigail, 292n10

Thernstrom, Stephan, 292n10

Third Reader, 133

Thirteenth Amendment, 12, 15, 20, 28, 257

Thompson, C. H., 297n16

Thompson, Daniel C., 2, 270, 289n2, 308n3

Thompson, Joseph, 145t

Thompson, Sue, 165, 300n5

Three-fifths-of-all-slaves rule, 16

3M company, 261

Tilden, Samuel, 17

Title III of Higher Education Act, 8, 10, 240, 242, 243, 252, 255–61, 265, 267, 273, 279; amount of subsidy for black colleges, 256; application for, 278; arguments against, 259–60; faculty development and, 221; impact of, 107–8; justification for assistance, 256–57, 258–59; for non-black minorities, 256

Title IX of Higher Education Act, 244

Tocqueville, Alexis de, 15, 290n4

Toomer, Jean, 88

Top-10-percent plan, 282, 309n3

Torrence, Ridgely, 296n27

Total Institutions (Wallace), 27

Tougaloo College, 5, 56, 84, 298n24; degrees awarded by, 118; faculty of, 226–28; mission statement of, 60–61; rank by enrollment, 4, 303n1; rules at, 87

Traditionally white colleges: attended by Blacks in nineteenth century, 32; black faculty in, 105; black graduates of, 184, 185, 185t, 188t, 189t, 191; black studies programs at, 113; comparative view of black colleges and, 124–25; desegregation and, 114–15; distance from home to, 202t; education/occupation of students' fathers, 201t; education/occupation of students' mothers, 200t; family income of students, 106, 202t, 203, 204t; as first choice, 212t; high school rank of students, 198t; included in study, 297n24; majors in, 209t, 210t; recruitment of black students by, 9, 119, 170, 218, 285; remedial work needed by students, 199t; satisfaction assessment in, 208–10, 211t, 213t, 214t; self-confidence of students, 207t; student degree plans and life goals, 205t

Tregre, Calvin S., 302n40

Trent, William J., Jr., 2, 93–94, 289n4
Tribally Controlled Community College
  Assistance Act, 307n2
Tucker, Anne Laurie Derricotte, 299n21
Tuition, 6, 8, 66, 77, 106, 250, 254, 271–72;
  rapid increases in, 9; at Talladega, 139
Tuition tax credits, 248, 250, 251
Tulane University, 11t
Turner, Lorenzo, 89
Turner, Thomas W., 89
Tuskegee Institute, 90, 93, 295n5; curriculum of, 63, 66; donations to, 67; endowments in, 65, 144; introduction of
  college-level program, 74–75
Tuskegee University, 79, 303n6; Congressional appropriations for, 260; degrees
  awarded by, 118; distance traveled to,
  199; endowments in, 276; faculty size,
  122; graduate programs in, 3; non-black
  students in, 104; rank by enrollment, 4,
  303n1

UNCF. See United Negro College Fund
Underwood, John, 83
UNIA (Universal Negro Improvement
  Association), 30, 111
United Church of Christ, 98
United Methodist Church, 96, 269
United Nations Educational, Scientific,
  and Cultural Organization, 84
United Negro College Fund (UNCF), 2,
  108, 122, 123, 165, 249, 253, 279, 283; creation and early accomplishments of, 93–
  95; crucial role in fundraising, 265–67;
  endowments and, 276, 277; faculty
  development and, 229, 231; formula for
  distribution of funds, 266; foundation
  and corporate gifts, 261, 262–63, 264,
  304n8; name change, 295n22; percentage male enrollment, 166; research by,
  267; revenue patterns for member colleges, 254–55; salaries in member
  schools, 6; small colleges in, 234, 235t;
  Texas College and, 238, 239, 240, 241, 242
Universal Negro Improvement Association
  (UNIA), 30, 111
University of Alabama, 116, 153
University of Arkansas, 257
University of California, Los Angeles
  (UCLA), 196, 248
University of Florida, 281

University of Massachusetts, 281
University of Mississippi, 110
University of North Carolina, 32
University of Pennsylvania, 32
University of Saint Thomas, 286
University of Texas at Austin, 281–82
University of Texas Law School, 280
University of the District of Columbia,
  292n3
University of Virginia, 281
University of Wisconsin, 171

Vassar College, 285, 286, 292n2
Veterans, 79t, 83
Veterinary medicine, 3
Vietnam War, 8, 154–55
Virginia, 13, 14, 15, 19, 39, 100
Virginia Seminary and College,
  123
Virginia Union University, 3, 4, 79,
  138, 298n24, 303n1
Virginia v. Rives, 291n9
Vision Plan, 166
Voorhees College, 4, 297n22
Voorhees Industrial School, 74
Voting rights, 15, 16, 18–19, 29
Voting Rights Act of 1965, 108

Walden College, 91
Wallace, DeWitt, 169
Wallace, Samuel E., 27, 291n18
Wall Street Journal, 10
Wal-Mart Stores, 262
Warren, Earl, 99, 120
Wartburg College, 297n24
Washington, 281
Washington, Booker T., 49, 62, 63, 64, 65,
  294n11
Washington Post, 10, 249
Watkins, Dayton J., 187t
Watkins, Shirley R., 187t
Watts riots, 110
Wayne State University, 303n6
Weaver, Robert, 112
Webster, David S., 220, 304n2
Wellesley College, 168, 285, 292n2
Wesley, Charles H., 89, 112
Wesleyan University, 113, 297n24
West, Togo D., Jr., 187t
Western Freedmen's Union Commission,
  37

West Virginia, 19, 50
West Virginia State College, 53, 104, 257
White colleges. *See* Traditionally white
    colleges
White House Initiative on Historically
    Black Colleges and Universities, 120,
    260
White students: desegregation impact on,
    103–4; in early twentieth century, 76; in
    high school, 72; high school rank and
    test scores of, 197; in historically black
    colleges, 2, 53, 104, 178–79
White supremacy, 18, 27
Whitla, Dean K., 227
Who's Who Among African Americans, 182–
    83, 190t, 302n2
Wightman, Linda, 309n6
Wilberforce University, 4, 33, 51, 138,
    292n3
Wiley College, 4, 122, 235t, 242
William and Flora Hewlett Foundation, 5,
    228, 230t, 261, 264
William and Mary College, 32
Williams, Alma Rene, 296n23, 307n12
Williams College, 238, 244
Wilson, William Julius, 189t
Wilson, Woodrow, 21–22
Winston, Judith, 187t
Witherspoon, John, 32
Wolanin, Thomas R., 244–45, 256, 306n2,
    307nn1,3
Women: college attendance in early
    twentieth century, 76; college atten-
    dance in nineteenth century, 33–34;
    doctorates received by, 158; increased
    enrollment by, 2; as percentage of stu-
    dents, 197; as trustees, 269; white, 33–
    34, 292n2

Women's colleges, 97, 285–86, 292n2. *See
    also specific institutions*
Woodruff, Hale, 60, 147
Woodson, Carter G., 89, 90, 112
Woodson, Robert L., 189t
Woodward, C. Vann, 18, 291n8
Woolseley, Theodore, 294n4
Woolworth's, 109
World War I, 23, 29, 76, 81–83
World War II, 77, 78, 93, 122, 125, 127
Wright, Walter Livingstone, 86
Wynn, Cordell, 164–65, 166, 175, 180,
    240, 269, 300nn2,3,4,6

Xavier Preparatory School, 174
Xavier University, 123, 268, 273, 283;
    degrees awarded by, 118; endowments
    in, 177–78, 276; enrollment by racial
    and ethnic status, 180t; enrollment size,
    163t, 173, 175; environment of, 5; fac-
    ulty size, 122; graduate programs of, 3;
    graduates of, 192; high school rank of
    students, 163t, 178, 179t; history of, 174;
    improvement of science department,
    176–77, 301n34; institutional strategy
    in, 272; leadership in, 160, 173–80, 270;
    non-black students in, 53, 104; operat-
    ing budget in, 10; rank by enrollment,
    4, 303n1; recruitment by, 220; risk toler-
    ance at, 179t; SAT scores of students,
    162, 163t, 179t; selected characteristics
    of, 161t; as supplier of medical students,
    173, 176, 284; Title III funds for, 257,
    258; tuition in, 106

Yale University, 32, 113
Young, Andrew, 7, 290n11
Younger, Paul, 94